Evidence

BY

Ruth Cannon
LL.B, B.C.L. (Oxon.), B.L.

AND

Niall Neligan
D.BS (N.U.I) B.L., B.A. (Hons) (N.U.I.)

DUBLIN
THOMSON ROUND HALL LTD
2002

Published in 2002 by
Round Hall Ltd.
43 Fitzwilliam Place
Dublin 2
Ireland

Typeset by
Devlin Editing, Dublin

Printed by
MPG Books, Cornwall

A CIP catalogue record for this book is available from the British Library

ISBN 1-85800-306-7 (hardback)
ISBN 1-85800-276-1 (paperback)

GRIFFITH COLLEGE DUBLIN
South Circular Road, Dublin 8.
Tel.4545640 Fax: 4549265

Evidence

WITHDRAWN

RTC

UNITED KINGDOM
Sweet & Maxwell Ltd
London

AUSTRALIA
Law Book Co. Ltd.
Sydney

CANADA and USA
Carswell
Toronto

NEW ZEALAND
Brookers
Wellington

SINGAPORE and MALAYSIA
Sweet & Maxwell
Singapore and Kuala Lumpur

To our parents

Conal and Catherine Cannon
and
Maurice and Dymphna Neligan

ACKNOWLEDGMENTS

Writing a book can be a frustrating and time consuming exercise, and yet the same time rewarding, educational and enlightening. We often wondered why recipients of Oscars spend so much time thanking everyone when accepting their award; it often transpires that everyone from the hair stylist to the fitness instructor gets a mention. Thankfully the authors neither have hair stylists nor fitness instructors to thank, but there are many who deserve recognition and praise.

Firstly, we would both like to thank our parents: Conal and Catherine Cannon, and Maurice and Dympna Neligan to whom this book is dedicated. This book is a tribute to their foresight in offering their children the best education available, at Sandymount High School and Clongowes Wood College respectively. After natural love, affection and security, a good education is the best gift a parent can bestow upon a child. We would both like to thank our siblings, Robert and Mary Cannon; and Maurice, Patrick, Dara and Donal Neligan, in their own way they too have played a role in shaping our respective views of the world.

In a professional capacity, we would first of all like to thank Mr Justice Joseph Finnegan, President of the High Court, for taking the time to write the foreword for this book. Mr Justice Finnegan is known not only for the scope of his legal knowledge, but also for his generosity and helpfulness towards the younger members of the profession. In decisions such as *M.F.M. v. P.W.* (unreported, High Court, June 22, 2001) he has laid down fundamental principles of our law in relation to legal professional privilege. We are honoured that he kindly accepted our request. We would also like to thank Mr Maurice Gaffney SC and Mr Felix McEnroy SC, consumate gentlemen and great colleagues, for their advice and encouragement during the past year.

We would both like to thank our respective masters for their patience and tolerance. The help and assistance afforded to Niall by Mr Tony Barr BL, Ms Pauline Codd BL and Mr Jim Kelly BL reminds him of an adage widely attributed to Mr Ken Connolly BL: "A devil is not for Christmas, it's for life!". Ruth would like to express her gratitude to Mr Gavin Ralston SC and Mr Alex Owens SC. Gavin's willingness to share his encyclopaedic knowledge with his devils has already been recognised by Michael McGrath BL in the foreword to his excellent book on liquor licensing law and Ruth wholeheartedly reaffirms Michael's comments.

From an academic perspective, we would both like to thank Mr Bruce Carolan, Head of the Department of Legal Studies at the Dublin Institute of Technology for giving us the opportunity to lecture at the institute and develop our research. The department of Legal Studies at the DIT is one of the finest repositories of legal learning and scholarship in Britain and Ireland and deserves a lot of credit. In addition we would like to thank fellow Department member Dr Fergus Ryan whose kindness and willingness to help his colleagues is truly exceptional.

No book on Irish evidence law would be complete without a recognition of the outstanding work of Declan McGrath BL, Averil Deverell, Lecturer in Law at Trinity College and Lecturer in Evidence Law at the Honourable Society of King's Inns. Over the past decade, Declan has taken this hitherto largely uncharted area of law and made it his own. His articles on evidence law in the *Irish Jurist* and the *Dublin University Law Journal*, not forgetting his outstanding contributions to the *Annual Review of Irish Law*, have clarified the complex and difficult topics of corroboration, legal professional privilege and public interest privilege. The authors wish Declan the very best with his publications in this field in the future and look forward to the appearance of a companion volume to his excellent work (with Dr. Hilary Delany) *Civil Procedure in the Superior Courts*, dealing with our criminal procedural system.

The authors would also like to thank Professor Yvonne Scannell, Declan's colleague in Trinity, for her continuing encouragement and support. Yvonne, you had faith in us when no one else did!

Finally, we would especially like to thank Catherine Dolan of Round Hall for all her help and support, and for giving us the opportunity to write this book. In addition we would like to thank Dave Ellis, Terri McDonnell, Therese Carrick and all the staff of Round Hall Sweet & Maxwell who have always been a pleasure to deal with.

Ruth Cannon
Niall Neligan

Law Library, September 15, 2002

FOREWORD

It is a pleasure to write the foreword to this book. It provides a comprehensive and meticulously careful exposition of the current law of evidence in this jurisdiction. It is a formidable work and deals fully with recent statutory interventions, including the Criminal Evidence Act, 1992, the Children Act, 1997 and all recent developments in case law on the law of evidence. It will prove indispensable to practitioners in both the criminal and civil courts and become a touchstone to which recourse will be had whenever a case is being prepared for trial and in whatever court. This volume will find a welcome on the library shelves of every solicitor's office and in the chambers of every barrister and Judge and I have no doubt in each such location it will soon become dog eared from frequent reference. Students will ignore it at their peril.

The authors are to be applauded for the structured and comprehensive manner in which they have dealt with their topic. The underlying concepts and their rationales are dealt with in a lucid manner and their development and application in practice expounded in the detail which practioners require.

This is a formidable work on a broad, intricate and technical topic but which is so organised and written as to make that topic intelligible and accessible and for this the authors are to be congatulated and thanked.

It is without hesitation that I recommend this learned work to practitioners and students alike and I wish it the success which it so richly deserves.

Mr. Justice Joseph Finnegan
President of the High Court
The High Court

GRIFFITH COLLEGE DUBLIN
South Circular Road, Dublin 8.
Tel.4545640 Fax: 4549265

CONTENTS

Table of Statutes

Statutory Instruments

Rules of Court

E.U. Conventions

Table of Cases

Chapter 1

INTRODUCTION AND BASIC CONCEPTS

An item of evidence may be defined as something that tends to prove or disprove a particular fact, in the sense that it makes the existence or non-existence of that fact more likely. An alternative definition of evidence describes it as information that may be used to help prove or disprove the truth or existence of some matter in legal proceedings.

The law of evidence lays down rules to determine what items of evidence may be called to prove salient facts in a trial. Phipson[1] has described the rules of evidence as being:

> "concerned not with the statement of rights and obligations which is the function of the substantive law but with the methods and means whereby rights and obligations are established and remedies given".

The law of evidence states which side bears the burden of proving particular facts in a criminal or civil trial. It lays down the standard to which those facts must be proved and details the range of permissible ways in which this may be done. In criminal proceedings and civil trials before a jury, the law of evidence also determines the particular roles of the judge and jury in relation to the evaluation of facts.

The primary objective of the law of evidence is to assist in the ascertainment of the truth in legal proceedings.[2] However, the law of evidence is also influenced by other objectives, such as the efficient operation of the trial process. The concept of fairness has also contributed significantly to the development of the law of evidence and in this jurisdiction the development of evidence law must take account of the constitutional right to a fair trial and fair procedures.

This chapter provides an introduction to the topics covered in this work and explains some basic concepts of evidence law.

1.1 Facts in issue

In a criminal trial, "facts in issue" are those facts which the prosecution must prove or disprove in order to win a conviction. The ingredients of the offence of murder, for instance, are facts in issue in a trial for that offence. In order to prove that someone has committed a murder it is necessary to show:

[1.] Phipson "Law of Evidence" (14th ed. Sweet and Maxwell, London, 1990).
[2.] Wright "The Law of Evidence: Present and Future" (1942) 20 *Can. Bar Rev.* 714.

1. that he has committed an act;

2. that this act has caused the death of another individual;

3. that the death of the individual occurred within a year and a day of the act being performed; and

4. that he had an intention to kill this person at the time of committing the act.

Defences, such as intoxication, provocation and self-defence, are not automatically facts in issue in a criminal trial. It is up to the defence to make them facts in issue by showing the court that there is some evidence to support their existence. Once the defence has done this, the particular defences become facts in issue in the case, and the prosecution must disprove their existence in order to get a conviction. Defences in both criminal and civil trials are facts put in issue by the defence.

In a civil action, the facts in issue are any facts that the plaintiff must prove in order to succeed in his claim, together with any facts that the defendant must prove in order to establish a defence. For example, in a negligence claim, the facts in issue are as follows:

1. duty of care;

2. breach of duty;

3. damage caused by that breach; and

4. any applicable defences, such as *volenti non fit injuria*, contributory negligence, etc.

Facts in issue are also known as principal facts or *factum probandum*.

1.1.1 Facts relevant to the facts in issue

Facts relevant to the facts in issue are facts that tend to make the existence or non-existence of particular facts in issue more likely. Facts relevant to facts in issue are also known as circumstantial evidence, evidentiary facts or *factum probans*.

1.1.2 Collateral issues

Issues relating to the admissibility of evidence or the competence or credibility of witnesses are regarded as collateral or side issues in a trial.

1.1.3 Collateral facts

Collateral facts are facts which are not relevant to facts in issue but which are relevant to a collateral issue. They are also known as subordinate facts.

1.2 Types of evidence

As stated above, evidence is information whereby facts in issue, facts relevant to facts in issue, or collateral facts may be proved.

1.2.1 Oral testimony of witnesses

The best-known type of evidence is oral testimony given in a courtroom by witnesses on oath. Most individuals are competent to testify. In the past there were difficulties in relation to children's evidence but these have been largely resolved by the Criminal Evidence Act 1992 and the Children Act 1997, which allow children and mentally handicapped witnesses to give unsworn evidence in criminal and civil proceedings provided that they are capable of giving an intelligible account of events.

The normal rule is that all competent witnesses can be compelled to testify in any proceedings. However, because of the right to silence, an accused in a criminal trial cannot be compelled to testify. A spouse of the accused can be compelled to testify for the defence but is only compellable for the prosecution in respect of a limited category of offences. Witnesses normally have to answer any question asked of them and if they refuse to answer questions, they may be imprisoned for contempt of court. In addition, individuals who are asked to disclose relevant documents are obliged to do so. However, in certain limited situations, individuals may be able to claim privilege from disclosing documents or answering questions. For example, a witness other than the accused cannot be compelled to answer a question or disclose a document where to do so would expose him to criminal proceedings, a penalty or forfeiture. The one exception is the accused, who cannot refuse to answer questions on the ground that the answers might incriminate him in relation to the particular offence with which he is charged.

Witnesses give their testimony for their own side first, and are then cross-examined by counsel for the other side. There is a rule that witnesses are confined to testifying to facts of which they have personal knowledge, except for an expert witness who may testify as to his opinion. There is also a related rule that witnesses cannot give evidence of what other people have told them. As Mr Justice Stareleigh remarked to Sam Weller: "What the soldier said, is not evidence."[3] This is known as the hearsay rule and it prevents out-of-court statements being adduced in evidence to prove the truth of their content.

Similarly, witnesses cannot normally give evidence of previous consistent statements made by them in order to enhance their credibility. However, there are a number of situations in which witnesses are exceptionally allowed to disclose these statements. For example, a witness in a rape trial is allowed to adduce evidence of a voluntary complaint made within a reasonable time after the offence.

1.2.2 Real evidence

However, it is also possible for information to be proved in other ways, *e.g.* by real evidence. For example, a murder weapon may constitute an item of real

---

[3.] *"The Pickwick Papers"* Charles Dickens Ch. XXXIV.

evidence. However, real evidence normally requires oral testimony in order to make its significance clear.

1.2.3 Documentary evidence

In addition, documents may also be put in evidence. However, the hearsay rule prevents documents being put in evidence to prove the truth of their contents. This means that it may not be possible to use information in a document to prove facts in court proceedings. Ideally, the person who wrote the document should be available to give oral testimony of the facts in question themselves. If they are not so available the information in the documents may be excluded.

It can be seen that the hearsay rule can operate quite harshly. It is not confined to preventing out-of-court statements made in documents from being admitted, but also applies to prevent witnesses from giving testimony of oral statements that have been made to them by third parties who are not available to testify. However, it should be noted that if the information in the document or the out-of-court oral statement comes within one of the exceptions to the hearsay rule, it may be admitted.

Even if a document comes within one of the exceptions to the hearsay rule, it is still necessary to produce the original of the document. Copies of documents can only be adduced under one of the exceptions to this rule. Also, it is necessary to provide proof of authorship of the document, which may require a handwriting expert.

The law of evidence has updated itself with modern technology. A video recording of the crime taken by a security camera can be shown to the jury. Alternatively, photographs of the crime scene or aftermath or a tape recording of the criminal's voice may be shown. Videotapes and photographs do not have to satisfy the best evidence rule and copies of them may be adduced.

1.3 Relevance[4]

The primary test that evidence has to satisfy in order to be admitted is one of relevance. In order for evidence to be admitted, it must be relevant to the existence or non-existence of a fact in issue. Either it must tend to prove the facts in issue or it must tend to prove facts, which are relevant to the facts in issue. Alternatively, where admissibility or credibility is in issue, evidence may be relevant if it is relevant to collateral facts.

The most famous definition of relevance is that given by Sir James Stephen in his *Digest of the Law of Evidence*.[5] He said that a fact is relevant to another if:

[4.]   Wigmore "*A Treatise on the Anglo American System of Evidence*" (3rd ed., Boston, 1940) paras.
       9-16; Egglestone, 4 Melbourne U.L.R. 180; Montrose, 70 L.Q.R. 527; Choo (1993) Crim. LR 114.
[5.]   (12th ed., MacMillan & Co., London, 1946)

"according to the common course of events one either taken by itself or in connection with other facts either proves or renders probable the past, present or future existence or non-existence of the other".[6]

In *D.P.P. v. Kilbourne*[7] Lord Simon stated:

"Evidence is relevant if it is logically probative or disprobative of some matter which requires proof...relevant evidence...is evidence which makes the matter which requires proof more or less probable."

Tapper[8] explains the conflicting decisions on relevance as follows:

"Relevance is an absolute concept; either proof of one fact makes the existence of another more probable, or it does not. It is however often regarded as variable, and evidence regarded as more or less relevant. This seems to relate more to the cogency (weight) of the evidence".[9]

He cites *R. v. Wilson*[10] to the effect that:

"lack of relevance can be used to exclude evidence not because it has absolutely no bearing on or upon the likelihood or unlikelihood of a fact in issue but because the connection is considered too remote. Once it is regarded as a matter of degree, competing policy considerations can be taken into account. These include the desirability of shortening trials, avoiding emotive distractions of marginal significance, protecting the reputations of those not present before the court and respecting the feelings of a deceased's family. None of these matters would be determinative if the evidence in question were of significant probative value."

1.4 Admissibility

The general rule is that, though evidence has to be relevant at the very least in order to be admitted, all relevant evidence is admissible.

This principle, however, is subject to a number of exceptions. Certain exclusionary rules are recognised by the law of evidence, which preclude the admission of relevant evidence. It must be remembered that the ascertainment of truth is only one of the considerations behind the law of evidence and that considerations of fairness and practicality may justify the exclusion of certain evidence even where it is relevant.

The best-known exclusionary rule is the hearsay rule, which excludes evidence of out-of-court statements that are adduced to prove the truth of their content. Out-of-court statements are not subject to the safeguard of cross-examination and are, therefore, seen as suspect. However, a large number of exceptions to the hearsay rule have been developed. For example, a confession

---

6. Art. 1.
7. [1973] A.C. 729.
8. *"Cross & Tapper on Evidence"* (9th ed., Butterworths, London, 1999).
9. At p. 56
10. [1991] 2 N.Z.L.R. 707 at 711.

is an out-of-court statement which may be admitted in evidence under an exception to the hearsay rule.

Other exclusionary rules, such as the rule excluding evidence of the accused's bad character, have developed out of the need to prevent the jury being unduly influenced by highly prejudicial evidence. Evidence of the accused's bad character can only be admitted by the prosecution in examination-in-chief if its probative value or relevance is so high as to outweigh its prejudicial value.

The prosecution is also precluded from raising the accused's bad character in cross-examination. However, the prosecution is entitled to ask the accused questions about his bad character when such evidence would have been admissible in examination-in-chief, or when the accused has raised his good character, given evidence against a co-accused, or cast unnecessary imputations on the character of a prosecution witness.

In addition, considerations of fairness necessitate that unconstitutionally obtained evidence be automatically excluded from use in criminal proceedings. In the case of evidence which has been unlawfully obtained, where the unlawfulness does not amount to a breach of constitutional law, the trial judge has a discretion to decide whether or not to exclude the evidence.

The courts are particularly protective of the accused in relation to the issue of confessions. A confession that is involuntary due to a threat, inducement or oppression, may be set aside. In addition, a judge has a discretion to exclude a confession if it has been obtained in breach of the Judges' Rules or the Custody Regulations[11] and, of course, a confession will be automatically excluded if it has been obtained as a result of a breach of an accused's constitutional rights.

Evidence may also be excluded as a result of the person who is asked to provide it claiming privilege. The best-known privilege is legal professional privilege, which allows individuals to refuse to disclose the contents of communications with their lawyers for the purpose of legal advice or the contents of any communications made by them or their lawyers for the purpose of litigation.

However, the State may be able to preclude the disclosure of information on the ground of public interest privilege. In order for a successful claim of public interest privilege to be made, it is necessary for the court to be satisfied that, in the particular case before them, the public interest in favour of the privilege outweighs the public interest of the administration of justice in the ascertainment of truth. Other privileges are the privilege against self-incrimination mentioned already, sacerdotal privilege and counselling privilege.

Questions of admissibility may be determined by way of a *voir dire* or trial within a trial. The procedure for the *voir dire* was laid down in *State v. Treanor.*[12] The trial proper is adjourned at the point at which the disputed

---

[11]   The Criminal Justice Act 1984 (Treatment of Persons in Custody) Regulations 1987
       (S.I. No. 119/87).

evidence would normally have been put before the jury. The jurors will be requested to withdraw while the *voir dire* is being held.

In some cases the evidence in question will be of such importance to the prosecution's case that the issue of its admissibility must be determined prior to the swearing of the jury. However, in *Attorney General v. McCabe*[13] it was suggested that, as a rule, the *voir dire* should be carried out during the trial rather than before the trial.

Nonetheless, in *People (D.P.P.) v. McCann*[14] the suggestion was made that a *voir dire* should usually be held at the beginning of the trial because it was easier for the jury to hear all the admissible evidence together rather than to have their task broken up by a *voir dire*. This was reaffirmed in *People (D.P.P.) v. Quinn*.[15]

The defence may request that the jury remain present throughout the *voir dire*. However, in *R. v. Hendry*[16] it was held that the trial judge has a discretion to ignore such a request. Also, even if particular evidence is held admissible as a result of the *voir dire,* it is possible for the defence to call subsequent evidence in the trial so as to undermine its weight.

1.5   The relationship of judge and jury in the criminal trial[17]

The general rule in a criminal trial is that questions of law are decided by the judge and questions of fact by the jury. However, occasionally in a criminal trial, the judge may have to decide on questions of fact. For instance, questions of fact may arise in the *voir dire* in relation to the admissibility of a confession. Foreign law is seen as a question of fact rather than a question of law, but any decisions on the rules of foreign law will of course be made by the judge.

When all evidence is heard and closing speeches have been made, the trial judge must provide the jury with directions on the substantive law and the law of evidence together with a summary of the evidence. He must remind them of the essential elements which must be proved in order to convict. If a term such as "intention" has a particular legal meaning, he must explain that meaning. He must direct them as to the burden of proof in relation to each fact in issue and the standard of proof. He has to be careful if commenting on the failure of an accused in a criminal trial to call evidence or to testify. Warnings must be given in respect of certain types of evidence.

In addition, the purposes for which certain types of evidence may be used are restricted, and this must be pointed out to the jury. Previous consistent statements and evidence of the accused's bad character admitted under section 1(f)(ii) and (iii) of the Criminal Justice (Evidence) Act 1924 can only be taken into account in assessing credibility. A confession by an accused may be taken

---

[12.] [1924] 2 I.R. 193.
[13.] [1927] I.R. 129.
[14.] [1998] 4 I.R. 397.
[15.] Court of Criminal Appeal, *ex tempore*, March 23, 1998.
[16.] (1988) 88 Cr. App. R. 187.
[17.] See Grier [1992] Crim. LR 204, McConville [1973] Crim. LR 164.

into account as evidence against him but it may not constitute evidence against a co-accused.

Finally, if the accused has adduced evidence of his good character, the judge may have to give a good character direction.

Lord Hailsham in *R. v. Lawrence*[18] stated that the trial judge's summing up:

> "must include references to the burden of proof and the respective roles of jury and judge. But it should also include a succinct but accurate summary of the issues of fact as to which a decision is required, a correct but concise summary of the evidence and arguments on both sides and a correct statement of the inferences which the jury are entitled to draw from their particular conclusions about the primary facts."

The judge cannot tell the jury to find a particular fact to be present. In *D.P.P. v. Stonehouse*[19] it was held that a trial judge had erred in directing the jury that certain conduct of the accused was sufficiently proximate to constitute an attempt.

1.6 Sources of the law of evidence

1.6.1 The common law

In *R. v. H.(A.)*[20] Lord Griffiths recognised that the common law rules of evidence sometimes appeared anomalous because they had been developed in a different era:

> "In the past, when jurors were often uneducated and illiterate and the penal laws were of harsh severity, when children could be transported and men were hanged for stealing a shilling and could not be heard in their own defence, the judges began to fashion rules of evidence to protect the accused from a conviction that they feared might be based on emotion or prejudice, rather than on a fair evaluation of the facts of the cases against him. The judges did not trust the jury to evaluate all the relevant material, and evolved many restrictive rules which they deemed necessary to ensure that the accused had a fair trial in the climate of those times. Today, with better educated and more literate juries, the value of those old restrictive rules of evidence is being re-evaluated, and many are being discarded or modified…"

The principles of the common law of evidence were laid down in the seventeenth and eighteenth centuries. Many of the rules developed during that period have now been abolished by statute or modified by judicial decision. However, a considerable number remain – for example, the hearsay rule and the rule prohibiting the admission of the accused's bad character.

[18.] [1982] A.C. 510.
[19.] (1982) 77 Cr. App. R. 13.
[20.] [1995] 2 Cr. App. R. 437 at 452.

1.6.2 The Constitution

The Irish Constitution has had a considerable impact on the law of evidence in this jurisdiction. Article 34 of the Constitution states as follows:

> "[J]ustice shall be administered in courts established by law by judges appointed in the manner provided by this constitution and save in such special and limited cases as may be prescribed by law, shall be administered in public."

This includes the common law rights of *audi alteram partem* and *nemo iudex in causa sua*. The term "constitutional justice" was first coined in *McDonald v. Bord na gCon*[21]:

> "In the context of the Constitution, natural justice might be more appropriately termed constitutional justice and must be understood to import more than the two well-established principles that no man shall be judge in his own cause and *audi alteram partem*."

In *Glover v. BLN (No. 2)*[22] it was stated that constitutional justice required fair procedures to be followed in criminal and civil cases.

In addition, Article 38 of the Constitution says that no person shall be tried on any criminal charge save in due course of law. This is similar in nature to the "due process" clause in the Fifth Amendment of the U.S. Constitution. In *State (Healy) v. O'Donoghue*[23] Gannon J said that this phrase contained, *inter alia*, "basic principles of justice which are inherent in the proper course of the exercise of the judicial function".

The right to trial in due course of law has been held to include a number of common law principles such as the presumption of innocence. It also includes the principles of natural justice. In *State (Howard) v. Donnelly*[24] it was held that the maxim *audi alteram partem* applied in respect of the accused in a criminal trial. In *Gill v. Connellan*[25] the accused's conviction was quashed because he had been granted inadequate opportunity to cross-examine the witnesses against him at his trial. It was stated that the accused must be provided with an effective opportunity to meet the case against him. In *State (Walshe) v. Murphy*[26] it was held that the maxim *nemo iudex in causa sua* was also inherent in Article 38.

In *State (Healy) v. O'Donoghue*[27] it was held that the right to legal assistance in criminal cases was part of the concept of due course of law and fair trial. Article 38 also includes the right to trial with reasonable expedition and the right not to have one's previous convictions adduced.

---

[21] [1965] I.R. 217.
[22] [1973] I.R. 432
[23] [1976] I.R. 325.
[24] [1966] I.R. 51.
[25] [1987] I.R. 541.
[26] [1981] I.R. 275.
[27] [1976] I.R. 325.

In *Heaney and McGuinness v. Ireland*[28] it was held that the right of the accused to silence was a concomitant of the right to freedom of expression in Article 40.1 rather than being implied in Article 38.

Article 38 only applies to criminal trials; however, similar rights to "fair procedures" are regarded as inherent in Article 40.3 of the Constitution in respect of any proceedings where a party is at risk of having his good name, his person or property, or any of his personal rights jeopardised.[29] This includes tribunal proceedings as well as civil proceedings.

Furthermore, in *Macauley v. Minister of Posts and Telegraphs*[30] it was held that the right to litigate was a personal right contained in Article 40.3 of the Constitution.

The most important facet of the Constitution in relation to evidence law has been its prohibition on the admissibility of unconstitutionally obtained evidence. Unconstitutionally obtained evidence is not admissible unless there are extraordinary excusing circumstances. There are a number of constitutional rights, breach of which may make evidence obtained as a result inadmissible, such as the right to liberty and the right to inviolability of the dwelling.

1.6.3 Statute law

The decisions of the common law courts of the eighteenth and nineteenth centuries remain the foundation on which the Irish law of evidence is based. However, statute law has intervened to create exceptions to the principles laid down by these courts in certain circumstances.[31]

Firstly, statutes have been passed to facilitate the testimony of certain witnesses excluded at common law. The common law was reluctant to recognise the competence of parties to proceedigns and their spouses to appear as witnesses. In addition many child witnesses were excluded at common law becasue they failed to understand the nature and consequence of an oath. Statute has intervened to facilitate the testimony of these individuals. The Evidence Act 1851, the Evidence Amendment Act 1853 and the Evidence Further Amendment Act 1869 provide for the competence and compellability of parties to civil proceedings and their spouses. Section 1 of the Criminal Justice (Evidence) Act 1924 renders an accused in criminal proceedings competent to testify in his own defence, while Part IV of the Criminal Evidence Act 1992 lays down a comprehensive set of rules governing the competence and compellability of an accused's spouse. The rules in relation to competence of children and mentally retarded persons are governed by Part V

[28.] [1996] 1 I.R. 580.

[29.] *Re Haughey* [1971] I.R. 217.

[30.] [1966] I.R. 345.

[31.] There are currently plans afoot to incorporate the European Convention on Human Rights into Irish law by means of statute. For discussions on the potential consequences of such incorporation, see Ni Raifeartaigh (2001) 7(2) Bar Rev 111 and Bacik (2001) 11(1) ICLJ 18.

of the Criminal Evidence Act 1992 in relation to criminal proceedings and by Part III of the Children Act 1977 as regards civil proceedings.

The Criminal Procedure Act 1865 sets out important rules in relation to the examination of witnesses. Despite its name, this statute applies in both criminal and civil proceedings. Section 3 deals with adducing previous inconsistent statements to disprove the testimony of hostile witnesses. Sections 4 and 5 of the same Act deal with proof of previous inconsistent statements made by witnesses for the other side. Section 6 of the Criminal Procedure Act 1865 permits a witness for the other side to be questioned in respect of his previous convictions. However, in relation to cross-examination of the accused in a criminal case, the application of section 6 is limited by the Criminal Justice (Evidence) Act 1924. Sections 1(e) and 1(f) of this statute regulate the circumstances in which the accused's bad character may be raised in the course of his cross-examination, if he decides to testify.

There are a number of important statutory exceptions to the rule against hearsay. Nineteenth century exceptions include the Bankers Book Evidence Act 1897, the Marriages (Ireland) Act 1844 and the Registration of Births and Deaths (Ireland) Act 1863. More recently Part II of the Criminal Evidence Act 1992 provides for the admission of hearsay evidence in criminal proceedings in a number of important new situations. Section 23 of the Children Act 1997 also facilitates the admission of hearsay evidence in civil cases concerning the welfare of a child or a person with a mental disability.

Statute has also laid down a number of exceptions to the best evidence rule in relation to documentary evidence. This rule has been abolished in respect of criminal proceedings by section 30 of the Criminal Evidence Act 1992. The rule still applies in respect of civil proceedings, but there are a number of important exceptions contained in the Documentary Evidence Act 1925, the Bankers Books Evidence Act 1879, the Documentary Evidence Act 1868 and the Evidence Act 1851.

Recent statutes have also altered the common law on corroboration. Section 7 of the Criminal Law (Rape) Amendment Act 1990 removes the need for a compulaory corroboration warning in respect of the evidence of a complainant in sexual offence proceedings. Section 28 of the Criminal Evidence Act 1992 makes a corroboration warning discretionary in respect of the unsworn evidence of children. However, section 10 of the Criminal Procedure Act 1993 adds a new corroboration warning requirement in respect of uncorroborated confession evidence.

The Criminal Justice Act 1984 (Treatment of Persons in Custody Regulations 1987[32] have significant implications for the admissibility of confession evidence. Section 7(3) of the Criminal Justice Act 1984 gives the trial judge the discretion to exclude a confession obtained in breach of the Regulations.

[32.] (S.I. No. 119/87).

Chapter 2

BURDEN AND STANDARD OF PROOF

2.1 Introductory concepts

2.1.1 Facts in issue and the burden of proof

In a criminal or civil trial, there will always be certain facts in issue which are material to the resolution of the dispute.

For example, in a criminal trial for murder, the facts in issue will be, at the very least, the following: whether someone has been killed; whether such person has been killed as a result of the accused's conduct; and whether the accused intended to kill that person at the time. Depending on the particular circumstances of the case, other facts in issue may include whether the accused was acting in self-defence and whether the accused was insane at the time. The question in relation to each fact in issue is, which party bears the burden of proving it?

2.1.2 The burden of proof varies in relation to different facts in issue

For example, in a civil action for negligence, duty, breach and damage will all be facts in issue. The presence or absence of contributory negligence may also be a fact in issue – it will materially affect the resolution of the dispute. In such an action, the plaintiff bears the burden of proving the first three facts in issue: duty, breach and damage. However, the defendant bears the burden of proving contributory negligence on the part of the plaintiff.

In the negligence example given above, the burden of proof with regard to some facts in issue lies on the plaintiff and in relation to other facts in issue lies on the defendant. The phrase "the burden of proof" is not used in the abstract, but rather in relation to a particular fact in issue.

2.1.3 The purpose behind the rules on the burden of proof

The rules in relation to the burden of proof are inspired by different considerations in criminal and civil cases. In a criminal trial, the law recognises the presumption of innocence, that an accused shall not be convicted without safeguards. In a criminal trial, the requirement of proof beyond reasonable doubt acts as a safeguard.

In a civil trial, the aim of the burden of proof is to resolve a deadlock and to keep the parties on even terms; which that is why the standard of proof is less.

2.1.4 Legal burden of proof

The legal burden in relation to a fact in issue is the obligation to prove that fact beyond reasonable doubt (in a criminal case) or on the balance of probabilities (in a civil case or in relation to the insanity defence in criminal cases). The legal burden is also known as the probative burden[1] or the persuasive burden,[2] on the ground that if an individual fails to satisfy the legal burden of proof on a particular fact, that fact is regarded as not having been proved. In criminal cases, the burden of proving the vast majority of the facts in issue lies on the prosecution. However in some limited situations the burden of proving certain facts in issue lies on the accused.

Normally, the rule in criminal cases is that laid down in *Woolmington v. D.P.P.*[3] the golden thread running through the criminal law is that the prosecution have to prove every fact in issue and the defence have to disprove nothing. However, this principle has been departed from both in relation to the defence of insanity, and also when statute either expressly or impliedly puts the burden of proving particular facts in issue on the accused.

It is uncertain to what extent such departures are permissible in Ireland, however, because the principle in *Woolmington* appears to be enshrined in our Constitution, according to *O'Leary v. Attorney General*[4] This will be returned to later.

2.1.5 Evidential burden of proof[5]

There is also what is known as the evidential burden. This is the obligation to adduce a prima facie case in relation to a fact in issue. In other words it is not necessary for the side bearing this burden to go so far as to prove the existence of the fact conclusively but they must produce some evidence that it exists.[6]

In *Jayasena v. R.*[7] Lord Devlin said that the evidential burden is satisfied by:

> "such evidence as, if believed and left uncontradicted and unexplained, could be accepted by the jury as proof".[8]

[1.] *D.P.P. v. Morgan* [1976] A.C. 182.
[2.] Wigmore called it "the risk of non-persuasion".
[3.] [1935] A.C. 462.
[4.] [1991] I.L.R.M. 454 (H.C.) and [1995] 2 I.L.R.M. 259 (S.C.).
[5.] The distinction between the legal and evidential burdens was first made by Glanville Williams in *Criminal Law* (The General Part) (2nd ed., 1961) Ch. 23 para. 287, 288; see also Williams (1977) 127 N.L.J. 156.
[6.] The evidential burden is also known as the burden of adducing evidence which probably gives the most accurate depiction of its function: Phipson, *Law of Evidence* (14th ed., Sweet and Maxwell, London, 1990).
[7.] [1970] A.C. 618 at 624.
[8.] Enough evidence to justify tribunal to find in favour of a person on point, although not to require them to do so, is a prima facie case.

In *Bratty v. Attorney General for Northern Ireland*[9] Lord Morris indicated that the evidential burden would be satisfied if there was:

> "sufficient evidence, fit to be left to a jury, on which a jury might conclude that the appellant had acted unconsciously and involuntarily or which might leave a jury in reasonable doubt whether this must be so".

It must be enough to raise a reasonable doubt or as Lord Devlin in *Bratty* said, to "suggest a reasonable possibility". The person who decides whether an evidential burden has been fulfilled is the judge rather than the jury.

(1) Evidential burden placed on accused in criminal cases in relation to defences[10]

As stated above, in criminal cases the legal burden in relation to the vast majority of facts in issue rests on the prosecution rather than the accused (the *Woolmington* principle). However, the *Woolmington* principle does not prohibit an evidential burden being placed on the accused in relation to certain facts in issue, namely defences.

It is important to note that although the *Woolmington* principle imposes the legal burden of proof in criminal trials on the prosecution in relation to every fact in issue, it does not stop an evidential burden being imposed on the accused.

If the accused wants to argue that a defence, *e.g.* self-defence, mistake, automatism, provocation, intoxication or duress, exists on the facts, then the accused bears an evidential burden in relation to that defence. He must satisfy the judge that there is a prima facie case that that defence exists on the facts. He must make this defence a fact in issue. Once this prima facie case is established, the prosecution then bears the legal burden of disproving the defence beyond reasonable doubt.

Walsh J. distinguished between the legal and evidential burden in relation to the defence of self-defence in *People (Attorney General) v. Quinn*:[11]

> "Before the possible defence can be left to the jury as an issue there must be some evidence from which the jury would be entitled to find that issue in favour of the appellant. If the evidence for the prosecution does not disclose this possible defence then the necessary evidence will fall to be given by the defence. In such a case, however, where it falls to the defence to give the necessary evidence it must be made clear to the jury that there is a distinction, fine though it may appear, between adducing the evidence and the burden of proof and that there is no onus whatever upon the accused to establish any degree of doubt in their minds."

It has been argued that the accused bears the evidential burden in relation to any statements he makes, which are other than mere denials of an allegation

---

9.   [1961] A.C. 386.
10. Williams (1977) 127 N.L.J. 156 and 182.
11. [1965] I.R. 366.

necessary for the prosecution case. This would bring alibi or accident within the evidential burden requirement. In *R. v. Johnson*[12] the Court of Appeal indicated obiter that alibi should be treated as a defence. In *Bratty v. Attorney General for Northern Ireland*[13] the defence of automatism was treated as raising an evidential burden.[14] Furthermore, Lord Kilmuir in *Bratty* said that the accused bore an evidential burden in relation to proving accident.

In *People (D.P.P.) v. Kavanagh*[15] the Court of Criminal Appeal affirmed that, in the case of duress, the accused bore an evidential burden but not a legal one. In the case of a defence of duress, the defendant must put forward "such material as makes the issue fit and proper to be left before a jury". This amounted to placing the evidential burden on the defendant. However, once this evidential burden was satisfied by the defendant, the legal burden was on the prosecution to disprove this beyond reasonable doubt.

The evidential burden in relation to the defence of provocation was discussed in *People (D.P.P.) v. Davis*[16] where it was stated that the defendant must point to:

> "evidence of some sort suggesting the presence of all the elements of the defence. This can be produced either through direct evidence or by inference on the evidence as a whole, but before leaving the issue to a jury the judge must satisfy himself that an issue of substance, as distinct from a contrived issue, or a vague possibility, has been raised."

The evidential burden in the case of provocation was not satisfied in the *People (D.P.P.) v. Halligan*[17] where the Court of Criminal Appeal agreed with the trial judge that no evidence had been adduced to show provocation.

The case of *D.P.P. v. Morrissey*[18] accords with the above decisions. This was a drunk driving case. The accused argued that the prosecution had failed to show that the vehicle was in a public place at the time of the accused being stopped. O'Higgins J. said that the accused was effectively raising a defence insofar as he was saying that his vehicle could have left the public road at some stage prior to being stopped and that he bore an evidential burden in relation to this.

(2) There is an evidential burden on prosecution to show a case to answer

As stated, in criminal cases, the prosecution normally bears the legal burden in relation to most facts in issue. However, it must be noted that the prosecution also bears an evidential burden in relation to those facts. At the end of the prosecution case, the defence will usually make a submission of no case to

---

[12.] [1961] 3 All E.R. 969.

[13.] [1963] A.C. 386.

[14.] Although often dealt with in criminal law textbooks under the heading of a defence, it could be argued that in fact this "defence" is a denial of the *actus reus* and *mens rea*.

[15.] Unreported, Court of Criminal Appeal, May 19, 1999.

[16.] Unreported, Court of Criminal Appeal, October 23, 2000.

[17.] Unreported, Court of Criminal Appeal, July 13, 1998.

[18.] Unreported, Court of Criminal Appeal, July 10, 1998.

answer and, if the prosecution cannot prove a prima facie case at this stage, the accused will go free.

In civil cases, the defendant can make an application for a non-suit.[19] In the case of a civil trial without a jury, the judge will then ask the defendant if he wants to give evidence. If the defendant does not want to give evidence, the question of liability is decided there and then on the balance of probabilities. In *Cranny v. Kelly*[20] a judgment was set aside because the judge had failed to follow proper procedure in relation to this. Even though the defendant had not given evidence, the judge had considered whether or not the evidential burden had been satisfied. If the defendant wants to give evidence, on the other hand, the judge must consider whether the plaintiff has satisfied the evidential burden, and if he has, then the judge may go on to hear the defendant's evidence.

In *D.P.P. v. Morrissey*[21] a District Justice stated a case to the High Court asking whether he had been correct to accede to a submission of no case to answer in a drunk driving case. The High Court held that the prosecution had produced sufficient evidence to raise a prima facie case.[22]

(3) The evidential burden may arise in relation to presumption of law

A third example of an evidential burden being imposed occurs in criminal trials where a presumption of law operates against the accused. For example, an accused may be charged with incest and may argue that the other party was not his child. Assuming the child to have been born to the accused's wife during their marriage, there is a presumption of law that the child is the accused's. However, as with all presumptions of law, this may be rebutted.

There is a rule that when a presumption of law operates against the accused in a criminal case the accused only has an evidential burden to fulfil in order to rebut the presumption; in other words, he only has to adduce prima facie evidence of the child's illegitimacy; he does not have to prove it on the balance of probabilities or beyond reasonable doubt. See further para 2.5 on Presumptions.

2.1.6 The tactical burden of proof

The tactical burden of proof does not compel the person on whom it is placed to produce evidence, not even a prima facie case. It merely makes it advisable that he should do so in order to rebut the weight of the other party's evidence

---

19. *O'Toole v. Heavey* [1993] 2 I.R. 544; *Hetherington v. Ultra Tyre Service Ltd* [1993] 2 I.R. 535; *Cranny v. Kelly* [1998] 1 I.R. 54.

20. [1998] 1 I.R. 54.

21. Unreported, Court of Criminal Appeal, July 10, 1998.

22. A submission of no case to answer was successful in *People (D.P.P.) v. Barnwell*, unreported, Flood J., Central Criminal Court, January 24, 1997. The principles to be applied in deciding this question are laid down in *R. v. Galbraith* [1981] 2 All E.R. 1060, which was approved in *Barnwell*. For two applications of these principles, see *People (D.P.P.) v. Nolan*, unreported, Central Criminal Court, November 27, 2001; *People (D.P.P.) v. M.*, unreported, Central Criminal Court, February 15, 2001.

on the point. Even if the person subject to the tactical burden does not adduce evidence, the judge/jury may still find in his favour.

Fennell[23] gives a good description of the tactical burden:

> ₹ "[T]here may come a point in the course of a trial when the legal burden upon an issue seems, in the light of the evidence so far adduced, to have been satisfied. In such circumstances there is a real sense in which considerations of prudence or good tactics – but not of law – impose an obligation upon the opponent. He is then sometimes said to bear a tactical burden of proof." ⅄

For example, once the prosecution has raised sufficient evidence to defeat the defence submission of no case to answer, it may be said that a tactical burden has passed to the accused to rebut this evidence. He is not obliged to do so, but it may be wise for him to do so.

Tactical burdens also arise in the case of circumstantial evidence and presumptions of fact. The tactical burden is sometimes also known as the provisional burden.

When faced with a tactical burden in relation to a particular point, the opponent must call evidence or take the consequences. However failure to discharge a tactical burden does not automatically cause the person to lose on the point.

In *People (Attorney General) v. Oglesby*[24] Kenny J. referred to the doctrine of recent possession as raising a tactical burden on the accused:

> "The so called doctrine is a convenient way of referring to the inferences of fact which, in the absence of any satisfactory explanation by the accused, may be drawn as a matter of common sense from other facts. It is a way of stating what a jury may infer and references to it as a doctrine are misleading because they give the impression that possession of recently stolen property raises a presumption against the accused or casts some onus on him."

Another example of judicial recognition of the tactical burden is to be found in the judgment of Lord Cross in *D.P.P. v. Morgan*:

> "If [the prosecution] adduces evidence to show that intercourse took place and that the woman did not consent to it then in the absence of any evidence from the defendant the jury will certainly draw the inference that he was aware that she was not consenting. So, as a practical matter he is bound – if he wishes to raise this point – to give evidence to the effect that he believed that she was consenting and as to his reason for that belief, and the weaker those reasons are the more likely the jury is to conclude that he had no such belief...[however] there is never any question of any evidential burden with regard to [the issue of knowledge of consent] being on the accused or of the judge withdrawing it from the jury."[25]

---

23. Fennell, *The Law of Evidence in Ireland*, (Butterworths, Dublin, 2002) at p. 28.
24. [1966] I.R. 162.
25. [1976] A.C. 182 at 217.

2.1.7 Shifting the burden of proof

The term "shifting the burden of proof" is quite commonly used to refer to any common law or statutory rule which imposes a burden of proof on the accused in a criminal case or the defendant in a civil case. The thinking is that the burden of proof in these cases would normally be on the prosecution or the plaintiff, so that when the accused or defendant is called on to prove something, this is exceptional and involves a "shifting" of the burden of proof.

The use of the phrase "shifting the burden of proof" in this context is incorrect and should be avoided. The phrase is only appropriate in one limited situation – where a rebuttable presumption of law operates. This will be discussed later.

2.1.8 Standard of proof

Finally, to note the concept of the standard of proof: if the burden of proof relates to the question of who has to prove a particular fact in issue, the standard of proof refers to the degree to which they have to prove it. In criminal cases, the standard of proof is beyond reasonable doubt, except in those very limited circumstances where the legal burden falls on the accused. In those situations, they merely have to prove the particular fact on the balance of probabilities. In civil cases, the standard is always on the balance of probabilities. This will be returned to later.

2.1.9 Conclusion

In conclusion, the burden of proof exists in relation to a particular fact in issue. It is the obligation on one particular side to prove or disprove the existence of a particular fact in issue. If they fail to do this, this fact in issue will be presumed not to exist. This may materially affect the success or failure of the particular trial.

Different rules regarding the allocation of the burden of proof apply in relation to criminal and civil proceedings. These will be discussed separately.

2.2 The legal burden of proof in criminal cases

2.2.1 The general rule

The burden of proving or disproving every fact in issue in a criminal case is on the prosecution. There are a number of very limited exceptions to this. The starting point here is the principle in *Woolmington v. Attorney General*[26] Mr. Woolmington was accused of killing his wife. The trial judge said that once the prosecution had proved that W fired the shot which killed his wife, the onus was on him to show that it was an accident, *i.e.* that he had no intention to kill. The House of Lords rejected this absolutely since it tended to

---

[26.] [1935] A.C. 462.

shift the legal burden onto the accused in relation to the *mens rea* of the offence.

The House of Lords formulated the general principle that, in criminal trials, the onus lies on the prosecution to prove every ingredient of the offence and to disprove anything consistent with innocence. In other words the prosecution have the burden of proof in relation to each and every fact in issue.

Viscount Sankey L.C. stated:

> "Throughout the web of the English criminal law one golden thread is always to be seen, that it is the duty of the prosecution to prove the prisoner's guilt... If, at the end of, and on the whole of the case, there is a reasonable doubt, created by the evidence given by either the prosecution or the prisoner, as to whether the prisoner killed the deceased with a malicious intention, the prosecution has not made out the case and the prisoner is entitled to an acquittal. No matter what the charge or where the trial, the principle that the prosecution must prove the guilt of the prisoner is part of the common law of England and no attempt to whittle it down can be entertained."

In *People v. Berber*[27] the judge directed the jury that if they thought that the accused's explanation might not be true, they should convict. This gave the impression that it was up to the accused to prove his innocence and was rejected by the Court of Criminal Appeal.

In *People (Attorney General) v. Oglesby*[28] the accused was charged with receiving stolen goods. The trial judge in his summing up to the jury said that they had to ask themselves whether the accused had raised a reasonable doubt in their minds as to his innocence. If that was the case, they should acquit. If the accused had failed to raise a reasonable doubt, they should convict him. Kenny J. said that the trial judge's remarks may have led the jury to believe that the burden of proof was on the accused – that he had the burden of disproving the prosecution's allegations. It was argued by the prosecution in *Oglesby* that when an accused is found in possession of recently stolen goods he is presumed to have stolen them and the burden shifts to him to give an explanation. This was rejected by Kenny J. who affirmed the *Woolmington* decision.[29]

Woolmington was also affirmed in Irish law in the case of *People (Attorney General) v. Quinn*.[30] Quinn raised the defence of self-defence to a manslaughter charge. The judge directed the jury that when the accused relies on self-defence, it is sufficient if he raises a doubt in the minds of the jury. This was criticised by the Supreme Court which said that all the accused had to do in relation to a defence was to satisfy the evidential burden and raise a prima facie case. Once there was enough evidence of the issue of self-defence,

---

27. [1944] I.R. 405.
28. [1966] I.R. 162.
29. Also *Attorney General v. Finnegan* [1933] I.R. 292, which stated that the legal burden did not shift to the prosecution even though the tactical burden might shift.
30. [1965] I.R. 366.

whether raised by the prosecution or the defence, the judge had to put the issue to the jury and the prosecution had to negative it beyond reasonable doubt.[31]

> "When the evidence in a case, whether it be the evidence offered by the prosecution or by the defence, discloses a possible defence of self-defence the onus remains throughout upon the prosecution to establish that the accused is guilty of the offence charged. The onus is never upon the accused to raise a doubt in the minds of the jury. In such case the burden rests on the prosecution to negative the possible defence of self-defence which has arisen, and if, having considered the whole of the evidence, the jury is either convinced of the innocence of the prisoner or left in doubt whether or not he was acting in necessary self-defence they must acquit."

Walsh J. further remarked:

> "Before the possible defence can be left to the jury as an issue there must be some evidence from which the jury would be entitled to find that issue in favour of the appellant. If the evidence for the prosecution does not disclose this possible defence then the necessary evidence will fall to be given by the defence. In such a case, however, where it falls to the defence to give the necessary evidence it must be made clear to the jury that there is a distinction, fine though it may appear, between adducing the evidence and the burden of proof and that there is no onus whatever upon the accused to establish any degree of doubt in their minds."

He concluded:

> "In a case where there is evidence, whether it be disclosed in the prosecution case or in the defence case, which is sufficient to leave the issue of self-defence to the jury the only question the jury has to consider is whether they are satisfied beyond reasonable doubt that the accused killed the deceased (if it be a case of homicide) and whether the jury is satisfied beyond reasonable doubt that the prosecution has negatived the issue of self-defence. If the jury is not satisfied beyond reasonable doubt on both of these matters the accused must be acquitted."

Quinn was affirmed in *People v. Clarke*[32]; and in *Attorney General v. Byrne*.[33] In *People (D.P.P.) v. Bambric*[34] and *People (D.P.P.) v. Davis*[35] it was again emphasised that there was no onus on the accused in relation to a defence, in this case the defence of provocation. In *People (D.P.P.) v. Kavanagh*[36] it was held that there was no legal burden in relation to duress, only an evidential one.

---

31. This mirrors the approach of the U.K. courts in *Mancini v. D.P.P.* [1942] A.C. 1 (defence of provocation) and *R. v. Gill* [1963] 2 All E.R. 688 (defence of duress). The evidential burden in relation to a defence may be satisfied by *any* evidence adduced in the case, whether adduced by the prosecution or the accused.
32. [1995] I.L.R.M. 355.
33. [1974] I.R. 1.
34. [1999] 2 I.L.R.M. 71.
35. Unreported, Court of Criminal Appeal, October 23, 2000.
36. Unreported, Court of Criminal Appeal, May 18, 1999.

This principle was recently evidenced in *D.P.P. v. Crimmins*,[37] a case stated by a District Justice as to whether or not she could convict an accused who had not been formally identified as the offender. O'Caoimh J. held that she could only convict if satisfied beyond all reasonable doubt. She would have to be satisfied that the offender was the accused. This could be because of his identification in court or at an identification parade or because of the evidence of a witness. There was no need for the accused to be in court in order for her to be satisfied beyond reasonable doubt of his guilt.

Article 6(2) of the European Convention on Human Rights protects the presumption of innocence. Its potential application in U.K. law has been recognised following the enactment of the Human Rights Act 1998.[38]

2.2.2 O'Leary v. Attorney General

The most important Irish decision on *Woolmington is O'Leary v. Attorney General*.[39] This case involved a constitutional challenge to section 3(2) of the Offences Against the State (Amendment) Act 1972. This section provides that a statement by a high-ranking garda officer that he believes the accused to be a member of an unlawful organisation shall be evidence that the accused is a member. Furthermore, section 24 of the Offences Against the State Act 1939 provides that proof of possession by the accused of an incriminating document shall be "evidence, until the contrary is proved", that the accused is a member.

Mr O'Leary was convicted by the Special Criminal Court of membership of the I.R.A. He argued that these two sections infringed the constitutional presumption of innocence in that they placed the legal burden of proving non-membership of an unlawful organisation on the accused.

Both the High Court and the Supreme Court held that the challenged sections were constitutional. Although both courts recognised the constitutional presumption of innocence, and saw it as a concomitant of this presumption that statutes not place the legal burden on the accused, they felt that these particular sections did not place a legal burden on the accused, but merely an evidential one.

Costello J. in the High Court started by accepting the constitutional presumption of innocence, which he located in the right to trial in accordance with law in Article 38.

> "It seems to me that it has been for so long a fundamental postulate of every criminal trial in this country that the accused was presumed to be innocent of the offence with which he was charged that a criminal trial held otherwise than in accordance with this presumption would prima facie be one which was not held in due course of law."[40]

---

37. Unreported, High Court, O'Caoimh J., June 8, 2000.
38. *R. v. D.P.P., ex parte Kebilene*, [1999] 3 W.L.R. 1. See further Stannard 51 N.I.L.Q. 560.
39. [1993] 1 I.R. 102, (HC) 2 I.L.R.M. 259 (SC).
40. [1993] 1 I.R. 103, 107, 259 (Supreme Court).

He also pointed out that not all impositions of the burden of proof on the accused infringe the presumption of innocence. Statutes may merely impose an evidential or a tactical burden on the accused and this is acceptable.

However, he made it clear that if a statute shifted the legal burden, it might be unconstitutional:

> "If the effect of the statute is that the court must convict the accused should he fail to adduce exculpatory evidence then its effect is to shift the legal burden of proof (thus involving a possible breach of the accused's constitutional rights) whereas if its effect is that notwithstanding its terms the accused may be acquitted even though he calls no evidence because the statute has not discharged the prosecution from establishing the accused's guilt beyond reasonable doubt then no constitutional invalidity could arise."[41]

He also pointed out that a shifting of the legal burden might in certain circumstances be constitutionally permissible. Reference was made to a decision of the European Court of Human Rights[42] where a statutory presumption placed the legal burden on the accused. This was upheld by the court as a justifiable and proportionate restriction on the presumption of innocence.[43]

Turning to the particular statutory provisions in issue in the case, Costello J. felt that section 3(2) did not shift the legal burden:

> "[It] cannot be construed as meaning that the court of trial must convict the accused without exculpatory evidence…the accused need not give evidence, and he may ask the court to hold that the evidence does not establish beyond reasonable doubt that he is a member of an unlawful organisation."

Neither did section 24 shift the legal burden, even though it included the words "until the contrary is proved". Section 24 did not mean that the court must convict in the absence of exculpatory evidence:

> "The court may evaluate and assess the significance of the evidence of possession and if it has a reasonable doubt as to the accused's guilt it must dismiss the charge, even in the absence of exculpatory evidence".

Problems with this judgment arise from Costello J.'s use of the term "evidential burden" which he uses not in the sense explained earlier but in the sense of "tactical burden". A tactical burden arises when the prosecution fulfil their evidential burden on a particular point. At this stage it becomes wise for the defence to call evidence to rebut the prosecution case, or else the jury may decide against them. However, while it might be advisable for the defence to call evidence, they are not obliged to do so. Even if they do not do so, the jury may possibly still decide in their favour.

---

41. At p. 111.
42. *X. v. United Kingdom* 5124/71 referred to in Jacobs, The European Convention on Human Rights pp. 113-114.
43. See further Ni Raifeartaigh (1995) 5 I.C.L.J. 135; O'Higgins & O'Braonáin, (1992) 2 I.C.L.J. 178 and for the U.S. position see Dripps (1987) 75 Cal L.R. 1665.

A single Supreme Court judgment was delivered by O'Flaherty J. He quoted extensively from Costello J.'s judgment. He emphasised that, in construing statutes, the courts are obliged to give them a constitutional interpretation where possible. Most of the argument at this stage related to section 24. Counsel for the accused, Mary Finlay S.C., argued that section 24 put the legal burden on the accused because of its use of the words "evidence until the contrary is proved". O'Flaherty J. rejected this:

> "The important thing to note about the section is that there is no mention of the burden of proof changing".

The jury is not bound to convict in the absence of exculpatory evidence. The consequence of *O'Leary* is that statutory provisions expressly imposing the legal burden of proof on the accused risk unconstitutionality. However, the courts will always interpret them so as to avoid a transfer of the legal burden wherever possible. Even if this construction is impossible it appears that statutes which shift the legal burden may still be constitutional if their encroachment on the presumption of innocence is justifiable and proportionate. Costello J. stated:

> "[I]t seems to me that the Oireachtas is permitted in certain circumstances to restrict the exercise of the right because it is not to be regarded as an absolute right whose enjoyment can never be abridged".

Kelly[44] argues that the judgment of O'Higgins C.J. in *Re the Criminal Jurisdiction Bill*[45] recognises the need to balance in Article 38.1 individual rights against the requirements of an ordered society. This could justify the peculiar knowledge principle. In fact, the insanity defence may be seen as an example of this principle in operation.

In *Hardy v. Ireland*[46] section 4(1) of the Explosive Substances Act 1883 was held to be constitutional. Section 4(1) provides that anyone who makes or knowingly has control or possession of an explosive substance "under such circumstances as to give to a reasonable suspicion that he is not making it or does not have it under his control for a lawful object" is guilty of a felony unless he can show that this was for a lawful purpose. Murphy J. saw this shifting of the legal burden as permissible. He said that this provision gave the accused "a particular defence of which he can avail if he proves the material facts on the balance of probabilities".

Statutory provisions which merely impose a tactical burden on the accused (*i.e.* they make it advisable for him to call evidence but not necessary for him to do so) are permissible under the Constitution. Costello J. also says that statutes which impose an evidential burden on the accused are acceptable.[47] However, it is uncertain what Costello J. means by the term "evidential

---

44. "The Irish Constitution" (4th ed., Butterworths, Dublin, 2001).
45. [1977] I.R. 152.
46. [1994] 2 I.R. 550.

burden" in this context. It would appear that he merely uses this phrase to refer to the tactical burden mentioned above.

2.2.3   Exceptions to Woolmington

In the light of *O'Leary* it would appear that any exceptions to Woolmington may be unconstitutional as infringing the presumption of innocence. This concern was anticipated by Davitt P. in *Attorney General v. Shorten*,[48] in which he stated in relation to an implied statutory exception:

> "I do not feel at all happy about the application in criminal cases of …the peculiar knowledge principle…I found it very hard to regard resorting to the 'peculiar knowledge' principle even in its modified form or to any similar principle as other than attempts to whittle down the presumption of innocence."

However, exceptions to *Woolmington* may possibly be justified if their encroachment on the presumption of innocence is justifiable and proportionate. The full consequences of *O'Leary* in this regard remain to be determined.

Lord Sankey in *Woolmington* specifically recognised the insanity defence and certain statutory exceptions as permissible enchroachments on the presumption of innocence.

(1) Insanity defence[49]

When an accused wants to raise a defence of insanity, he bears the legal burden. He must convince the jury of his insanity on the balance of probabilities. Note the reduced standard of proof.

This was laid down in *McNaghten*[50] case, the first decision to recognise the insanity defence.

> "The jurors ought to be told in all cases that every man is presumed to be sane, and to possess a sufficient degree of reason to be responsible for his crimes, until the contrary be proved to their satisfaction; and that to establish a defence on the ground of insanity, it must be clearly proved that, at the time of the committing of the act, the party accused was labouring under such a defect of reason, from disease of the mind, as not to know the nature and quality of the act he was doing, or, if he did know it, that he did not know he was doing what was wrong."

In *Attorney General v. Boylan*[51] the accused was charged in the Central Criminal Court with murder. He argued that at the time of the murder he had

---

[47.] See further, *D.P.P. v. Byrne*, unreported, Superior Court, December 16, 2001. Section 50(8) of the Road Traffic Act 1961 (as inserted by s. 11 of the Road Traffic Act 1964) was interpreted as merely placing an evidential burden (in the true sense) on the accused and therefore being constitutionally permissible.

[48.] [1961] I.R. 304.

[49.] For discussion of the insanity defence see Dwyer (1996) 2 Bar Rev. 9.

[50.] *McNaghten v. Cave* (1843) 10 Cl. & Fin. 200.

[51.] [1937] I.R. 449.

been insane. The trial judge stated that the onus of proving insanity rested on the accused. It was argued that once the defence of insanity had been raised the burden lay on the prosecution to disprove it. This was rejected by Sullivan C.J. in the Court of Criminal Appeal:

> "It is said that the judge should have told the jury that, if the result of the evidence was to leave them in doubt as to the sanity of the accused, they should give the accused the benefit of the doubt, and find him to have been insane. This court is satisfied that that contention cannot succeed. The opinion given by the judges in McNaughton's [*sic*] case is clear – that the presumption that every man is sane continues until 'the contrary is proved to the satisfaction of the jury, and clearly proved'."[52]

However, it was recognised by Sullivan C.J., citing the case of *Sodeman v. The King*[53] that the standard of proof which the accused had to fulfil when proving insanity was proof on the balance of probabilities:

> "In *Sodeman v. The King*, the Judicial Committee of the Privy Council decided that the burden of proof resting upon an accused who sought to establish his insanity was not so onerous as the burden of proof resting upon the prosecution to prove the facts which they had to establish, and that the burden which rested upon an accused in such a case was not higher than that which rested upon a plaintiff or defendant in civil proceedings."[54]

In *People (Attorney General) v. Fennell (No.1)*[55] a trial judge stated that the accused must prove beyond reasonable doubt that he was insane in order to be able to avail of the defence of insanity. This was inconsistent with the dicta in *Boylan* but nonetheless it was upheld by the Court of Criminal Appeal.

(2) Express statutory exceptions

In the United Kingdom Parliament is sovereign, which allows the legislature to enact a law which puts the legal burden on the accused in relation to a particular fact in issue. T his is not possible in Ireland anymore because of *O'Leary*. As Costello J. remarked, there are a number of statutes which purport to place the burden of proof on the accused. Some examples follow.

The Misuse of Drugs Act 1977, section 15(2), provides that the onus of proving lawful possession shall be on the defendant.

The School Attendance Act 1926, section 18(2), provides that if a parent prosecuted under this Act wants to avail of the defence that their children were receiving suitable elementary education at home, they must bear the burden of providing this. In *D.P.P. v. Best*[56] Denham J. held that this statutory shifting of the burden of proof was justified on the grounds of the common good as

---

52. *Ibid.*, p. 457.
53. [1936] W.N. 190.
54. *Attorney General v. Boylan* [1937] I.R. 457, 458.
55. [1940] I.R. 445.
56. [2000] 1 I.L.R.M. 1.

protecting the child's right to a certain minimum education. She also referred to the fact that this was a matter within the special knowledge of the parents.

The Criminal Justice Act 1984, section 4(2), provides that:

> "[t]he accused person shall be presumed to have intended the natural and probable consequences of his conduct, but this presumption can be rebutted".

In *People (Attorney General) v. Dwyer*[57] it was held that this provision merely shifted an evidential burden. In *People (D.P.P.) v. Cotter*[58] the trial judge had indicated that up to accused to prove on balance of probabilities that she had not intended the natural and probable consequences of her acts. This was held to be incorrect.

In *Rock v. Ireland*[59] the Supreme Court refused to find that sections 18 and 19 of the Criminal Justice Act 1984 infringed on the presumption of innocence. They merely shifted the tactical or evidential burden not the legal burden.

(3) Implied statutory exceptions

Traditionally, statutes which prohibited the doing of an act subject to exceptions (in specified circumstances or by persons of specified classes or with specified qualifications or with the licence or permission of specified authorities), were understood as impliedly placing a burden of proof on the accused to show that he comes within the exception.

In *R. v. Jarvis*[60] Lord Mansfield said that it was a "known distinction" that:

> "what comes by way of proviso in a statute must be insisted on by way of defence by the party accused; but where exceptions are in the enacting part of a law, it must appear in the charge that the accused does not fall within any of them".

It primarily related to pleadings but was later taken as setting rules for the burden of proof in trials.

In *R. v. Turner*[61] the accused was prosecuted for having game in his possession without any authorisation. The game laws provided for certain matters which would allow an individual to qualify as being legitimately in possession of game. It was held that it was for the accused to adduce that he qualified under the game laws. In coming to this decision Lord Ellenborough focused on the relative ease and difficulty of proof and disproof. It was easy for the accused to prove he came within the qualifications if he actually did so, but it was difficult for the prosecution to disprove this fact. Bayley J. stated that:

---

[57]. [1972] I.R. 416; *People (D.P.P.) v. Murray* [1977] I.R. 360.
[58]. Unreported, Court of Criminal Appeal, June 28, 1999.
[59]. [1998] 2 I.L.R.M. 35.
[60]. (1756) 1 East 643.
[61]. (1816) 5 M. & S. 206.

"if a negative averment be made by one party, which is peculiarly within the knowledge of the other, the party within whose knowledge it lies, and who asserts the affirmative, is to prove it and not he who asserts the negative".

This case was the foundation of the peculiar knowledge principle. In the application of this principle it has been held in *Apothecaries Co. v. Bentley*[62] that an apothecary charged with practising without a certificate bears the burden of proving that he has a certificate and in *R. v. Ewens*[63] that an accused found with drugs in his possession must prove that he had been given a prescription for those drugs.

R. v. Edwards[64] described the principle as follows:

"The common law has evolved an exception to the fundamental rule that the prosecution must prove every element of the offence charged. It is limited to offences arising under enactments which prohibit the doing of an act save in specified circumstances or by persons of specified classes or with specified qualifications or with the licence or permission of specified authorities. Whenever the prosecution seeks to rely on this exception, the court must construe the enactment under which the charge is laid. If the true construction is that the enactment prohibits the doing of acts, subject to provisos, exemptions and the like, then the prosecution can rely upon the exception."

In *Edwards* the accused was convicted of selling alcohol without a licence.

The House of Lords in *R. v. Hunt*[65] took a wider view of the scope of implied statutory exceptions to Woolmington. Hunt was charged with the unlawful possession of morphine contrary to the Misuse of Drugs Act 1971. Morphine was a prohibited substance under that Act. However, a lot of pharmaceutical products contain morphine and subsequent legislation[66] was passed which said that the prohibition did not apply to preparations containing less than 0.2 per cent morphine. Hunt alleged that the burden was on the prosecution to prove that the substance in his possession was more than 0.2 per cent morphine and they had failed to do this. The prosecution claimed that the statute impliedly imposed the burden of proof on this issue on *Hunt*.

The statute in question did not fall within the definition in *Edwards*. It was not an enactment "which prohibited the doing of an act save in specified circumstances or by specified persons or subject to specified conditions or subject to the obtaining of a licence".

The House of Lords agreed on this. However, they also pointed out that the formula in *Edwards* was not intended to be conclusive, and went on to look at the wording of the statute and policy considerations in seeking the legislature's implied intention.

However, on the facts of this case the language of the statute was uncertain, and policy considerations did not point towards placing the burden of proof on

---

62. (1824) 1 C. and P. 538.
63. [1967] 1 Q.B. 322.
64. [1975] Q.B. 27.
65. [1987] 1 All E.R. 1.
66. Misuse of Drug Regulations 1973 (S.I. 1973/797).

the accused. The substance was in the possession of the police and the accused would have practical difficulties in proving its morphine content. The prosecution, however, would have no such difficulty. So in the circumstances, the House of Lords found no implied statutory placing of the burden of proof on the accused.

The *Hunt* test involves looking closely at the particular piece of legislation in hand. If the wording of the statute does not clearly indicate on whom the burden should lie, the court may have regard to matters of policy including practical considerations and in particular the ease or otherwise that the respective parties would encounter if required to discharge the burden. So "peculiar knowledge" may come in at this stage. Under the *Edwards* test it did not come in at all. However the *Hunt* approach, while taking peculiar knowledge into account as part of its statutory interpretation test, does not accord it the all-important role that Irish courts do.

An example of an implied statutory placing of the burden on the accused outside the context of Edwards is to be found in the case of *Nimmo v. Alexander Cowan & Sons Ltd.*[67] Section 29(1) of the Factories Act 1961 (U.K.) provided that a safe working place shall, so far as reasonably practicable, be provided and maintained. It did not fit within the Edwards test because the reasonably practicable issue did not appear to be an exception. This was recognised by Lord Griffiths and the Court of Appeal in Hunt. The words were an integral part of the definition of the offence rather than a qualification or excuse.

The most important Irish case is *Minister for Industry and Commerce v. Steele.*[68] A wartime order prohibited the selling of sausages with more than a 65 per cent pork content without a ticket. The accused was caught selling pork sausages and could not produce a ticket. Beyond saying there was some pork in the sausages, it was impossible to prove their exact content scientifically. The accused nonetheless argued that the onus was on the prosecution to prove the 65 per cent content. This was rejected by the Supreme Court.

Once it was shown that there was pork in the sausages, the onus shifted to the accused to show that the pork content was less than 65 per cent. The accused had better opportunities of proving the truth on this point. The Supreme Court said that the burden shifted on this point because of the peculiar knowledge of the accused. However, in order for the peculiar knowledge principle to operate, the Supreme Court felt that the prosecution must first fulfil an evidential burden and make out a prima facie case that the sausages were prohibited. They had done so here by showing that the sausages were described by the accused as "pork sausages".

O'Byrne J. delivering the judgment of the Supreme Court quoted from Stephen's *Digest of the Law of Evidence*[69] to the effect that if one party had

---

[67.]   [1968] A.C. 107.
[68.]   [1952] I.R. 304.
[69.]   Stephens, Sir James Fitzjames, (9th ed., MacMillan & Co., London), Article 96.

peculiar knowledge of a particular matter, the burden shifted to him to prove that matter:

> "The burden of proof as to any particular fact lies on that person who wishes the court to believe in its existence, unless it is provided by any law that the burden of proving that fact shall lie on any particular person; but the burden may in the course of a case be shifted from one side to the other, and in considering the amount of evidence necessary to shift the burden of proof the court has regard to the opportunities of knowledge with respect to the fact to be proved which may be possessed by the parties respectively."

The problem with this quote was that Stephen in particular appeared to be referring to the civil burden and his comments about the peculiar knowledge principle may have been restricted to civil cases only.

O'Byrne J. also quoted *Taylor on Evidence*[70] to similar effect:

> "[W]here the subject matter of the allegation lies peculiarly within the knowledge of one of the parties, that party must prove it, whether it be of an affirmative or a negative character, and even though there be a presumption of law in his favour."

It is worth noting, however, that the above dictum in *Taylor* had been cut down by Palles C.B. in *Graham v. Belfast and NC Railway Co.*[71] O'Byrne J. does not refer to that case.

In *People (Attorney General) v. Shribman*[72] the accused were charged under the Emergency Powers (Control of Export) Order 1940 with conspiring to export certain articles without a licence. They claimed that it was up to the prosecution to prove that they had no licence. Maguire P. held that the accused bore the onus of proving that they had a licence, stating that:

> "[i]t is well settled that when an offence consists of doing something which persons are not permitted to do unless duly qualified and under special circumstances, the onus of disproving the qualification does not rest on the prosecution".

He referred to the dictum of Gibson J. in *R. (Sheahan) v. Justices of Cork*:

> "Does the statute make the act described an offence subject to particular exceptions, qualifications etc., which, where applicable, make the prima facie offence an innocent act? Or does the statute make an act, prima facie innocent, an offence when done under certain conditions? In the former case the exceptions need not be negatived: in the latter, words of exception may constitute the gist of the offence."[73]

---

70. Taylor, *A Treatise on the Laws of Evidence as Administered in England and Ireland* (12th ed., Sweet and Maxwell, London, 1931).
71. [1901] 2 I.R. 13.
72. [1946] I.R. 431.
73. [1907] 2 I.R. 5 at 11.

In *Attorney General v. Duff*[74] it was held on a different ground that the onus of proving the existence of the licence was on the defendant because of the peculiar knowledge principle.

However, this should be contrasted with the subsequent case of *Mc Gowan v. Carville*[75] where the Supreme Court refused to apply the peculiar knowledge principle. This was a case where the accused was charged with driving a vehicle without a licence. The question was whether the burden of proving that he had no licence was on the prosecution, or whether the onus was on the accused to prove he had a licence.

Davitt P. felt that the onus of proof would only shift if the prosecution could show some evidence that the accused was without a licence. However, the prosecution had not showed this on the facts of the case:

> "If in the case of a prosecution such as this evidence is given that the defendant at a certain time and place drove a mechanically propelled vehicle on a public road, and that on being stopped and asked by a member of the garda to produce his licence he failed to do so, or that having so failed and promised to produce it at a specified garda station he again failed to do so, then I think that the court would be entitled to hold that having regard to the means of knowledge possessed by the complainant and defendant respectively the onus had shifted to the defendant. It may not be possible in all cases to stop a driver and ask for his licence. In such a case if the identity of the driver is established and evidence given that no licence has been issued to him by the licensing authority in whose area he resides or carries on business then I think that the court would again be entitled to hold that the onus of proof had shifted."[76]

He refused to apply the peculiar knowledge principle without some evidence that the accused was without a licence. Otherwise,

> "every person who drives a mechanically propelled vehicle on a public road is prima facie committing an offence. There is no need to stop him and ask for his licence. Provided he is seen and recognised, or can otherwise be identified, he can be prosecuted and made to establish his innocence by proof that he had at the material time a valid driving licence".[77]

He pointed out that in *Steele* it could be inferred that some portion of the meat consisted of pork from the fact that it was being sold as pork sausages.

The Supreme Court, affirming the judgment of Davitt P., found that the burden was on the prosecution. The Gardaí. had failed to fulfil the prima facie case requirement necessitated by *Steele*. In addition, there was no difficulty in the Gardaí. proving the absence of a licence; they merely had to check the records and see if one had been issued.

However, Maguire C.J. delivered a strong dissent. He felt that the prosecution had made a sufficient prima facie case. A.'s failure to produce his

---

74. [1941] I.R. 406.
75. [1960] I.R. 330.
76. At p. 344.
77. At p. 343.

licence on the spot raised a prima facie case that he had not got one. However, the main difficulty with this argument is that A. was not requested by the Gardaí. to produce his licence. Arguably, if he had been so requested, and failed to do so, this would be a sufficient prima facie case. Maguire C.J. also felt that it was easier for the accused to show he had a licence than it was for the Gardaí. to show he was without one.

The subsequent case of *Attorney General v. Shorten*[78] also should be noted. Here the accused was charged with making a false declaration to the effect that his motor car had not been used by him or with his consent during a specific period. The accused's motor car had been seen on the road. It was argued that a prima facie case had been satisfied. Again, it was held that the onus of proving that the accused was not the driver was on the prosecution because the possession of a licence was not a matter peculiarly within the knowledge of the defendant. Davitt J. expressed dissatisfaction with the peculiar knowledge principle; he pointed out that the accused was not charged with a breach and therefore the decision in *McGowan v. Carville* was not strictly applicable.

The final case on the peculiar knowledge principle in this jurisdiction is *Bridgett v. Dowd*.[79] Here the accused was charged with illegally carrying merchandise by road. Statute prohibited the merchandise in question from being carried without a licence except within a restricted area. The prosecution had shown that the lorry was on the road, that it was owned by the accused, and that he had no licence. It was held that the onus of proof was on the accused to show that the merchandise had only been carried within that area. The prosecution had shown a prima facie case by proving that A had no licence.

2.3   Burden of proof in civil cases

In civil cases, the law seeks to hold a neutral balance between the parties and ensure that the party with the best case wins. In civil cases, the legal burden of proof will normally lie on the person asserting that a particular fact in issue is true. In *Joseph Constantine Steamship Line v. Imperial Smelting Corporation*[80] this rule was described by Maugham V.-C. as "an ancient rule founded on considerations of good sense and it should not be departed from without strong reason".

In *Amos v. Hughes*[81] it was stated that the burden of proof is usually on the party who would be unsuccessful if no evidence at all were adduced on the point.

In *Abrath v. North Eastern Railway Co*[82] Bowen L.J. stated that "[i]f the assertion of a negative is an essential part of the plaintiff's case, the proof of the assertion still rests upon the plaintiff".

[78.] [1961] I.R. 304.
[79.] [1961] I.R. 313.
[80.] [1942] A.C. 154 at 174.
[81.] Nisi Prius 1835.
[82.] (1883) 1 Q.B.D. 440 at 457; affirmed (1886) 11 App. Cas. 247 (H.L.).

The legal burden of proof will normally be shown by the pleadings. If that party has asserted that fact in the pleadings, then he must prove it. In a contract case, the plaintiff bears the burden of proving the contract, the performance of any conditions precedent, the breach of contract and loss. The defendant must prove any facts that go beyond a mere denial of the plaintiff's case, such as infancy, fraud, mistake, undue influence. A party relying on an exclusion clause in the contract will normally have to prove that he can avail of it. *The Glendarroch* [83] involved a contract for the sale of goods with a clause exempting the vendor where the goods were lost at sea. It was held that the vendor would have to prove that he came within the exemption from duty of care, breach of duty and that he had suffered damage as a result of the breach clause.

In negligence actions, the plaintiff bears the burden of proving duty, breach, damage. The defendant bears the burden of proving any facts that go beyond a mere denial of the plaintiff's case, such as *volenti non fit injuria* or contributory negligence.

Hanrahan v. Merck Sharp and Dohm[84] states that the ordinary rule is that a person who alleges a tort must prove all the ingredients of that tort and it is not for the defence to prove anything. However, Henchy J. also stated that:

> "it would be palpably unfair to require a plaintiff to prove something which is beyond his reach and which is peculiarly within the range of the defendant's capacity of proof".

If a defence goes beyond a denial of the plaintiff's allegations and asserts some new fact, *e.g.* contributory negligence or *volenti non fit injuria* in negligence actions, or frustration or mistake in contract actions, then the defendant must prove that fact. He has made it a fact in issue and now he must prove it. This is known as the defendant raising an affirmative defence. An affirmative defence is a defence that raises facts in issue which do not form part of the plaintiff's claim.

Courts generally look at precedents relating to the area of substantive law in question in allocating the burden of proof. If such precedents are not available, the courts allocate the burden of proof, having regard to the policy behind the particular rule of substantive law in question. Relative difficulties of proof may be taken into account.

In *Joseph Constantine Steamship Line v. Imperial Smelting Ltd*[85] a ship on charter was destroyed by an explosion. The cause of the explosion was unclear. The charterers claimed damages from the owners. The owners raised the argument that the charter contract had been frustrated. However, even if all the other requirements of frustration were satisfied, the defence would not apply if the accident was not caused by the fault of the owners.

[83.] [1894] P. 226.
[84.] [1988] I.L.R.M. 631.
[85.] [1942] A.C. 154.

Was lack of fault part of the frustration defence or was it something additional that could be used to prevent the frustration defence applying? The question was whether the onus was on the owners to show lack of fault as part of raising the frustration defence, or whether, once the frustration defence had been raised, the burden of proving that the explosion was caused by the fault of the owners lay on the charterers.

In other words, there was a material fact, namely the cause of the explosion. If the accident was caused by the fault of the owners, frustration would be inapplicable. If it was not so caused, frustration would apply. The question was, who bore the burden in relation to this fact – the plaintiff charterers or the defendant shipowners?

The House of Lords held that the burden was on the plaintiff charterers to prove fault on the part of the shipowners. The reason for this is that it is easier to prove fault than it is to prove absence of fault. If the burden was placed on the shipowners, then they would have to prove absence of fault and this is nearly impossible to prove.

In *Levison v. Patent Steam Carpet Cleaning Ltd*[86] the plaintiffs sued the defendants to whom they had left their Chinese carpet for cleaning. The defendants pleaded the contract, which exempted them from liability for negligence but not for any fundamental breach of contract. The question was whether the onus was on the plaintiffs to prove that there had been a fundamental breach or whether the onus was on the defendants to prove that there had been no fundamental breach. The Court of Appeal held that the onus was on the defendants – they had much greater opportunities in relation to this, the loss having happened within their sphere of control. This was even though it required asking the defendants to prove a negative.

It appears that in some cases, even where facts are clearly ingredients of the offence, the burden of disproving them may be shifted to the defendant in civil cases if they are peculiarly within his knowledge. In *Mahony v. Waterford, Limerick and Western Railway Co.,*[87] where the plaintiff was suing for goods damaged by wilful misconduct of servants while in transit, it was held that the burden was on the defendant to disprove wilfulness even though it was one of the ingredients of the tort. Palles C.B. said that these facts were peculiarly within the knowledge of the defendant.

In *Gilligan v. Criminal Assets Bureau*[88] and *Murphy v. GM PB PC Ltd*[89] it was argued that sections 3 and 4 of the Proceeds of Crime Act 1996, which require a respondent to show that property is not the proceeds of crime in order to prevent an interlocutory freezing order, were unconstitutional. It was held by O'Higgins C.J. in the latter case that:

> "there is nothing unfair or contrary to any concept of equality of arms in the onus shifting in a civil action on the attaining of certain proofs. It is quite

86. [1978] Q.B. 69.
87. [1900] 2 I.R. 273.
88. [1998] 3 I.R. 285.
89. Unreported, O'Higgins J., High Court, June 4, 1999.

reasonable in the context where it appears to the Court that the goods are the proceeds of crime that the person in possession be asked to account for them. The Respondent is in a unique position to account for the property."[90]

The doctrine of *res ipsa loquitur* should also be noted.[91] This greatly affects the burden of proof in negligence actions. If the damage suffered arises out of something in the control of the defendant or his servants, and the accident is such as does not happen in the ordinary course of things if people take proper care, then the onus of proof shifts to the defendant to show that the accident was not caused by lack of due care on his part.

Examples of situations in which *res ipsa loquitur* will apply are as follows:

1. If a bag of flour falls from the window of a warehouse owned by D, it will be presumed it did so due to the lack of care of D. The accident is such as would not happen in the ordinary course of things if due care was taken. The onus shifts to D to show due care.

2. If a car driven by D climbs on to the pavement, it will be presumed, on similar reasoning, that this occurred due to D's want of care. Similarly, if stones are found in buns made by D or if a slippery substance is found on D's shop floor, it will be presumed that this occurred due to D's want of care. Such things do not usually happen without negligence.

Res ipsa loquitur is based on the premise that negligence on the part of the defendant can be very difficult for the plaintiff to prove. Often, only the defendant will be aware of the true cause of the accident and whether he was negligent or not. To try to ensure justice despite this, the law will shift the burden of disproving negligence to the defendant when the plaintiff has shown a prima facie case of negligence, *i.e.* when he has shown that the accident is such as would not in the ordinary course of events happen if the defendant had taken proper care.

Res ipsa loquitur operates in similar fashion to the peculiar knowledge principle in certain respects. Some commentators feel that *res ipsa loquitur* merely transfers an evidential burden, or maybe only a tactical burden, to the defendant. However, others appear to regard *res ipsa loquitur* as transferring the legal burden. In other words, unless the defendant adduces evidence to the contrary, he will be presumed negligent.

It is also worth noting that some evidence writers treat *res ipsa loquitur* under the heading of presumptions rather than in the context of chapters on the burden of proof. However, presumptions and the burden of proof are inextricably linked. A rebuttable presumption of fact, for instance, shifts the burden of proof. Once the basic fact is proved, the presumed fact will be presumed in the absence of evidence from the other side. So, at first, the burden is on one party to prove the basic fact. Once he has discharged this, the

---

90.   At p. 84.
91.   (1997) I.L.T. 121.

burden shifts to the other party to disprove the presumed fact. This is the only context in which we talk about the burden "shifting".

There are a number of Irish cases pertinent to the *res ipsa loquitur* doctrine. In *Mullen v. Quinnsworth*[92] Mrs. Mullen slipped on some cooking oil on the floor of the defendant's supermarket. In the ordinary course of events, cooking oil is not found on the floor of a supermarket. Mrs. Mullen should have been able to raise r*es ipsa loquitur.* This would mean that the defendants would be presumed negligent. They would have the burden of raising evidence to prove that they were not negligent. However, in the proceedings the presumption of *res ipsa loquitur* was not raised.

In *O'Reilly v. Lavelle*,[93] the presumption was pleaded successfully. The defendant's animals got out onto the road and the plaintiff's car crashed into them. Because farm animals do not, in the ordinary course of events, wander unattended along the highway, the onus was on the defendant to prove that their presence on the road was not caused by his negligence.

2.4   Standard of proof

This is the degree to which the party who has the burden of proof has to prove or disprove certain facts. There are different standards of proof. In criminal cases, the prosecution has a higher standard of proof than the defence. In civil cases, the standard is the same no matter which party has the burden of proof.

2.4.1 Standard of proof in criminal cases

Whenever the legal burden is on the prosecution (and this will be the vast majority of the time), the burden is to prove the fact in issue beyond all reasonable doubt. In order to avoid a reasonable doubt in convicting, the jury must be of the view that the facts are inconsistent with any rational explanation other than guilt. Judges are obliged to make this very clear in their summing up.

Proof beyond reasonable doubt was defined by Lord Denning in *Millar v. Minister for Pensions*[94] as follows:

> "It need not reach certainty, but it must carry a high degree of probability. Proof beyond a reasonable doubt does not mean proof beyond the shadow of a doubt. The law would fail to protect the community if it admitted fanciful possibilities to deflect the course of justice. If the evidence is so strong against a man as to leave only a remote possibility in his favour, which can be dismissed with the sentence 'of course it is possible but not in the least probable' the case is proved beyond reasonable doubt, but nothing short of that will suffice."

[92.]   [1990] 1 I.R. 59.
[93.]   [1990] 2 I.R. 372.
[94.]   [1947] 2 All E.R. 372.

(1) Correct directions on standard of proof for prosecution in criminal cases

In *R. v. Hepworth*[95] Lord Goddard said that a judge would be safe if he said, "You must be satisfied beyond reasonable doubt". A statement to the effect that "You must feel sure of the prisoner's guilt" would also be acceptable.

In *Ferguson v. R*[96] the formula "satisfied beyond reasonable doubt so that you feel sure of the accused's guilt" was held to be sufficient by the Privy Council. However the Privy Council in that case also recognised that there was no one form of words which must be used.

In *People (Attorney General) v. Byrne* it was stated that the jury should be told that:

> "the accused is entitled to the benefit of the doubt and that when two views on any part of the case are possible on the evidence, they should adopt that which is favourable to the accused unless the State has established the other beyond a reasonable doubt".[97]

Kenny J. also stated that the degree of proof in criminal cases should be contrasted with that in a civil case. However, it was established in *People (D.P.P.) v. Shortt*[98] that there was no obligation on judges to do this.

In *People (D.P.P.) v. Cotter*[99] the trial judge said that the standard of proof in criminal cases was not moral certitude but rather something short of a mathematical or moral certainty, namely proof beyond reasonable doubt. This was held to be correct.

In *People (D.P.P.) v. C.*[100] the Court of Criminal Appeal held that if there was a conflict between pre-trial statements of a witness and evidence given by that witness at trial, there was no obligation on the trial judge to direct the jury to accept the version most favourable to the accused. Murray J. stated that to direct the jury to rely on one version rather than another would be to usurp its function.

(2) Incorrect directions on standard of proof for prosecution in criminal cases

In *People (Attorney General) v. Byrne*,[101] the trial judge told the jury that they must be "satisfied" of the accused's guilt. This was held to be wrong. One may

---

[95.] [1955] 2 Q.B. 600.

[96.] [1979] 1 W.L.R. 94.

[97.] [1974] I.R. 1, 9. However, note the decision of McGuinness J. in *People (D.P.P.) v. Kiely*, unreported, Central Criminal Court, March 21, 2001, in which she relied on the earlier authorities of *People (Attorney General) v. Berber* [1944] I.R. 405 and *People (Attorney General) v. O'Connor* [1935] Ir. Jur. Rep. 1 in coming to the conclusion that it was not essential for a trial judge to state that the accused be given the benefit of the doubt. See also on this point *People (D.P.P.) v. Rawley* [1997] 2 I.R. 265.

[98.] Unreported, Court of Criminal Appeal, July 23, 1996.

[99.] Unreported, Court of Criminal Appeal, June 28, 1999.

[100.] [2001] 3 I.R. 345.

[101.] [1974] I.R. 1.

be satisfied of something and still have a reasonable doubt. This was also held by the U.K. courts in *R. v. Hepworth*.[102]

In *R. v. Law*[103] the words "pretty certain" were held to be insufficient. In *R. v. Head*[104] the words "reasonably sure" were inadequate. In *R. v. Gray*[105] the jurors were asked to see if the evidence satisfied the standard of proof that they would use in their everyday business affairs. This was held to be insufficient.

In *People (D.P.P.) v. Cremin*[106] the trial judge said that doubt on any one matter before the jury did not entitle the accused to an acquittal. The Court of Criminal Appeal held that this was a misdirection and quashed the conviction. In *People (D.P.P.) v. Morrissey*[107] the Court of Criminal Appeal criticised a trial judge who had told the jury that they were allowed to choose between the prosecution and the defence evidence. He should have referred to reasonable doubt.

(3) Should the judge explain reasonable doubt?

In *R. v. Ching*[108] the jury requested clarification as to the meaning of "proof beyond reasonable doubt" and the judge provided this. His direction was later found to be correct; however, the Court of Appeal pointed out that in most cases judges should not try to define "beyond reasonable doubt". Most judicial summaries of the phrase tend to lead to confusion. However, the case in question was an exceptional case where the jury had requested help.

Kenny J, in *People (Attorney General) v. Byrne*[109] said that it was useful to explain exactly what "being entitled to the benefit of the doubt" meant. However, in contrast to this Lord Goddard in *R. v. Hepworth and Fearnley*[110] said that judges should avoid expressions like "giving the benefit of the doubt":

> "It is not a question of giving the benefit of a doubt; if the jury are left with any degree of doubt whether the prisoner is guilty, the case has not been proved."

The accused in *People (D.P.P.) v. Kelly*[111] was charged with sexual offences. The trial judge instructed the jury that the onus of proof was on the prosecution and told them that if they were satisfied of the accused's guilt beyond reasonable doubt, they should find him guilty. This was held to be inadequate. The Court of Criminal Appeal said that the trial judge should have explained what "satisfied beyond reasonable doubt" meant and told them that they could only convict if they had no reasonable doubt as to guilt. However, it

---

[102]. [1983] Crim. L.R. 474.
[103]. [1961] Crim. L.R. 52.
[104]. (1961) 45 Cr. App. R. 225.
[105]. (1973) 58 Cr. App. R 177.
[106]. Unreported, Court of Criminal Appeal, *ex tempore*, May 10, 1999.
[107]. Unreported, Court of Criminal Appeal, July 10, 1998.
[108]. (1976) 63 Cr. App. Rep. 7.
[109]. [1974] I.R. 1.
[110]. [1955] 2 All E.R. 918.
[111]. Unreported, Court of Criminal Appeal, December 13, 1999.

should be noted that a model direction by the Court of Criminal Appeal in *People (D.P.P.) v. Cotter*[112] uses the phrase "satisfied beyond reasonable doubt" without explaining fully what this means.[113]

(4) Standard of proof when legal burden on accused

When the legal burden is placed on the accused in a criminal case, *e.g.* insanity, he merely has to fulfil the civil standard of proof on the balance of probabilities (see below). He does not have to prove this beyond reasonable doubt. This was affirmed by the Court of Criminal Appeal in *Attorney General v. Boylan*.[114] It was affirmed in the United Kingdom in *R. v. Carr-Briant*.[115]

The issue of the standard of proof to be placed on the accused in criminal cases where he bears the legal burden was discussed in *Convening Authority v. Doyle*[116] by the Court Martial. Again, it affirmed *R. v. Carr-Briant*: the standard of proof is on the balance of probabilities.

In *Boylan* the direction of the trial judge as to the standard of proof on the balance of probabilities was affirmed by the Court of Criminal Appeal. In relation to the standard of proof which the accused must meet, the trial judge said that:

> "such a thing as insanity can never be proved to demonstration in the way one would prove a mathematical problem.... It is necessary that it should be proved to your reasonable satisfaction – it is necessary that the accused should satisfy you, as reasonable men, that at the time this act was committed he was insane. Gentlemen, do not approach that question in an arbitrary, detached way. Approach it in the same way that you would approach some problem that you had to solve in your ordinary, everyday life.... Supposing you had, for the purpose of your business, or for the purpose of some important affair in your own lives, to determine whether or not upon this occasion the accused was insane. Assuming you had to do that, and you had to determine it upon the evidence that has been produced before you, would you for the purpose of your own business be satisfied that the accused was insane? If so, that is sufficient."[117]

2.4.2 *Standard of proof in civil cases*

The standard of proof for all parties on whom the burden is placed in civil proceedings is the balance of probabilities. This applies in nullity cases too, but not to contempt of court proceedings leading to committal; here, because of the threat of imprisonment, the criminal standard applies. Normally, the balance of probabilities standard applies to tribunals but in some cases it may

---

[112.] Unreported, Court of Criminal Appeal, June 28, 1999.

[113.] See most recently *People (D.P.P.) v. Kiely*, unreported, Court of Criminal Appeal, 21 March 2001 where McGuinness J. upheld an unorthodox explanation of "beyond reasonable doubt" given by a trial judge. See also *People (D.P.P.) v. Cahill*, unreported, Court of Criminal Appeal, July 31, 2001.

[114.] [1937] I.R. 449.

[115.] [1945] K.B. 607.

[116.] [1996] 2 I.L.R.M. 213.

[117.] Quoted by Sullivan C.J., at pp. 456-457.

be higher. *e.g.* the Kerry Babies Tribunal, which had an intermediate standard of proof.

The best definition of proof on the balance of probabilities was given by Denning L.J. in *Miller v. Minister for Pensions*:[118] there should be a reasonable degree of probability, but not as high as required in a criminal case. The evidence should be such that the jury can say, "We think it more probable than not". However, it is not enough for the probabilities to be equal:

> "It must carry a reasonable degree of probability, but not so high as is required in a criminal case. If the evidence is such that the tribunal can say 'we think it more probable than not' the burden is discharged, but if the probabilities are equal it is not."

Morris L.J. in *Hornam v. Neuberger Products Ltd*,[119] an action for damages for breach of warranty and fraud, stated that there was some difference of approach in civil actions depending on the type of civil action:

> "Though no court and no jury would give less careful attention to issues lacking gravity than to those marked by it, the very elements of gravity become a part of the whole range of circumstances which have to be weighed in the scale when deciding as to the balance of probabilities."

Some similarity exists between this approach and that of O'Flaherty J. in *O'Laoire v. Medical Council*:

> "[T]here is but one standard of proof in civil cases though, of necessity, it is a flexible one. This flexibility will ensure that the graver the allegation the higher will be the degree of probability that is required to bring home the case against the person whose conduct is impugned."[120]

Re H. (Minors)[121] involved an application for a care order in respect of a child by a local authority. The child had alleged that her stepfather had been raping her. The stepfather had been acquitted of her rape. What was the appropriate standard of proof to take into account in the care order application? The House of Lords stated as follows *per* Lord Nicholls:

> "Where the matters in issue are facts the standard of proof required in non-criminal proceedings is the preponderance of probability, usually referred to as the balance of probability. This is the established general principle…. The balance of probability standard means that a court is satisfied an event occurred if the court considers that, on the evidence, the occurrence of the event is more likely than not. When assessing the probabilities the court will have in mind as a factor, to whatever extent it is appropriate in the particular case, that the more serious the allegation, the less likely it is that the event occurred and, hence, the stronger should be the evidence before the court concludes that the allegation is established on the balance of probability. Fraud is usually less likely than

---

118. [1947] 2 All E.R. 372.
119. [1957] 1 Q.B. 247.
120. Unreported, Supreme Court, July 24, 1992.
121. [1996] 1 All E.R. 1.

negligence. Deliberate physical injury is usually less likely than accidental physical injury. A stepfather is usually less likely to have repeatedly raped and had non-consensual oral sex with his under age stepdaughter than on some occasion to have lost his temper and slapped her. Built into the preponderance of probability standard is a generous degree of flexibility in respect of the seriousness of the allegations. Although the result is much the same, this does not mean that where a serious allegation is in issue the standard of proof is higher. It means only that the inherent probability or improbability of an event is itself a matter to be taken into account when weighing the probabilities and deciding whether, on balance, the event occurred. The more improbable the event, the stronger must be the evidence that it did occur before, on the balance of probability, its occurrence will be established."[122]

Lord Lloyd dissented, stating that:

"In my view the standard of proof...ought to be the simple balance of probability however serious the allegations involved.... It would be a bizarre result if the more serious the anticipated injury, whether physical or sexual, the more difficult it became for the local authority to satisfy the initial burden of proof."[123]

Cross has suggested the solution in *Re J.S. (a minor)*[124] as a compromise:

"[T]he claimant must satisfy the court that it is reasonably safe in all the circumstances of the case to act on the evidence before the court, bearing in mind the consequences which will follow."

In *Hearn v. Collins* O'Sullivan J. said that the standard of proof on the balance of probabilities:

"should be applied with some degree of flexibility and that the court should require allegations of particular gravity to be clearly established in evidence".[125]

2.5 Presumptions[126]

Presumptions are inextricably linked to the concept of the burden of proof. There are four different types of presumptions:

1. rebuttable presumptions of law;
2. irrebuttable presumptions of law;
3. presumptions of fact; and
4. presumptions without basic facts.

[122.] *Ibid.*, p. 15.
[123.] *Ibid.*, p. 8.
[124.] [1981] Fam. 22.
[125.] Unreported, High Court, February 3, 1998.
[126.] For the constitutionality of presumption in the light of *O'Leary v. Attorney General*, see O'Higgins & O'Braonáin (1992) 2 I.C.L.J. 179.

2.5.1 Rebuttable presumptions of law

These are the most common form of presumption. As already stated, they operate to shift the burden of proof from one party to another. They operate as follows: once the basic fact is proved (all presumptions of law have basic facts that must be proved before they swing into operation) another fact (a *presumed fact*) is automatically presumed. The onus of proof then swings to the other party to adduce evidence to rebut the presumed fact.

This is best illustrated by an example, *e.g.* the presumption of death. There is a rebuttable presumption of law that once someone has been missing for seven years, they are dead. The basic fact that must be proved is that the person has been missing for seven years. Once this is shown the presumption swings into operation and the fact of that person's death is presumed. The other party must bring evidence to rebut the presumption if he wishes to win on this point.

Other examples of presumptions of law are the presumption of legitimacy; the presumption of marriage, the presumption known as *omnia praesemunter rite esse actio, res ipsa loquitur* and the presumption against suicide. These will be discussed later.

Rebuttable presumptions of law can be legal or evidential presumptions.[127] Legal presumptions shift the legal burden of proof; evidential burdens shift the evidential burden of proof. The practical difference between the two is as follows: it is easier to rebut an evidential presumption because you merely have to raise a prima facie case that the presumed fact is not true. In order to rebut a legal presumption you have to rebut the truth of the presumed fact on the balance of probabilities (in a civil case) or beyond reasonable doubt (if you are the prosecution in a criminal case).

It appears that a legal presumption can never operate against the accused in a criminal case so as to fix him with the legal burden of disproving the presumed fact. Cross points out[128] that:

> "it is hard to believe, since the decision in Woolmington, that an English court would be prepared to apply a common law presumption so as to cast a persuasive burden upon the accused in a criminal case".[129]

Only evidential presumptions operate against the accused in a criminal case. So if, on the facts, any of the common law presumptions are applicable as against the accused in a criminal case, they are to be construed as being evidential presumptions only, *i.e.* only imposing a duty on the accused to raise a prima facie case in rebuttal.

[127.] Glanville Williams distinguished between evidential and persuasive presumptions.

[128.] *Cross & Tapper on Evidence* (9th ed., 1999), p. 124.

[129.] However, there is some authority to the contrary *R. v. Curgerwen* (1865) L.R. 1 C.C.R. 1; *R. v. Audley* [1907] 1 K.B. 383 and in Australia the placing of a legal burden on the accused by way of presumption is permissible: *R. v. Bonnor* [1957] V.L.R. 227. On the constitutional problems involved in the U.S. in doing this see Jeffries and Stephan, (1979) 88 Yale L.J. 1325.

(1) Presumption of accidental death

This was raised in the Irish case of *Harvey v. Ocean Accident Guarantee Corporation.*[130] Mr. Harvey had put out to sea in a small boat. His body was washed up weeks later. The life assurance company argued that his death was suicide. In the circumstances it was impossible to say either way. The court held that where someone died and the precise circumstances of death were unknown, there was a presumption that that person's death was by accident rather than suicide. The burden was on the assurance company to prove suicide and, since they could not do this, they had to pay out under the policy.

Holmes L.J. saw this presumption as a development of the presumption of innocence:

> "The death can only be reasonably accounted for in one of two ways – immersion in the water by accident or design; and an innocent cause ought to be presumed as against what would be prima facie a crime. There is ample authority that the presumption against crime is applicable in a civil action."[131]

(2) Presumption of marriage

This presumption has three facets.

Firstly, there is a presumption that if a marriage was celebrated between people who intended to marry, all the formal requirements in relation to the ceremony must have been fulfilled. It appears that in civil cases this presumption may have to be rebutted beyond reasonable doubt.[132] This case, *Mahadervan v. Mahadervan,* also illustrates that the presumption can operate in favour of foreign marriages as well as in English ones. In *Piers v. Piers*[133] the House of Lords applied this presumption. There was no evidence that a special licence was obtained, but it was held that it should be presumed to have been obtained unless otherwise shown.[134]

Secondly, there is a presumption that if a formally valid marriage was celebrated, the parties to the marriage had full capacity to enter into it, *e.g.* they were of full age and not married already.

Thirdly, there is a presumption that if two people have cohabited together and been treated by others as man and wife, there is a valid marriage between them.

In *Mulhern v. Clery*[135] a landowner in Macroom lived with a humble peasant widow for some years and had five children by her. He built a mansion on his estate and moved in to it with their children. The widow never lived in the mansion, but had a sixth child by the landowner two years after he moved out.

[130.] [1905] 2 I.R. 1 See also *Walcott v. American Life & C; O'Hagan v. Sun Life Insurance Co of Canada* [1932] I.R. 741; *R. v. Cardiff City Coroner, ex p Thomas* [1970] 1 W.L.R. 1475.

[131.] At 132.

[132.] *Mahadervan v. Mahadervan* [1964] P. 233.

[133.] (1849) 2 H.L. Cas. 331.

[134.] In *Re Estate of McLoughlin* 1 L.R. Ir. 421.

[135.] [1930] I.R. 649.

There was no documentary evidence of marriage between the couple. It was argued that the presumption of marriage should operate in this situation.

However, the court refused to treat this presumption as applicable. Fitzgibbon J. felt that it was rebutted by the words used by the landowner in his will, in which he had described his children as "reputed" and the woman "Margaret Swyney, widow" rather than his wife. Kennedy C.J. held that the presumption did not arise on the facts because there was no evidence that the couple had been treated by others as man and wife. Murnaghan J. dissented, being of the view that the presumption did arise and was not rebutted.

It should be noted that the presumption of marriage cannot be used against the accused in a prosecution for bigamy. In this instance, *R. v. Kay*[136] establishes that the existing valid marriage must be proved.

(3) Presumption of death if missing for seven years[137]

If someone has been missing for seven years, if there are persons who would be likely to hear from him during that period and none of those persons have heard from him, and if all other due enquiries have been made and produced nothing, that person will be presumed to be dead.

However, the presumption did not apply in *Chard v. Chard*,[138] where a husband would have been unlikely to have heard from his estranged wife in the past seven years because he had been in prison.

Authority is divided on when exactly the missing person is presumed to have died under this presumption. Some cases indicate that he will be presumed dead as of the date of trial[139]; other cases indicate that he will be presumed to have died at some stage during his seven-year absence[140] However, no precise date of death is presumed.[141]

The presumption was applied in *Re Bonis Doherty*.[142] Doherty bought shares in 1919 and was never heard from again by the firm. Advertisements in Irish and British newspapers were not replied to. In 1961, the Minister for Finance applied to the court, claiming that D. was dead and he was entitled to the shares as *bona vacantia*. Kenny J. held he was so entitled. The minister did not have to prove that D. was actually dead; he could rely on the presumption of death. D. had not contacted the stockbrokers for over thirty years.

Kenny J. said:

> "I think that the firm of stockbrokers who had purchased these shares for James Doherty could reasonably be expected to have heard from him about them during the last forty years. Even if the name which he gave was false, I cannot

---

136. (1887) 16 Cox C.C. 292.
137. Treitel 17 M.L.R. 530; Stone 44 M.L.R. 516.
138. [1956] P. 259.
139. *Re Rhodes, Rhodes v. Rhodes* (1887) 36 Ch.D. 586l.
140. *Chipchase v. Chipchase* [1939] P. 391and *Re Aldersey; Gibbon v. Hall* [1905] 2 Ch. 181.
141. See *Re Phene's Trusts* (1870) 5 Ch. App. 139, 144: where the court was not prepared to say whether death presumed to have taken place at the end or the beginning of the 7-year period.
142. [1961] I.R. 219.

think of anybody who would be more likely to hear from him than the firm which he had instructed to purchase the shares and to retain the share certificate and receive the dividends. I think that this is a case in which the legal presumption of death arises…"[143]

In McMahon v. McElroy[144] Chatterton V.-C. referred to the presumption that an individual's death was presumed seven years after last hearing from him. However, this presumption was inappropriate in the instant case where there was no one who could be expected to hear from him.

"If it be shown that Hugh Morgan has not been heard of by persons who might reasonably be expected to have heard of him, and if proper inquiries be made as to the place of his residence in America, and it is found that he has disappeared from it, and cannot be traced, I should not hesitate to presume him dead."[145]

(4) Presumption of intestacy[146]

It appears that where someone is missing for seven years and was not missing when last heard of, there is a presumption that he died intestate and without issue. The cases which support this are *Re Webb's Estate*[147] and *Re Bonis Doherty*[148] in which Kenny J. presumed that Doherty died intestate, unmarried and without known next of kin.

(5) Presumption of legitimacy

There is a presumption that a child born to, or conceived by, a wife in lawful wedlock with a husband alive at the date of conception, is the child of the husband, in the absence of evidence to the contrary. This applies even if the couple are living apart, though not if a court order of separation has been granted (see below). In *R. v. Hemmings*[149] the presumption of legitimacy was invoked against the accused, who was charged with incest.

The presumption may be rebutted by contrary evidence including non-access, impotence, contraceptive use, blood groups and genetic fingerprinting, cohabitation by the wife with another man at the relevant time, or by an admission of paternity by another man.

In civil cases, it has been argued[150] that the presumption must be rebutted by evidence of illegitimacy beyond reasonable doubt because of the stigma attached to a finding of illegitimacy. However, arguably, the Status of Children

---

[143.] *Ibid.*, p. 222.

[144.] (1869) I.R. 5 Eq. 1.

[145.] *Toher v. Purcell* (1931) L.J. (I.F.S.) 143.

[146.] Also note in relation to multiple deaths the statutory presumption in section 5 of the Succession Act 1965. Where two or more people die in circumstances rendering it uncertain which of them survived the other, they are deemed to have died simultaneously. This can be compared with section 184 of the Law of Property Act 1925: where two or more people died in circumstances rendering it uncertain which of them survived the other, the younger shall be presumed to be the survivor.

[147.] (1869) I.R. 5; Eq. 235.

[148.] [1961] I.R. 219.

[149.] [1939] 1 All E.R. 417.

[150.] *Blyth v. Blyth* [1966] A.C. 643.

Act 1987 has removed the need for proof beyond reasonable doubt in civil cases in Ireland. In the United Kingdom, section 26 of the Family Law Reform Act 1969 specifically says that the presumption can be rebutted on the balance of probabilities.

(6) Presumption of illegitimacy

Where a wife and husband are separated by court order before the conception of the child, the child will be presmed to be illegitimate. In *Hetherington v. Hetherington*[151] the presumption was rebutted by evidence that the wife and husband had sexual intercourse during the period of separation.

(7) *Omnia prasemunter rite esse acta* (presumption of validity of a purportedly official act)

On proof or admission of the basic fact that a public or official act has been performed, it is presumed, in the absence of evidence to the contrary, that the act has been regularly and properly performed. Similarly, it is presumed that the person performing the act has been properly appointed. Note that all the presumptions so far have imposed a legal burden in civil proceedings. However, this maxim only imposes an evidential burden in civil cases.

In *Martin v. Quinn*[152] the accused was charged with failure to provide a urine sample to a medical practitioner. The accused argued that the doctor who requested the sample was not a medical practitioner. The court held that since the individual was performing an official act, there was a presumption that he had been validly appointed. The accused must adduce prima facie evidence to rebut this.

In *People (D.P.P.) v. Farrell*[153] the maxim was also raised. Normally, an extension of detention under the Offences Against the State Act 1939 must be authorised by a Chief Superintendent. An ordinary Superintendent can only do this if authorised by the Commissioner. It was held that the above presumption did not apply in respect of an extension of detention under a section such as this one. It did not apply where the alleged official act involved the exercise of an extraordinary power. Here it was not sufficient to presume that the Commissioner's authorisation had been given. Written record of such authorisation had to be provided.

However, in *Minister for Agriculture v. Cleary,*[154] a case which involved the illegal sale of fertiliser, an issue arose as to whether two Department officials, who gave evidence, were validly appointed. The court distinguished *Farrell*[155] and applied the presumption.

---

151. (1887) 12 P.D. 112.
152. [1980] I.R. 244.
153. [1978] I.R. 13.
154. [1988] I.L.R.M. 294.
155. [1978] I.R. 13.

Arguably, this maxim cannot be used in a criminal case to establish an essential element of the offence. The accused in *R. v. Dillon*[156] was charged with negligently permitting prisoners to escape from custody. The Privy Counsel refused to allow the prosecution to rely on the maxim to prove that the prisoners were in custody.

(8) *Res ipsa loquitur*

This maxim has been dealt with already when looking at the burden of proof in civil cases. It only applies to negligence actions. It is uncertain whether this presumption shifts the legal, equitable or tactical burden.

2.5.2 Irrebuttable presumptions of law

These are effectively rules of substantive law expressed in terms of presumptions. *e.g.* section 41 of the Road Traffic Act 1961. Section 41 stated that a certificate of blood alcohol content from a doctor shall be conclusive evidence of the alcohol content in the accused's blood. This made the offence in question effectively one not of driving over the alcohol limit but of driving at a time when one's alcohol content as subsequently certified by a doctor was found to be over the limit. There is nothing wrong with creating such an offence.

However, the courts in future should be careful to avoid expressing the substantive law in the language of irrebuttable presumptions because a similar provision to section 41 was recently found unconstitutional in the case of *Maher v. Attorney General.*[157] It was held that the provision in question deprived the accused of the right to rebut the truth of the certificate by preventing him from adducing evidence to rebut the prosecution case. It therefore infringed his constitutional right to a fair trial.

2.5.3 Presumptions of fact

These presumptions operate in a similar way to presumptions of law. However, they do not shift the legal or evidential burden but merely the tactical burden. In other words, they operate as follows: One party proves the basic fact. This raises a tactical presumption of the presumed fact. This allows the judge or jury to find in favour or against the presumed fact as they think fit. The other party is not strictly obliged to adduce evidence to rebut the presumed fact. He may still win on the point even though he does not adduce any evidence. However, it is usually advisable for him to adduce evidence.

Presumptions of fact are merely examples of a common process in the law: that of drawing inferences from facts. You get it all the time in relation to circumstantial evidence. An example of a common presumption of fact is the

---

[156.] [1982] A.C. 484.
[157.] [1973] I.R. 40.

presumption of guilt in relation to handling stolen goods: if someone is caught with stolen goods there is an inference of fact that he knows they are stolen.

There is also a presumption of continuance of life: where someone is alive on a particular date, an inference may be drawn that he was alive on a subsequent date. The strength of the inference diminishes as the date of the sighting goes back further and further into the past. Finally, there is a presumption of unseaworthiness: when a ship sinks shortly after leaving port, an inference may be drawn that it was unseaworthy at the time of leaving port.

Another example of a presumption of fact is to be found in the maxim *omnia praesumunter contra spoilatorem*. This maxim allows a court to draw adverse inferences against a wrongdoer from his destruction of or failure to produce relevant evidence or documents. For example, if there is difficulty in valuing items because they have been wrongfully destroyed by one party, this uncertainty will be resolved against the wrongdoer.[158]

2.5.4 *Presumptions without basic facts*

These are merely rules of evidence that deal with the placing of the legal burden of proof, *e.g.* the presumption of innocence in criminal cases, which places the legal burden of proof in relation to all facts in issue on the prosecution.

Another example is the presumption of sanity in criminal trials, which states that the legal burden of proof is on the accused if he wants to raise the defence of insanity.

[158.] For the application of this maxim, see *Armory v. Delamirie* (1722) 1 S..T.R.A. 504; *Seager v. Copydex Ltd* [1969] 2 All E.R. 718; *Gray v. Haig & Son* (1855) 20 Beav. 219; and most recently *O'Mahony v. Bon Secours Hospital*, unreported, Superior Court, July 13, 2001.

Chapter 3

PROOF OF FACTS WITHOUT EVIDENCE

There are three ways in which facts may be proved without evidence: they may be presumed in a party's favour under a presumption of law in the absence of any evidence rebutting that presumption; they may be judicially noticed; and, finally, they may be proved by formal admission.

3.1 Judicial notice[1]

The term "judicial notice" is used to refer to a process whereby a court may accept the existence of a fact without requiring it to be proved, either because the fact is common and indisputable knowledge or because it can be ascertained from sources of incontrovertible reliability.

Once a matter has been judicially noticed, the jury must accept it as proven. In addition, judges in subsequent cases will also be compelled to judicially notice the issue.

Lord Sumner in *Commonwealth Shipping Representative v. P & O Branch Services*[2] described the doctrine as follows:

> "Judicial notice refers to facts which a judge can be called upon to receive and to act upon either from his general knowledge of them, or from inquiries to be made by himself for his own information from sources to which it is proper for him to refer."

As this dictum indicates, there are two heads of judicial notice.

3.1.1 Judicial notice of facts which are matters of common knowledge

If facts are matters of common and indisputable knowledge, they may be judicially noticed, thus relieving the side asserting them from the necessity of having to prove them. The rationale for this head of the doctrine of judicial notice is based on that of common sense and the saving of time and expense.

In *R. v. Luffe*[3] judicial notice was taken of the fact that a baby cannot be conceived and born in two weeks. In *Bryant v. Foot*[4] judicial notice was taken of the fact that value of money decreases over time. In *Nye v. Niblett*[5] the fact

---

[1]   See further on this issue Nokei 74 L.Q.R. 59.
[2]   [1923] A.C. 191 at 212.
[3]   (1807) 8 East 193.
[4]   (1868) L.R. 3 Q.B. 497.
[5]   [1918] 1 K.B. 23.

that cats are domestic animals was judicially noticed. *Bridlington Relay Ltd v. Yorkshire Electricity Board*[6] was a case where judicial notice was taken of the fact that television is a standard feature of domestic life. In *Re Oxford Poor Rate*[7] judicial notice was taken of the fact that one of the objects of Oxford University is the advancement of learning.

The doctrine of judicial notice was applied by an Irish court in *Byrne v. Londonderry Tram Co.*,[8] in which judicial notice was taken of the fact that a passenger travelling on the driver's platform in a tram was acting in an unauthorised manner.

Holmes L.J. stated in the above case that:

> "it is not necessary in the trial of an action to give formal evidence of matters with which men of ordinary intelligence are acquainted".[9]

The doctrine of judicial notice had already been applied in Ireland by Palles C.B. in *Robinson v. Jones*,[10] where he held that judicial notice could be taken of the fact that a postcard is the sort of document which anyone may read. This decision was later followed by the United Kingdom courts in *Huth v. Huth*.[11]

However, in *Kearney v. King*[12] a court refused to take judicial notice of the fact that the word "Dublin" on a bill of exchange meant Dublin, the capital city of Ireland. Interestingly, Cross[13] points out that this case has sometimes been incorrectly explained as saying that courts will not take judicial notice of the fact that Dublin is located in Ireland.

As a general rule, the courts are reluctant to take judicial notice of the situation of towns, buildings and streets or boundaries, which may have to be proved by evidence. In *Attorney General v. Kirk*[14] an Irish Circuit Court judge refused to take judicial notice of the boundary of County Louth. In *Kirby v. Hickson*[15] a court would not take judicial notice of the fact that Russell Square in London was within 20 miles of Grosvenor Square. In *Theaker v. Richardson*[16] a court refused to take judicial notice of the fact that husbands read their wives' letters.

In contrast to this, in *Waters v. Cruickshank*[17] O'Dalaigh C.J. held that, as Ireland was an agricultural country, the judge could take judicial notice of the price of yearlings in a particular year.

---

6. [1965] 1 All E.R. 264.
7. (1857) 8 E. & B. 184.
8. [1902] 2 I.R. 457.
9. Ibid., 480.
10. (1879) 4 L.R. Ir. 391.
11. [1915] 3 K.B. 32.
12. (1819) 2 B & Ald 301
13. *Cross and Tapper on Evidence* (9th ed. 1999) p. 76 fn. 17.
14. [1955-56] Ir. Jur. Rep. 59.
15. (1850) 14 JP 370.
16. [1962] 1 All ER 229
17. [1967] I.R. 378

Arguably, some courts are too ready to take judicial notice of a particular fact. A question mark hangs over the case of *Burns v. Edman*[18] and its conclusion that judicial notice should be taken of the fact that criminals have unhappy lives.

3.1.2 Judicial notice of facts instantly verifiable from unimpeachable sources

To some extent this head of judicial notice is influenced by public policy considerations.

In *Duff Development Co. Ltd v. Government of Kelatan*[19] the government of Kelatan applied for an order against the enforcement of an arbitration award on the ground that Kelatan was an independent sovereign state. The judge received a letter from the Secretary of State confirming this and correctly took judicial notice of the fact after reading the letter. The House of Lords said:

> "It has for some time been the practice of our courts, when such a question is raised, to take judicial notice of the sovereignty of a state, and for that purpose (in case of any uncertainty) to seek information from a Secretary of State; and when information is so obtained the court does not permit it to be questioned by the parties."[20]

In this case, if the courts had required the question of whether Kelatan was an independent sovereign state to be proved, they might have infringed on the executive power to determine foreign relations.

In *Read v. Bishop of Lincoln*[21] a judge consulted various sources to see if the mixing of communion wine with water was contrary to the law of the Church of England. Lord Halsbury stated that "where it is important to ascertain ancient facts of a public nature the law does permit historical works to be referred to".[22]

Judicial notice may be taken after enquiry of the practice of conveyancers and other professionals.

Judicial notice is taken of all statutes, but not necessarily of statutory instruments, which may have to be proved in court unless they are particularly well known in legal circles. In *State (Taylor) v. Circuit Court Judge for Wicklow*,[23] judicial notice was taken of the fact that Part III of the Road Traffic Act 1933 had been brought into operation by statutory order by a certain date. Davitt P. recognised that not all statutory instruments may be judicially noticed. This particular statutory instrument, however, might be judicially noticed by a District Justice who spent most of his time administering it.

---

18. [1970] 2 QB 541
19. [1924] AC 797
20. Per Lord Cave at 805.
21. [1892] A.C. 644.
22. *Ibid.*, at 653.
23. [1951] I.R. 311.

Davitt P. stated:

> "There is no doubt that a judge is entitled to bring to the determination of any issue his own knowledge relevant thereto, not his private or particular knowledge as an individual but his general knowledge as a lawyer and a judge."[24]

However, *People (Attorney General) v. Kennedy*[25] held that statutory instruments made under the Emergency Powers Act must be proved.

In *McQuaker v. Goddard*[26] a court had to consider whether a camel was a domestic animal. In deciding this question, the judge heard expert witnesses but also consulted reference works. Clauson L.J. followed Stephen's *Digest of the Law of Evidence*[27] which stated:

> "No evidence of any fact of which the court will take judicial notice need to be given to the party alleging its existence; but the judge, upon being called upon to take judicial notice thereof, may, if he is unacquainted with such fact, refer to any person or to any document or book of reference for his satisfaction in relation thereto."

Clauson L.J. said that the judge in this case had not been receiving evidence as such; he had merely heard the witnesses to form his view on a matter of which he was supposed to have complete knowledge.

3.2 Formal admissions

There is a special category of admission in a civil case known as a formal admission. The inclusion of information in pleadings or in a letter sent to the other party's legal adviser constitutes a formal admission of that information in a civil case. Once made, a formal admission cannot subsequently be contradicted by the person who has made it. Formal admissions, however, are binding only for the purposes of the case in which they are made. The concept of a formal admission is not recognised in criminal proceedings in this jurisdiction.[28]

---

24. p. 322.
25. [1946] I.R. 517.
26. [1940] 1 K.B. 687.
27. (12th ed., MacMillan & Co., London, 1946), Article 12.
28. *R. v. Riley* (1896) 18 Cox C.C. 285.

Chapter 4

REAL EVIDENCE

Real evidence consists of material, tangible evidence, such as a chattel, the demeanour or appearance of a witness, a view, a tape recording or computer printout, or a photograph.[1] Real evidence does not usually stand alone. In order to make such objects relevant, the court will usually need to hear oral evidence explaining their significance. Expert evidence in particular is frequently adduced to explain the significance of real evidence.

4.1 Material objects[2]

A chattel is an example of real evidence. For example, in a murder case, the murder weapon may be an item of real evidence. However, its significance will only become apparent by testimony Similarly, in a trial for handling stolen goods, the goods in question constitute real evidence. However, they only become significant to the facts in issue once testimony is given identifying them as stolen property.

In a civil action under the Sale of Goods and Supply of Services Act 1980 for breach of an implied condition that goods sold be of merchantable quality, the goods in question may constitute real evidence, and testimony may be given by experts as to whether or not they are of merchantable quality or not. In *R. v. Wright*[3] it was recognised that the trial judge has discretion to allow the jury to take material objects put before the court into the jury room if he feels it is appropriate.

In *Line v. Taylor*,[4] an animal liability action, one of the issues was whether the dog that had attacked the defendant was of a vicious disposition. In order to determine this fact, it was permitted to bring the dog into court to be examined.

Sometimes it may be impossible to produce the material objects at the trial, perhaps because they are perishable objects or because they have been lost. However, in contrast to the rule in relation to documents, the court may accept secondary evidence of material objects. Photos, replicas, or the oral evidence

---

[1.] For a critical discussion of the rules relating to real evidence, see further Nokei 65 L.Q.R. 57.
[2.] Under the Criminal Procedure Act 1997 the prosecution must not only provide witness statements to the accused in the trial on indictment, they must also give a list of exhibits, *i.e.* documents and material objects.
[3.] [1993] Crim. L.R. 607.
[4.] (1862) 3 F. & F. 731.

of someone who has seen the object, can constitute admissible secondary evidence of material objects.

However, the non-production of the relevant object may affect the weight to be attributed to it by the court. The police in particular have a duty to preserve all objects in their possession relevant to the commission of a crime. In addition, if the value of a material object is an issue, *Armory v. Delamire*[5] demonstrates that a presumption operates against the party who fails to produce it.

4.2   A view

A view consists of an out-of-court inspection of either the place of the crime or of some object, relevant to the facts in issue, which it is impossible to bring to court. A view may be part of the evidence in either a criminal or civil case. Photographs or a video of the view may be acceptable.

A view of an object may be taken if it is too large to be produced in court. The classic example of such an object would be a motor vehicle. In *Buckingham v. Daily News*,[6] which involved a civil action for negligence arising out of an injury caused by a machine, the machine was inspected. The object in question should be brought as near to the court as possible. In *London General Omnibus Co v. Lovell*[7] the bus in question was parked outside the courthouse and viewed there.

In a criminal case, the judge, jury and defendant should always be invited to be present at a view. The defendant may decline to attend, in which case the view may take place without him. The entire jury must see the view. In *R. v. Gurney*[8] the nature of particular street lighting was relevant to the facts in issue. The trial judge asked one of the jurors to go and view the street lighting and report on it to his colleagues. This was held to have been improper.

This rule has been modified somewhat in civil cases, where the scene of the accident is a public place. In *Salsbury v. Woodland*[9] it was held that the judge is entitled to attend the scene of the accident on his own without notifying the parties, provided that the scene of the accident is a public place. However, the application of this principle to criminal cases was discouraged in *Parry v. Boyle*.[10] In this case, magistrates hearing the case summarily had visited the scene of a road accident in the absence of the accused. It was held that they should normally be accompanied by the accused in such circumstances. It is a serious matter not to inform an accused of a view and his conviction may be set aside as a result.

---

5. [1722] All E.R. Rep. 121.
6. [1956] 2 Q.B. 534.
7. [1901] 1 Ch. 135.
8. [1976] Crim. L.R. 567.
9. [1970] 1 Q.B. 324.
10. (1983) Cr. App. Rep. 310.

It has been established since the case of *R. v. Martin*[11] that normally the judge or jury is not entitled to ask questions at a view. This was affirmed in *R. v. Karamat*.[12] Questions may be put to a witness in court afterwards regarding the view.

4.3 Appearance or voice

The appearance or voice of the accused may constitute real evidence, particularly when the issue of identification of the criminal is in issue. In personal injury cases, the accused may be physically examined in order to assess the quantum of damages awardable.

4.4 Demeanour

The demeanour of the accused and other witnesses in court is an item of real evidence which may be relevant to their credibility.

4.5 Documents

Documents may constitute real evidence if their relevance does not depend on the words contained in them. For example, a stolen deed or cheque may be shown to the court in order to prove that it bears the fingerprints of the accused. In this situation, the documents are real evidence.

4.6 Statements made by mechanical devices

Automatic recordings also constitute real evidence. *The Statue of Liberty*[13] involved a civil action concerning a collision between two ships. The issue was whether a film of radar echoes coming from the two ships at the time of the collision could be admitted to prove how the collision occurred. The film had been produced by a machine, without human intervention. It was held that it could be admitted as an item of real evidence.

The decision was premised on the basis that tape recordings and photographs were generally admissible. Sir Jocelyn Simon stated:

> "It would be an absurd distinction that a photograph should be admissible if the camera were operated by a photographer, but not if it were operated by a trip or clock mechanism".[14]

This case was followed in *Owen v. Chesters*,[15] where evidence of what appeared on the visual display of a breath testing device was held to be real evidence.

[11.] (1872) L.R. 1 C.C.R. 378.
[12.] [1956] A.C. 256.
[13.] [1968] 2 All E.R. 195.
[14.] At p. 196.
[15.] [1985] Crim. L.R. 156.

4.7 Photographs

Sir Jocelyn Simon in *The Statue of Liberty*[16] referred to the admissibility of photographs. Photographs have been admissible in evidence since the case of *R. v. Tolson.*[17] This involved a prosecution of a woman for bigamy. Witnesses were permitted to look at photos of the prisoner's first husband to identify him as the person named in the certificate of marriage. In *R. v. Cook*[18] Watkins L.J. said that the correctness of the ruling in *Tolson* had never been doubted.

The general view is that photographs do not infringe the hearsay rule because they are scenes or situations reproduced by mechanical and chemical devices within the meaning of *The Statue of Liberty*. The attitude is that the camera never lies, and therefore a photo is not hearsay. However, this view has been questioned by at least one commentator. If they are hearsay, on what basis are they admissible in this jurisdiction? In this regard, it is worth noting that Watkins L.J. in *R. v. Cook* was of the view that the photograph and photofit were in a class of their own to which neither the rule against hearsay nor the rule against narrative applied.

However, in order for a photo to be admitted in evidence it is necessary first to prove its authenticity. The photographer must prove that he took the photograph and the person who has developed the photo must also give a statement to the effect that the negatives were untouched. If the camera is instamatic, there is of course no need for this.

The photo may be of a deceased in a murder or manslaughter trial, or it may actually show the occurrence of the crime. A witness not actually present at the scene of the crime may be allowed to identify the criminal from a photograph of the crime as someone previously known to them. Alternatively, the jury may be asked to look at the photos and decide whether or not they are of the accused. In *R. v. Dodson*[19] the jury were allowed to look at men in the dock and compare them with men in photos taken by a security camera of an armed robbery at a building society in order to identify the men.

In *R. v. Blenksinsop*[20] it was stated that a *Turnbull* direction on identification was not usually necessary in the case of identification from photos. However, in *Dodson* the judge was obliged to warn the jury of the dangers of identifying criminals from photos, in particular with regard to the possibility of changes in a person's appearance over time, the quality of the photos and the fact that they may be only seeing the person in the photos from a particular angle. However, in *R. v. Downey*[21] it was stated that this warning did not always have to be given.

One unresolved issue in evidence law relates to the status of photofits and sketches. Are they real evidence or are they hearsay? In *R. v. Cook*[22] it was

---

[16.] Also known as *Sapporo Maru (Owners) v Statue of Liberty (Owners)* [1968] 2 All E.R. 195.
[17.] (1864) 4 F. & F. 103.
[18.] [1987] 2 W.L.R. 775.
[19.] [1984] 1 W.L.R. 971.
[20.] [1995] 1 Cr. App. R. 7.
[21.] [1995] 1 Cr. App. R. 547.

stated that photofits were analogous to photos. However, it has subsequently been argued that this decision is wrong.[23]

4.8 Tape recordings

Tape recordings and videotapes have also been admitted under the same principles as photographs. Like the admission of photographs, this is based on the principle, summarised by Marshall J. in *R. v Maqsud Ali*,[24] that it is wrong to deny to the law of evidence the advantages of new techniques.

This principle was recently affirmed by Lord Taylor C.J. in *R v. Clare and Peach*,[25] where he stated that, in relation to new technology:

> "the courts must be vigilant to ensure that no unfairness results [but] they should not block steps which enable the jury to gain full assistance from the technology".

A tape recording is admissible as evidence of the sounds or conversation recorded in it. This has been established since the case of *R. v. Maqsud Ali*.[26] In this case, two individuals were charged with the murder of the wife of one of them. Both the accused had gone voluntarily to the police station. While in a room on their own at the station, they engaged in a conversation between themselves in Punjabi. A hidden mike in the room picked up this conversation, which amounted to a confession to murder. The tape recording was admitted in evidence. It is worth noting that the tape recording in this case was admissible even though it had been obtained through eavesdropping. In *R. v. Senat*[27] a tape obtained through telephone tapping was admitted.[28]

However, before a tape recording can be admitted in evidence it is necessary to show that it is authentic. It will be necessary to define the circumstances in which the tape was made and outline who had control of it afterwards. A prima facie case of authenticity must be made out before the judge before the tape can be played to the jury.

As with material objects, a copy of the tape may be admitted if the original is unavailable. In addition, if there is no copy of the tape, an individual who has heard it can give evidence of what he has heard on the tape. The primary evidence rule, which applies in relation to written documents, does not apply

---

22. [1987] Q.B. 417.
23. Tapper, Cross and Tapper on Evidence (9th ed., Butterworths, London, 1999) at p. 676.
24. [1966] 1 Q.B. 688.
25. [1995] 2 Cr. App. R. 333 at 339.
26. [1966] 1 Q.B. 688.
27. [1968] 52 Cr. App. R. 282.
28. It should be noted that a trial judge has a general common law discretion to exclude any evidence obtained illegally or by unfair means. In addition, unconstitutionally obtained evidence is automatically inadmissible. See Chapter 5.

in relation to videotapes, tape recordings or photos. For this reason, these types of evidence are perhaps better categorised as real evidence.[29]

The jury may be permitted access to hear the tape during its deliberations at the discretion of the judge. The normal procedure is for the jury to go back into the court to hear the tape. *R. v. Tonge*[30] confirms this. *R. v. Rampling*[31] establishes that the issue of whether or not to give the jury a transcript of the tape, is up to the discretion of the judge. If the recording is of poor quality or is of a conversation in a foreign language the judge is more likely to make a transcript available.

People v. Prunty[32] is an Irish decision on the use of tape recordings in court. The applicant was charged with various offences relating to the payment of a ransom by the family of a wealthy solicitor. Part of the evidence related to telephone calls about the payment of a ransom. The voice of the accused was identified at the trial from recordings made. The process of tracing the calls was also put in evidence. An objection was taken to the method of proof of the tracings on the ground that part of the proof of such tracings was established by hearsay evidence.

The Court of Criminal Appeal said that in a trial where a significant part of the evidence consisted of a tape recording and the tape was shown to be authentic, defects in sound quality or disputes as to the identity of the speakers were no grounds for excluding it from the evidence, although they might be relevant to its weight. The recording was held admissible.

4.9 Video recordings

Video recordings are admissible as real evidence on the same basis as photos and tape recordings. Once again, the authenticity and provenance of the recording must be established. If the original recording is not available, a copy is admissible. However, the authenticity of the copy must be proved. In *Kajala v. Noble*[33] a copy of a B.B.C. tape, on which the appellant was shown taking part in a disturbance, was held admissible. The Court of Appeal held that the secondary evidence rule only applied to written documents and not to tapes or film.

In *Braddish v. DPP*[34] the accused was charged with a robbery and arrested on the basis of video camera footage. He requested a copy of the video. Six months later he was told that the videos had been returned to the owners. He argued before the Supreme Court that his further prosecution should be restrained because the Gardaí. had parted with possession of the videotape. The Supreme Court restrained the further prosecution of the accused. It was no justification that the prosecution was not relying on the videotape; the accused

---

29. Although they fall within the definition of "document" given in s. 30(3) of the Criminal Evidence Act 1992: see ante. para 5.1.1.
30. [1993] Crim. L.R. 876.
31. [1987] Crim. L.R. 823.
32. [1986] I.L.R.M. 716.
33. (1982) 75 Cr. App. R. 149.
34. Unreported, Supreme Court, May 18, 2001.

was entitled to see it, as it might exculpate him. Hardiman J. said that the videotape was real evidence and that the Gardaí. were not entitled to dispose of it before trial. They had to seek out and preserve all evidence, which had an evidential bearing on guilt and innocence.

The duty to preserve and disclose evidence must be interpreted according to what is reasonable on the facts of each case. If no copy of the videotape is available, a witness may be allowed to give evidence of what he has seen on the video. In *Taylor v. Chief Constable of Cheshire*[35] witnesses had seen a video recording of an event. This recording had been accidentally erased before trial. The court said the witnesses could give evidence of what they had seen on the video. However, the jury must be given a warning in these circumstances and, if only part of the recording has been erased, the court will be very suspicious.

As with photographs, it is permissible for witnesses, experts, and the jury to identify the accused from videos. Normally, no evidence is admissible to explain a tape or video recording and it should be shown to the court without comment. However, there are exceptions to this in the case of experts and identifying witnesses. In *R. v. Clarke*[36] the witness was an expert in facial identification. Using a special technique, he superimposed video photos of the bank robber over photos of the accused and showed that they were a perfect match. His evidence was held admissible.

As with tape recordings, the judge has a discretion to allow a jury back into court to see a videotape that has already been shown to them.

4.10 Re-enactments

It has also been argued that videos and views of re-enactments should constitute a form of real evidence. In *Li Shu-Ling v. R.*[37] the defendant agreed to take part in the re-enactment of a killing he had admitted to carrying out. The re-enactment was recorded on video, with a commentary by the defendant. At trial, the defendant sought to stop this being admitted. It was held that the re-enactment should be regarded as a confession and that, provided it satisfied the rules for confessions, it was admissible.

One unresolved question in relation to re-enactments, which was sidestepped in *Li Shu-Ling v. R.*, is whether they involve real or testimonial evidence. If they are regarded as testimonial evidence, they are inadmissible under the hearsay rule, unless one of the exceptions (such as confessions) applies. It is worth noting that re-enactments may contain inaccuracies, which could mislead the court. In *R. v. Quinn and Bloom*,[38] a prosecution for disorderly conduct, a re-enactment of a striptease show by the defence was prohibited on the ground that slight differences in movement of dancers or snakes might change the character of show.

---

35. [1986] 1 W.L.R. 1479.
36. [1995] 2 Cr. App. R. 425.
37. [1989] AC 270.
38. [1962] 1 Q.B. 245.

Chapter 5

DOCUMENTARY EVIDENCE

A document is anything with writing on it. This definition is not confined to paper but includes stone, a computer disk or anything else which has things written on it. Darling J. in *R. v. Day*[1] stated that "[a]ny written thing capable of being evidence is properly described as a document ... and it is immaterial on what the writing may be inscribed".

The Criminal Evidence Act 1992 defines tape recordings, films and photos as documents for the purposes of that Act. However, these are different from traditional documents in the sense that they are seen as objective and not subject to the hearsay rule. Therefore they have been dealt with in the chapter on real evidence (Chapter 4).

A written document is an out-of-court statement, so if its relevance depends on the truth of its contents, it must come under an exception to the hearsay rule in order to be admissible. In addition, there are special additional admissibility requirements, which apply only to written documents.

5.1 Best evidence rule

The best evidence rule requires a party who is seeking to rely on the contents of a written document, to adduce primary evidence of the contents of that document. This rule is a survivor of the best evidence principle, which required a party to produce the best evidence that the case would allow.

Primary evidence is usually the original document. A copy of an enrolled document issued by the court or official having lawful custody of the original may also constitute primary evidence. Therefore, the contents of a private document, *e.g.* a will, which has been filed or enrolled in a public registry or court, may be proved by a copy issued by that registry or court.

5.1.1 *Abolition in criminal cases*

This requirement has been abolished in respect of criminal cases by section 30 of the Criminal Evidence Act 1992, which states as follows:

> "(1) Where information contained in a document is admissible as evidence in criminal proceedings, the information may be given in evidence, whether or not

---

[1] [1908] 2 K.B. 335.

the document is still in existence by producing a copy of the document or the material part of it authenticated in such manner as the court may approve.

(2) It is immaterial for the purposes of this section how many removes there are between the copy and the original or by what means (which may include facsimile) the copy produced or any intermediate copy was made."

Information is defined by the 1992 Act as being "any representation of fact, whether in words or otherwise".

Section 30(3) states that a document "includes a map, a plan, a graph, a drawing, a photograph or a reproduction in permanent legible form by a computer of information in non-legible form".

It also includes "a film, a sound recording or a video recording".

The above section constitutes a hugely significant legislative change insofar as it involves the complete abrogation of the best evidence rule in criminal proceedings. In *Carey v. Hussey*[2] the applicant had been prosecuted for breach of a safety order. The prosecution wanted to adduce a photocopy of the safety order, but the applicant objected. Kearns J. stated that section 30 gives the judge a very wide discretion to accept, not just photocopies, but also faxes in criminal cases. The photocopy was held to be admissible.[3]

The best evidence rule, requiring production of the original of a document, still exists in civil proceedings in this jurisdiction. However, as recognised by Ackner L.J. in *Kajala v. Noble*,[4] there are a large number of exceptions to this rule, allowing secondary evidence to be adduced:

"The old rule, that a party must produce the best evidence that the nature of the case will allow, and that any less good evidence is to be excluded, has gone by the board long ago. The only remaining instance of it is that, if an original document is available in one's hands, one must produce it; that one cannot give secondary evidence by producing a copy. Nowadays we do not confine ourselves to the best evidence. We admit all relevant evidence. The goodness or badness of it goes only to weight, and not to admissibility."

5.1.2 *Exceptions to best evidence rule: proving documents by secondary evidence*

Secondary evidence may be oral evidence, a photocopy, or a microfilm copy. It may also be a copy of a copy. As stated in *Gilbert (Dec'd) v. Ross*[5] "There are no degrees of secondary evidence".

[2.] Unreported, High Court, Kearns J., December 21, 1999.
[3.] It may be argued that photocopies of documents may be admitted even in civil cases; *R. v. Wayte* (1982) 76 Cr. App. R. 110. After all, the rationale for the best evidence rule is the risk of an error appearing in a copy made by hand. However, if the copy has been made by a mechanical device, this is not usually applicable.
[4.] (1982) 75 Cr. App. R. 149 at 152.
[5.] 10 L.J. Exch. 201.

(1) Where the original document has been destroyed

Secondary evidence may be used if the original document has been destroyed[6] or lost. If the original document has been lost, it must be shown that a thorough search has been made before secondary evidence will be admitted.

An example of a lost document being proved by secondary evidence is to be found in *In Bonis McQuillan*.[7] A testator handed his will to his executors, who mislaid it. However, a copy of the will had been made by the local priest before it was handed over. The testator's son applied to court for grant of probate of this copy will. Secondary evidence of the will was allowed.

(2) Where the production of original document is physically or legally impossible

An example of production of the original being physically impossible would be where it was an inscription on a monument. In *Owner v. Bee Hive Spinning Co Ltd*[8] a notice on a factory wall could not legally be removed because the management was obliged to display it at all times. In such cases the document may be proved by secondary evidence.

(3) Where the original document is in hands of third party not legally obliged to disclose it

If the document is in the hands of a third party who is outside the jurisdiction or who is able to claim privilege in respect of the document, it may be proved by secondary evidence.

However, the mere fact that a third party who is legally obliged to produce the document has failed to do so, does not justify proving the document by secondary evidence.[9] The party seeking the document should serve a subpoena on the third party and, if he still fails to produce it, initiate contempt of court proceedings.

(4) Where original is in the possession or control of the other party to the case who has been served with a notice to produce and has failed to comply with it

In *R. v. Morgan*[10] a conviction was quashed because copies of letters, the originals of which were in the possession of the other party, had been admitted in evidence without a notice to produce having been served.

Failure of the other side to comply with a notice to produce will allow secondary evidence to be given of the relevant documents. However, the notice must give the other side a reasonable time to produce the documents.

---

6. This has been established since Leyfield's case (1611).
7. [1954] I.R. Jur. 10.
8. [1914] 1 K.B. 105.
9. Unless the third party is able to avail of diplomatic immunity, in which case the document may be proved by secondary evidence.
10. [1925] 1 K.B. 752.

(5) Section 14 of the Evidence Act 1851: public documents

Section 14 of the Evidence Act 1851 provides that whenever any book or other document is of such a public nature as to be admissible in evidence on its mere production from the proper custody and no statute exists which renders its contents provable by means of a copy, an examined or certified copy is admissible if production of the originals would entail a high degree of public inconvenience.

In *Mortimer v. McCallan*[11] Alderson J. said that the books of the Bank of England would cause so much inconvenience to be produced that they might be proved by secondary evidence.

(6) Entries in the register of birth, deaths and marriages

Copies of entries in the Register of Births, Deaths and Marriage are admissible under an exception to the rule.[12]

(7) Bankers' Books Evidence Act 1879[3]

This provides that copies of entries in bankers' books are admissible as prima facie evidence of the original entries and of the matters, transactions and accounts therein recorded. The term "bankers' books" includes cash books, accounts books, day books, ledgers and all other books used in the ordinary business of the bank. *R. v. Dadson*[14] held that letters in a correspondence file were not books and could not be admissible.

(8) Documentary Evidence Act 1925

This act provides for the proof of state documents by a Stationery Office copy.

(9) Where the other side has admitted the contents of the documents

Where the other side has admitted the contents of documents, the best evidence rule no longer applies and copies of the documents may be adduced.

(10) Photos, tapes or films

The best evidence rule was never applied in the context of photos, tapes or films. This was recognised in *Kajala v. Noble*,[15] where it was stated that the primary evidence rule was "limited and confined to written documents in the strict sense of the term, and has no relevance to tapes or films".

---

[11] (1840) 9 L.J. Exch. 73.
[12] Marriage (Ireland) Act 1844, Registration of Births and Deaths (Ireland) Act 1863.
[13] As amended by the Bankers Book of Evidence Act 1959. See Dunne and Davies "The Bankers Books Evidence Acts" (1997) Bar Rev. 297.
[14] (1983) 77 Cr. App. R. 91.
[15] (1982) 75 Cr. App. R. 149.

(11) Section 2 of the Documentary Evidence Act 1868

As amended by section 2 of the Documentary Evidence Act 1882, section 2 of the Documentary Evidence Act 1868 allows secondary evidence of statutory instruments and ministerial orders.

(12) Section 7 of the Evidence Act 1851

Section 7 of the Evidence Act 1851 provides for secondary evidence of proclamations, treaties and Acts of State of foreign countries.

5.2 Rule requiring proof of authenticity or authorship

The authenticity of a document may be proved either by direct oral testimony from its author or a witness, or by opinion evidence identifying the signature or handwriting. If copies of a document are tendered, there must be someone able to swear that the copy is an accurate one.

5.2.1 Criminal cases

The principles relating to proof of authenticity in criminal cases were summarised in *R. v. Wayte*:

> "Where the party affected by the evidence contends that the document is not genuine, his counsel will in general ask for and be granted an opportunity to have the document examined, but it is almost inevitable that the issue raised concerning the genuineness of the document will have to be left to the jury in the end. It may be that in very rare cases there will have to be a trial within a trial on the issue of admissibility...but...where the party producing the document and arguing for its admissibility contends that it is genuine, [that] issue will invariably be left to the jury."[16]

5.2.2 Handwriting comparisons

Section 8 of the Criminal Procedure Act 1865, which, despite its name, applies to both criminal and civil proceedings, states as follows:

> "Comparison of a disputed handwriting with any writing proved to the satisfaction of the judge to be genuine shall be permitted to be made by witnesses, and such writings, and the evidence of witnesses respecting the same, may be submitted to the court and jury as evidence of the genuineness or otherwise of the writing in dispute."

People (D.P.P.) v. Malocco[17] related to the requirement of proof of handwriting in criminal cases. Malocco was charged with forging documents. His signature had been proved by witnesses. He claimed that the trial judge should have

---

16. (1983) 76 Cr. App. R. 110 at 118.
17. Court of Criminal Appeal, May 23, 1996.

required his signature to be proved by a handwriting expert. This argument was rejected.

5.3   Rule requiring proof of due execution

A document more than 30 years old coming from proper custody is presumed to have been duly executed and made on the date it bears, duly sealed, and any alteration or erasure is presumed to have been made before execution. In the case of a will, this principle is modified by the Succession Act 1965, which provides that any alteration to or erasure in a will is presumed to have been made after execution. Public documents are exempt from proof of execution.

In criminal cases, the formal validity of a document is rarely important. Issues regarding due execution tend to come up in civil proceedings. Section 14 of the Stamp Act 1891 specifically provides that the absence of a stamp cannot affect the admissibility of a private document in criminal proceedings.

Chapter 6

WITNESSES: COMPETENCE AND COMPELLABILITY

The general rule is that all persons are competent witnesses[1] and that a competent witness may be compelled to testify in all proceedings. The effect of a person being regarded as compellable is that he can be imprisoned for contempt of court if he refuses to attend or, if attending, refuses to answer any questions put to him[2]. It is no defence that the prospective witness's reluctance to testify comes from having been intimidated by one of the parties to the case.

As will be seen, however, there are certain situations in which an individual may be regarded as incompetent to testify. In addition, in very limited cases, a person who is competent may not be compellable.[3]

Special rules apply regarding compellability of an accused and/or his spouse in a criminal case[4]. Problems regarding competence may arise in relation to the evidence of children and mentally handicapped witnesses, as well as those suffering from mental illness or disorder. These situations will be considered in turn.

6.1 Competence and compellability of the accused

6.1.1 Competence for the defence

At common law, the accused was incompetent to testify in his own defence. This was changed by the Criminal Justice Act 1898. The relevant provisions were reproduced by the Irish Free State in section 1 of the Criminal Justice (Evidence) Act 1924. They allow an accused to give evidence in his own defence if he so wishes.

---

1. There used to be many categories of incompetent witnesses but most of them have been abolished either by the common law or by statute. *Omychund v. Barker* (1745) 1 Atk. 21 held that non-Christians and atheists were permitted to take the oath. People with criminal convictions were allowed to give evidence by the Civil Rights of Convicts Act 1828. Parties to civil proceedings and their spouses were permitted to testify by the Evidence Act 1851, the Evidence (Amendment) Act 1863, and the Evidence (Further Amendment) Act 1869. The Criminal Evidence Act 1898 allowed an accused to give evidence in his own defence.

2. Sometimes a witness may be permitted to refuse to answer questions on the ground of privilege, see *supra*, Chap. 16.

3. However, even if a witness is not compellable, if he opts to take the oath and give evidence, he must answer all non-privileged questions asked of him or risk contempt of court.

4. A plaintiff or defendant in a civil case has been competent and compellable since the nineteenth century; *supra*, n.1

6.1.2   *Competence for the prosecution*

However, these statutory provisions only deal with the entitlement of the accused to give evidence in his own defence. Obviously, an accused would not want to give evidence against himself; but he might very well want to give evidence for the prosecution against a co-accused. The question of whether or not an accused is entitled to give evidence for the prosecution remains regulated by the common law. According to the common law, an accused is not competent to give evidence for the prosecution against a co-accused. The one exception is in the case of a prosecution for public nuisance under the Evidence Act 1877.[5]

If the prosecution wants one of the accused to give evidence for them against the other, they must first ensure that the prospective witness ceases to be an accused. One way in which an individual can cease to be an accused, and thus become both competent and compellable for the prosecution, is by pleading guilty. Alternatively, he could be acquitted on the ground there is no case to answer, or a verdict of *nolle prosequi* could be entered against them. The final way in which an individual could cease to be an accused in the particular matter is if the judge responds to a request by either side to sever the indictment, so as to have the charges relating to him tried separately from those relating to his co-accused.[6]

6.1.3   *Compellability of the accused*

The Criminal Justice (Evidence) Act 1924 distinguishes between the competence and compellability of the accused and, in so doing, diverges from the normal rule that all competent individuals are compellable. An accused cannot be compelled to give evidence in his defence.

Furthermore, his failure to give evidence cannot be the subject of comment by the prosecution. Section 1(6) Criminal Justice (Evidence) Act 1924 states that "The failure of any person charged with an offence to give evidence may not be made the subject of any comment by the prossecution". Such comments may result in a subsequent conviction being set aside. In *People v. Maples*[7] the Court of Criminal Appeal ordered a re-trial on the ground that the prosecution had commented unfavourably on the accused's failure to testify. It was held that once such comments have been made by the prosecution, the trial judge cannot remedy the situation by telling the jury to disregard these comments. The jury must be discharged and a retrial ordered.

---

[5]   In relation to this offence, an accused is both competent and compellable to testify for the prosecution against a co-accused.

[6]   It is also worth noting that evidence given by an accused when testifying in his defence, either during examination in chief or in cross-examination, becomes evidence for all purposes in the case and the prosecution may rely on this evidence against a co-accused.

[7]   Unreported, Court of Criminal Appeal, February 26, 1996

Although the judge may comment on the accused's failure to give evidence, he must be very careful not to give the jury the impression that the accused's silence indicates that he is guilty. [8]

6.1.4 Cross-examination of the accused

As with all witnesses, if an accused opts to give evidence, he may be cross-examined. However, special rules apply in relation to the cross-examination of the accused. Under section 1(e) of the Criminal Justice (Evidence) Act 1924, the accused is obliged to answer questions even though they may incriminate him in relation to the offence charged.[9]

However, section 1(f) prohibits the prosecution from asking the accused questions, the answers to which may indicate his bad character. This is in line with the general principle in criminal trials that the bad character of the accused should not be admissible in evidence. However, section 1(f)(i), (ii) and (iii) provide that the accused may be asked questions about his bad character in a limited number of situations, in particular where he has put his good character in issue, cast imputations on the character of prosecution witnesses, or given evidence against a co-accused.[10]

6.2 Competence and compellability of spouse of the accused[11]

Originally, the spouse of an accused was not competent to testify either for the defence or the prosecution. This stemmed from the fact that husband and wife were regarded as a single legal unit. Because the accused had been precluded from testifying by the common law, his spouse was similarly excluded.

The Criminal Justice (Evidence) Act 1924 made the spouse of an accused a competent witness in his defence. However, there were a number of uncertainties in relation to the law after the Act. Firstly, although it was clear that the spouse was a competent witness for the defence, it was not clear whether she could be compelled to testify. Secondly, post-1924 case law indicated that a spouse might be competent to testify for the prosecution in certain cases, but it was uncertain what conditions had to be fulfilled before this competency arose. Finally, it was also unclear whether, in situations where the spouse was competent to testify for the prosecution, she could actually be compelled to do so.

Fortunately, it is not necessary to struggle through the inconsistent case law on these points, because the current rules in relation to the competence and

---

8. See *R. v. Sparrow* [1973] 1 WLR 488. Also *R. v. Bathurst* [1968] 2 Q.B. 99, 107; *R. v. Mutch* [1973] 1 All E.R. 178; *Waugh v. R.* [1950] A.C. 203.

9. Section 1(e) places a limitation on the operation of the privilege against self-incrimination in relation to the accused.

10. The precise scope of section 1(f) is discussed in more detail later in Chapter 14.

11. These rules only apply to spouses of the accused in criminal proceedings. Spouses of parties in civil proceedings have been competent and compellable in those proceedings since the nineteenth century; *supra*, n.1.

compellability of a spouse of the accused have been comprehensively enumerated by the Criminal Evidence Act 1992.

6.2.1 *Criminal Evidence Act 1992: Competence and compellability for the defence*

Section 21 of the Criminal Evidence Act 1992 states that the spouse of an accused is always a competent witness for the defence. Section 22 goes on to add that the spouse is also a compellable witness for the defence.

6.2.2 *Criminal Evidence Act 1992: Competence for the prosecution*

Section 21 of the Criminal Evidence Act 1992 states that a spouse is competent to testify for the prosecution. The only situation in which a spouse is incompetent to testify for the prosecution is if she herself is a co-accused. In this case, she is precluded from testifying, not because she is the spouse of an accused, but because she is an accused in her own right.

6.2.3 *Criminal Evidence Act 1992: Compellability for the prosecution*

The normal rule under the 1992 Act is that a spouse is not compellable for the prosecution. However, section 22 of the Criminal Evidence Act 1992 lists a number of limited situations in which a spouse may be compelled to testify for the prosecution.

These situations are as follows:

1. If the offence is one of violence to the spouse, a child of the spouse or a person under 17;

2. If the offence is a sexual offence in relation to a child of the spouse or a person under 17; and

3. If the offence consists of attempting or conspiring to commit or of aiding, abetting, counselling, procuring, or inciting the commission of, either of the above offences.

Of course, if the spouse is a co-accused, he or she cannot be compelled to testify for the prosecution, even in the above situations.[12] Furthermore, section 26 of the Criminal Evidence Act 1992 states that section 22 does not affect the right to marital privacy. The effects of section 26 have yet to be considered.

6.2.4 *Constitutionality of section 22*

Arguably, section 22 of the Criminal Evidence Act 1992 is unconstitutional, insofar as it makes a spouse of an accused compellable for the prosecution in certain situations. It goes against the recommendations of the Law Reform

---

[12] Because a co-accused is not competent to testify for the prosecution. See above, at para 6.1.2

Commission to the effect that in no case whatsoever should an accused's spouse be compellable for the prosecution.

In defence of section 22, other commentators have argued that it would be unconstitutional not to compel a spouse to testify for the prosecution in the situations specified in that section. Arguably, giving a spouse a choice as to whether or not to testify actually puts more pressure on them and results in greater destruction of marital harmony than a straightforward compellability provision.

Probably the most cogent justification for section 22 is that it protects the right of the victim to justice. This right was first recognised by O'Hanlon J. in *S. v. S.*[13] It was further developed by Walsh J. in the case of *D.P.P. v. J.T.*[14] In that case, Walsh J. suggested that the Constitution required that a wife be a compellable witness for the prosecution in any case where her husband was charged with sexual assault on their children. Insofar as the Criminal Justice (Evidence) Act 1924 operated to prevent this, it should be regarded as unconstitutional. The above statement was *obiter* because, in this case, the wife had voluntarily given evidence for the prosecution. Section 22 of the 1992 Act was, to a large extent, a response to this decision.

On the reasoning in the above cases, the compellability provisions in section 22 might one day be held unconstitutional on the grounds that they are too narrow. The victim's right to have justice done could apply to compel the spouse to testify in relation to crimes outside those specified in section 22. Therefore the victim may have a constitutional right to compel a spouse to give evidence independently of the 1992 Act. It is worth noting Claire Jackson's[15] argument to the effect that spouses should be generally compellable for the prosecution, subject to a judicial discretion to exempt them if the importance of their testimony is outweighed by the risk of either damage to the marital relationship or harshness to the other spouse.

6.2.5 *Former spouses*

A former spouse is one who has either got a decree of judicial separation or who has entered into a separation agreement with his or her spouse. Section 23 of the 1992 Act makes clear that a former spouse is competent and compellable to testify for the prosecution. There are two exceptions. First, if the former spouse is a co-accused, he or she can never testify for the prosecution because of the rule that an accused cannot testify for the prosecution. Secondly, a former spouse is not compellable in relation to offences committed by his or her former spouse at a time when the marriage is subsisting, unless:

---

13. [1983] I.R. 68; in this case O'Hanlon J. held that a spouse was entitled to call evidence to rebut the presumption of legitimacy. Any common law rule to the contrary was contrary to fair procedures as well as to the "paramount public policy of ascertaining truth and doing justice".
14. (1988) 3 Frewen 141.
15. Jackson (1993) 15 D.U.L.J. 202, 208-209.

1. the offence is one of violence to the former spouse, a child of the former spouse or a person under 17;

2. the offence is a sexual offence in relation to a child of the former spouse or a person under 17; and

3. the offence consists of attempting or conspiring to commit or of aiding, abetting, counselling, procuring, or inciting the commission of, either of the above offences.

6.3   Competence of children[16]

Originally, children's evidence in both criminal and civil proceedings had to be given on oath. In order to give such evidence, the child had to understand the nature and consequences of an oath. In addition, a mandatory corroboration warning had to be given in relation to the sworn evidence of children in criminal cases.

In the Canadian case of *R. v. Bannerman*[17] Dixon J. said that the child must understand that there is a moral obligation involved in taking an oath. In *R. v. Hayes*[18]it was held that there was no need for the child to know of the existence of God in order to take the oath. The test was whether the child had sufficient appreciation of the solemnity of the occasion and the added responsibility to tell the truth involved in taking an oath over and above the responsibility to tell the truth in the context of normal social conduct.

If the child had not heard of an oath, but was capable of understanding its nature and consequences, the trial judge was obliged to adjourn the case for such time as was necessary in order to enable the child to be properly instructed in the meaning and importance of the oath, and then to swear him.

In *Attorney General v. O'Sullivan*[19] the accused was convicted of sodomy in relation to a 10-year-old boy. The question was whether the boy was capable of understanding the nature and meaning of an oath. The court said that it was not necessary to hold a preliminary inquiry; the trial judge could decide this question in the course of giving evidence.

The Children's Act 1908 took a step forward in allowing, for the first time, the unsworn evidence of children in criminal cases. The unsworn evidence of children was admissible under this Act provided that the child understood the concept of a duty to speak the truth. However, the Act further provided that such evidence required corroboration before it could be relied on.

The rules in relation to the competency of children have been relaxed in criminal cases by the Criminal Evidence Act 1992 and in civil cases by the Children Act 1997.

[16.] It should be noted that the issue in this area has related to the competence of children rather than their compellability. In any situation where a child is competent, they are also compellable.

[17.] (1966) 48 C.R. 110.

[18.] [1977] 2 All E.R. 288.

[19.] [1930] I.R. 553.

6.3.1 Criminal Evidence Act 1992

Section 27 of the Criminal Evidence Act 1992 provides that in any criminal proceedings the evidence of a person under 14 years of age may be received otherwise than on oath or affirmation if the court is satisfied that he is capable of giving an intelligible account of events which are relevant to those proceedings. The old test laid down by the Children Act 1908, "understanding the concept of a duty to speak the truth", has therefore been abolished and replaced by a new and more easily satisfied test which is whether the child is capable of giving an intelligible account of events.

It should be noted that the wording of section 27 makes it clear that in order to avail of this facility, the child must be under 14 years of age. In *R. v. Lee*[20] a finding of a trial judge, that a fifteen year old girl could give unsworn evidence, was held to be incorrect.

Of course, children under 14 can, alternatively, give evidence on oath providing that they satisfy the tests laid down in *R. v. Bannerman* and *R. v. Hayes*. However, there is no longer any advantage for a child in giving evidence on oath. Section 28 of the Criminal Evidence Act 1992 abolishes the requirement laid down in the Children Act 1908 that the unsworn evidence of a child be corroborated. Such evidence may be admitted in the absence of corroborating evidence.

There is no longer any obligation on the judge to give a corroboration warning in respect of children's evidence. Section 28 of the Criminal Evidence Act 1992 states that it is up to the discretion of the trial judge whether to give such a warning. It also states that the unsworn evidence of a child may be treated as corroboration.

The Criminal Evidence Act 1992 also provides for the evidence of children to be given through live TV link. Section 13 states that, in relation to a sexual offence or an offence involving violence, a person under 17 years (other than the accused) will be automatically allowed to give evidence through live TV link, unless the court sees good reason to the contrary.

However, it is worth noting that it will be very difficult for the accused to show good reason why this evidence should not be given.[21] It is arguable that a fairer solution would have been to place the onus on the prosecution, in every case, to show good reason why the child should testify in this way.[22]

In cases where evidence is being given through a live TV link, no wigs or gowns shall be worn. The court may opt to ask questions through an intermediary, who should put the questions to the witness in a way that is appropriate to the age and mental ability of that witness.

[20.] [1988] Crim. L.R. 525.

[21.] The defence will only be able to show this through psychiatric examination of the child, which is likely to cause him or her added trauma.

[22.] In the United States the prosecution must show that the video link evidence is necessary on the facts of the particular case: *Maryland v. Craig* 497 U.S. 836 (1990).

In *Donnelly v. Ireland*[23] it was argued that the giving of evidence by live TV link was unconstitutional because it breached a requirement in the Constitution that witnesses give their evidence in the presence of the accused. The Supreme Court held that the provisions relating to TV link evidence were constitutional. The witness was available for cross-examination, although not in the same room as the accused. The physical demeanour of the witness was evident to all those watching, including the accused. The accused had no constitutional right to physically confront the person giving evidence against him.

Under section 16 of the Criminal Evidence Act 1992, a video-recording of any evidence given by a person under 17 years of age through a live TV link at the preliminary examination, and a video-recording of any statement made by a person under 14 years of age during an interview with the Garda Síochána or "any other person who is competent",[24] are stated to be admissible as evidence of any fact in relation to which direct oral evidence would have been admissible.

Where the facilities are not available in the District Court to conduct a video link during the preliminary examination, section 17 provides that the matter may be transferred to a Circuit Court or to another District Court where such facilities are in place. The court has a discretion not to admit the video recording if the interests of justice necessitate its exclusion. In considering whether, in the interests of justice, the video recording ought not to have been admitted, the court shall have regard to all the circumstances, including any risk that its admission will result in unfairness to the accused.

6.3.2 Children Act 1997

Part III of the Children Act 1997 reforms the rules relating to evidence of children in civil cases. Prior to this Act there was no provision for children to give unsworn evidence in civil cases. In *Mapp v. Gilhooley*[25] a trial judge in civil proceedings was held to have acted improperly in hearing the unsworn evidence of an eight-year-old child.

Section 28(1) of the Children Act 1997 mirrors section 27 of the Criminal Evidence Act 1992. It allows the unsworn evidence of children under 14 in all civil cases if the child is capable of giving an intelligible account of events relevant to the proceedings. The child's evidence may corroborate any sworn or unsworn evidence given by another person.[26]

The 1997 Act also allows for the evidence of children to be given through live TV link in civil cases concerning the welfare either of a child or of a person with a mental disability such as to make independent living impossible. The leave of the court must be sought before this can be done. Unlike the

---

[23] [1998] 1 I.R. 321.

[24] The expression "anybody else who is competent" may include a child psychologist.

[25] Unreported, Supreme Court, April 23, 1991.

[26] Section 28(4); the insertion of this last clause may have been a mistake since corroboration require-ments do not normally apply in civil proceedings.

Criminal Evidence Act 1992, there is no presumption that children under 17 are entitled to give their evidence by live TV link.[27] No guidelines are given as to when such leave will be granted.

In addition to permitting evidence by TV link, the court may direct that any questions be put through an intermediary. Questions put to the child by an intermediary should be in words that convey to the child, in a way that is appropriate to his age or mental condition, the meaning of the questions.[28]

6.4 Competence of mentally handicapped persons

In order to give sworn evidence, mentally handicapped persons must be capable of satisfying the tests in *R. v. Bannerman* and *R. v. Hayes* in order to show that they understand the nature and consequences of an oath.

6.4.1 Criminal cases

However, legislation also makes provision for the unsworn evidence of mentally handicapped persons in criminal and civil cases. Section 27 of the Criminal Evidence Act 1992 operates to allow the evidence of a mentally handicapped person to be received otherwise than on oath or affirmation if the court is satisfied that he is capable of giving an intelligible account of events that are relevant to the proceedings.

Mentally handicapped people are also entitled to give video link evidence in criminal cases involving violence or sexual offences, unless the prosecution shows good reason to the contrary. Video recordings of any statements made by them in preliminary examination or to a member of the Gardaí or other competent person are also admissible.

In *O'Sullivan v. Hamill*[29] the applicant was charged with having sexual intercourse with a person who was mentally impaired, contrary to section 5(1) of the Sexual Offences Act 1993. The applicant wanted this person to give evidence and the judge made an order that she should be permitted to give her deposition by live TV link under the Criminal Evidence Act 1992. The judge did not hold any inquiry prior to making this order.

The applicant said that the judge should have heard evidence to the effect that the victim had a mental handicap prior to making the order. O Higgins J. said that an inquiry to establish mental handicap was necessary for unsworn evidence to be given but not before video-link evidence. The trial judge had the right to grant video link evidence, not just in respect of mentally impaired witnesses, but in any case where he felt there was good reason to do so; O'Higgins J. said that he was happy that good reason had been shown.

[27.] The Criminal Evidence Act 1992 only allows such evidence to be given in the case of trials for offences of violence or sexual offences.

[28.] Section 23 of the 1997 Act also allows for the admission of the hearsay evidence of children.

[29.] Unreported, High Court, February 25, 1998.

6.4.2 Civil cases

Section 28(3) of the Children Act 1997 provides that mentally disabled persons may give unsworn evidence in any civil proceedings if they are capable of giving an intelligible account of events which are relevant to the proceedings. This evidence can corroborate evidence given by another person.

Section 21 also seems to have been intended to allow mentally handicapped persons to give evidence by video link in proceedings concerning their welfare, subject to the permission of the judge. However, section 21, although specifically including proceedings where the welfare of a mentally handicapped person is in issue, only applies, on the face of it, to children. Although section 28, which provides for unsworn evidence in civil cases, specifically states that it applies to mentally handicapped persons as well, there is no parallel clause in existence in relation to section 21, and one suspects a mistake on the part of the drafters of the Act. It remains to be seen whether the court will take a purposive approach to section 21 so as to allow mentally handicapped persons to avail of the video link provisions in civil cases concerning their welfare.

Finally, it should be noted that in any case where a mentally retarded person is competent to give sworn or unsworn evidence, he is also compellable.

6.5   Competence of persons suffering from mental illness

In relation to persons suffering from mental illness, provided they understand the nature and consequences of an oath, it is up to the court to decide whether they are capable of testifying. As with children and mentally retarded persons, if a person suffering from mental disorder is competent, he is also compellable.

In *R. v. Hill*[30] a person under the delusion that he was surrounded by spirits was allowed to testify on the ground that he was capable of understanding the nature of an oath. Lord Campbell C.J. stated:

> "If there be a delusion in the mind of a party tendered as a witness, it is for the judge to see whether the party tendered has a sense of religion and understands the nature and sanction of an oath; and then if the judge admits him as a witness, it is for the jury to say what degree of credit is to be given to his testimony."

In this situation the witness's evidence was allowed because he had:

> "a clear apprehension of the obligation of an oath, and was capable of giving a trustworthy account of any transaction which took place before his eyes, and he was perfectly rational upon all subjects except with respect of his particular delusion."

---

[30]. (1851) 2 Den. 254.

Finally, the decision of *Attorney General v. Lannigan*[31] dealt with the question of whether the jury had to be present when the competency of children, mentally retarded and mentally disordered persons was being assessed. The fear is that these potential witnesses might say something damaging to the accused and that this statement might influence the jury even if they were declared incompetent. In this case, the Court of Criminal Appeal held that the right to have the jury present was the right of the accused; he could waive that right, and have the issue determined in the absence of the jury.

6.6 Diplomatic staff

Section 5(1) of the Diplomatic Relations Immunities Act 1967 provides that diplomatic agents or non-national members of administrative and technical staff, as well as their non-national families, are not obliged to give evidence as witnesses in either criminal or civil proceedings in this jurisdiction. As with the accused, and the accused's spouse (in relation to most offences), they are in an unusual category insofar as they are competent but not compellable.

---

[31] [1958] Ir. Jur. Rep. 59.

Chapter 7

WITNESSES: EXAMINATION-IN-CHIEF AND CROSS-EXAMINATION

7.1 General rules in relation to witness evidence

The evidence of a witness is normally taken on oath. No religious belief is necessary in order to take an oath, and, indeed, in *R.v Hayes*[1] Bridge L.J. said that:

> "it is unrealistic not to recognise that in the present state of society amongst the adult population the divine sanction of an oath is probably not generally recognized."

An oath is valid so long as the person taking it appreciates the solemnity of the occasion and the additional moral obligation, over and above the everyday obligation, to speak the truth, which arises in such a situation. Many people with no religious beliefs opt to take the oath. However, if a witness does not want to take an oath, the Oath Acts 1888-1909 provide that he can make a solemn affirmation instead.

The normal rule in civil cases, as laid down in *Shea v Wilson & Co*,[2] is that a judge has no right to call witnesses without the consent of the parties. However, in the case of proceedings relating to the care and custody of a child, there may be an exception to this rule. The judge's function in wardship proceedings is a quasi-inquisitorial one. Carney J. in *Eastern Health Board v. Mooney*[3] said that a District Court judge is entitled to call foster parents and compel them to testify in proceedings under the Child Care Act 1991, even if the parties do not consent.

At common law, the witness has to be physically present in the courtroom in order to give oral evidence. However, the Criminal Evidence Act 1992 provides for the reception of video-link evidence in criminal proceedings. Section 29 of the 1992 Act provides that persons resident outside the State may give evidence through a live TV link in any criminal proceedings other than one in which they are charged.[4]

In addition section 13 of the 1992 Act provides that in any proceedings relating to a sexual offence or an offence involving violence, the court may

---

1.   [1997] 1 W.L.R. 234.
2.   (1916) 50 I.L.T.R. 73.
3.   Unreported, High Court, Carney J., March 20, 1998.
4.   See O'Malley (1999) I.C.L.R. 57.

grant leave to a person other than the accused to have the proceedings heard by video link. In the case of a witness under 17, or a mentally handicapped person, the court shall grant such leave unless they see good reason to the contrary. In all other cases, the decision is at the discretion of the court. In addition there are special rules allowing the admission of video recordings made in relation to prior evidence of child witnesses and mentally handicapped witnesses.[5]

In *Donnelly v. Ireland*[6] it was argued that the giving of evidence by live TV link was unconstitutional because it breached a requirement in the Constitution that witnesses give their evidence in the presence of the accused. The Supreme Court held that the provisions relating to TV-link evidence were constitutional. The witness was available for cross-examination, although not in the same room as the accused. The physical demeanour of the witness was evident to all those watching, including the accused. The accused had no constitutional right to physically confront the person giving evidence against him.

The Court of Criminal Appeal in *Attorney General v Joyce v Walsh*[7] recognized that a witness in this jurisdiction is entitled to give his evidence in any language. Kennedy C.J. stated:

> "It would seem to me to be a requisite of natural justice, particularly in a criminal trial, that a witness should be allowed to give evidence in the language which is his or her vernacular language, whether that language be English or Irish, or any foreign language, and it would follow, if the language used should not be a language known to the members of the court, that means of interpreting the language to the court (judge and jury) and also, in the case of evidence against a prisoner, that means of interpreting it to the prisoner, should be provided."[8]

In this case the accused were allowed to give their evidence in Irish.

7.2 Witnesses: Examination-in-chief

The process of examination-in-chief involves the witness being asked questions by the party who has called him. Counsel conducting the examination-in-chief should beware of asking leading questions, as well as the rule against narrative. The witness may be entitled to refer in court to previous statements made by him in order to refresh his memory. Finally, if the witness shows a lack of willingness to co-operate, an application may be made to have him declared a hostile witness.

---

5. These are discussed in more detail in paras 6.3 and 6.4.
6. [1998] 1 I.R. 321.
7. [1929] I.R. 526.
8. At p. 531.

7.2.1 The rule against narrative

This rule prevents a witness being asked in examination-in-chief about former oral or written statements made by him that are consistent with his evidence. The rule against narrative is distinct from the rule against hearsay.

The hearsay rule prohibits out-of-court statements being adduced to prove the truth of their content in situations where the maker of the statement is not available to testify. Such statements are known as hearsay. The rule against hearsay is often justified by the fact that, because the maker of the statement is not available, it is not possible to use the process of cross-examination to assess possible defects attaching to the statement.

The rule against narrative prohibits a witness being asked by his own side about consistent out-of-court statements made by him in order to enhance his credibility.[9] The rationale for prohibiting narrative is different from that used in relation to hearsay; in the case of narrative, the maker of the out-of-court statement is available to be questioned on it. The reason for excluding narrative is different. Narrative is excluded because it is of no real help in relation to any of the issues before the court. The fact that a witness has made previous consistent statements does not really boost his credibility in any way. As Humphreys J. pointed out in *R. v. Roberts*[10]:

> "It is of no real help to the court or jury in assessing the credibility of [the defendant's] evidence to learn that he has previously told other persons what his defence may be."

The danger is that juries may ascribe undue importance to previous consistent statements and mistakenly believe that the more often the story is repeated, the more likely it is to be true. There are also practical considerations involved in excluding narrative, such as the fact that it takes up unnecessary court time and expense.

Nevertheless, there are some exceptional situations in which previous consistent statements of a witness are admissible. It should be noted, however, that these situations are exceptions to the rule against narrative and not to the rule against hearsay. The statements are admitted solely for the purpose of bolstering the credibility of a witness who has already given evidence of the facts contained in them.[11] The one exception is where the statements are admitted as *res gestae*, because statements in this category are exceptions to both the hearsay rule and the rule against narrative. The exceptions to the rule against narrative are set out below.

---

9.   It should be noted that the rule against narrative only prohibits statements that boost the credibility of an accused. It does not prohibit evidence of prior inconsistent statements as these do not boost credibility.

10. [1942] 1 All E.R. 187.

11. Another way of putting this is that previous statements of a witness admitted under the exceptions to the rule against narrative (except for the *res gestae* exception) are admitted as evidence going to the witness's credibility, rather than as evidence of the truth of their contents.

(1) Exception 1: Doctrine of recent complaint in sexual cases[12]

The doctrine of recent complaint applies only to sexual offences. It allows previous statements by the victim to be put in evidence to bolster her credibility, provided that those statements satisfy certain conditions: the complaint must be voluntary,[13] and must have been made at the first possible opportunity.[14]

It has been held that a complaint may be voluntary even if it was made in answer to a question, so long as the question is not of a leading nature. If the question merely anticipates a statement, which the complainant was about to make, it is not rendered inadmissible by the fact that the questioner happened to speak first. However, it is up to the judge to decide whether or not this was the case. The relationship of the questioner to the complainant may be taken into account in deciding whether the complaint is voluntary.

The complaint must be made at the first reasonable opportunity after the defence. Again, this issue is a matter of degree, to be decided by the judge. In *D.P.P. v. Moloney*[15] an objection was made to the admission of a complaint on the ground that it had not been made at the first opportunity. However, the Court of Criminal Appeal held that the trial judge was in the best position to decide this and that they would not interfere with his decision.

In *D.P.P. v. McDonagh*[16] the complainant got a taxi to the garda station immediately after her rape. She told the taxi driver that she had been raped. She made a complaint of rape as soon as she got to the garda station. The defence argued that once she had made a complaint to the taxi driver, she couldn't rely on the complaint she had made to the Gardaí. This was rejected, and it was stated that the complaint to the Gardaí should be regarded as having been made at the first reasonable opportunity.

In *D.P.P. v. Brophy*[17] the accused was charged with indecent assault. The complainant had alleged that an indecent assault occurred at the accused's home. She informed her father and some friends the next day. She had encountered her mother and some other friends after the event but had failed to inform them. It was held that the complaint was not admissible under the doctrine of recent complaint because it had not been made at the first reasonable opportunity.

In *D.P.P. v. Kiernan*[18] the alleged rape occurred on a Friday. The victim told the accused's girlfriend, who didn't believe her. She didn't tell her parents, but intended to tell her boyfriend whose brother was a social worker. She didn't tell her boyfriend at her first meeting with him on the Saturday. However, the next day she met him again and told him. It was held that the complaint had

---

12. See further, Foley (2001) 11(3) I.C.L.J. 20; (2001) 15 I.L.T. 234.
13. *R. v. Osborne* [1905] 1 K.B. 551.
14. *D.P.P. v. Brophy* [1992] I.L.R.M. 709.
15. Unreported, Court of Criminal Appeal, *ex tempore* November 8, 1999.
16. Unreported, O'Flaherty J., July 27, 1994.
17. *supra*, n.12.
18. Unreported, Morris J., March 11, 1994.

been made too late but that if she had told her boyfriend on Saturday, it would have been made within a reasonable time.

However, in cases of systematic abuse, the courts are much more lenient as regards the time of making the complaint. In *O'Connor v. Smith*[19] a 13-year-old girl made an allegation that her uncle had abused her one year earlier. It was held that given the circumstances of the case, the age of the complainant and the fact that the abuse was ongoing, the delay was not unreasonable.

In *C.B. v. D.P.P.*[20] the accused was charged in 1993 with the indecent assault and rape of his daughters between 1962-74. The first complaint made by the daughters was over 20-30 years later, after their mother had died. They explained the delay on the ground that they were anxious for their mother's peace of mind. It was held that the complaint had been made at the first reasonable opportunity.

It is important to note that a complaint is admissible under the doctrine of recent complaint only to show consistency and enhance the credibility of the complainant. This means that if the terms of the complaint are not consistent with the complainant's testimony, there is no point in adducing it. Furthermore, as with all exceptions to the rule against narrative, the complainant has to testify in order for the complaint to be admitted.

In *People (D.P.P.) v. Gavin*[21] the accused was convicted of sexual assault. A complaint made by the victim to the Gardaí had been admitted in evidence. The victim had told him that he had awoken to find the accused in his bed and that the accused's hand was on his groin. However, this was not the behaviour that the complainant had alleged in his testimony. On appeal, McGuinness J. said that this complaint should not have been admitted. The purpose of admitting recent complaint is to demonstrate consistency, but here there was no consistency between the two accounts.[22]

The evidence admissible under the doctrine of recent complaint is not limited to the fact of complaint. *R. v. Lillyman*[23] involved a prosecution for an attempted rape. The victim complained to her mistress. The mistress was allowed to give detailed evidence of what the girl said to her; otherwise the jury would not be able to assess the witness's evidence and decide whether or not the complaint was actually made. However, as emphasised by McGuinness J. in *Gavin,* the judge must make clear to the jury that they ought not to treat the complaint as evidence of the facts complained of.

There is one exception to this, insofar as evidence of a complaint may be taken into account in order to negative consent in a rape case. However, whether this is admissible by way of exception to the rule against hearsay, as

---

[19]   Unreported, Barr J., December 19, 1994.
[20]   Unreported, Budd J., October 9, 1995.
[21]   Unreported, Court of Criminal Appeal, July 27, 2000.
[22]   The decision in *Gavin* may be contrasted with that in *People (D.P.P.) v Jethi* (2000), Court of Criminal Appeal, February 7, 2000. Here there were minor discrepancies between the testimony of the victim and the complaint; however, the court admitted the complaint.
[23]   [1896] 2 Q.B. 167.

circumstantial evidence of the fact of complaint, or merely as evidence of credibility, is uncertain.

Other situations in which evidence of previous consistent statements are admissible are as follows:

(2) Exception 2: To rebut an allegation of recent fabrication

The allegation must be one of recent invention or reconstruction. It does not have to be an allegation of conscious dishonesty. However, on the other hand, pointing out a contradiction or inconsistency between something said at trial and something said on a previous occasion will not amount to an allegation of recent fabrication so as to justify the admission of a previous consistent statement by the witness.

(3) Exception 3: As evidence of a previous identification

This includes evidence of a previous formal or informal identification (assuming the informal identification was not in breach of the accused's right to fair procedures). Evidence that a witness previously identified the accused from a photograph is also admissible for these purposes provided that the photo does not come from the police files, because this would alert the jury to the fact that the accused has previous convictions.

(4) Exception 4: Under the *res gestae* exception[24]

This phrase in fact contains a number of different exceptions. What they have in common is that they are all connected with a particular act in some way, and operate to clarify that act.[25]

(a) Spontaneous statements made by participant/observer of relevant event, relating to that event

The statement must be so clearly made in circumstances of spontaneity or involvement in the event that the possibility of concoction can be disregarded. The event must be so unusual or startling as to dominate the thoughts of the maker of the statement.

The leading modern case on this subset of the *res gestae* rule is *R. v. Andrews*.[26] Andrews was charged with manslaughter and burglary. He and an accomplice covered by a blanket knocked on the door of the victim's flat and, when the victim opened the door, stabbed him. Then, no longer covered by the blanket, they stole property from the flat. The victim went to the flat below for help, bleeding profusely from a deep stomach wound. Before dying, he named

---

24. Choo, *Hearsay and Confrontation in Criminal Trials* 112-139; Ormerod [1998] Crim. L.R. 301; Callendar [1998] Crim L.R. 337.

25. The *res gestae* rule is discussed in considerably more detail in the context of the hearsay rule, at para 11.3.2.

26. [1987] 1 All E.R. 513.

his assailant. The question was, whether the victim's statement could be admitted.

In this case, Lord Ackner stated as follows:

> "(1) the primary question which the judge must ask himself is: can the possibility of concoction or distortion be disregarded? (2) To answer that question the judge must first consider the circumstances in which the dramatic statement was made, in order to satisfy himself that the event was so unusual or startling or dramatic as to dominate the thoughts of the victim, so that his utterance was an instinctive reaction to that event, thus giving no real opportunity for reasoned reflection. In such a situation the judge would be entitled to conclude that the involvement or pressure of the event would exclude the possibility of concoction or distortion, providing that the statement was made in conditions of approximate but not exact contemporaneity. In order for the statement to be sufficiently "spontaneous", it must be so closely associated with the event which has excited the statement that it can fairly be stated that the mind of the declarant was still dominated by the event (4) Quite apart from the time factor, there may be special instances in the case, which relate to the possibility of concoction or distortion…in the instant appeal the defence relied on the possibility that the deceased had a motive of his own to fabricate or concoct, namely…malice. (5) As to the possibility of error in the facts narrated in the statement, if only ordinary fallibility of human recollection is relied on, this goes to the weight to be attached to and not to the admissibility of the statement and is therefore a matter for the jury. However, here again there may be special features that may give rise to the possibility of error… in such circumstances the trial judge must consider whether he can exclude the possibility of error."[27]

(b) Statement by person performing relevant act, accompanying or explaining it

The act must be relevant to a fact in issue and the statement must be made by the person performing the act. The statement must be contemporaneous with the act, and must explain it. However, if the act is a continuing one, such as staying abroad away from creditors, contemporaneity is more easily satisfied.

In *Cullen v. Clarke*[28] the plaintiff sought to prove a fact in issue, namely that he was unable to obtain employment due to an injury at work. He sought to do this by referring to an oral statement made to him by a person from whom he had sought work and been refused. The statement was admissible under this category of *res gestae*.

Kingsmill Moore J. stated:

> "The statements accompanying an act may be offered as showing the mind of the actor at the time of the doing of the act…. When the motive or reason of a person for doing an act, or the intention with which he does it, is relevant to the

---

27. Lord Ackner at pp. 300-301.
28. [1963] I.R. 368.

issue, his statement made at the time of the doing of the act is evidence of his motive, reason, or intention."[29]

(c) Statement by person relating to state of mind or emotion at time of making statement

The statement must be contemporaneous with the emotion, *i.e.* it must state that the maker has this particular emotion at the time of making the statement and not that he has had it in the past. The statement must relate to the state of mind of the maker and must be relevant to a fact in issue. There is no requirement that the maker of the statement be the accused, nor that he perform an act. A statement made by a person as to his intention is also admissible under this exception as evidence of the existence of such intention at the time when the statement was made. In *R. v Moghal*[30] a statement made by someone else saying that she intended to kill the victim was admissible on behalf of the accused under this exception.

(d) Statement by person relating to physical sensations at time of making statement

In *Aveson v. Lord Kinnaird*[31] the issue was whether or not the wife of one of the parties had been in good health when a policy of life assurance had been taken out on her life. It was held that statements of bodily symptoms made by the lady in question at the relevant time were admissible in order to determine her state of health.

7.2.2 Refreshing memory in court

Another issue, which may arise in examination-in-chief, is that of refreshing memory. Where the side calling the witness has copies of statements previously made by the witness, they can of course give these statements to the witness to read over prior to going into court, in order to to refresh his memory.

In *People (D.P.P.) v. Donnelly*[32] the accused was convicted of sexual assault. The complainant had been given her statement by the Gardaí a number of days before the trial and had spent time memorising it. It was held that there was no reason why witnesses should not be shown their statements in advance. However, in such cases, the trial judge may have to give a warning. It should also be noted that in *R v. Westwell* it was held that the prosecution should inform the defence if witnesses have refreshed their memory out of court.[33]

However, if the witness needs to have access to notes or statements previously made by him in order to refresh his memory in the courtroom,

---

29. At p. 379.
30. (1977) 65 Cr. App. R. 56.
31. (1805) 6 East 188.
32. Unreported, Court of Criminal Appeal, February 22, 1999.
33. [1976] 2 All E.R. 812.

certain conditions must be satisfied. It is important to note that the witness in this case is not putting the document before the court; the document is merely used by the witness to refresh his memory. The document itself is not evidence in the case.[34]It is the witness's subsequent oral testimony, which is evidence, even in cases where the witness has no recollection of the events and is merely giving evidence as to the accuracy of what is recorded.[35]

The conditions that must be fulfilled in order for a witness to refresh his memory in court are as follows:

1. The document must have been either made by the witness himself or checked and certified by him as accurate when the facts were still fresh in his memory.

2. The document must have been made or certified more or less contemporaneously with the evidence.

3. The document must be available for inspection by the court/counsel/jury.

4. Ideally, the document must be the original but this is not strictly necessary if it is impossible to produce the original.

7.2.3 Hostile witnesses

The issue of hostile witnesses may also occur in examination-in-chief. Normally, it is not possible to attack the credibility or character of one's own witness, or to refer to any previous inconsistent statements or bias on his part. However, it is possible to do such things in relation to a witness for the other side. However, if a witness is declared hostile, it is possible for counsel to treat him as if he were a witness for the other side being cross-examined by counsel.

Who is a hostile witness? An unfavourable witness is not a hostile witness – there must be something more. *People (Attorney General) v. Hannigan*[36] established that if a judge feels that a witness has no desire to tell the truth, then the witness must be declared hostile. In coming to a conclusion on this point, the judge will take into account the demeanour and attitude of the witness, his willingness to co-operate, and any previous inconsistent statements made by him.

People (Attorney General) v Taylor[37] outlines the procedure that needs to be followed before a witness can be categorised as hostile. It is necessary for counsel to apply to the judge and put before him the material on which it is

---

[34.] If there is cross-examination on parts of the document, other than those used to refresh memory, the document may be put in evidence, but, in this case, it is only admissible to show credibility, and its contents are not evidence of the facts stated: *R. v. Virgo* (1978) 67 Cr. App. R. 323.

[35.] The refreshing memory rule should not be confused with Part II of the Criminal Evidence Act 1992, which provides that a previous statement made by a witness with personal knowledge of the matters in the document may be admitted into evidence, where that document was created or received by someone else in the course of a trade or business. Documents admitted under this exception to the hearsay rule actually become evidence in the case, and the person who compiled them does not have to be available to give evidence.

[36.] [1941] I.R. 252.

[37.] [1974] I.R. 97.

sought to have the witness declared hostile. This should be done in the absence of the jury. If the application is successful the witness is declared hostile and may be cross-examined.

Declaring a witness hostile allows his examination-in-chief to be conducted in the manner of a cross-examination. The matter is governed by the Criminal Procedure Act 1865. A hostile witness may be asked leading questions. Under section 3 of the Criminal Procedure Act, the witness may be asked about previous inconsistent statements. Section 4 provides that these statements may be put before the court if denied by the witness. However, the witness must first be given the statement and asked if he has made it and then told about the circumstances in which the statement was made.[38] Under section 3 of the Criminal Procedure Act, the evidence of a hostile witness may be contradicted by other evidence.[39] However, section 3 of the Criminal Procedure Act precludes counsel from asking about the previous bad character of a hostile witness. Neither is it possible to adduce evidence of the witness's doubtful veracity (apart from previous inconsistent statements). Section 6, however, provides that a witness may be asked whether he has been convicted of any felony/misdemeanour, and if he denies this, evidence to the contrary may be adduced. There is some doubt, however, as to whether this section was intended to apply to hostile witnesses.

In *Taylor* the applicant's conviction was quashed because the trial judge had confused the rules applying to hostile witnesses. He had not followed the correct procedure for determining witnesses hostile. Counsel for the prosecution should have made a formal application to have the witness declared hostile, and this had not been done. In addition, the trial judge had not followed the correct procedure for cross-examining a witness on their previous inconsistent statements. He should have asked the witness whether she had, at another specified time and in other specified circumstances, made a contrary statement.

7.3 Witnesses: Cross-examination

Unlike a hostile witness, a witness for the other side may be asked about any aspect of his bad character. However, this is somewhat limited by the rule in relation to the finality of collateral questions, which is set out below.

---

[38] *Taylor* established how this should be done. The witness should be asked whether he had on a different specified occasion made a contrary statement. If he denies this, he must stand down from the box while the previous statement is proved. He is then put back into the box and the statement is put to him for identification, with attention drawn to the section of the statement which is relied on for the purpose of contradicting him. If he admits the contradiction, the earlier statement is evidence of the facts contained in it. If he denies the contradiction, the earlier statement is evidence of facts going to credibility.

[39] If a witness is unfavourable, rather than hostile, his evidence can still be contradicted by other evidence.

7.3.1   Rule in relation to finality of collateral questions

The rule is as follows: once an answer has been received in cross-examination to a question on a collateral issue, that answer is final and the other side can't adduce evidence to contradict it.

(1) What is a collateral issue?

This raises the question: what is a collateral matter? A collateral matter tends to be an issue relating to the credibility of a witness rather than the facts of the case. In *Attorney General v. Hitchcock*[40] it was stated that in deciding whether something was a collateral issue, it was necessary to ask the following question: "Is the matter one on which you would be allowed to introduce evidence-in-chief?". In other words, is it relevant to the facts in issue?

If the answer is no, the matter is a collateral issue. If the answer is yes, the matter is not a collateral issue, and evidence can be adduced to rebut the witness's answer.

In *Hitchcock*, a maltser was charged with the use of a cistern in breach of statutory requirements. A key witness gave evidence that the cistern had been used. The witness was asked whether or not he had told a man named Cook, that he had been offered a bribe to say this very thing. The witness answered, no, he had not told Cook this. The defence wanted to call evidence to rebut the witness's answer but were not permitted. This was a collateral matter; it would have been different if the question had asked whether the bribe had been accepted.

The rule in relation to the finality of collateral questions surfaced in the Irish case of *D.P.P. v. Barr*.[41] This involved a prosecution for indecent assault in the Phoenix Park. The victim was asked whether she had ever been at the crime scene on a previous occasion. She said that she had not. The defence sought to call evidence of Mr. Curley to the effect that the victim had participated in a robbery in that area on a previous occasion. This application failed; it was unlikely that such evidence would have been admissible in examination-in-chief. It simply was not relevant to whether or not the offence had been committed.

The rule against the finality of collateral questions has been the subject of particular controversy in rape cases. The question is whether the victim's past sexual history is relevant to the facts in issue or is a mere collateral matter. Questions about the complainant's demeanour or previous sexual history have on occasion been held relevant to the question of consent.

In *R. v. Viola*[42] the accused was convicted of a rape, which had occurred in the complainant's flat shortly before midnight. Two questions were put to the victim. She was asked about the presence of two men in her flat shortly before the alleged rape and about her flirtatious conduct towards them. Secondly, she

---

[40]   [1847] 1 Exch. 91.
[41]   Unreported, Court of Criminal Appeal, March 2, 1992.
[42]   [1982] 3 All E.R. 73.

was asked about the presence of a naked man in her flat a few hours after the rape.

The question for the court was whether evidence could be adduced to contradict the complainant's answers to these questions. The Court of Appeal overturned the trial judge on this and held that such evidence would have been admissible in examination-in-chief. The complainant could be cross-examined on her answers. The Court of Appeal said as follows:

> "The judge had been wrong to exclude the cross-examination because the two incidents went to the issue of consent and could not be regarded as so trivial as to allow the judge to say that no injustice could be done by excluding them from evidence."

In *R. v. Fenlon*[43] the complainant was asked whether she had had sex with any other man during the five days prior to the rape. She answered no. The question was whether further cross-examination could take place. It was held that the court must weigh the risk of injustice to the accused if cross-examination were not permitted, against competing considerations of fairness to, and the protection of, the complainant.

In that case, it was taken into account that the complainant was only 14 years old and had attempted to commit suicide. In the circumstances, her answers were taken as final. However, other cases, such as *R. v. Cox*,[44] contradict *Fenlon* and say that the primary factor is that of doing justice to the accused rather than protecting the complainant.

Section 3 of the Criminal Law (Rape) Act 1980 and section 13 of the Criminal Law (Rape) (Amendment) Act 1990 are relevant in the above situations. They state that where the accused pleads not guilty, no evidence may be adduced about the victim's previous sexual experience without the consent of the trial judge. The trial judge will grant leave to cross-examine on such matters if he feels that it is unfair to the accused to refuse. The concept of unfairness is defined in section 3(2)(b) which states that it is unfair not to allow such questions or such evidence if they may raise a reasonable doubt as to the accused's guilt. An application for leave should be heard by the trial judge in the absence of the jury.

In *People (D.P.P.) v. Moloney*[45] it was argued that the trial judge had erred in not permitting cross-examination as to previous sexual history. However, the court said that previous sexual history was only relevant to the issue of consent. In this case, the complainant was under age and, therefore, consent did not arise. Also, the accused had denied that he had ever had sexual intercourse and therefore consent was not an issue.

---

[43]. (1980) 71 Cr. App. R. 307.
[44]. (1986) 84 Cr. App. Rep. 132.
[45]. Unreported, *ex tempore*, November 8, 1999.

(2) Exceptions to collateral issues rule

However, there are a number of situations in which cross-examination may be engaged in and evidence may be sought to rebut answers to collateral questions.

Firstly, previous inconsistent statements of a witness may be put in evidence. Sections 4 and 5 of the Criminal Procedure Act 1865 state that such statements are admissible. If a witness under cross-examination denies a previous oral or written statement, which is relevant to an issue in the case and inconsistent with his or her testimony, this statement may be proved against him. However, the witness must first be given the statement and asked if he has made it and then told about the circumstances in which the statement was made.[46]

Secondly, previous convictions of a witness may be put in evidence despite being collateral matters. Section 6 of the Criminal Procedure Act 1965 says that a witness may be questioned as to whether or not he committed a crime. If he denies this fact, evidence may be adduced in rebuttal.[47]

Thirdly, evidence may be adduced at common law to contradict a witness's denial of bias or partiality and to show that he is prejudiced. *R. v. Mendy*[48] involved a trial for assault. A man was observed taking notes at the trial. He left and spoke to a witness who was being kept outside. The witness denied that he talked to this man. It was held that evidence was admissible to contradict this on the ground that the witness's behaviour indicated bias or partiality.

If it is denied that a witness has accepted a bribe, evidence is admissible in rebuttal, because this issue tends to show bias. However, if a witness merely denies that he was offered a bribe, this is different, as shown by *Attorney General v. Hitchcock.*[49]

Fourthly, evidence can be called as to a witness's reputation for untruthfulness. A party may call a witness to give evidence that in his opinion a witness for the other party is not to be believed. But the witness so called is merely allowed to state his belief, and cannot give evidence of any facts which form the basis for this belief.

Finally, evidence may be given of a physical or mental disability suffered by the witness, such as poor eyesight,[50] which affects his reliability.

---

[46] *People (Attorney General) v. Taylor* [1974] I.R. 97 established how this should be done. The witness should be asked whether he had, on a different specified occasion, made a contrary statement. If he denies this, he must stand down from the box while the previous statement is proved. He is then put back into the box and the statement is put to him for identification, with attention drawn to the section of the statement which is relied on for the purpose of contradicting him. If he admits the contradiction, the earlier statement is evidence of the facts contained in it. If he denies the contradiction, the earlier statement is evidence of facts going to credibility.

[47] It should be noted that a defence counsel may be reluctant to use section 6 because of fear of the accused losing his shield under section 1(f)(ii) of the Criminal Justice (Evidence) Act 1924 and becoming liable to be cross-examined about his bad character. See Chap. 14.

[48] (1976) 64 Cr. App. R. 64.

[49] [1847] 1 Exch 91.

[50] *Toohey v. Metropolitan Police Commissioner* [1965] A.C. 595 at 609.

Chapter 8

OPINION EVIDENCE

8.1 Introduction[1]

An opinion is an inference drawn from facts. For example, a doctor may infer from the fact that his patient has a sharp pain on the right side of his stomach the diagnosis that the patient has appendicitis.

The general rule is that opinion evidence is inadmissible. Witnesses should confine their testimony to stating facts, rather than giving opinions. It is for the court alone to draw inferences from facts. It is the job of a witness to give the facts, not to draw inferences from them.

Non-expert opinion evidence is admissible as regards the testimony of eyewitnesses. Often it is impossible to separate fact from opinion in such testimony. Expert opinion evidence may be admissible in relation to a matter that is beyond the ordinary knowledge of the jury.

In respect of both types of evidence it has been said that the ultimate issue rule applies. An opinion cannot be given as regards an "ultimate issue" in the case.

An ultimate issue is an issue which has to be proved before guilt can be shown, *e.g.* that the plaintiff was unfit to drive in a prosecution for unfitness to drive. The ultimate issue rule was applied in relation to non-expert witnesses in the United Kingdom case of *R. v. Davies*,[2] where it was held that a witness could not describe the plaintiff as being unfit to drive. This would be expressing an opinion on an ultimate issue in the case.

However, as regards expert evidence, at any rate, the ultimate issue rule is no longer strictly applied and the courts allow it to be avoided by mere semantics. For example, instead of using the precise words "unfitness to drive" in the example above, the expert could say, "In my opinion his ability to drive was seriously impaired".

In Ireland, it appears that the case of *Attorney General (Ruddy) v. Kenny*[3] has seriously undercut the ultimate issue rule in relation to non-expert witnesses too.

---

1. See also London, 60 L.Q.R. 201.
2. [1962] 3 All E.R. 97.
3. (1960) 94 I.L.T.R. 185.

8.2 Non-expert opinion evidence

Non-expert opinion evidence is admissible as regards eyewitnesses' testimony when it is impossible to separate fact from opinion in this testimony.

The words of a witness testifying as to perceived facts are always coloured, to some extent, by his opinion as to what he perceived. A non-expert witness may give opinion evidence on matters in relation to which it is impossible, or virtually impossible, to separate his inference from the perceived facts on which those inferences are based.

For example: John is hit with a stick by a man while walking down the street. He is asked in court to describe the man and he says that he is a tall, dark man. What John is really doing is giving his opinion that his attacker was a tall, dark man. He believes that his attacker was tall because his female companion looked significantly small beside him. He believes that his attacker was dark because his hair appeared dark in the shade of a nearby building. He believes that his attacker was male because he was dressed in male attire and had signs of hair on his upper lip.

However, maybe John's attacker was not tall, but merely appeared so because his companion was only 4 foot 10 inches tall. Maybe his hair was not dark, but auburn or light brown and was merely temporarily darkened by his standing in the shade. Maybe "he" was not even a man. When John says that his attacker was a tall dark man he is merely giving his opinion as to this. He is drawing inferences from facts. He would not know for certain that his attacker was a tall dark man unless he caught him, measured him and checked that he was six foot or over, looked at his hair in a variety of lights and checked to see that "he" had the necessary male equipment.

This example proves the point that wherever an eyewitness gives testimony, the eyewitness merely gives an opinion as to what he has seen. This kind of opinion evidence is permissible, however, because if it were not allowed, eyewitnesses could never give testimony at all.

An eyewitness can give evidence of a person's age, appearance, health, bodily or emotional state or reaction to an event or set of circumstances. All this evidence is, of course, opinion evidence involving inferences drawn by the eyewitness from facts perceived by him. However, it is admissible.

United Kingdom courts, however, have imposed restrictions on the kinds of evidence that can be given by eyewitnesses. In the United Kingdom, an eyewitness is allowed to be asked as to whether someone was drunk, *i.e.* he may be asked to give his opinion as to whether someone was drunk. However, he is not allowed to be asked whether someone was so drunk as to be unfit to drive. This was established in *R. v. Davies*,[4] where it was held that, on a charge of driving when unfit through drink, a non-expert may properly give his general impression as to whether the accused had taken drink. However, he was not allowed to say whether the accused was unfit to drive, because this

---

[4.] [1962] 3 All E.R. 97.

was an ultimate issue in the case. It was also felt that the question of degree of drunkenness was an issue better left to an expert.

In Ireland, a non-expert witness can give his opinion as to whether someone was unfit to drive. The case of *Attorney General (Ruddy) v. Kenny* was a prosecution for drunken driving. Davitt P. stated that drunkenness was a condition that did not require special diagnosis, so a non-expert could give his opinion on whether someone was too drunk to drive. In Ireland, it is permissible for an ordinary witness to testify not only that someone was drunk, but also as to the degree of drunkenness, *e.g.* that he was so drunk as to be unfit to drive.

8.3 Expert opinion evidence[5]

Opinion evidence is also admissible if it is given by someone who is an expert in the particular matter on which he gives his opinion and it is on a matter of expertise. A matter of expertise is some issue outside the ordinary knowledge of the jury.

8.3.1 Who is an expert?

The issue as to who is or is not an expert is a question for the trial judge. The person purporting to be an expert must be properly qualified in the subject calling for expertise. Expertise may have been acquired through study, training or experience. There is no requirement that the expertise should have been acquired professionally or in the course of a business.

In *R. v. Silverlock*[6] a solicitor who had studied handwriting as an amateur for 10 years was permitted to give evidence of his opinion to establish whether certain handwriting was that of the accused.

8.3.2 What is a "matter on which expertise is necessary"?

Expert opinion evidence is admissible wherever the drawing of certain inferences calls for an expertise which the tribunal of fact does not possess. The matter on which the expert opinion is given must be a "matter calling for expertise". Such matters can include accident investigation, blood tests, breath tests, fingerprint identification, genetic fingerprinting, the genuineness of works of art, and the state of public opinion. Foreign law is usually proved by the evidence of an expert.

Expert opinion is admissible in relation to standards of professional competence, market values, and customary terms of contract. It is particularly useful in medical and psychiatric matters, which are beyond the experience of the jury. Where the triers of fact can form their own opinion without the

---

5. See further Heeney (2002) 7(3) Bar Rev. 120; Barr (1999) 4(4) Bar Rev. 185; Pigot (1996) GILS 1.
6. [1894] Q.B. 766.

assistance of an expert, the matter in question being within their own experience and knowledge, the opinion of an expert is inadmissible because unnecessary.

8.3.3 *"Indecent" or "obscene" not usually words calling for expertise*

The jury shouldn't normally need expert evidence to determine whether something satisfies the legal definition of indecent or obscent, *i.e.* it tends to deprave and corrupt. However, in a very limited fact situation expert evidence may be admissible to help the jury decide whether something is likely to deprave or corrupt children.

D.P.P. v. A and BC Chewing Gum[7] has been described as.a unique case, being "highly exceptional and confined to its own circumstances".[8] The accused was charged with publishing for gain obscene battle cards, which had been sold together with packets of bubble gum. The High Court held that evidence of experts in child psychiatry concerning the likely effect of the cards on children should be admitted. Lord Parker C.J. stated that

> "when considering the effect of something on an adult, an adult jury may be able to judge just as well as an adult witness called on the point. But certainly when you are dealing here with children of different age groups, any jury and any justices need all the help they can get, information which they may not have as to its effect on different children".[9]

8.3.4 *Expert opinion not admissible to show intention or lack of it but admissible to show that accused had no capacity to form necessary intention*

The opinion of a psychiatrist is not admissible to show that the accused did not intend to commit the crime; however, it is admissible to show lack of capacity to form the intent to cause the crime.

In *R. v. Chard*,[10] it was held that, in a trial for murder, the judge had properly refused to admit the evidence of a medical witness on the intention of the accused to kill or do grievous bodily harm because, there being no question of insanity or diminished responsibility, the jury were able on the basis of their ordinary experience to judge for themselves the state of the accused's mind at the time of the crime.

In *R. v. Toner*[11] it was held to be permissible for a doctor to give evidence, in a trial for attempted murder, that the accused was suffering from a low blood sugar condition, which would have prevented him from forming the necessary intention to kill.

---

7.   [1968] 1 Q.B. 159.
8.   Keane, *The Modern Law of Evidence* (4th ed., Butterworths, London, 1996) at p. 457.
9.   At 164-165.
10.   (1971) 56 Cr. App. R. 268.
11.   (1991) 93 Cr. App. R. 382.

The expert evidence of a psychiatrist or psychologist is admissible on the issue of the reliability or truth of a confession to support an argument that no reliance can be placed on the confession because the accused is suffering from a mental disorder.

8.3.5 *Expert opinion admissible to show insanity, diminished responsibility or automatism*

It is also admissible to show insanity or diminished responsibility, or automatism (sleepwalking), these matters not being within the range of the ordinary juryman's experience.

8.3.6 *Expert evidence not admissible to show provocation*

Expert evidence is generally inadmissible on the issue of an accused's credibility or to establish that he was likely to have been provoked.

In *R. v. Turner*[12] United Kingdom courts were called upon to clarify the limits of psychiatric evidence. The accused was charged with murder. He claimed that he was deeply in love. He struck her with a hammer when she told him that she was sleeping with other men for money and that her baby was not his child.

The evidence of the psychiatrist was to show that the accused had a deep emotional interest in the relationship and her confession of infidelity would lead to blind rage and that subsequent to killing her he would act like a person in blind grief. The Court of Appeal held that this evidence should be excluded. Matters of personal relationships, where there is no mental disorder present, are within the ordinary experience of the jury and they should be left to draw their own inferences.

In *Turner* reference was made to the case of *Lowery v. R.*[13] In this case, both L and K were charged with murder. There was no motive and the murder could have been committed by either or both of the accused. Psychiatric evidence was allowed in this case at the instance of K to show that L had the most aggressive behaviour.

It is very hard to reconcile *Lowery* and *Turner*. *Turner* said that *Lowery* was limited to its own special facts; Lawton J. stated:

> "We don't consider this case as authorising that you need to call a psychiatrist in all cases, because such authorisation would usurp the authority of the court".[14]

Turner was approved by the Irish courts in *D.P.P. v. Kehoe*. In this case a Dr. Behan was called to support the defence of provocation to a murder charge. The accused had gone back to his ex-girlfriend's house, where he went into a spare room and saw her new boyfriend. He lost his temper and killed him. It

---

[12.] [1975] Q.B. 834.
[13.] [1974] A.C. 85.
[14.] At p. 842.

was held that while the evidence of a psychiatrist is relevant regarding insanity, it should be confined to this defence rather than being extended to the defence of provocation.

8.4 Miscellaneous issues on expert evidence

8.4.1 *What happens if expert has no personal knowledge of facts of case on which his opinion is based?*

It is important that the facts on which the expert's opinion is based be proved by admissible evidence. If an expert relies on the existence of some fact, that fact must be proved. The expert will normally have no personal knowledge of the facts upon which his opinion is based. However, the expert is entitled to rely on such facts in the process of forming an opinion. The expert should state the assumed facts upon which his opinion is based, and examination-in-chief and cross-examination of the expert should take the form of hypothetical questions.

In *English Exporters (London) Ltd v Eldonwall Ltd,*[15] an application was made by landlords for the determination of a reasonable interim rent under the Landlord and Tenant Act 1954. In this case, it was held that a professional valuer was entitled to express opinions that he had formed as to values, even though the formation of those opinions had been influenced by matters of fact of which he had no first-hand knowledge but had learned about from sources.

8.4.2 *Can expert base his opinions on writings of others?*

An expert can fortify his opinion by referring to works of authority, learned articles, research papers, letters and other similar material written by others and comprising part of the general body of knowledge falling within the field of expertise of the expert in question.

H. v. Schering Chemicals Ltd[16] involved the issue of whether the drug Primodos had caused certain personal injuries and whether the defendants had been negligent in manufacturing and marketing it. It was held that expert witnesses were entitled to refer to the results of research into the drug, and to articles and letters about the drug in medical journals. Bingham J. held as follows:

> "if an expert refers to the results of research published by a reputable authority in a reputable journal the court would ordinarily regard those results as supporting inferences fairly to be drawn from them, unless or until a different approach was shown to be proper."[17]

---

[15] [1975] 1 Ch. 415.
[16] [1983] 1 All E.R. 849.
[17] At p. 853.

Chapter 9

WITNESSES: SUSPECT EVIDENCE –
CORROBORATION AND OTHER SAFEGUARDS

9.1 Introduction: Solutions to problem of suspect evidence

Certain types of evidence, although admissible, are suspect. In other words, they frequently turn out to be untrue or incorrect. These types of evidence are as follows:

1. accomplice evidence, when the accomplice is testifying on behalf of the prosecution[1];

2. evidence given by the alleged victim of a sexual offence;

3. children's evidence;

4. confessions;

5. identification evidence.

There are a number of solutions, which have been adopted by the courts in criminal cases to minimise the problems attaching to such evidence.

9.1.1 Solution 1: Withdrawing evidence from jury in absence of corroborative evidence

In some limited situations, corroborative evidence[2] must actually be present in order for the jury to convict on certain evidence. If the corroborative evidence is not present, the judge must direct the jury to find the accused innocent.

Corroborative evidence must actually be present before a jury can convict on a charge of perjury[3] or the procuration of girls for prostitution.[4] Sections 1(4) and 2(2) of the Treason Act 1939 further provide that no person

---

[1]. It is clear that there is no mandatory warning requirement when the accomplice is testifying on his own behalf. However, Keane "*The Modern Law of Evidence*" (5th ed., Butterworths, London, 2000) indicates that the trial judge has a discretion to give a warning when an accomplice is testifying on his own behalf, *e.g.* if the accomplice is a co-accused.

[2]. Corroborative evidence may be defined as independent evidence pointing to the accused's guilt. The question of what constitutes corroborative evidence is discussed in more detail, at para. 9.2.1.

[3]. *R. v. Boulter* (1852) 5 Cox C.C. 543; the common law states that a person cannot be convicted of perjury on the uncorroborated evidence of one witness alone.

[4]. Section 3 of the Criminal Law Amendment Act 1885 (as amended by s. 8 of the Criminal Law Amendment Act 1935) provides that a person cannot be convicted, upon the uncorroborated evidence of one witness, of the crime of procuration of women to have unlawful carnal knowledge or to become prostitutes, or to procure unlawful carnal knowledge by intimidation, false pretences or the administration of drugs.

shall be convicted, on the uncorroborated evidence of one witness, of the charge of treason, or of encouraging, harbouring or comforting persons guilty of treason. In addition, certain offences under the Road Traffic Act 1961 require corroboration where speed of a vehicle is proved by the opinion of a witness.

9.1.2 *Solution 2: Compulsory corroboration warning*

An alternative, and more common, solution in Ireland in relation to suspect evidence has been to require a corroboration warning to be given by the judge to the jury in his summing up. This warning is required by common law in respect of accomplice evidence. Section 10 of the Criminal Procedure Act 1993 further requires a warning where confession evidence is relied upon.

The precise form of compulsory corroboration warning will be discussed later. Basically, it points out to the jury that it is dangerous to convict on such evidence in the absence of corroboration; however, if they are satisfied of the accused's guilt beyond reasonable doubt, they can go on and convict even in the absence of corroborative evidence. In these circumstances, if the proper warning has been given, the jury's conviction cannot be overturned even in the absence of corroborative evidence. So there does not have to be corroborative evidence present in order to convict on accomplice evidence or confession evidence, but a corroboration warning should be given in such cases, and if it is not given, the conviction may be overturned.

9.1.3 *Solution 3: Discretionary corroboration warning*

A distinction should be drawn between cases where a corroboration warning is compulsory and situations where the question of whether or not to give such a warning is merely left to the discretion of the trial judge. This third approach has been taken in the case of evidence of victims of sexual offences and the evidence of children; the judge has a discretion to give a corroboration warning in such cases.

Originally, at common law a corroboration warning was compulsory in relation to the evidence of complainants in sexual offence cases and also in relation to the sworn evidence of children. Unsworn evidence of children was only admissible if there was actual corroborative evidence present on the facts; a mere corroboration warning was insufficient here.

However, matters have been changed by statute[5] and the position now is that a corroboration warning is no longer compulsory in respect of the evidence of sexual complainants or the sworn evidence of children. Instead, the decision whether or not to give such a warning is left to the trial judge's discretion. As regards the unsworn evidence of children, the rule that corroboration must be

---

[5.]   The relevant provisions are s. 28 of the Criminal Evidence Act 1992 (in respect of the evidence of children) and s. 7 of the Criminal Law Rape (Amendment) Act 1990 (in respect of the evidence of complainants in sexual offence cases).

present in order to convict on such evidence has also been abolished and a corroboration warning in respect of this evidence is discretionary.

What these three solutions to the problem of suspect evidence have in common is that they all rely on the notion of corroborative evidence, separate and distinct independent evidence that points towards the accused's guilt. In cases where the corroboration warning features, corroborative evidence is not actually required in order to convict, but the warning makes it clear to the jury that it is dangerous to convict in the absence of corroborative evidence.

9.1.4 Solution 4: Different type of warning

However, there are other solutions to the problem of suspect evidence, which do not necessarily involve the concept of corroboration. One such solution has been adopted to deal with the problem of identification evidence. Identification evidence is often proved to be wrong after the fact. The problem is that often those who make the identification are genuinely mistaken. The court's solution to the problem has been to compel the judge to give a special warning in all cases where identification evidence is involved.

Precise requirements have been laid down in relation to this warning, which must be tailored to the facts of the particular case. Firstly, the judge must talk about the dangers of identification evidence generally; how quite genuine identifications may later prove to be wrong. Secondly, any risks attaching to the particular identification in question must be pointed out: whether the witness had good eyesight; the duration of the observation; the circumstances of the observation, etc.

The warning given in identification cases is similar to a corroboration warning insofar as it was also developed to cope with the problem of suspect evidence. However, the identification warning is not a corroboration warning as such, since it makes no reference to the need for corroborative evidence. It is an alternative solution to the problem of suspect evidence, and one which does not involve a search for corroboration. The special rules in relation to identification evidence will be considered in detail later.

However, the concept of corroboration is still relevant in relation to the following kinds of suspect evidence: evidence of accomplices; confessions; evidence of complainants in sexual cases; the sworn and unsworn evidence of children. It is proposed to look at the special rules relating to these categories later.

9.2 Defining corroborative evidence and the corroboration warning

9.2.1 What is corroborative evidence?

As we have seen, the concept of corroborative evidence or, as it is also known, corroboration, has been used as a solution to problems of suspect evidence. It therefore becomes necessary to ascertain what requirements evidence must fulfil in order to amount to corroboration. *People(Attorney General) v.*

Williams[6] defined corroborative evidence as "independent evidence of material circumstances tending to implicate the accused in the commission of the crime".

And in *Attorney General v. Levison*[7] O'Byrne J. provided an alternative description of this concept as being "evidence of any material circumstance tending to connect the accused with the crime and to implicate him in it".

In order to amount to corroboration the evidence must fulfil the following requirements:

1. It must implicate the accused in a material particular, *i.e.* it must tend to show that the accused was guilty of the offence charged.

2. It must be admissible.

3. It must be credible.[8]

4. It must be independent, *i.e.* it must come from a source other than the witness whose evidence requires corroboration.

These requirements conform with *Williams, Levison* and the United Kingdom case of *R. v. Baskerville*,[9] which described corroboration, in similar terms, as:

> "independent testimony which implicates the accused by tending to connect him with the commission of the crime...which confirms in some material particular not only the fact that the crime has been committed but also that A. committed it."

It should be noted that the Irish courts have established in *D.P.P. v. Hogan*[10] that it is irrelevant whether or not the corroborative evidence accords with the other evidence given against the accused, so long as it shows that he was implicated in the crime.

The requirement of independence means that the corroborative evidence must emanate from a new source. Evidence of prior complaints by the witness whose testimony requires corroboration may sometimes be admissible at trial to bolster the credibility of that witness,[11] but it cannot constitute corroboration because it does not come from an independent source. This rule is demonstrated by a number of cases which date from the days when a corroboration warning was mandatory in relation to the evidence of victims in sexual cases.

In *R. v. Whitehead*[12] the victim had told her mother of the rape directly after its occurrence. It was argued that evidence of this complaint could be admitted as corroboration of her testimony in court. This was rejected because the complaint was not independent evidence of the accused's guilt. In the Irish

---

6.   [1940] I.R. 195.
7.   [1932] I.R. 158.
8.   *D.P.P. v. Kilbourne:* corroboration can only be afforded by a witness who is otherwise to be believed.
9.   [1916] 2 K.B. 658.
10. [1994] 2 I.L.R.M. 74.
11. Under the doctrine of recent complaint, see para 7.2.1.
12. [1929] 1 K.B. 99.

case of *People (Attorney General) v. Cradden*[13] the argument that evidence of recent complaints in sexual matters was admissible as corroboration of the victim's testimony was similarly rejected. However, in *R. v. Redpath*[14] evidence of the distressed condition of the victim following the alleged rape was held to be independent evidence.

It is crucial to the concept of corroboration that the corroborative evidence should show the accused to be guilty of the offence charged, *i.e.* "implicate him in a material particular". This requirement is illustrated by the case of *R. v. James*.[15] The accused was charged with rape. There was medical evidence that someone had had intercourse with the victim and the trial judge directed that this was corroboration. This was rejected on appeal because the evidence in question only showed that someone had had intercourse with the victim; it did not point towards that person being the accused or that the intercourse was non-consensual, both of which facts need to be shown in order for the accused to be guilty of rape. The evidence was not corroborative because it did not show that the accused was guilty.

In the *People v. D.*[16] the Court of Criminal Appeal was required to consider whether particular evidence constituted corroboration. The accused had been charged with the indecent assault of his ten-year-old daughter. The trial judge had referred medical evidence of interference with the victim's hymen and said that this constituted corroboration. The Court held this to be incorrect, on the ground that the medical examination had occurred a year later and therefore the doctor's evidence did not directly implicate the accused. Similarly, in the case of *People (D.P.P.) v. Donnelly*[17] it was held that evidence of blood stains on the complainant's bed could not provide corroboration of her allegations of sexual assault against the appellant.

R. v. Redpath[18] provides a contrast on this point also. Here, a bystander gave evidence that the accused approached the child victim and that shortly afterwards the bystander saw the child in a distressed condition. It was held that this evidence pointed towards the accused having sexually assaulted the child; it was corroboration since it tended to implicate him in a material particular.

However, in the Irish case of *People (Attorney General) v. Trayers*[19] the accused was charged with unlawful carnal knowledge of an under age-girl. It was held that the fact that the accused had gone to her house to try to settle the case, and also the fact that he had admitted being out with her on a number of occasions, were not corroboration since they did not point to the accused's guilt. Such behaviour was consistent with his innocence.

---

13. [1955] I.R. 130.
14. (1962) 46 Cr. App. R. 319.
15. (1971) 55 Cr. App. R. 299.
16. Unreported, Central Criminal Court, July 27, 1993.
17. Unreported, Court of Criminal Appeal, February 22, 1999.
18. (1962) 46 Cr. App. R. 319.
19. [1956] I.R. 110.

An example of an Irish case in which corroboration was found to exist is *People (D.P.P.) v. Reid*.[20] The accused was charged with rape. It was a pre-1991 offence so the Rape Act 1990 did not apply and corroboration was necessary. The victim claimed that the accused had forced her into his house and raped her in the sitting room with the TV on to muffle her cries. Corroboration was found in the cumulative effect of the following pieces of evidence:

1. the fact that the victim had severe injuries to her genitalia – this indicated sexual intercourse without consent;

2. the fact that her parents and Gardaí had noted her distress – again this pointed to sexual intercouse without consent; and

3. the fact that when the Gardaí called to the accused's house, they did indeed find the television set at an extraordinarily high volume – this accorded with the victim's testimony and did indeed point to the rape having been carried out by the accused.

This case is an example of corroboration being provided by the cumulative effect of a number of different pieces of evidence.

One issue in relation to corroboration is whether the evidence of one accomplice can corroborate that of another. This is the issue of mutual corroboration and was dealt with in the U.K. case of *D.P.P. v. Kilbourne*.[21] Generally, the answer is no. However, under *Kilbourne* accomplices are divided up into three different classes:

1. persons implicated either as principals or accessories to the offence charged;

2. handlers of stolen goods, in a trial for larceny; and

3. principals or accessories to another offence committed by the accused.

According to the House of Lords in *Kilbourne,* an accomplice in one class can corroborate the evidence of an accomplice in another class. The thinking here is that there is less danger of collusion.

Kilbourne was alleged to have committed sex offences against young boys in 1971. The problem was that the boys were regarded as accomplices to the crime of buggery, and, as such, their evidence required corroboration. The accusations of the 1970 boys were contained in a single count. All the 1970 victims were accomplices in class 1; they were accessories to the offence charged and could not corroborate one another. However, the indictment contained other counts relating to boys who had been abused by the accused in 1971. They belonged to class 3, being parties to another offence committed by the accused. As such, it was held that their evidence could corroborate the evidence of the 1971 boys.

---

[20] [1993] 2 I.R. 186.
[21] [1973] A.C. 729.

Mutual corroboration was allowed in a similar situation in *D.P.P. v. Boardman*.[22] However, it would appear that the accomplices have to be from different *Kilbourne* classes if the evidence of one is to corroborate the other. As regards mutual corroboration between witnesses other than accomplices, there was a common law rule that the evidence of one child could not corroborate the evidence of another child; however, this has been abolished by section 28(3) of the Criminal Evidence Act 1992.

Another issue is whether failure on the part of the accused to testify could amount to corroboration. It was established by *R. v. Jackson*,[23] that failure to testify cannot be so treated. It is undecided whether or not silence of the accused when charged with an offence can amount to corroboration.[24]*People v. Quinn*[25] indicates that the silence of an accused when charged cannot amount to corroboration in this jurisdiction. In this case, the accused was taken to Newbridge Garda Station and charged with unlawful carnal knowledge of the complainant. When told of the charges against him, he said, "I will not make any statement". The trial judge said that this amounted to corroboration but this finding was later overturned by the Court of Criminal Appeal on the basis that such a rule would be contrary to the privilege against self-incrimination.

R. v. Lucas[26] establishes that lies told by the accused in or out of court can amount to corroboration provided they meet the following conditions: they must be deliberate; they must relate to a material issue; and, the motive for the lie must be a realisation of guilt. However, the court recognises that sometimes people lie out of shame or as a wish to conceal scandal from family, or to bolster up a just cause. The statement must be shown to be a lie by independent evidence (evidence coming from a source other than the person who is to be corroborated). *R. v. Lucas* also illustrates that the fact that the accused's testimony is untruthful cannot be treated as corroboration.

Can evidence of the accused's propensity to commit an offence of this nature amount to corroboration? Yes, provided that such evidence is admissible.[27] In *D.P.P. v. Boardman*[28] the head of a language school was accused of assaults on two of his pupils, S. and H. Evidence of the assault on H was admissible at the trial of S and vice versa, because the striking similarities between the two allegations meant that each had high probative effect in relation to the other. Once S.'s evidence was admissible, it could corroborate H.'s and vice versa.

---

22. [1975] A.C. 421.
23. [1953] 1 All E.R. 872.
24. Keane, *The Modern Law of Evidence* (5th ed., Butterworths, London, 2000) thinks that the absence of protest of innocence can sometimes be corroboration. *Cross and Tapper on Evidence* (9th ed., Butterworths, London, 1999) disagrees.
25. [1955] I.R. 57.
26. [1981] 3 W.L.R. 122.
27. The admissibility of evidence showing the accused is of bad character is severely restricted. See Chapters 12-14. Such evidence may, however, be admissible on a number of grounds, in particular if its probative value is so high as to outweigh the prejudices caused by its admission.
28. [1975] A.C. 421; *D.P.P. v. Kilbourne* [1973] A.C. 729 is another example of corroboration being provided by evidence of the accused's previous misconduct.

Arguably, the rules in relation to what constitutes corroborative evidence are too strict and exclude valuable testimony. It has been argued that any evidence that tends to show that a witness is telling the truth should be capable of corroborating that witness, whether or not it indicates that the accused is guilty of the crime charged.[29]In this regard it may be noted that *People (D.P.P.) v. Reid*[30] hints at a more liberal approach in this jurisdiction. Keane J. in this case gave a broader definition of corroboration as "concurring circumstances which give greater probability to the evidence of the prosecutrix".

Finally, it has been recognised that a trial judge has a discretion to withdraw potentially corroborative evidence from the jury where such evidence is of questionable reliability. In *People (D.P.P.) v. Morrissey*[31] the applicant was convicted of sexual offences relating to the daughter of a woman with whom he had cohabited. The mother gave evidence corroborating that of the daughter, although there were inconsistencies between the mother and the daughter's evidence. The Court of Criminal Appeal said that the mother's evidence could not constitute corroboration, because there had been a conspiracy between the mother and the daughter, stating that:

> "Corroboration must come from independent evidence. The mere fact that two parties in conspiracy with each other give the same evidence does not make the evidence of one corroboration of the evidence of the other."[32]

9.2.2   What form should corroboration warning take?

Whenever a corroboration warning is required, or when the judge decides to exercise his discretion to give a warning, it should take the following form: The judge must point out that it is dangerous to convict on evidence of this type unless corroborated, but that the jury can, however, convict, even in the absence of corroborating evidence, if they are satisfied of the guilt of the accused beyond all reasonable doubt.

The judge must then outline the rules relating to what constitutes corroboration. It is important to note that he does not have to actually use the word corroboration, so long as he explains what it is. It appears from *People (D.P.P.) v. Reid*[33] that it is not strictly necessary for the judge to go through the evidence in the case and point out what pieces of evidence are capable of constituting corroboration. However, it is advisable for him to do so.

The degree and gravity of the warning required may vary depending on the degree and gravity of the risk involved in accepting the evidence, on the particular facts of the case. In *People (Attorney General) v. Berber*[34] the Court of Appeal stated that the fact that the accomplice had previously made false

---

[29]. This has been the approach taken by the Canadian courts in *Vetrovec v. The Queen* [1982] 1 S.C.R. 811.
[30]. [1993] 2 I.R. 186.
[31]. Unreported, Court of Criminal Appeal, July 10, 1998.
[32]. At p. 20
[33]. [1993] 2 I.R. 186.
[34]. [1944] I.R. 405.

accusations against the accused should have been brought to the attention of the jury. The fact that the witness has been given immunity from prosecution, has yet to receive a sentence or has been pressurised into testifying, or indeed has been previously convicted of perjury or has a general reputation for untruthfulness, may also be taken into account. The degree of complicity of the accomplice in the crime may also be a factor.

In *People (D.P.P.) v. Hogan*[35] a trial judge's corroboration warning was challenged on the grounds that he had erred in failing to explain to the jury exactly why it was necessary to be careful in relation to accomplice evidence. It was held that on the facts of the case this was not necessary; it was abundantly clear from other passages in the summing up, which stated that the witness had got a reduction in sentence for co-operating with the police, exactly why it was necessary to be careful of that witness's evidence. The judge in that case had:

1. warned the jury of the dangers of acting upon the uncorroborated evidence of an accomplice;

2. furnished the jury with a full description of what was meant in law by corroboration; and

3. laid before them the the matters capable of being corroborative.

This was entirely correct; in fact the direction was seen as a model one.

It should be noted that the question of whether a witness is an accomplice is normally a matter for the jury. If there is evidence pointing in favour of a witness being an accomplice, the judge should make the warning conditional on the jury deciding that the witness is an accomplice. However, if the witness is an accomplice on any reasonable view of the evidence, the judge's corroboration warning should be absolute and not conditional. This was the view of the majority in *D.P.P. v. Carney*,[36] a prosecution arising out of a robbery at the Monument creameries. O'Byrne J. felt that "on any reasonable view of the evidence, the witness was an accomplice"; therefore the matter should not have been left to the jury and the warning should have been absolute. However, Dixon J. dissented and felt that the question was one for the jury.

Having defined corroboration and discussed the requirements for a valid corroboration warning, the next question is when such a warning is necessary. As stated above, a corroboration warning is compulsory in the case of accomplice evidence and confessions, and discretionary in the case of evidence of complainants in sexual offences and children's evidence. It is proposed to consider each type of evidence in turn.

---

35. [1994] 2 I.L.R.M. 74.
36. [1955] I.R. 324.

9.3   Situations in which the corroboration warning is necessary

9.3.1   Accomplice evidence

The rule requiring a corroboration warning in respect of accomplice evidence first originated as a rule of practice and crystallised into a rule of law in the early 20th century. In *Attorney General v. Levison*[37] O'Byrne J. described it as "such an invariable practice as now to amount to a rule of law".

(1) Rationale for requiring corroboration

As recognised in the Irish case of *Dental Board v. O'Callaghan,*[38] an accomplice may attempt to transfer the blame in order to put himself in a more favourable position in the eyes of the judge and jury. Alternatively, he may be looking for more favourable treatment from the prosecution and may, on occasion, have been promised an immunity from prosecution or a lighter sentence in return for his testimony. He may be actuated by malice or may want to shield the real culprit by implicating an innocent party. Finally, there is the argument that an accomplice is by definition a criminal and, as such, his moral standards and credibility have been called into doubt. The danger is that the accomplice may be able to lull the jury into a false sense of security. Because of his knowledge of the details of the crime, he may be able to concoct a plausible story which it is difficult to shake on cross-examination.

(2) Who is an accomplice?

For the above reasons, a corroboration warning is compulsory at common law in the case of evidence given by an accomplice. This raises the question – who is an accomplice? A starting point is the threefold categorisation laid down in *Davies v D.P.P.*[39] and reaffirmed in *R. v. Kilbourne.*[40] An accomplice is either:

1. a party to the offence charged, either as principal or accessory;

2. a handler of stolen goods, in respect of a trial for larceny; or

3. an accomplice to another offence committed by the accused, of which evidence is admissible under the principles of similar fact evidence.

This distinction was criticised in the Australian case of *McNee v. Kay*[41] where a wider definition of accomplice was recommended. Scholl J. argued that anyone who was chargeable in relation to the behaviour alleged in the indictment, where the offence with which he was charged was of such a nature that he might be tempted to lie or to deflect prosecution from himself, should be regarded as an accomplice.

---

[37]   [1932] I.R. 158.
[38]   [1969] I.R. 1.
[39]   [1954] A.C. 378.
[40]   [1973] A.C. 729.
[41]   (1953) V.L.R. 520.

The Irish case of *Attorney General v. Linehan*[42] stated that a narrow or precise definition of accomplice should be avoided. However, it was felt that the term definitely included anyone implicated either as principal or accessory in the offence charged. The degree of involvement can be quite small. In this case a woman was charged with the murder of her granddaughter's illegitimate child. Evidence showed that the granddaughter could have been involved. She was regarded as an accomplice. In *People (Attorney General) v. Carney*[43] it was held that a very slight degree of complicity as either a principal or an accomplice would be enough to necessitate the accomplice warning.

People (D.P.P.) v. Murtagh[44] established that in a prosecution for the offence of subornation of perjury, the perjurer is an accomplice of the suborner. The trial judge must consequently give a warning. Similarly, when an individual is on trial for the offence of attempting to pervert the course of justice by incitement, the person alleged to have been so incited is an accomplice. In contrast, in *Dental Board v O'Callaghan*[45] it was held that a police spy who participates in the entrapment of the criminal is not an accomplice.

A woman upon whom an abortion is performed is also regarded as an accomplice,[46] as is a willing participant in a sexual offence. *Attorney General v. Durnan* held that when an accomplice gives evidence, his or her spouse, when corroborating the evidence, is in the same position as the accomplice and a corroboration warning should be given.[47] If the spouse testifies for the prosecution, there is no need for a corroboration warning to be given.

The case of *D.P.P. v. Diemling*[48] involved false imprisonment and murder. The accused's daughter, Kia Bailey, had been in the house when these offences were carried out. She had purchased medical supplies, attended the injuries of the criminal, and assisted in the destruction of evidence. The trial judge instructed the jury, however, that she was not an accomplice and her evidence did not require corroboration. This was overturned on appeal. There was evidence that Kia Bailey was an accessory after the fact. She knew of the victim's death, and her subsequent activities could be construed as intended to aid her father's escape. It was found that in the circumstances it was for the trial judge to direct the jury that in the event of their finding that Kia was an accessory after the fact, there was a sufficient degree of complicity to make her an accomplice, and in that event they should follow the warning. If they were not satisfied that she was an accessory after the fact, they should disregard the warning.

The issue of accomplice corroboration arose in *People (D.P.P.) v. Ward*.[49] Paul Ward was charged before the Special Criminal Court with the murder of

---

42. [1929] I.R. 19.
43. [1955] I.R. 324.
44. [1990] I.R. 339.
45. [1969] I.R. 181.
46. *Attorney General v. Levison* [1932] I.R. 158.
47. See also *R. v. Allen* [1965] 2 Q.B. 295.
48. Unreported, Court of Criminal Appeal, May 4, 1992.
49. Unreported, Special Criminal Court, November 27, 1998.

the crime journalist Veronica Guerin. The case against him was based largely on the evidence of his accomplice, Charles Bowden. Bowden admitted loading and preparing the gun used in Guerin's murder. He alleged that Ward had helped plan the murder and had been responsible for disposing of the motorcycle and gun. Bowden's evidence was uncorroborated.[50]It was argued by the defence that Bowden was no ordinary criminal and no ordinary accomplice, but a supergrass, equivalent to a terrorist informer who has been given his freedom and a new life, and that, as such, his evidence must be treated with the greatest of suspicion.

The court said that Bowden must be treated as an ordinary accomplice. However, even on this basis the corroboration warning applied. The trial, being one before the Special Criminal Court, did not involve a jury; the guilt of the accused fell to be decided by a panel of three judges. The Special Criminal Court was therefore in a position of having to give itself a corroboration warning. However, despite recognising the dangers of uncorroborated accomplice evidence, it chose to ignore the dangers and to convict on Bowden's uncorroborated evidence.

Barr J., delivering the judgment of the courts, described Bowden as:

> "a self-serving, deeply avaricious and potentially vicious criminal.... The court readily accepts that he would lie without hesitation and regardless of the consequences for others if he perceived it to be in his own interest to do so."[51]

They said that the real motivation behind Mr. Bowden's evidence was:

> "a cold dispassionate assessment of his grievous situation at that time and amounted to a decision on his part to extricate himself as best he could from what he probably perceived as the reality of his situation then."[52]

However, they took the view that this same self-interest would probably lead him to tell the truth. He was:

> "clever enough to realise and he has been told in terms that the information he furnished would be thoroughly checked out. He knows that if he is found to be lying as to any material fact much of the situation he has salvaged for himself and his family may be jeopardised. The Court accepts that Bowden is fully aware that it is in his best interest to tell the truth about those involved in the murder and that he is likely to have done so unless...it appeared to him that it might be in his interest to lie and wrongly implicate the accused."[53]

The court placed emphasis on the fact that most of Bowden's evidence about the background to the crime had not been challenged by the accused. It was pointed out that Bowden's account of all events up to the actual murder was consistent with the evidence as given by the accused. The court said that Bowden's evidence about the murder was consistent with the facts as known.

[50.] The only evidence relied on to corroborate it, Ward's confession, had been held inadmissible in an earlier decision of the Special Criminal Court on this matter.

[51.] At p. 22.

[52.] At p. 24.

[53.] At p. 25.

There was nothing suggesting that it might have been in Bowden's interest to lie. There were some minor lies told'by Bowden but these were unimportant.

The Court of Criminal Appeal[54] subsequently set aside Paul Ward's conviction on the ground that the Special Criminal Court should not have relied on the accomplice evidence of Charles Bowden. Murphy J. stated that the Special Criminal Court had correctly given themselves a corroboration warning but had failed to pay attention to it. Normally, a corroboration warning is given by a judge to a jury, who are supposed to follow it. However, the jury has the right to ignore the warning and convict on uncorroborated evidence without risk of that conviction subsequently being overturned. However, Murphy J. said that matters were different in the context of a trial without jury. A conviction by a panel of judges, based on uncorroborated accomplice evidence, may be set aside if that accomplice evidence is clearly unreliable.

The issue of accomplice testimony also came before the Special Criminal Court in *People (D.P.P.) v. Meehan*.[55] Meehan was charged with the murder of Veronica Guerin and also in relation to drugs and firearms offences. Again, one of the main prosecution witnesses was Charles Bowden. His evidence in relation to the murder was rejected here because of his tendency to lie to suit his interests, but was accepted in relation to the drugs and firearms offences. Mr. Bowden's wife gave evidence supporting him. However, it was held that an accomplice warning should also be given in relation to her evidence under the principle laid down in *Attorney General v. Durnan*.[56] A warning was also given in relation to the evidence of a friend of the Gilligan gang, even though he was not strictly speaking an accomplice.

(3) Who decides whether someone is an accomplice – the judge or the jury?

In *People (Attorney General) v. Carney*[57] the Supreme Court held that where it was clear that someone was an accomplice, the corroboration warning should be unconditional. However, if there was some evidence on which a reasonable jury could find a witness to be an accomplice, then the issue should be left to them in the form of a conditional warning, defining the term "accomplice", and telling them that if they were satisfied that the witness was an accomplice, they should heed the words of the corroboration warning.[58] However, Dixon J. dissented. He felt that even where the evidence was strongly in favour of a finding that the witness was an accomplice, if a reasonable jury could take the view that the witness was not, the matter should be left to them. In the

---

54. *D.P.P. v. Ward*, unreported, Court of Criminal Appeal, March 22, 2002.
55. *People (D.P.P.) v Meehan*, unreported, Special Criminal Court, July 29, 1999.
56. [1934] I.R. 308.
57. [1955] I.R. 324.
58. A conditional warning of this type was given in *People (D.P.P.) v. Diemling*, unreported, Court of Criminal Appeal, May 4, 1992.

subsequent cases of *People (D.P.P.) v. Lynch*[59] and *People (D.P.P.) v. Conroy*[60] the Supreme Court has established that material issues of fact should be left to the jury unless it would be perverse of them to take the view that the witness was not an accomplice.

(4) Supergrass trials[61]

In the United Kingdom a supergrass is defined as a person who has repeatedly taken part in serious criminal enterprises and who agrees to give evidence for the prosecution against alleged participants in these same crimes.

The term is not confined to terrorists and includes members of large criminal gangs. In the United Kingdom supergrass evidence must be corroborated before an accused can be convicted on it.[62] The Northern Ireland Court of Appeal has adopted a similar approach in *R. v. Crumley*,[63] where they stated that it was possible, but very difficult, for a jury to convict on the uncorroborated evidence of a supergrass. It is worth noting that the Special Criminal Court in *People v. Ward*[64] appeared to share this view, although they held that the accomplice in that case, Charles Bowden, was not a supergrass.

A corroboration warning has also been made compulsory in respect of confession evidence.

9.3.2 Confession evidence

Section 10 of the Criminal Procedure Act 1993 states that where, at a trial of a person on indictment, evidence is given of a confession made by that person and that evidence is not corroborated, the judge shall advise the jury to have due regard to the absence of corroboration. It shall not be necessary for a judge to use any particular form of words under this section.

Prior to this there was no mandatory corroboration warning at common law in the case of confessions. This was confirmed by the Supreme Court in *People v. Quilligan (No. 3).*[65] A strong dissent was delivered by McCarthy and Egan JJ., who felt that a warning analogous to the identification warning should always be given in these cases. However, the majority of the Supreme Court said that it was within the discretion of the trial judge to give a corroboration warning at common law, although there does not appear to have been any previous common law basis for this statement.

The question is now otiose since a warning has been made compulsory in this situation. It is uncertain what precise form this warning must take. It appears that it must refer to the concept of corroboration, and state that the jury must not convict in the absence of such evidence. It has yet to be decided,

---

[59] [1982] I.R. 64.
[60] [1986] I.R. 460.
[61] See further *Ingoldsby* (1999) T.C.L.R. 29.
[62] *R. v. Turner* (1975) 61 Cr. App. R. 67.
[63] (1986) 7 N.I.J.B. 1.
[64] Unreported, Special Criminal Court, November 27, 1998.
[65] [1993] 2 I.R. 305.

however, whether the warning must satisfy the same strict standards as the corroboration warning given in accomplice evidence cases.

9.4   Situations in which the corroboration warning is discretionary

9.4.1   Children's evidence

The relevant provision in relation to corroboration of children's evidence is section 28(1) of the Criminal Evidence Act 1992, which abolishes the absolute requirement of corroboration in respect of unsworn evidence of children and makes a corroboration warning discretionary in relation to child evidence generally.

Section 28 repeals section 30 of the Children Act 1908, which requires corroboration of the unsworn evidence of a child. Any requirement that the jury be given a compulsory corroboration warning by the judge about convicting on the evidence of a child is also abolished. Wherever a child's evidence is concerned, it shall be for the judge to decide, in his discretion, having regard to all the evidence given, whether the jury should be given such a warning.

Section 28 also states that if the judge decides, in his discretion, to give such a warning as aforesaid, it shall not be necessary to use any particular form of words. Finally, unsworn evidence received by virtue of section 28 may corroborate evidence given by any other person.

9.4.2   Evidence of complainants in sexual offence cases

At common law, a corroboration warning was compulsory in respect of the evidence of complainants in sexual offence cases. This originally developed as a rule of practice and crystallised into a rule of law. In *People (Attorney General) v. Cradden*[66] the Court of Criminal Appeal stated that the warning was "a rule of practice with the force of a rule of law"

(1) Rationale for corroboration in respect of such evidence

According to Hale, an accusation of a sexual offence is easily made and hard to defend. As against this, the unpleasant nature of the criminal process operates to discourage people from making false claims of sexual offences. It may also be argued that, though sexual offences are difficult to defend, equally they are hard to prove. Hale's rationale was strongly criticised by McGuinness J. in *People (D.P.P.) v. Kiernan.*[67] There is also a fear that sympathy for the victim may affect the reasoning process of the jury. However, it is worth noting that a requirement of corroboration in such cases may actually work against the accused by confusing the jury and distorting the effect of the judge's

---

[66.]   [1955] I.R. 130.
[67.]   The judgment was approved by the Court of Criminal Appeal, unreported, ex tempore, October 19, 1998.

summing up. A jury experiment carried out by the London School of Economics in the early 1970s found that a jury was actually more likely to convict where a full corroboration warning had been given.[68]

(2) Section 7 Criminal Law Rape (Amendment) Act 1990

However, section 7 of the Criminal Law Rape (Amendment) Act 1990 makes a corroboration warning discretionary in relation to the evidence of sexual offence victims. Section 7 also states that if a judge decides, in his discretion, to give the warning, it shall not be necessary for him to use any particular form of words.

Reference is also made in the 1990 Act to the discretionary warning as being "such a warning as aforesaid", which indicates that when the trial judge decides to exercise his discretion, the warning given should be the same as before. In *D.P.P. v. Cornally*[69] the Court of Criminal Appeal stated that where a corroboration warning was given under section 7, it was necessary to point out to the jury the issues capable of amounting to corroboration. In addition, *People (D.P.P.) v. D.* reaffirms the application of the *Baskerville* definition of corroboration in this context. However, in *People (D.P.P.) v. Murphy*[70] the appellant had been convicted of sexual assault. He appealed, alleging that the trial judge had given a corroboration warning and that the definition of corroboration was incorrect. The trial judge had said that dirt on the appellant's body and clothes was corroborating evidence. It was recognised that this was not corroborating evidence because it failed to implicate the accused. However, the Court of Criminal Appeal refused to set the conviction aside on the ground that the trial judge needn't have said anything about corroboration at all. This case may herald a more relaxed approach to the question of corroboration.

In *People (D.P.P.) v. Kiernan*[71] the Court of Criminal Appeal had to consider what type of warning should be given in such cases. The warning given by the trial judge, Mc Guinness J., was approved. She had explained the meaning of corroboration and pointed out which evidence was capable of being corroborative. In addition, she had pointed out certain problems with the corroborative evidence, and warned the jury that inconsistencies can weaken the effect of corroborative evidence.

(3) Subsequent application of section 7

In *People v. Molloy*[72] the Court of Criminal Appeal criticised a trial judge for failing to give a corroboration warning in a rape case. It was stated that where the charge was supported by the evidence of the complainant alone without

---

[68.] LSE Jury Project, "Juries and the Rules of Evidence" [1973] Crim. L.R. 208.

[69.] Unreported, Court of Criminal Appeal, *ex tempore*, November 7, 1994.

[70.] Unreported, Court of Criminal Appeal, *ex tempore*, November 3, 1997.

[71.] Unreported, Court of Criminal Appeal, *ex tempore*, October 19, 1998.

[72.] Unreported, Court of Criminal Appeal, July 28, 1995.

collateral forensic evidence or other form of corroboration, it is a prudent practice for the trial judge to give a corroboration warning.

However a change in approach was demonstrated by the subsequent decision of the Court in *People (D.P.P.) v. JEM*.[73] The applicant was appealing against his conviction for sexual assault on the ground that the trial judge had failed to give the jury a warning. Denham J. said that the warning was no longer mandatory. She approved the United Kingdom decision of *R. v. Makanjuola*[74] and emphasised that the decision whether or not to give a discretionary warning was primarily a matter for the trial judge, who should only give such a warning if there was some evidence indicating that the victim's testimony was unreliable.

In *Makanjuola* the Court of Appeal stated that statute had intended to make the warning discretionary, and the judge must exercise his discretion. The factors to be taken into account in this regard would depend on the circumstances of the case, the issues raised, and the content and quality of the witness's evidence. If a warning were given, there would need to be an evidential basis for stating that the evidence is unreliable, *e.g.* false accusations made by the victim in the past, a grudge held by the victim against the defendant, or evident lies in his testimony. Subsequent Court of Appeal decisions have recognised other grounds making a complainant's evidence unreliable: jealousy; purported retractions; serious inconsistencies in his evidence; evidence of the allegations being retaliatory; false memory syndrome. It has also been emphasised that a child sexual complainant is not in a special category as regards the exercise of this discretion. In *R. v. R. (John David)*[75] the Court of Appeal held that there was nothing to indicate that a discretionary corroboration warning was required just because the complainant was a child.

It is now proposed to go on and consider the special non-corroboration warning which has been developed to deal with the problems of identification evidence.

9.5 Identification evidence safeguards

9.5.1 Identification warning

Originally a warning was not required in the case of identification evidence. The first change in this approach came with the United Kingdom case *R. v. Turnbull*.[76] In this case, the Court of Appeal laid down guidelines for visual identification evidence. Failure to follow these guidelines resulted in a conviction being quashed if, on all the evidence, the verdict was unsafe or unsatisfactory.

[73.] Court of Criminal Appeal, February 1, 2000.
[74.] [1995] 3 All E.R. 730.
[75.] [1996] Crim. L.R. 909.
[76.] [1976] 3 All E.R. 549.

In cases of visual identification it was stated that the judge should:

1. warn the jury of the need for caution in identification evidence;
2. instruct the jury as to why it is necessary to be cautious with such evidence, namely, because judicial experience has shown this category to be particularly vunerable to error;
3. point out that often an identification witness, even when mistaken, can be honest and very convincing;
4. direct the jury to examine closely the circumstances of the identification, *e.g.* the distance of the observer from the criminal, the light, the date and time of observation, and whether the witness had seen the accused before;
5. remind the jury of any weaknesses in the identification;
6. direct that if the quality of the identification evidence is fairly good, identification by one witness can provide support for an identification by another (analogous to mutual corroboration);
7. withdraw the case from the jury and direct an acquittal when the quality of the identification evidence is poor;
8. identify supporting evidence to the jury. Supporting evidence is not necessarily the same as corroboration. Significantly, the term "corroboration" was not used in *Turnbull*.

The guidelines were stated to apply "whenever the case against the accused depends wholly or substantially on the correctness of one or more identifications of him". They had to be followed in all identification cases, even if the opportunities of observation were good and/or even if the accused was identified at a formal identification parade. However, they did not apply if the witness had not actually identified the accused, but had merely given a description, even a photo-fit description, which was consistent with the accused's appearance.

The above principles apply outside the context of visual identification to cases of voice identification. In a recent U.K. case, *R. v. Hersey*,[77] the accused was convicted of a robbery which lasted 15 minutes and involved conversation with the shopkeeper he was robbing. The shopkeeper recognised the voice of the masked robber as that of the accused, a customer. The accused and some volunteers read a passage and the shopkeeper picked out the accused's voice. Counsel sought to call evidence on the reliability of the identification and, in particular, the effect of stress on the pitch of the voice. The Court of Appeal refused to admit such evidence on the facts of the case but indicated that they might take a different approach in future cases.

Subsequent Irish cases have to a large extent followed *Turnbull*. In *People v. Casey (No. 2)*[78] it was held that wherever the verdict depends substantially on the correctness of visual identification of the accused, the attention of the jury

---

77. [1998] Crim. L.R. 281.
78. [1963] I.R. 33.

should be drawn in general terms to the fact that in a number of cases visual identification had subsequently been found erroneous.

This warning is not confined to cases where the identification is by only one witness. The direction should:

1. state that, often, honest witnesses with good observation opportunities have made incorrect identifications, even on an identification parade;

2. carefully examine the identification evidence in the light of all the circumstances;

3. indicate the need for particular caution;

4. point out that the jury must be satisfied beyond all reasonable doubt of the correctness of the identification.

In *People (Attorney General) v. Stafford*[79] it was argued that an identification warning was not necessary where the identification was made by someone who already knew the accused and could be expected to recognise him accurately. This was rejected. Even in cases of recognition, as distinct from identification, the warning must be given.[80] This followed the dictum of Lord Widgery C.J. in *Turnbull* to the effect that mistakes in recognition of close relatives and friends are sometimes made. *Stafford* was followed in *D.P.P. v. McNamara*,[81] where a conviction was overturned because the trial judge failed to give a warning in respect of recognition evidence.

People v. Fagan[82] developed and expanded *Casey*. In this case an informal identification parade was held, and the judge gave the warning set out in *Casey*. However, it was held that this was insufficient. A stronger and fuller warning should have been given in the circumstances:

1. The judge should have pointed out that this was an identification made on an informal identification parade.

2. It was not enough to merely say generally that the jury should examine the identification in the light of all the circumstances; the judge must point to particular circumstances which weaken the quality of the identification and he had failed to do this here.

There was also a suggestion that an explanation should have been given as to why a formal identification parade was not held. This has been developed in later cases into the view that the accused has some kind of entitlement to a formal identification parade. This semi-right to an identification parade is a parallel doctrine to the warning requirement and operates as a further protection against mistaken identifications.

---

[79]. [1983] I.R. 165.

[80]. However, a formal identification parade will not usually be required in respect of recognition evidence. In-court identification will suffice.

[81]. *People (D.P.P.) v. McNamara*, unreported, Court of Criminal Appeal, March 22, 1999.

[82]. 1 Frewen 375.

People (D.P.P.) v. O'Reilly[83] was an example of an informal identification. The accused was charged with larceny and the principal witness against him was an 85-year-old woman. She had been brought to Edgeworthstown in a garda car, where she identified the applicant. She had also been given a photograph in advance of the parade. The trial judge merely gave the basic *Casey* warning. The defence challenged the conviction on two grounds. Firstly, there should have been an explanation as to why a formal identification parade was not held. Secondly, the trial judge's warning was inadequate. O'Flaherty J., delivering the judgment of the Court of Criminal Appeal, found in favour of the appellant on two grounds. Firstly, the warning was inadequate because it was not related to the particular facts of the case. *Casey* was not a stereotyped formula. The infirmities surrounding informal identification parades in general, and this informal identification parade in particular, should have been put to the jury. Also, the advanced age of the identifying victim, her state of shock at the time of the original observation, and the limited duration of that observation, should have been noted. Secondly, the circumstances of the case were such that fair procedures required a formal identification parade be held, and the argument that it was more beneficial to the accused not to hold one, was constitutionally unsatisfactory.

9.5.2 Right to formal identification parade and other fair procedures

By stating in *People (D.P.P.) v. O'Reilly* that there was some kind of right to a formal identification parade implicit in the constitutional doctrine of fair procedures, O'Flaherty J. was rejecting the view previously expressed by the Supreme Court in *Attorney General v. Martin*.[84] In this case, the Supreme Court had held that there was no rule of law requiring the holding of a formal identification parade. O'Flaherty J. reinterpreted this case as actually saying that the right to a formal identification parade will depend on all the circumstances of the case.[85]

O'Flaherty J. stated that the court should take into account whether a formal parade is impossible or impracticable. A formal parade would normally be required if the identifier had been in shock, had had limited observation opportunities, or had not known the offender prior to the commission of the crime. In the circumstances of this case, a formal parade should have been held.

O'Flaherty J. went on to lay down the requirements for a formal identification parade. There should be assembled eight or nine people of similar age, height, appearance, dress, and walk of life as the suspect. The parade should be supervised by a garda who had not been concerned in the

---

[83.] [1990] 2 I.R. 415.

[84.] [1956] I.R. 22.

[85.] In *People v. Mills* [1957] I.R. 106 a witness at an identification parade had previously been shown a number of photos from which she picked out the accused. She subsequently identified him at the parade. It was held that the judge should warn, as part of the identification warning, that her evidence might be coloured by having subsequently picked out the photo.

actual investigation. Full details should be kept about the other people in the parade (the foils) and the witness should not see the suspect in advance of the holding of the parade.

The case of *People (D.P.P.) v. O'Hanlon*[86] provided further guidance in relation to the composition of an identification parade. In this case, the applicant was convicted of armed robbery. The robbery had been carried out by two men wearing head coverings. One was tall and one was short. A garda was able to identify the applicant by looking at the security video of the incident. An identification parade was held consisting of 13 persons – the applicant and 12 volunteers from Baldonnell Military Base. The witness identified the applicant as the shorter of the two men in the shop. He also asked each of the men to say a particular phrase. It was argued that some of the other people on the identification parade were two or three inches taller than the applicant, who was 5 foot 5 inches. The court said that that was not a great discrepancy. It was argued that because all the foils came from Baldonnel Military Base, they had a military bearing. This was rejected. Also it was argued that only two of them came from Dublin, but this was rejected because the identifier had formed his conclusion before hearing them speak.

The constitutional right to an identification parade was subsequently examined in *People (D.P.P.) v. Maples*.[87] In this case, the Court of Criminal Appeal rejected the argument that there was an automatic constitutional right to a formal identification parade. However, an identification parade was a police procedure, which, if carried out, should be done in accordance with fair procedures. The constitutional right to fair procedures may necessitate a formal identification parade in all the circumstances of the case. Here, the suspect had refused to take part in a formal parade. He was outraged at having been subsequently exposed to an informal parade. He claimed that he had a constitutional right to a formal identification parade and that the right had not been waived by his refusal to participate, because he hadn't realised the consequences of non-participation. O'Flaherty J., once again delivering the judgment of the Supreme Court, pointed out that if a suspect refused to take part in a formal identification parade, he had to live with the consequences. He had no automatic constitutional right, as such; his only protection came from the doctrine of fair procedures, and given his behaviour, this had not been infringed by the holding of an informal parade.[88]

People (D.P.P.) v. Rapple[89] related to identification from photographs. The appellant was charged with robbery and the victim described his assailant as having a tattoo of a bird on his hand between the thumb and forefinger. He was shown a series of photographs and identified the appellant as his attacker. The appellant was found to have a similar tattoo. The appellant refused to participate in a formal identification parade and, therefore, there was an

---

[86]. Unreported, Court of Criminal Appeal, October 12, 1998.
[87]. Unreported, Court of Criminal Appeal, February 26, 1996.
[88]. It is uncertain how much, if at all, *Maples* cuts down the dicta in *People (D.P.P.) v. O'Reilly.*
[89]. [1999] 1 I.L.R.M. 113.

informal identification. The victim was taken for a drive along a particular route. The accused was positioned on the route and the victim identified him as his attacker. It was held that the Gardaí were entitled to hold an informal identification parade, where the option of a formal identification parade was refused. However, the particular informal identification must be just and reasonable in the circumstances.

In *People v. Cooney*[90] two identification parades had been held in which a number of witnesses identified the appellant. However, these parades were inadmissible because the appellant had been in unlawful custody at the time they were held. The judge excluded evidence of the parades but allowed the witnesses to identify the accused in court. The court said that in-dock identifications had for a long time been recognised as unsatisfactory, because the identity of the accused tended to be patently obvious to the witness identifying him. Such identifications should usually be confined to recognition cases. However, even in pure identification cases, the trial judge had a discretion to admit evidence of an in-dock identification. It was held in this case that the in-dock identification was justified. Wherever an in-dock identification took place, it was necessary to warn the jury of the particular dangers attaching to it. However, the trial judge had done this.

Failure to hold a formal identification parade is only one of the ways in which the accused's right to fair procedures may be breached in the context of identification evidence. In *Braddish v. D.P.P.*[91] the accused was convicted of robbery. A member of the Gardaí looked at a videotape of the robbery and identified the accused as the criminal. The prosecution were unable to produce the video for the accused's solicitor. However, stills were produced in court. Hardiman J. held that the fact that the videotape was unavailable should have precluded further prosecution of the accused, since it was the only identification evidence on which the prosecution were relying. It was held to be contrary to the accused's right to fair procedures to rely on an identification made from a videotape which was not available to be produced.

It may be seen that there are two ways in which the frailty of identification evidence is remedied. The first is the compulsory warning, which has to be quite detailed. Irish courts are moving towards the extensive warning requirements laid down in *Turnbull*. The second way is by holding that fair procedures may require a formal identification parade in the circumstances. However, these principles have been modified in cases where the witness knew the accused already before the crime.

9.5.3 Recognition evidence

People v. Meehan[92] involved an in-dock identification: a witness identified the accused as a person he had met on a considerable number of previous

---

[90.] [1998] 1 I.L.R.M. 321.
[91.] Unreported, Supreme Court, May 18, 2001.
[92.] Unreported, Special Criminal Court, July 29, 1999.

occasions in relation to the importation of drugs. It was held that an in-dock identification was permissible in this case, as the witness knew the accused well. In-court identification was permissible in recognition cases.

In *People (D.P.P.) v. Farrell*[93] the applicant had been charged with possession of a controlled drug for supply. The case against him depended to a large extent on the identification evidence of two Gardaí. The Gardaí knew the applicant previously and felt that the person they saw was the applicant. They had had a good opportunity to observe him. The Court of Criminal Appeal said that there was no obligation to hold an identification parade because this was a case of recognition evidence and in *People (D.P.P.) v. O'Reilly* it had been recognised that there was no need to hold such parades in recognition cases. This was affirmed in *People v. Kavanagh*.[94]

In *People (D.P.P.) v. Smith*[95] the applicant was alleged to have engaged in joyriding and, while doing so, caused damage to a garda patrol car. It was held that the only evidence against the applicant was visual identification evidence given by four members of the Gardaí who had known the applicant prior to the incident. It was argued that the trial judge's warning was inadequate. The court said that an identification warning must still be given in cases of recognition, but its terms may vary depending on the nature of the case and the evidence available. In this case, the trial judge's warning was upheld. In *People v. Murphy*[96] it was held that where a witness had previous acquaintance with the accused, such as in a recognition case, it was necessary to alert the jury to this fact.

Section 18 of the Criminal Evidence Act 1992 provides that where a person is accused of an offence of violence or a sexual offence and evidence is given by a person through a live television link under section 13(1), then, if evidence is given that the accused was known to the witness before the date on which the offence is alleged to have been committed, the witness shall not be required to identify the accused at the trial of the offence, unless the court in the interests of justice directs otherwise. Section 18 further provides that, in any other case, evidence by a person other than the witness that the witness identified the accused at an identification parade as being the offender, shall be admissible as evidence that the accused was so identified.

9.5.4   Identification from photos and videotapes

People (D.P.P.) v. Rapple[97] established that photos may be shown to a witness at the outset where the police are trying to find a suspect. However, they may not be shown where the person in them is a suspect and the police have a formal identification parade in store for him. If a witness has been shown photographs at the outset and previously identified a suspect, then his evidence

[93.] Unreported, Court of Criminal Appeal, *ex tempore*, July 13, 1998.
[94.] Unreported, Court of Criminal Appeal, *ex tempore*, July 7, 1997.
[95.] [1999] 2 I.L.R.M. 161.
[96.] Unreported, Court of Criminal Appeal, *ex tempore*, November 1997.
[97.] [1999] ILRM 113.

at a subsequent identification parade may be coloured by this. His identification is consequently weaker. The jury's attention should be drawn to the fact that the identifying witness has previously been shown photographs.

In *People (D.P.P.) v. O'Callaghan*[98] the accused was charged with robbery arising out of a bank raid. He was identified by one of the security guards. During the raid the guard had recognised the robber as someone who had come in to the bank a few days earlier and had looked suspicious. He then played back the video of that particular day and identified the accused as that person. It was argued on appeal that the trial judge should have dismissed the prosecution case on the ground of no case to answer. Also, it was argued that a correct warning was not given. Both arguments were rejected. It was pointed out that the witness was a trained security officer. He had suspected the men immediately the first time they entered and had watched them closely. This had allowed him to identify the accused during the robbery.

Also, if the photo or videotape has not been followed up by a subsequent identification parade, *Braddish v. D.P.P.*[99] indicates that the photo or videotape must be available for examination by the defence, otherwise the identification cannot be relied on.

9.5.5 Discretion to withdraw weak identification evidence

In *People v. Kavanagh*[100] it was recognised by the Court of Criminal Appeal that the trial judge had the discretion to withdraw identification evidence from the jury if it is extremely weak. In *People (D.P.P.) v. Cahill*[101] the applicants were charged with robbery and possession of a firearm. The case against the first applicant was based exclusively on identification evidence and the case against the second applicant was based largely on such evidence. Their appeals were allowed by the Court of Criminal Appeal.

It was held that there was no rule of law or practice requiring visual identification to be proved by means of an identification parade. In some cases it may not be possible or practicable; in other situations a suspect may refuse. In the case of the first applicant, he had refused the opportunity of a formal identification parade and, therefore, it was appropriate to arrange for an informal parade. However, as each of the three witnesses had failed to identify him at the garda station, subsequent in-court identifications were of negligible value. The case against the first applicant should have been withdrawn from the jury at the close of the prosecution's case.[102]

---

[98]   Unreported, Court of Criminal Appeal, July 30, 1990.
[99]   Unreported, Supreme Court, May 18, 2001.
[100] Unreported, Court of Criminal Appeal, *ex tempore*, July 7, 1997.
[101] Unreported, Court of Criminal Appeal, July 30, 2001.
[102] It is worth comparing this case with *People (A.G.) v. Mazure* [1946] I.R. 448 in which it was held that a judge has no discretion to withdraw accomplice evidence from the jury even if such evidence is extremely weak.

9.6   Other types of suspect evidence

As seen above, *R. v. Turnbull* extended the categories of evidence in respect of which a judicial warning could be given. A further extension was made in *R. v. Spencer*,[103] in which it was held that a trial judge can give a warning in respect of any evidence wherever there is evidence to suggest that a witness's testimony is questionable. This was followed by the Special Criminal Court in *People (D.P.P.) v. Meehan*,[104] where what appears to have been a corroboration warning was also given in relation to the evidence of a friend of the Gilligan gang, even though he was not strictly speaking an accomplice.

[103.] [1986] 2 All E.R. 928
[104.] Unreported, Supreme Criminal Court, July 29, 1999.

Chapter 10

CIRCUMSTANTIAL EVIDENCE

Circumstantial evidence may be contrasted with direct evidence. Direct evidence refers to testimony in relation to facts in issue of which a witness has personal knowledge. Circumstantial evidence is evidence of facts from which it is possible to infer the facts in issue. Another way of putting this is that circumstantial evidence is evidence of facts relevant to facts in issue. *R. v. Taylor, Weaver and Donvan*[1] established that it is no derogation of evidence to say it is circumstantial.

Examples of circumstantial evidence in the case of a theft, for instance, would be as follows:

1. The presence of the defendant's fingerprints at the scene of the crime.

2. The fact that he was found in possession of a large amount of money without being able to give any reason for this.

Other examples of circumstantial evidence in a murder trial would be as follows:

1. The fact that the accused had an intense dislike of the victim.

2. The fact that he lied about his alibi.

3. The fact that he was in the area at the time and lied about this.

10.1 Circumstantial evidence of matters occurring before alleged offence

Circumstantial evidence may concern matters occurring before the alleged offence:

> "In a prosecution for murder, you can prove previous acts or words of the accused to show that he entertained feelings of enmity to the deceased and this is evidence not merely of the malicious mind with which he killed the deceased but of the fact he killed him…it is more probable that men are killed by those who have some motive for killing them than by those who have not."[2]

Wigmore[3] calls this type of circumstantial evidence "prospectant" circumstantial evidence.

[1.] (1928) 21 Cr App Rep 20.
[2.] *R. v. Ball* [1911] A.C. 47 at 68 *per* Lord Atkinson.
[3.] Wigmore, "A Treatise on the Anglo-American System of Evidence" (3rd. ed., Little Brown, Boston, MA, 1940) Vol 1A para 43.

Evidence that an individual, such as the victim, was in the habit of acting in a particular way can constitute circumstantial evidence from which facts in issue may be inferred. In *Joy v. Philips Mills & Co Ltd*[4]*a* stable boy was found dead near a horse. It was held that evidence might be called that the boy had been in the habit of teasing the horse in order to show how his death had been caused.

Phillimore L.J. stated:

> "Wherever an inquiry has to be made into the cause of death of a person and there being no direct evidence, recourse must be had to circumstantial evidence, any habit evidence as to the habits and ordinary doings of the deceased, which may contribute to the circumstances by throwing light on the probable cause of death."[5]

Examples of circumstantial evidence being constituted by matters occurring before the alleged offence are as follows:

1. Evidence of motive[6]

2. Evidence of planning for a crime, *e.g.* the purchase of poison;

3. A declaration of intention to do something made by the victim or accused;

4. Evidence of the speed at which the accused was driving a few minutes before the accident may be admitted as circumstantial evidence of the speed he was travelling at the time of the accident[7];

5. Sometimes evidence of the accused's past misconduct may be admissible as circumstantial evidence but because of the prohibition on adducing evidence regarding the bad character of the accused, this evidence can only be admitted if its probative value outweighs its prejudicial effect.

10.2 Circumstantial evidence of facts contemporaneous with offence

Evidence of facts contemporaneous with the offence may also be circumstantial evidence. For example, the fact that the accused was intoxicated may support an inference that he was driving dangerously.

In addition, someone's capacity may be relevant. For example, the fact that a doctor would find it relatively easy to get hold of particular drugs might be circumstantial evidence that he was the person who had committed a murder shown to have been caused by the administration of those drugs.

The fact that the accused was present in the area at the time of the crime may be circumstantial evidence against him. In *Woolf v. Woolf*[8] the fact that a couple occupied the same hotel bedroom for two nights was circumstantial evidence from which adultery could be inferred.

---

4. [1916] 1 K.B. 849.
5. At p. 854.
6. Motive can allow *actus reus* to be inferred as well as *mens rea*.
7. *Beresford v. St Albans Justices* (1905) 22 T.L.R. 1.
8. [1931] P. 34.

The finding of the accused's fingerprints at the scene of the crime constitutes strong circumstantial evidence in the absence of an explanation for them.[9] The fact that the accused's blood or DNA corresponds to blood or DNA found on the victim's body may also constitute circumstantial evidence. The fact that the accused's style of spelling corresponded to that written on paper in which the victim's body had been wrapped constituted circumstantial evidence against him in *R. v. Voisin*.[10]

On a charge of theft or of handling stolen goods, it has been laid down in a series of cases[11] that the accused's possession of recently stolen property may entitle the jury to find that he is guilty in the absence of any satisfactory explanation.

Kenny J. in *People (Attorney General) v. Oglesby*[12] stated that there was no doctrine of recent possession, as such; it was simply:

> "a convenient way of referring to the inferences of fact which, in the absence of any satisfactory explanation by the accused, may be drawn as a matter of common sense from other facts. It is a way of stating what a jury may infer and references to it as a doctrine are misleading because they give the impression that possession of recently stolen property raises a presumption against the accused or casts some onus on him."

Dowling v. Dowling[13] involved an action for money lent. The defendant denied the loan and said that he had not borrowed any money from the plaintiff. He gave evidence that the plaintiff was very badly off. The court held that this was circumstantial evidence, which made the loan less likely. It was held that the evidence had been properly admitted.

Pigot C.B. held as follows:

> "[I]n my own experience...it has been the constant practice of judges to receive such evidence...in such cases proof that a party was in such circumstances that he could not has been received as evidence that he did not pay the money in question...Evidence of this nature is plainly admissible; for the simple reason, that it constitutes, or forms part of, circumstantial evidence, from which the jury are entitled to form their judgment as to the fact of payment and as to the credibility of testimony."[14]

He pointed out that circumstantial evidence was often the only way of resolving a conflict in testimony.

Finally, possession of real[15] or personal[16] property at a particular time is circumstantial evidence from which ownership of that property may be inferred.

---

9.   *R. v. Castleton* (1909) 3 Cr. App. R. 74.
10. [1918] 1 K.B. 531.
11. *R. v. Schama* (1914) 11 Cr. App. R. 45; *R. v. Hepworth* [1955] 2 Q.B. 600.
12. [1966] I.R. 162.
13. 10 Ir. Com. Law Rep. 236.
14. At 239.
15. *Doe d Graham v. Penfold* (1838) 8 C. & P. 536.
16. *Robertson v. French* (1803) 4 East 130.

10.3 Circumstantial evidence provided by evidence of matters after the crime

Retrospective circumstantial evidence allows inferences to be drawn from subsequent behaviour or events. Wigmore[17] calls this "retrospectant" circumstantial evidence.

In *Gumbley v. Cunningham*[18] the proportion of alcohol in the accused's blood four hours after the accident was such that the court could infer that he had been over the limit at the time of the accident, given the normal rate of elimination of alcohol.

In *R. v. Onufrejczyk*[19] evidence of the death of the victim and the accused's guilt could be inferred from the accused's bizarre and suspicious behaviour after the offence.

In civil cases, one party's failure to give evidence or call witnesses may amount to circumstantial evidence.[20] In *Bessela v. Stern*[21] a defendant's failure to deny the plaintiff's claim of a promise to marry was sufficient to constitute circumstantial evidence on this point. The failure of a party in a civil case to testify may also constitute circumstantial evidence against him. In *Boyle v. Wiseman*[22] Alderson B. said that the failure of a party to testify in a civil case "gives colour to the evidence against him".

However, in relation to criminal cases, the position is very different. The accused in a criminal case has a right to silence. If a judge in a criminal case wishes to comment on an accused's refusal to give evidence, he must be careful in so doing. In *R. v. Martinez Tobon*[23] it was stated that the judge's direction on this point should be based on that in *R. v. Bathurst*[24]; it should state that the accused is under no obligation to testify and that the jury should not automatically assume that he is guilty just because he doesn't testify.

In particular cases, the judge may feel it appropriate to make a stronger comment on the accused's failure to testify. However, the nature and strength of such comment must be a matter for the discretion of the judge and will depend upon the circumstances of the individual case. [25]

At common law, the accused's failure to explain a particular matter may sometimes be evidence from which facts against him may be inferred. However, in *R. v. Burdett*[26] Abbot C.J. remarked:

[17.] Wigmore "A Treatise on the Anglo-American system of Evidence" (Tillers Revn, 1983) Vol V para 43.
[18.] [1989] A.C. 281.
[19.] [1955] 1 Q.B. 388.
[20.] *British Railways Board v. Herrington* [1972] AC 877 at 930 *per* Lord Diplock.
[21.] (1877) 2 C.P.D. 265.
[22.] (1855) 10 Exch. 647 at 651.
[23.] [1994] 2 All E.R. 90.
[24.] [1968] 2 Q.B. 99 at 107.
[25.] See *R. v. Sparrow* [1993] 1 W.L.R. 488. Also *R. v. Bathurst* [1968] 2 Q.B. 99; 107 *R. v. Hutch* [1973] 1 All E.R. 178; *Wang v. R.* [1950] A.C. 203.
[26.] (1820) 4 B. & Ald. 95 at 120.

> "No person is to be required to explain or contradict until enough has been proved to warrant a reasonable and just conclusion against him, in the absence of explanation or contradiction; but when such proof has been given, and the nature of the case is such as to admit of explanation or contradiction if the conclusion to which the prima facie case tends is to be untrue, and the accused offers no explanation or contradiction, can human reason do otherwise than adopt the conclusion to which the proof tends"

Lies told by the accused can amount to circumstantial evidence. In *R. v. Goodway*[27] the accused lied to the police about where he was at the time of the offence and this was taken as circumstantial evidence against him. However, a direction should be given to the jury that they must be satisfied that there was no innocent motive for the lie.

10.4 Convictions based entirely on circumstantial evidence

The courts have warned about a conviction being based entirely on circumstantial evidence. However, in *McGreevy v. D.P.P.*[28] the House of Lords refused to lay down a rule that a conviction could not be based on circumstantial evidence.

In *Teper v. R.* [29] Lord Normand gave a warning:

> "Circumstantial evidence may sometimes be conclusive, but it must always be narrowly examined, if only because evidence of this kind may be used to cast suspicion on another. Joseph commanded the steward of his house 'put may cup, the silver cup in the sack's mouth of the youngest' and when the cup was found there Benjamin's brethren all too hastily assumed that he must have stolen it. It is necessary before drawing the inference of the accused's guilt from circumstantial evidence to be sure that there are no other co-existing circumstances which would weaken or destroy the inference."

One piece of circumstantial evidence on its own is not sufficient. It is the cumulative effect of circumstantial evidence that gives it probative force. In *R. v. Exhall*[30] Pollock C.B. described the cumulative effect of circumstantial evidence as being similar to a multi-stranded rope:

> "One strand of the cord might be insufficient to sustain the weight, but three stranded together may be of quite a different strength. Thus it may be in circumstantial evidence – there may be a combination of circumstances, no one of which would raise a reasonable conviction or more than a mere suspicion, but the three taken together may create a conclusion of guilt with as much certainty as human affairs can require or admit of".

Lord Simon in *D.P.P. v. Kilbourne*[31] said that circumstantial evidence "works by cumulatively, in geometrical progression, eliminating other possibilities".

[27.]   [1993] 4 All E.R. 894.
[28.]   [1973] 1 W.L.R. 276.
[29.]   [1952] A.C. 480 at 489.
[30.]   (1866) 4 F & F 922, 929.
[31.]   [1973] A.C. 729 at 758.

In *People (Attorney General) v. Thomas*[32] the accused was travelling on board "The Munster" with his friend Humphries. They were drunk. They got into a fight and the friend was thrown into the sea. The ship turned around but he could not be found.

It was argued by counsel for the accused that the deceased had not been proved to be dead. Maguire C.J. held that the deceased had proved to be dead by circumstantial evidence. It was stated that circumstantial evidence could be used to show someone was dead: "[I]n homicide cases it is not necessary to produce the body of the victim if the fact of killing be otherwise clearly proved".

Maguire C.J. referred to previous judgments in *R. v. McNicholl*[33] and *People (Attorney General) v. Kirwan*,[34] which supported this. Sullivan C.J. in *Kirwan* had held:

> "The fact of death may be legally inferred from such strong and unequivocal circumstances of presumpion as render it morally certain, and leave no ground for reasonable doubt."

In this case:

> "There was evidence that the deceased had consumed 23½ pints of intoxicating liquor before going on the ship; there was further evidence that he continued drinking on board the ship between 9 and 12 o'clock at night. The jury might reasonably infer that he was therefore not in a good condition to sustain any great effort. He was also precipitated some 20 feet at least into the sea. The ship was 15 miles from land, and assuming he was not picked up that would be the minimum distance he would have to swim even if he knew what was the right direction which seems altogether improbable. There was evidence that the ship was turned and made a search for about an hour with its floodlights on and no sign was seen of Humphries. The sea was choppy and somewhat rough. There was another ship in the neighbourhood at the time of the search. The night was bright and the moon was out. There was a possibility that he might have been picked up, but if he was, it could only have been with the knowledge of those on board the other vessel and it is altogether incredible that all on board would have kept silent in the circumstances. If some other boat, even a small one, rescued Humphries, it is again incredible that such a remarkable rescue as this should not have become widely known in a matter of hours.... Humphries was returning to his mother's home. She has not heard from him since the fateful night. Even if a desire on Humphries' part to disappear happened to coincide with the opportunity to do so, there is a very cogent reason why he should have made it known that he was alive...surely Humphries, if alive, would not have allowed his friend to be placed in peril of his life when a word from him would save him."[35]

---

32. [1954] I.R. 319.
33. [1917] 2 I.R. 557.
34. [1943] I.R. 279.
35. At pp. 328-329.

CHAPTER 11

HEARSAY EVIDENCE

11.1 Introduction: The rule prohibiting hearsay evidence

One of the most famous definitions of the hearsay rule has been given in *Cross on Evidence*:

> "An assertion other than one made by a person while giving oral evidence in the proceedings is inadmissible as evidence of the truth of any fact asserted."[1]

The above definition has been approved by the House of Lords.[2]

The rule against hearsay limits the circumstances in which out-of-court statements may be put before a court. It states that such statements cannot be adduced in evidence if their relevance depends on an assumption that their contents are true. However, note *People (D.P.P.) v. O'Donoghue,*[3] in which the Court of Criminal Appeal held that the introduction of hearsay evidence in the accused's trial did not affect the validity of the conviction since it had not affected the outcome of the trial and the applicant had not objected to it at the time.[4] Contrast this with *Maloney v. Jury's Hotel plc,*[5] Supreme Court, November 12, 1999, unreported, where Barrington J. set aside a decision in civil proceedings on the ground that hearsay evidence had been improperly admitted at the trial.

---

[1] *Cross on Evidence* (6th ed., Butterworths London1985) at p. 38. This is reproduced in latest edition *Cross and Tapper on Evidence* (9th ed., Butterworths, London 1999) at p. 530 with the word "assertion" changed to "statement".

[2] *R. v. Sharp* [1988] 1 All E.R. 65 at 68.

[3] Unreported, July 29, 1991.

[4] See further: Tapper "Hearsay and Implied Assertions" (1992) 109 L.Q.R. 524; Pattenden "Conceptual Versus Pragmatic Approach to Hearsay" (1993) 56 M.L.R. 138; Hirst "Conduct, Relevance and the Hearsay Rule" (1993) 13 Legal Studies 54; Gunworth and Patterson "Reliability, Hearsay Evidence and the English Criminal Trial" (1986) 102 L.Q.R. 292; Guest "Scope of the Hearsay Rule" (1985) L.Q.R. 385; Tapper "Hillman Rediscovered" (1990) 106 L.Q.R. 441; Rein "The Scope of Hearsay" [1994] 110 L.Q.R. 431; Carter "Hearsay: Whether and Whether" (1993) 109 L.Q.R. 573.
U.K.: Law Reform Committee 13th Report on Hearsay Evidence in Civil Proceedings (Cmnd. 2964, 1966); Law Commission No. 216: The Hearsay Rule in Civil Proceedings (Cm. 2321); Law Commission: Evidence in Criminal Proceedings: Hearsay and Related Topics, Consultation Paper no. 138, 1995; Law Commission: Report on Evidence in Criminal Proceedings: Hearsay and Related Topics (Law Case No. 245) Cm. 3670, 1997; Zuckerman "The Futility of Hearsay" (1996) Crim. L.R. 4; Spencer "Hearsay Reform: A Bridge not Far Enough" (1996) Crim. L.R. 29;
Ireland: Law Reform Commission, "The Rule Against Hearsay" LRC Working Paper No 9 "Report on the Rule Against Hearsay in Civil Cases" (L.R.C.; 25-1988).

[5] Unreported, Supreme Court, November 12, 1999.

An example of an out-of-court statement being excluded as inadmissible hearsay is to be found in the case of *Teper v. R.*[6] Teper was convicted of arson of a shop belonging to his wife. His defence was one of alibi. A policewoman gave evidence that an unidentified female bystander had shouted to Teper, "Your place is burning and you are going away from the fire". It was held that this statement could not be admitted to establish Teper's presence at the crime scene at the relevant time.

The exclusionary rule was first developed in the seventeenth and eighteenth centuries[7] and its application in this jurisdiction has been confirmed by a series of post-1922 cases.[8] It applies at all stages of criminal and civil proceedings.

There are a variety of situations in which a party may seek to admit out-of-court statements in order to prove the truth of their content; firstly, where it is impossible for the maker of the statement to testify either because he is dead, or for other reasons; secondly, where it is inconvenient for the maker of the statement to come into court to testify; and thirdly, where the maker of the statement is available to give evidence in court but the side calling him wants the statement to be put before the court in addition to his oral testimony. The operation of the hearsay rule does not distinguish between these three situations. If the evidence is hearsay, it is prohibited in all three situations, unless it comes within one of the exceptions to the rule.[9]

11.1.1 Rationales for the hearsay rule[10]

Why is hearsay evidence prohibited in this way? One reason is that it breaches the principle of orality which is a fundamental component of our criminal justice system, namely, that truth is best ascertained by unrehearsed answers on oath or affirmation, and that each side should have the right to test the veracity of opposing witnesses by means of cross-examination.

A related justification for the rule against hearsay focuses on the dangers of admitting such evidence. As stated by Lord Normand in *Teper v. R.*:

> "It is not the best evidence and it is not delivered on oath. The truthfulness and accuracy of the person whose words are spoken to by another witness cannot be tested by cross-examination, and the light which his demeanour would throw on his testimony is lost."[11]

---

6. [1952] A.C. 480.
7. *Choo, Hearsay and Confrontation in Criminal Trials* (O.U.P., 1996), pp. 3-6.
8. *Gresham Hotel v. Manning* (1867) I.R.I.CL 125; *Cullen v. Clarke* [1963] I.R. 368; *Eastern Health Board v. MK* [1999] 2 I.R. 99.
9. In relation to the third situation, out-of-court statements by witnesses may be admitted under one of the exceptions to the rule against narrative. However, these statements can only be admitted to bolster the witness's creditability and are not admissible as evidence of the truth of their content, see para 7.2.1 above.
10. Baker, The Hearsay Rule (Pitman & Sons, London, 1950); Park (1987) 86 Mich. L.R. 51; Pattenden (1993) 56 M.L.R. 138.
11. [1952] A.C. 480 at 486-487.

The dangers attaching to hearsay evidence may be listed as follows: misperception, misunderstanding, forgetfulness and lies. A person giving evidence of an oral statement or a statement by conduct may either have misperceived it at the time it was made or, alternatively, his memory of its contents may be defective. There is a further danger present in respect of all types of out-of-court statements: without the maker present to explain its meaning, the statement may be misunderstood. Finally, there is the possibility that the person who made the out-of-court statement may have deliberately concocted or distorted it. In cases where the maker of the statement is not available to testify, cross-examination is not available to uncover these defects and it is extremely difficult to identify the weight, if any, that should be given to such evidence.[12]

As stated by Lord Bridge in *R. v. Blastland*:

> "Hearsay evidence is not excluded because it has no logically probative value…the rationale for excluding it as inadmissible, rooted as it is in the system of trial by jury, is a recognition of the great difficulty, even more acute for a juror than for a trained judicial mind, of assessing what weight can properly be given to a statement by a person whom the jury have not seen or heard and which has not been subject to any test of reliability by cross-examination."[13]

It has also been argued that the admission of hearsay evidence might lead to lengthier and more expensive trials and consequent jury confusion. Another fear is that the prosecuting and investigating authorities might be tempted to accord undue importance to out-of-court statements and that this would be at the expense of other evidence in the case.

11.1.2   Criticisms of the hearsay rule[14]

One of the most forceful criticisms of the hearsay rule is that it may operate to exclude highly probative evidence. In this respect its operation creates an unfairness, which becomes particularly apparent when the rule is used against an accused in a criminal trial.

In *R. v. Blastland*[15] the accused was charged with the murder of a boy. He admitted having engaged in homosexual activity with the victim on the evening in question at the murder scene. However, he said that he had run away when he saw someone else watching them. He gave a description of the watcher, which closely resembled Mark, a known homosexual. At one stage in the investigation, Mark had confessed to the crime. At the trial the defence was that Mark had committed the murder. Counsel for the defence wished to introduce evidence of out-of-court statements made by Mark, before the body

---

12.   See Barrington J., *Maloney v. Jury's Hotel plc*, unreported, Supreme Court, November 12, 1999, for a consideration of the above.
13.   [1986] A.C. 41; this view was shared by Lord Ackner in *R. v. Kearley* [1992] 2 A.C. 228.
14.   See (1988) 6(11) I.L.T. 1.
15.   [1986] A.C. 241.

was discovered, to the effect that a boy had been murdered. The House of Lords held that the evidence was inadmissible. Lord Bridge stated that the statements were prohibited by the rule against hearsay.[16]

A counterpart to *Blastland* is to be found in the nineteenth century Irish decision of *R. v. Gray*.[17] In this case, a deathbed confession by a third party that he, not the accused, had committed the murder was held to be inadmissible evidence under the hearsay rule.

Furthermore, as pointed out by Young C.J. in *R. v. Clune (No. 1)*:

> "it is notorious that in many cases the question whether evidence of a statement would infringe the hearsay rule depends on difficult criteria and nice distinctions".[18]

In particular, the number and variety of the exceptions to the rule against hearsay, coupled with the lack of any guiding principle governing their development, has led to severe criticism.

In the United Kingdom, statute has intervened to make hearsay evidence more readily admissible. The Irish Law Reform Commission has recommended statutory reform of the rule in this jurisdiction; however, this recommendation has yet to be followed by our legislature.

However, it is worth noting that the judiciary in other commonwealth jurisdictions have themselves taken active steps to reform the situations in which hearsay evidence may be admissible. The following dictum of Mason C.J. in *Walton v. R.*[19] demonstrates an interventionist judicial response to the above criticisms:

> "Where the dangers which the rule seeks to prevent are not present or are negligible in the circumstances of a given case there is no basis for a strict application of the [hearsay] rule. Equally, where in the view of the trial judge those dangers are outweighed by other aspects of the case lending reliability and probative value to the impugned evidence, the judge should not then exclude the evidence by a rigid and technical application of the rule against hearsay. It must be borne in mind that the dangers against which the rule is directed are often very considerable, as evidenced by the need for the rule itself. But especially in the field of implied assertions there will be occasions upon which circumstances will combine to render evidence sufficiently reliable for it to be placed before the jury for consideration and evaluation of the weight which should be placed on it, notwithstanding that in strict terms it would be regarded as inadmissible hearsay."

---

16. The other judges in the case held that the evidence was inadmissible because it was not sufficiently relevant. For a discussion of the concept of relevance and its susceptibility to judicial manipulation see para 1.3.
17. Discussed (1841) Ir. Cir. Rep. 76.
18. [1975] V.R. 723 at 750.
19. (1989) 166 C.L.R. 283.

11.1.3   The Constitution and the rule against hearsay

There have been comparatively few judicial pronouncements on the Constitution and this rule of evidence. The principle of orality on which it is based could be said to have a constitutional mandate. In *Eastern Health Board v. M.K.*[20] Denham J. said that the hearsay rule had been adopted to protect fair trial process. In this regard, the rule might be seen as a component of the constitutional right to a fair trial.[21]

McGuinness J. in *Gilligan v. Criminal Assets Bureau*[22] has also recognised its potential constitutional impact. The Proceeds of Crime Act 1996 allows-out-of court opinion statements of a member of the Gardaí to be adduced as evidence of the truth of their contents. McGuinness J. held that such statements could not be relied on without corroborating evidence. Otherwise constitutional justice might be infringed.

However, insofar as the hearsay rule prevents a defendant from introducing exculpatory evidence, its constitutionality may be subject to question.

11.2 Identifying hearsay evidence

The rule against hearsay prohibits the admission of evidence when the following criteria are present:

1. The evidence must contain a statement or statements made out-of-court.

2. The relevance of the evidence to the person adducing it must depend on one of these statements being true.

The hearsay rule applies whether or not the prohibited statement is written and oral, or even if it is a statement by conduct.

11.2.1   Oral statements

In *Teper v. R.*[23] the accused was convicted of maliciously, and with intent to defraud, setting fire to a shop belonging to his wife, in which he carried on a dry goods business. His defence was one of alibi. A policewoman gave evidence that an unidentified female bystander had shouted to a man resembling the accused and leaving the scene in a car, "Your place is burning and you are going away from the fire." As stated above, this evidence was inadmissible under the hearsay rule.

When the statement is analysed, it can be seen that it qualifies as hearsay under the above test. It is an out-of-court statement, and its relevance depends on it being true. It is relevant insofar as it indicated that Teper was leaving the scene in a hurry, which could allow the jury to infer that he had started the fire.

---

[20].   [1999] 2 I.R. 99.
[21].   However, note *Murphy v. GM, PB, PC Ltd*, unreported, High Court, June 4, 1999, in which O'Higgins J. stated that the hearsay rule was not a constitutional principle.
[22].   [1998] 3 I.R. 185.
[23].   [1952] A.C. 378.

Another example of an oral hearsay statement is to be found in *Cullen v. Clarke.*[24] A civil action, the plaintiff was suing his former employer for damages, claiming that an injury at work had left him unemployable. In order to prove this, he sought to refer to an oral statement made to him by a person from whom he had sought work and been refused; this person had allegedly said that he could not employ the plaintiff because of his past injury. The statement was obviously an out-of-court statement, and its relevance to the plaintiff's case depended on it being true. If the maker of the statement had been lying, and had in fact refused the plaintiff employment on another ground entirely, the statement would have been irrelevant to the plaintiff's case.[25]

In *Sparks v. R.*[26] a child who had been assaulted told its mother that its attacker had been a black man. At the accused's trial for the assault, the mother sought to give evidence of what the child said. However, the child's statement regarding its attacker was obviously hearsay and this evidence was held to be inadmissible.

In *R. v. Gibson*[27] the accused was charged with unlawful wounding. A central issue in the case was whether the accused had actually been the person who attacked the victim. In order to prove that the accused had in fact been the attacker, the prosecution sought to adduce evidence of a statement made by an identified woman after the attack. Pointing to the accused's door, she had said, "The person who threw the stone went in there." This evidence made it more likely that the attacker was in fact the accused. However, its relevance to the prosecution case depended entirely on it being true. If the woman was lying, or had been mistaken, there would have been no point in the prosecution adducing the evidence. On appeal, it was held that this statement was hearsay and should not have been admitted. The conviction was overturned.

11.2.2 Written statements

Myers v. D.P.P.[28] is the most notorious example of the application of the hearsay rule to written statements. The accused was charged with fraud involving the passing-off of stolen cars as models rebuilt from wrecked cars. In order to prove their case, the prosecution had to adduce evidence proving that the cars sold by Myers were stolen. The only way that this could be done was by reference to the number cast into the cars' cylinder blocks at the factory where they were made.

The records of that factory contained, in relation to each car manufactured by it, a card, filled out by an unidentifiable worker, on which the numbers on the particular cylinder block were stated together with the number of the car in

---

24. [1963] I.R. 368.
25. The hearsay in this case was, however, held admissible under one of the exceptions to the hearsay rule, namely, that it was part of the *res gestae*; for discussion of this point, see *supra*, see para 11.3.2.
26. [1964] A.C. 964.
27. (1887) 18 Q.B.D. 537.
28. [1965] A.C. 1001.

question. It was essential to the prosecution case to be allowed to put these cards in evidence. However, as hearsay evidence, they were held to be inadmissible. Their relevance to the prosecution case depended on the statements written on them being true.[29]

In *Patel v. Comptroller of Customs*[30] it was held that the words "produce of Morocco" inscribed on bags of coriander seed were hearsay, and could not be adduced to show that the produce came from Morocco. Similarly, in *Comptroller of Customs & Western Electric*[31] it was held that labels on, and words stamped into, various implements stating their country of origin were inadmissible hearsay when adduced to prove the country of origin of the goods.

11.2.3   Statement by conduct

Chandrasekara v. R.[32] established that statements by conduct could constitute hearsay. The victim of a murder had, shortly before dying, indicated who the murderer was by making signs. She was unable to say anything because her throat had been cut. When asked who had attacked her, she made signs indicative of driving oxen. She also pointed at a policeman and made signs of slapping her face. These signs were immediately interpreted as referring to A who drove oxen and who had been in trouble for slapping a policeman's face. She was asked a direct question whether it was A and she nodded her head. This statement was held to constitute hearsay. It was only relevant to the prosecution case if it was true.

11.2.4   Implied written and oral statements

The above cases all involved express statements. It has been held that implied statements also constitute hearsay.[33] An implied statement is an inference which can be drawn from another statement.

The first case to recognise that implied statements could be prohibited by the hearsay rule was *Wright d. Doe v. Tatham*.[34] This case related to the testamentary capacity of a wealthy English gentleman called Marsden, whose will in favour of an employee was being challenged by his next of kin, Admiral Tatham, on the grounds that Marsden was mentally incompetent at the time he made it. Letters written to the testator, by a person who was unable to give evidence in court, were sought to be adduced by the other side for the purpose

---

[29.]   This decision has been much criticised; and legislation has now been passed to render such statements admissible in criminal cases; *supra*, para 11.3.9.

[30.]   [1966] A.C. 356.

[31.]   [1965] 3 All E.R. 599.

[32.]   [1937] A.C. 220.

[33.]   Tapper "Hearsay and Implied Assertion" (1992) 109 L.Q.R. 524; Patterson "A Conceptual Versus Pragmatic Approach to Hearsay (1993) 56 M.L.R. 138; Guest "Scope of the Hearsay Rule" (1985) 101 L.Q.R. 385; Rein "The Scope of Hearsay" (1994) 110 L.Q.R. 431; Ormerod "Reform of Implied Assertion" (1996) 60 J. Crim. L. 201; Guest "Hearsay Revisited".

[34.]   (1837) 7 Ad. & El. 313.

of proving his mental competence. However, it was held that these letters were inadmissible because their importance derived from an implied statement by the writer of the letters in the letters that the person he was writing to was sane; it was held that, consequently, the letters could not be admitted.

The application of the hearsay rule to implied statements was confirmed by the House of Lords in *R. v. Kearley*.[35] The police suspected that Kearley was trading in illegal drugs. They found drugs hidden in a rabbit hutch, but not in sufficient quantities to raise the inference that he possessed drugs for the purposes of supply. While on the premises, police intercepted 15 telephone calls. Three of the callers asked for Kearley and for drugs. None of these callers appeared as witnesses at the trial. The prosecution proposed to call the police officer who had taken these calls to give evidence of them. It was argued that the request for the drugs implied a belief on the part of the caller that Kearley sold drugs, and that this was relevant to the facts in issue. The House of Lords held that evidence of what the callers believed was irrelevant, and, even if relevant, it was inadmissible hearsay.

Lord Ackner stated:

> "What is sought to be done is to use the oral assertion, even though it may be an implied assertion, as evidence of the truth of the proposition asserted. That the proposition is asserted by way of necessary implication rather than expressly cannot, to my mind, make any difference."[36]

There was a strong dissent by both Lord Griffiths and Lord Browne Wilkinson. Lord Griffiths said that to apply the rule against hearsay to the facts of *Kearley*:

> "hampers effective prosecution by excluding evidence which your Lordships all agree is highly probative and since it comes from the unprompted actions of the callers, is very creditworthy".[37]

None of these implied statements appear to have been intended to communicate that Kearley was a drug dealer. It is worth noting, however, that even though the statements did not appear to have been intended to communicate, this does not mean that they were not deliberately fabricated, or misunderstood.

It has been argued that the risk of fabrication is less in the case of implied statements.[38] However, Pattenden correctly points out:

> "Against any reduction in the risk of lying when an implied (as opposed to an express) assertion is offered in evidence must be set the increased risk of a misunderstanding. Is the interpretation which the party offering the statement puts on it correct? When X makes the non-assertive statement: "Is Z in there"

---

35. [1992] 2 A.C. 228. Also see Spencer [1993] C.L.J. 40; Tapper [1992] 109 L.Q.R. 524.
36. At p. 255
37. At p. 238.
38. Although this does not mean that such a risk is never present. As Pattenden points out (56 M.L.R. 138, 142), the callers in a situation such as Kearley "may have believed that they were participating in a hoax or may have wished to frame the accused".

does this imply that Z is not with X and nothing more, or that Z is not with X and X wants Z, or Z is in danger, or X wants to know where Z is? As for honest mistakes of perception and memory, the danger of these is the same whether the assertion is express or implied."[39]

Arguably, therefore, implied hearsay statements ought to be prohibited both as a matter of principle and a matter of policy.

11.2.5   Implied statements by conduct

However, in relation to statements implied from conduct, as opposed to statements implied from oral or written statements, there is a question as to whether or not these statements should be regarded as being subject to the hearsay rule.

Parke B. in *Wright v. Doe d. Tatham*[40] thought that such statements were hearsay. He gave the following examples of statements implied from conduct:

> "the supposed conduct of the family or relations of a testator, taking the same precautions in his absence as if he were a lunatic; his election, in his absence, to some high and responsible office; the conduct of a physician who permitted a will to be executed by a sick testator; the conduct of a deceased captain on a question of seaworthiness, who, after examining every part of the vessel, embarked in it with his family; all these, when deliberately considered, are, with reference to the matter in issue in each case, mere instances of hearsay evidence, mere statements, not on oath, but implied in or vouched by the actual conduct of persons..."

According to Parke B. such acts were implied statements and should not be admitted as evidence of the truth of their contents.

However, the inclusion of inferences from people's conduct within the hearsay rule on the ground that they are implied statements has been widely criticised. The difficulty with extending the hearsay rule to cover these statements is that it could then have a much wider application. It could be applied, for instance, whenever the jury is asked to make inferences from a person's demeanour. The fact that an accused was found near the scene of a murder and was visibly upset might be prohibited on the grounds that he was making an implied statement by conduct that he was upset and that to put forward this statement as true would be to breach the hearsay rule.

It must be remembered that, as "the devil knows not the mind of man", people's intention can only be determined by looking at their demeanour and conduct. There are therefore strong reasons why the hearsay rule should not be extended to include this type of evidence. As against this, it could be argued that such evidence may be fabricated or unreliable in the same way that evidence prohibited under the hearsay rule may be. However the chances of this happening in the case of implied statements by conduct is lower.

[39.] (1993) 56 M.L.R. 138, at p. 142.
[40.] 7 L.J. Ex. 340.

Tapper[41] has stated that conduct only comes within the hearsay rule if it was intended to assert something. However, the current author recognises that "the line between that which is primarily intended to assert, and that which is not, will often be difficult to draw". Adrian Keane[42] takes a similar view, saying that in the case of statements by conduct, there must have been an intention to make a statement in order for inferences from the conduct to constitute hearsay. The hearsay rule applies to assertions: statements made in such a way as to convey deliberately the impression that they are being made with the object of stating some information that is true. It also includes inferences drawn from those statements. But if the conduct was not intended to assert anything, then it does not come within the hearsay rule.

11.2.6   Out-of-court statements which are not hearsay

Assuming that there is an express or implied out-of-court statement (excluding implied statements by conduct), this alone is not sufficient to prohibit the evidence in question under the hearsay rule. A statement is only prohibited under the hearsay rule if its relevance to the party who seeks to adduce it depends on its contents being true. This can be easily determined by applying the following test: If the statement were untrue, would the party who is seeking to adduce it still want to do so?

The primary rationale behind the hearsay rule is that out-of-court statements cannot be admitted in evidence as proof of the truth of their contents, precisely because the truth of those contents cannot be tested by cross-examination and is therefore suspect. However, if the statement would be relevant whether or not it was true, or fabricated, or even if it had been misunderstood, then the hearsay rule does not apply because the probative value of the statement is not affected by the lack of cross-examination.

Examples of situations in which the truth or falsity of out-of-court statements was held to be irrelevant and in which the hearsay rule did not apply are as follows:

(1) Where the relevance of statement depends on the fact that it was made

First of all, evidence of an oral or written statement may be adduced to show that the person who made it was able to speak or able to write, if that fact is relevant to the case.

Another case in which the statement is sometimes explained as being relevant, irrespective of the truth of its contents, is the case of *Ratten v. R.*[43] The accused was charged with the murder of his wife. His defence was that his gun had gone off accidentally while cleaning it at home. A telephonist gave evidence that at 1.15 p.m. on the evening of the wife's death she had received a

---

41. *Cross and Tapper on Evidence* (6th ed. 1985, Butterworths London) pp. 459-475. The statement has been removed from the latest edition of this work.
42. Keane, *The Modern Law of Evidence*, (5th ed., Butterworths, London, 2000) p. 259.
43. [1972] A.C. 378.

call from the Ratten house which had been made by a distressed woman who had asked her to get the police quickly. It was held that this statement was not hearsay. The evidence rebutted the accused's evidence that no phone call had been made from the house that evening.[44]

(2) Where statement adduced to show its likely effect on others

A witness may give evidence of the terms of a defamatory statement without this being hearsay. In *Fullam v. Associated Newspapers*[45] a footballer sued for defamation in relation to a newspaper article. The admission of the article was not hearsay; it was admitted for the purpose of showing that it would lower the plaintiff in the eyes of right-thinking persons, which was one of the facts in issue in the case. However, it was stated that the jury should only look at the article for this limited purpose and that a specific warning was needed from the trial judge to the effect that they should not assume that any of the facts in it were true.

Lord Bridge in *R. v. Blastland*[46] stated:

"It is of course elementary that statements made to a witness by a third party are not excluded by the hearsay rule when they are put in evidence solely to prove the state of mind....of the person to whom it was made. What a person...heard may often be the best and most direct evidence of that person's state of mind. This principle can only apply, however, when the state of mind evinced by the statement is either itself directly in issue at the trial or of direct and immediate relevance to an issue, which arises at the trial".

In *Subramaniam v. Public Prosecutor*[47] the accused was charged with the unlawful possession of ammunition. He pleaded duress and sought to give evidence as to what the terrorists had said. It was held that his evidence on this point was inadmissible hearsay. On appeal, the evidence of the death threats was held to be admissible. This evidence merely went to show that the statement was made and not to show the truth or falsity of the information in the statements. They were not introduced to show that the assailants actually intended to kill the defendant.

The Privy Council stated:

"In ruling out peremptorily the evidence of conversation between the terrorists and the appellant the trial judge was in error. Evidence of a statement made to a witness by a person who is not himself called as a witness may or may not be hearsay. It is hearsay and inadmissible when the object of the evidence is to establish the truth of what is contained in the statement. It is not hearsay and is

---

[44.] However, although the fact of the phone call was certainly relevant, it is questionable whether the words "get the police quickly" should have been admitted since they may be seen as containing an implied statement that there was something badly wrong at the Ratten house. *Ratten* is probably best explained in this regard as either a case decided before *Kearley*, or as an example of the *res gestae* exception to the hearsay rule.

[45.] [1953-54] Ir. Jur. Rep. 79.

[46.] [1986] A.C. 41.

[47.] [1956] 1 W.L.R. 965.

admissible when it is proposed to establish by the evidence, not the truth of the statement, but the fact that it was made.

The fact that the statement was made, quite apart from its truth, is frequently relevant in considering the mental state and conduct thereafter of the witness or of some other person in whose presence the statement was made. In the case before their Lordships statements could have been made to the appellant by the terrorists, which, whether true or not, if they had been believed by the appellant, might reasonably have induced in him an apprehension of instant death if he failed to conform to their wishes.

A complete, or substantially complete version according to the appellant of what was said by him to the terrorists and by him to them...if believed, could and might have afforded cogent evidence of duress brought to bear upon the appellant. Its admission would also have meant that the complete story of the appellant would have been before the trial judge and assessors and enabled them more effectively to have come to a correct conclusion as to the truth or otherwise of the appellant's story."[48]

(3) Where the statement adduced to show its legal effect and this legal effect does not depend on it being true

One example of this is when out-of-court statements are adduced to show that a contract has been created. A person is contractually bound if he makes an oral statement that a reasonable man would regard as an acceptance of an offer. There is no need to prove the truth of such a statement in order to show that a contract exists. All that needs to be shown is that the statement was made, and it was objectively capable of bringing a contract into existence.

In *Director of Public Prosecutions v. O'Kelly*[49] the respondent had been arrested under the Road Traffic Act 1961. The member in charge at the time of the arrest did not give evidence. However, the prosecuting garda gave evidence to the effect that he had heard the member in charge tell the respondent why he had been arrested, that he had the right to call a solicitor, etc. It was argued that this evidence of compliance with the Custody Regulations was hearsay. McCracken J. said that there was no need to consider whether the words were true; the question was whether they had been said to the accused. The evidence was admissible not to prove that the accused had a right to a solicitor, but rather to prove that the appropriate information was given and therefore that the regulations were complied with.

(4) Statements produced by mechanical or other devices

Statements produced by mechanical or other devices may be admitted. Where information is recorded by mechanical means without the intervention of a human mind, the record made by the machine is admissible.[50]

---

48. At p. 970.
49. Unreported, High Court, February 11, 1998.
50. *The Statue of Liberty* [1968] 2 All E.R. 195.

(5) Statements adduced to prove falsity

There is an argument that a statement is not hearsay if adduced to prove falsity. In *Attorney General v. Good*[51] a wife's statement that her husband was away from home was received on the issue whether he intended to defraud his creditors.

In *R. v. Steel*[52] the accused was charged with murder. He wished to tender evidence of a false alibi given to the police by another man. The court expressed the view that this statement was hearsay. However, Tapper disagrees with this:

> "It is not adduced as evidence of its truth, and it is hard to see how the lack of any opportunity to cross-examine weakens any inference to be drawn from it, since the roles of cross-examiner and examiner-in-chief are effectively reversed."[53]

(6) Other situations sometimes classified as falling outside hearsay rule

(a) Use of statement as circumstantial evidence

The finding of an article with a particular person's name constitutes circumstantial evidence that that person was at or near the place where the article was found. The question is whether the writing on the article constitutes a statement, the relevance of which to the party adducing it depends on the statement being true. Arguably it does.

However, *Tapper* takes a different view, arguing that:

> "Writing on an object is admissible consistently with the hearsay rule when it is an identifying part of an object the identity of which is in issue. The writing is admissible not as an assertion of a state of fact, but as itself a fact, which affords circumstantial evidence on the basis of which the jury may draw an inference as it may from any other relevant circumstances."[54]

Guest[55] takes the view that in such a case the court is not relying on the statement on the article but rather on circumstantial evidence, namely that a person is more likely to possess something with his own name on it than any other person. The problem with this circumstantial evidence doctrine is that it seems to be dangerously near some of the situations that have been held to breach the hearsay rule. For example, in *Patel v. Comptroller of Customs*[56] it was held that writing on a container "Produce of Morocco" was inadmissible hearsay. Why should writing on an object stating the name of its owner be treated any differently?

[51.] (1825) M'Cle & Yo. 286.
[52.] [1981] 2 All E.R. 422.
[53.] (1922) 109 L.Q.R. 524, 529.
[54.] Ibid., at 530.
[55.] "The Scope of the Hearsay Rule" [1985] 101 L.Q.R. 385, at pp. 386-387.
[56.] [1966] A.C. 356.

R. v. Rice[57] is one case, however, where the circumstantial evidence approach can be seen as justified. The prosecution wanted to establish that Rice had flown from London to Manchester on a certain day. It was held that a used airline ticket with Rice's name on it, found where such tickets were normally returned after use, was admissible as evidence that someone of that name had travelled on the flight written on it.

The objection had been raised that the used ticket contained a statement by an unidentified ticket agent that a man by the name of Rice had made a booking on that flight and for that reason was hearsay. The Court of Appeal rejected that argument showing that the purpose of the introduction of the ticket was to show that a man called Rice had travelled on the flight and not that he had made the booking.

This distinction drawn by the Court of Appeal depended on the factual connection between the flight and the finding of the ticket. If there had been no evidence that the ticket had been handed in after the flight, the ticket would have been hearsay. In this case, the court could only have inferred that Rice had made the flight from the ticket agent's statement that a particular flight had been booked in the name of a Mr. Rice. On the other hand, because the ticket was found where tickets had been handed in after the flight, the court could infer that someone must have used the ticket to get on to the plane and that his name was Rice.

The circumstantial evidence argument was again made in the case of *R. v. Lydon*.[58] In this case, a paper was found at the scene of the crime. The paper had the words "Sean rules" written on it. The Court of Appeal admitted the paper, saying that they were admitting it as circumstantial evidence that a man called Sean had been at the scene of the crime rather than to show Sean ruled anything.

The words on the piece of paper were admissible:

> "not to prove the truth of what they asserted, but because they were more likely to have been written by someone called Sean than not, and afforded some circumstantial support to the identification of the evidence".

However, unlike *R. v. Rice*, this case is difficult to justify after the decision in *R. v. Kearley*.[59] The statement "Sean rules" could be regarded as raising an implied inference that the writer was called Sean. *Kearley* demonstrates that implied inferences which may be drawn from assertive statements are also prohibited by the hearsay rule.

---

[57] [1963] Q.B. 857.
[58] [1987] Crim. L.R. 407.
[59] [1992] 2 A..C. 228.

(b) Proving the state of mind of the person who made the statement

Lord Bridge in *R. v. Blastland*[60] stated:

> "It is of course elementary that statements made to a witness by a third party
> are not excluded by the hearsay rule when they are put in evidence solely to
> prove the state of mind either of the maker of the statement or of the person to
> whom it was made. What a person said or heard may often by the best and most
> direct evidence of that person's state of mind. This principle can only apply,
> however, when the state of mind evinced by the statement is either itself directly
> in issue at the trial or of direct and immediate relevance to an issue which arises
> at the trial."

On this principle, it has been held that a ludicrous statement may be admitted
to prove the insanity of the person who made it, and that a statement may be
admitted in order to show the state of mind of the person who made it, *e.g.* in
Ratten, to show that the wife was in a state of fear. In *Woodhouse v. Hall*[61] a
policeman was allowed to give evidence of an oral offer of immoral services to
him on premises in order to prove that the premises were being used as a
brothel.

However, as with *Lydon*,[62] the status of these examples must be uncertain
after *Kearley*, in which it was held that the statements of the phone callers
could not be admitted as evidence that they believed Kearley to be a drug
dealer.

(c) Opinion polls

In *Hanafin v. Minister for the Environment*,[63] it was stated that opinion polls
were not hearsay. This is clearly incorrect. However, such polls are probably
admissible under the *res gestae* doctrine.

11.3 Exceptional cases in which hearsay evidence is admissible[64]

The following are situations in which evidence comes within the hearsay rule
but is nonetheless allowed to be admitted. They should be distinguished from
the situations above where evidence does not constitute hearsay at all because
it is adduced to show the truth of its content.

---

60. [1986] A..C. 41.
61. (1980) 72 Cr. App. Rep. 39.
62. [1987] Crim. L.R. 407.
63. [1966] 2 I.R. 321.
64. Omerod "The Hearsay Exceptions" (1996) Crim. L.R. 16.

11.3.1 Admissions/confessions[65]

A statement by a party to the proceedings, which goes against their interests in the proceedings, is not regarded as coming under the hearsay rule. The thinking behind this exception is that people would not make statements against their interest unless they were true.

However, the person making the admission must be a party to the proceedings. This means that an admission of guilt in a criminal case by someone other than the accused is not admissible under this exception and remains prohibited hearsay.[66]

11.3.2 Res gestae exceptions[67]

Hearsay evidence is regarded as being admissible if it is part of the *"res gestae"*. Kingsmill Moore J. in *Cullen v. Clarke*[68] called this a "somewhat vague" principle. In *Ratten v. R.*[69] Lord Wilberforce said that the expression "like many Latin phrases, is often used to cover situations insufficiently analysed in clear English terms".

Lord Tomlin in *Homes v. Newman*[70] described it as "a phrase adopted to provide a respectable legal cloak for a variety of cases to which no formula of precision can be applied".

The *res gestae* principle contains a number of exceptions. What they have in common is that they are all connected with a particular act in some way, and operate to clarify that act. As Lord Normand remarked in *Teper v. R.*, sometimes

> "human action may be so interwoven with words that the significance of the action cannot be understood without the correlative words, and the dissociation of the words from the action would impede the discovery of truth".[71]

This explanation of the *res gestae* was adopted in this jurisdiction in *People (Attorney General) v. Crosbie.*[72] Nowadays, textbooks commonly divide *res gestae* into four parts:

[65.] See Chapter 17 for the rules governing the admissibility of confessions and admissions. Hardiman J., delivering the judgment of the Court of Criminal Appeal in *People (D.P.P.) v. O'Callaghan*, unreported, December 18, 2000, referred to Stone's description of the *res gestae* as "the lurking place of a motley crowd of conception in mutual concept and reciprocating chaos" (1939) 55 LQR 66. Hardiman J. went on to describe the term as having "no virtue of precison or historical connotation".

[66.] *R. v. Blastland* [1986] A.C. 41.

[67.] Choo, *"Hearsay and Confrontation in Criminal Trials"* (O.U.P., 1966) 112-139; Ormerod [1998] Crim. L.R. 301, Callendar [1998] Crim. L.R. 337; Allen [1987] C.L.J. 229.

[68.] [1963] I.R. 368.

[69.] [1972] A.C. 378.

[70.] [1931] 2 Ch. 112 at 120.

[71.] [1952] A.C. 480.

[72.] [1966] I.R. 490.

(1) Spontaneous statements made by participant/observer of relevant event, relating to that event, called "excited utterance" rule in U.S.

In *Thompson v. Trevanion*[73] the plaintiff sued for an assault on his wife. Holt C.J. held that:

> "what the wife said immediately upon the hurt received, and before she had time to devise or contrive anything for her own advantage, might be given in evidence".

The statements must be spontaneous in order to be admissible. A question arises as to the precise degree of contemporaneity which the statement must bear in relation to the relevant event.

In *R. v. Bedingfield*[74] Bedingfield was charged with murdering his mistress by cutting her throat. The victim, a laundress, came out of the building in which she had been with Bedingfield, into the yard, very frightened and bleeding from the throat. She put her hands up to her throat, and said to her two assistants, "Look what Bedingfield has done to me". She died ten minutes later.

It was held that the victim's statement was inadmissible, because it was made after her throat was cut and was not sufficiently contemporaneous "[I]t was something stated by her after it was all over, whatever it was, and after the act was completed".

Cockburn C.J. in *Bedingfield* also held that the statement was not admissible as a dying declaration[75] because it did not appear that the woman had been aware that she was dying:

> "Though she might have known if she had had time for reflection, here that was not so, for at the time she made the statement she had no time to consider and reflect that she was dying; there is no evidence to show that she knew it, and I cannot presume it."

However, the modern approach to this subset of the *res gestae* exception does not require the same degree of contemporaneity. The modern approach is based on the rationale that the most important issue, in deciding the degree of contemporaneity required, is whether the possibility of error or mistake can be disregarded. On this basis, *Bedingfield* was wrongly decided. As Lord Wilberforce in *Ratten* said, of that case:

> "[T]here could hardly be a case where the words uttered carried more clearly the mark of spontaneity and intense involvement".[76]

This branch of the res gestae exception constitutes the modern justification for admitting the wife's statement to the telephone operator in *Ratten*. As mentioned earlier, Ratten was accused of the murder of his wife. His defence

---

[73.] (1693) Skin. 402.

[74.] (1849)14 Cox C.C. 477; this decision was contrary to the earlier decision of *R. v. Foster* (1834) 6 Car. & P. 325.

[75.] See para 11.3.3.

[76.] [1972] A.C. 378.

was that a gun went off accidentally while he was cleaning it. The evidence established that the shooting of the wife, from which she died almost immediately, must have taken place between 1.12 p.m. and 1.20 p.m. A telephonist from the local exchange gave evidence that at 1.15 p.m. she had received a call from Ratten's house made by a sobbing woman who in a hysterical voice had said, "Get me the police, please."

The Privy Council held that the telephonist's evidence did not constitute hearsay. However, the modern explanation for the decision in *Ratten* is that the wife's statement was hearsay involving an implied assertion that the police were needed. On this view, *Ratten* is seen as a case where hearsay evidence was allowed because it came within the res gestae exception.

Not only was there a close association in place and time between the statement and the shooting, but the request for the police and the tone of voice used showed intrinsically that the statement was being forced from the wife by an overwhelming pressure of contemporaneous events. In this case, it was specifically held that in assessing the degree of contemporaneity required for this branch of the *res gestae*, the primary question must be whether the statement was made in such circumstances of spontaneity/involvement in the event that the possibility of concoction could be disregarded.

Lord Wilberforce said that the test of contemporaneity "should not be the uncertain one whether the making of the statement was in some sense part of the event or transaction."

Instead:

> "as regards statements made after the event it must be for the judge…to satisfy himself that the statement was so clearly made in circumstances of spontaneity or involvement in the event that the possibility of concoction can be disregarded. Conversely, if he considers that the statement was made by way of narrative of a detached prior event so that the speaker was so disengaged from it as to be able to construct or adapt his account, he should exclude it. And the same should in principle be true of statement made before the event. This may often be difficult to show. But if the drama, leading up to the climax, has commenced and assumed such intensity and pressure that the utterance can safely be regarded as a true reflection of what was unrolling or actually happening, it ought to be received".[77]

The leading modern case on this subset of the *res gestae* rule is *R. v. Andrews*.[78] Andrews was charged with manslaughter and burglary. He and an accomplice covered by a blanket knocked on the door of the victim's flat and, when the victim opened the door, stabbed him. Then, no longer covered by the blanket they stole property from his flat. The victim crawled to the flat below for help, bleeding profusely from a deep stomach wound. Before dying, he named his assailant. The question was, whether the victim's statement could be admitted in evidence as part of the *res gestae*.

---

[77]. At p. 389.
[78]. [1987] 1 All E.R. 513. See also "*Res Gestae* in the House of Lords: Concoction or Distortion" [1987] C.L.J. 229.

It was held that in deciding whether a statement is sufficiently spontaneous, the court must take account of the following:

1. Whether the possibility of concoction can be distorted.

2. The event must be so unusual or startling as to dominate the thoughts of the maker of the statement.

3. The event must continue to dominate the thoughts of the maker of the statement at the time of making the statement.

4. Error, malice and other human fallibilities.

In *Andrews* Lord Ackner stated as follows:

> "(1) the primary question which the judge must ask himself is: can the possibility of concoction or distortion be disregarded? (2) To answer that question the judge must first consider the circumstances in which the dramatic statement was made, in order to satisfy himself that the event was so unusual or startling or dramatic as to dominate the thoughts of the victim, so that his utterance was an instinctive reaction to that event, thus giving no real opportunity for reasoned reflection. In such a situation the judge would be entitled to conclude that the involvement or pressure of the event would exclude the possibility of concoction or distortion, providing that the statement was made in conditions of approximate but not exact contemporaneity. (3) In order for the statement to be sufficiently 'spontaneous', it must be so closely associated with the event which has excited the statement that it can fairly be stated that the mind of the declarant was still dominated by the event. (4) Quite apart from the time factor, there may be special instances in the case, which relate to the possibility of concoction or distortion... in the instant appeal the defence relied on the possibility that the deceased had a motive of his own to fabricate or concoct, namely... malice. (5) As to the possibility of error in the facts narrated in the statement, if only ordinary fallibility of human recollection is relied on, this goes to the weight to be attached to and not to the admissibility of the statement and is therefore a matter for the jury. However, here again there may be special features that may give rise to the possibility of error...in such circumstances the trial judge must consider whether he can exclude the possibility of error."[79]

Andrews mirrors the approach of the Irish Court of Criminal Appeal in *People (Attorney General) v. Crosbie*,[80] in which it was held that "the words were so clearly associated with the stabbing in time, place and circumstances that they were part of the thing done and so an item or part of real evidence and not merely a reported statement".

In *R. v. Carnall*[81] a victim was stabbed and took one hour to crawl to help. She named the accused twice as her attacker: once to witnesses and later to a police officer while in the ambulance. Her statements were held admissible under the above principle.

---

[79] At pp. 300-301.
[80] [1996] I.R. 490.
[81] [1995] Crim. L.R. 944.

(2) Statement by person performing relevant act, accompanying or explaining it

In order for the requirements of this branch of the *res gestae* to be satisfied, the act in question must be relevant to a fact in issue and the statement must have been made by the person who performed the act. The statement must be contemporaneous with the act and must explain it.

Gresham Hotel v. Manning[82] was a civil action for the obstruction of light to the windows of the hotel. The action contained no allegation of special damage. A servant gave evidence that guests coming to the hotel had refused to take rooms on the ground that they were dark. This evidence was obviously hearsay, but a question arose as to whether it was admissible under this facet of the *res gestae*. It was held that it was not. Even though the statements explained the acts of refusing to take the rooms, these acts were not in themselves relevant to any of the facts in issue in the absence of the statements.

O Brien J. stated as follows:

> "This evidence comes within the general rule, which excludes hearsay evidence, inasmuch as the statements and declarations given in evidence were no more than the hearsay expression of the opinion of third parties as to the manner in which the bedrooms were lighted, some of whom acted on that opinion by refusing to take the rooms, and leaving the hotel. It has, however, been contended by plaintiffs' counsel that the general rule against the reception of hearsay evidence is subject to an exception in case of declarations which accompany an act, and also explain or qualify it...[however] it is requisite, in order to render such declarations admissible, that the act which they accompany should be one that would be evidence in the case without any such declarations. And it follows, in our opinion, that if (as in the present case) the act without the accompanying declaration would not be admissible in evidence of the fact in controversy, then the union of the two cannot render them legal evidence.
>
> The statements and declarations of opinion received in evidence in this case were made by parties not examined upon oath, or subject to cross-examination; and, though they were accompanied by acts tending to show that those parties really entertained the opinions they so expressed, still their statements would not on that account be exempted from the general rule excluding hearsay evidence where the acts which they accompanied would not be evidence per se."

In *Cullen v. Clarke*[83] the plaintiff sought to prove a fact in issue, namely that he was unable to obtain employment due to an injury at work. He sought to do this by referring to an oral statement made to him by a person from whom he had sought work and been refused. It was held that this statement was hearsay. However, the statement was subsequently admitted under one of the exceptions to the hearsay rule, the *res gestae*. The act of the prospective

---

[82] (1867) I.R. 1 C.L. 125.
[83] [1963] I.R. 368.

employer in refusing the plaintiff work was a relevant act and the words spoken showed the mind of the actor at the time of doing the act.

Kingsmill Moore J. stated:

> "[T]here is no general rule of evidence to the effect that a witness may not testify as to the words spoken by a person who is not produced as a witness. There is a general rule, subject to many exceptions, that evidence of the speaking of such words is inadmissible to prove the truth of the facts which they assert; the reasons being that the truth of the words cannot be tested by cross-examination and has not the sanctity of an oath. This is the rule known as the rule against hearsay.
>
> The utterance of the words may itself be a relevant fact, quite apart from the truth or falsity of anything asserted by the words spoken. To prove, by the evidence of a witness who heard the words, that they were spoken is direct evidence, and in no way encroaches on the general rule against hearsay. In the present case the refusal of the employer to engage the workman is a relevant fact. A workman could give evidence that, on asking the employer for a job, the employer said 'no'.
>
> The statements accompanying the act may be offered as showing the mind of the actor at the time of the doing of the act. Here there is a breach of the hearsay rule, in so far as reliance is placed on the truth of the words uttered, a truth which is not sanctified by an oath or capable of being tested by cross-examination. But here resort can be had to another well-established practice, sometimes regarded as falling within the res gestae exception, sometimes as an exception to the hearsay rule. When the motive or reason of a person for doing an act, or the intention with which he does it, is relevant to the issue, his statement made at the time of the doing of the act is evidence of his motive, reason, or intention.
>
> As to the admissibility of declarations as to states of mind, where such declarations are made prior to or subsequent to an act and unconnected therewith, the authorities are not uniform, but the modern tendency is to admit such declarations [but they] must, I think be confined to cases where such words are the spontaneous and unrehearsed expression of contemporary feelings, words which reveal rather than declare the condition of the mind. A man's statement as to what are his motives, intention or otherwise his state of mind may be rehearsed, and may be false, and to admit such a statement as evidence of the true condition of his mind is contrary to the general hearsay rule and can only be allowed as an exception to that rule.
>
> Here the reasons or motives of a prospective employer were clearly relevant facts; and statements as to those reasons, certainly if made contemporaneously with the refusal to employ him, would, although hearsay, be admissible as coming within the exception already stated. But such statements, though admissible, must be acted on with caution; for the statements may be false. An employer, for instance, might refuse to employ a man because of gross disfigurement or because he was a foreigner, but he would hardly be likely to assign those reasons. He would be more likely to say that he had no job available."

Another example of a statement accompanying a relevant act being used to explain that act is to be found in the case of *Walters v. Lewis*,[84] where a witness was allowed to give evidence that he heard the defendant's wife say, "This money is to pay for the sheep", when handing it over.

Should the statements of the callers in *R. v. Kearley*[85] have been admitted on the basis that they explained the act of telephoning? Only Lord Oliver considered the issue of *res gestae* and he rejected it on the ground that the phone calls, by themselves, were not independently relevant:

> "To say that [the words] were admitted to explain an act which is, in itself, without significance is merely to conceal the true purpose of their admission."[86]

However, arguably the requirement that the acts be independently relevant is not always carried through in the cases. In *R. v. Edwards*[87] shortly before her murder by her husband, a wife had deposited an axe and a carving knife with her neighbour, saying that she felt safer with them out of the way. This statement was admissible despite the fact that the act which it explained might not have been independently relevant.

(3) Statement by person relating to state of mind or emotion at time of making statement

The statement must be contemporaneous with the emotion, *i.e.* it must state that the maker has this particular emotion at the time of making the statement and not that he has had it in the past. The statement must relate to the state of mind of the maker and must be relevant to a fact in issue. There is no requirement that the maker of the statement be the accused, nor that he perform an act.

In *R. v. Conde*,[88] in relation to a charge of murdering a child by depriving it of food, evidence of the child's complaints of hunger was held to be admissible.

In *R. v. Vincent*[89] a question arose as to whether a particular public meeting had caused alarm and a police officer was called to prove that a number of people had complained to him that the meeting had made them fearful and apprehensive. In order to prove the state of mind of the public, it was possible for a witness to give evidence of the feelings and emotions expressed to him by members of the public. In *Hanafin v. Minister for the Environment*[90] it was held that the results of a properly conducted opinion poll were admissible as evidence of the state of mind of the public on a particular date.

---

84. (1836) 7 C. & P. 344.
85. [1992] 2 A.C. 228.
86. At p. 265.
87. (1872) 12 Cox C.C. 230.
88. (1867) 10 Cox C.C. 547.
89. (1840) 9 C. & P. 275.
90. [1996] 2 I.R. 321.

A statement made by a person as to his future intentions is also admissible, under this exception, as evidence of the existence of such intention at the time when the statement was made. However, if the statement of intention is self-serving, it is not admissible.[91]

Sugden v. Lord St Leonards[92] has been explained on this ground. A testator had drafted his will, but after his death all that remained were holograph notes. These notes were held admissible as evidence of his intentions in relation to the will.

What if there is a time lapse between the making of the statement of intention and the time at which the issue of intention becomes relevant? In *R. v. Moghal*[93] a statement made by someone else saying that she intended to kill the victim was admissible by the defence, even though it had been made a number of months before the murder. In *R. v. Buckley*[94] a police officer was murdered and a statement by him made the day of his death, in which he had stated that he intended to go to the accused's house, was admitted in evidence.

However, in contrast to this, in *R. v. Wainright*[95] a murdered girl said, before she disappeared, that she was going to the accused's place. This statement was held inadmissible, on the grounds that "it was only a statement of intention which might or might not have been carried out".[96]

(4) Statement by person relating to physical sensations at time of making statement

This exception was first laid down in *Aveson v. Lord Kinnaird*.[97] The issue in this case was whether or not the wife of a party was in good health when a policy of life assurance was taken out in relation to her. It was held that statements of bodily symptoms made by the lady in question at the relevant time were admissible in evidence to determine this.

The statement must be contemporaneous, but the sensations do not have to be felt at the precise time the statement is being made. Salter J. in *R. v. Black*[98] stated:

> "Surely 'contemporaneous' cannot be confined to feelings experienced at the actual moment when the patient is speaking. It must include such statements as 'Yesterday I had a pain after meals'."

Statements under this exception are admissible as evidence of the existence of the particular physical sensation, such as pain, but are not admissible as

---

91. Crampton J. in *R. v. Petcherini* (1855) 7 Cox C.C. 79: "otherwise it would be easy for a man to lay grounds for escaping the consequences of his wrongful acts by making such declarations".
92. (1876) 34 L.T. 369.
93. (1977) 65 Cr. App. R. 56.
94. (1873) 13 Cox C.C. 293.
95. (1875) 13 Cox C.C. 171.
96. See also *R. v. Thomson* [1912] 3 K.B. 19. However, a different approach has been taken in Australia and in the United States: *Walton v. R..* (1989) 84 A.L.R. 59; *National Life Insurance Co. v. Hillman* 145 U.S. 284 (1892).
97. (1805) 6 East 188.
98. (1922) 16 Cr. App. R. 118

evidence of its possible causes. This is demonstrated by *Donaghy v. Ulster Spinning Co Ltd.*[99] A tinsmith died of compression of the brain following a concussion. He had told his wife and a doctor that he had been injured at work. The question was whether or not this statement could be admitted in evidence in a civil trial for compensation. It was held that statements by a deceased as to the cause of his pain could not be admitted. There is a distinction between statements as to bodily feelings and statements as to the cause of those bodily feelings.

Cherry L.J. himself gave judgment in the case saying:

> "I was always under the impression that in such cases the best, and in many cases, the only evidence that can be obtained, as to the nature and effects of an injury, is the statement of the injured man himself, and that evidence as to the nature of the injury includes not only the physical fact of the injury, but also the immediate cause…[which is] an additional part of the statement as to the nature of the injury."

He felt constrained to follow English precedent, but ended by saying:

> "It will have the effect of shutting out hundreds of cases where no other evidence of the nature of an injury is obtainable."[100]

This decision illustrates the harsh effects of the hearsay rule.

11.3.3 Statements of deceased persons

Certain statements of deceased persons may be admitted as an exception to the hearsay rule.

(1) Dying declarations regarding cause of death[101]

These are only admissible in criminal trials for murder or manslaughter.[102] In addition, they must be made by the victim of the crime. At the time the statement is made there must have been a settled hopeless expectation of death on the part of the victim.[103] It must also be shown that the victim would have been a competent witness were he alive.[104]

[99.] (1912) 46 I.L.T.R. 33.

[100.] *Ibid.*, at 34.

[101.] This doctrine was applied to admit the victim's hearsay statement by conduct in *Chandrasekara v. R.* [1937] A.C. 220 (P.C.)

[102.] *R. v. Hutchinson* (1822), cited in 2 B. & C. 608n (charge of using an instrument with intent to procure a miscarriage; the offence caused death but the dying declaration of the victim was not admissible). In *Eliza Smith v. Cavan* (1924) 58 I.L.T.R. 107 it was held that a dying declaration was inadmissible in a quasi criminal trial for compensation arising out of the murder of a witness. Judge Brown K.C. stated that "this is a quasi-criminal matter, and it might seem reasonable to admit a dying declaration in the circumstances particularly as no known individual has been implicated, but no precedent has been cited for allowing such evidence in any similar or analogous case and I refuse to allow it".

[103.] *R. v. Peel* (1860) 2 F. & F. 21; *R. v. Perry* [1909] 2 K.B. 697.

[104.] *R. v. Drummond* (1784) 1 Leach 337.

The rationale behind admitting dying declarations is set out by Eyre C.B. in *R. v. Woodcock*:

> "The principle on which this species of evidence is admitted is, that they are declarations made in extremity, when the party is at the point of death, and when every hope of this world is gone; when every motive to falsehood is silenced, and the mind is induced by the most powerful considerations to speak the truth; a situation so solemn and so awful is considered by law as creating an obligation equal to that which is imposed by a positive oath administered in a course of justice."[105]

However, as against this it must be pointed out that the reliability of such evidence may be suspect due to the declarant being weak and confused.

Most of the case law relates to the issue of whether the declarant was under a settled and hopeless expectation of death.

In *R. v. Mooney*[106] the accused was charged with manslaughter. He had been on good terms with his wife up to the time of her death. The wife, who was pregnant, woke complaining of a pain in her stomach. She was taken to hospital and told that she was dangerously ill. The issue was whether declarations made by her against her husband prior to her death there could be admitted. The issue was whether she had been under a settled hopeless expectation of death at the time she made these declarations. She had been told that she was dangerously ill and a clergyman had been sent for who warned her to prepare for death. She had been heard recommending her soul to God. The declarations were not admitted, as there was no evidence that she knew she was dying when she made them. The dying person had to be under a clear impression that they were in a dying state.

Pigot C.B. stated:

> "These declarations would not be evidence unless she was under a clear impression that she was in a dying state. It must be proved, to the satisfaction of the court, that she was dying, and that she was aware of the fact. We cannot, therefore, allow these declarations as evidence."

The dying declaration is only admissible insofar as it relates to the cause of the declarant's death. In *R. v. Gray*[107] a deathbed confession by a third party that he, and not the accused, had committed the murder was held to be inadmissible under this heading.

An unresolved question is whether the dying declaration can relate to the cause of someone else's death as a result of the same incident which caused the declarant's death. In *R. v. Baker*[108] the inhabitants of a house were poisoned. While the cook was dying, she said she had put nothing in the cake. This evidence was held admissible at the trial of the other servant in relation to the death of the master of the house.[109]

---

105. (1789) 1 Leach 500.
106. (1851) 5 Cox C.C. 318.
107. (1984) I.R. QR Rep. Cir.
108. (1837) 2 M. & Rob. 53.

If the victim dies before the declaration is finished, it may not be admissible. In *Waugh v. R.*[110] the deceased said, referring to the accused, "The man has an old grudge for me because..." and died. The declaration was held not to be admissible.

In *R. v. Fitzpatrick*[111] the deceased was assaulted and severely beaten. He reached home and was removed to hospital, where he died a month later. Ten days after his assault, he had made a statement to a police sergeant naming the accused as his assailant. The initial part of this statement was made in response to leading questions. Was it admissible?

Palles C.B. held the dying declaration to be admissible. Although leading questions were put to the victim in reference to his belief whether he was dying or not, no leading questions were put as to the matter for which the dying declaration is evidence, namely the cause of death. It appears from this case, however, that even if the entirety of the dying declaration had been made in response to leading questions, it would have been admissible. Palles C.B. stated that it was:

> "a settled rule of practice that the fact that a declaration was based on answers to questions went to the weight but never to the admissibility of the evidence.... Neither upon principle nor upon authority could it be held that a dying declaration was inadmissible only because it was cast in narrative form, although it had been given in answer to questions put."

In *R. v. Stephenson*[112] the accused was charged with the manslaughter of a girl by using an instrument to procure an abortion, which resulted in her death. The girl's dying declaration was admissible even though it had been made in response to questions. A dying declaration is not rendered inadmissible just because it was obtained in response to questions, although this may be a matter that goes to its weight. It was pointed out, in this case, that dying declarations should always be given close scrutiny by the jury:

> "The jury have no opportunity of seeing and hearing the declarant and forming their own judgment as to their reliability [it is rare] that the accused will have been present or had any opportunity for cross-examination...one of the dangers in admitting such declarations is the danger that omissions, failure to tell the whole story, or misrepresentations, or mere turns of phrase, may have the effect of giving a colour which could have been corrected by cross examination."[113]

(2) Declarations of deceased person that go against his interest

The rationale of this exception was laid down in the case of *Ward v. HS Pitt & Co.*[114] and is as follows: if a man makes a conscious statement to his own

---

[109.] *R. v. Hind* (1860) 8 Cox C.C. 300; *R. v. Murton* (1862) 3 F. & F. 492 appear to contradict the principle in *Baker*.
[110.] [1950] A.C. 203.
[111.] (1910) 46 I.L.T.R. 173.
[112.] [1947] N.I. 110.
[113.] *Ibid.*, at 116.
[114.] [1913] 2 K.B. 130.

hindrance, it is more likely than not that it is true. The exception may be subdivided into declarations against the deceased's pecuniary interest and declarations against his proprietary interest.

An example of a declaration against pecuniary interest is a declaration by the deceased acknowledging receipt of money on behalf of a third party. It is possible that an acknowledgment by a deceased of his tortuous liability could be admitted on the ground that it is a statement against his pecuniary interest, although Kennedy C.J. in his dissenting judgment in *Power v. Dublin United Tramways Company*[115] indicates otherwise.

An example of a declaration against proprietary interest is to be found in the case of *Flood v. Russell*.[116] This case concerned a statement by a wife, now deceased, to the effect that her husband, who predeceased her, had made a will giving her a life interest in certain real estate. This was a declaration against pecuniary/proprietary interest because, had there been no will, the wife would have got a much greater share on intestacy.

A declaration exposing someone to criminal liability is not admissible under this ground.[117] This has been established since the *Sussex Peerage Case*,[118] in which a statement of a deceased clergyman in relation to the marriage of one of the sons of King George III was held not to be admissible as a statement against interest, even though it would have exposed him to criminal liability under the Royal Marriages Act 1772.

In *Lalor v. Lalor*[119] a Mr. Delany had purchased certain leaseholds and re-assigned them to trustees for his sister Maria. Maria's husband claimed that he was the person supposed to get the equitable interest under the trust. He sought to admit evidence of a conversation he had with Delany, in which Delany had admitted this to be the case. Fitzgibbon J. refused to admit the evidence on the ground that the statements were not against Delany's interest at the time when they were made:

> "The fallacy of the argument for the defendant here seems to me to lie in the assumption that the supposed statements of Delany, made after the execution of the settlement, were prima facie against his interest. I am of opinion that the interest against which the statement appears to be made must, in order to supply that sanction which, after the death of the party, is accepted as a substitute for an oath, be an interest existing at the time of making the statement. Here, after the execution of the settlement, Delany could not have been heard to say that the payment or non payment of the purchase money had either discharged or kept alive any demand against Lalor, nor could the truth or falsehood of the statement have affected any then existing interest of Delany's."[120]

---

115. [1926] I.R. 302.
116. (1891) 29 L.R. Ir. 91.
117. *R. v. Gray* (1841) Ir. Cir. Rep. 76; *R. v. Blastland* [1986] A.C. 41. In *R. v. O'Brien* (1977) 76 D.L.R. (3d) 513, the Supreme Court of Canada refused to follow this and held that declarations against penal interest were admissible under this exception.
118. (1844) 11 Cl. & Fin. 85.
119. (1879) 4 L.R. 678.
120. *Ibid.*, at 681.

The statement must have been against the interest of the declarant at the time it was made. In addition, the declarant must have known that the statement was against his interest, although this requirement is often not applied in practice. An unresolved question is whether the declarant must have personal knowledge of the facts stated.

Once the condition for this exception is satisfied, the statement can be admitted to prove the truth of anything contained in it. In *Higham v. Ridgeway*[121] a statement by a deceased midwife that he had delivered a child on a certain day, and acknowledging payment of his fees, was held to be admissible evidence of the child's date of birth.

(3) Declarations of deceased persons as to pedigree

The declaration must have been on a matter of pedigree: dates and facts of births, marriages, deaths, legitimacy, failure of issue, intestacy, identity of an individual's parents. In addition the declarant must have been a blood relation of the person whose ancestry is in issue, or the spouse of a blood relation of that person.[122] There is no requirement that the declarant have personal knowledge of the subject-matter of his declaration. The fact that the declarant has an interest in the declaration being true goes to its weight rather than to its admissibility.[123]

The declaration must have been made before the dispute about pedigree had arisen. In *Butler v. Mountgarret*[124] a letter written in relation to a marriage was inadmissible because a controversy as to that marriage had already arisen.

In addition, the proceedings must be one in which a matter of pedigree is directly in issue. In *Haines v. Guthrie*[125] a question arose as to whether or not the defendant in an action for the price of goods sold was a minor. It was held that a statement made by the defendant's deceased father as to his age was improperly admitted because the proceedings did not relate to pedigree.

In *Palmer v. Palmer* a father devised lands to his son for life and then to his son's heirs according to their seniority. The third of A's son's children, in an action to gain possession of the lands, was permitted to prove the death of his two elder brothers by means of family repute under this exception. Sir Michael Morris stated that:

> "the case involved a question of pedigree so as to have made the proof by family reputation receivable, even within the principle laid down in Haines v Guthrie. It became necessary for the plaintiff here to displace the life estate by showing that the tenant for life had died: and that can be done by the testimony of a member of the family proving his relative's death as a matter of family reputation".[126]

[121.] (1808) 10 East 109.
[122.] A servant or friend does not count: *Johnson v. Lawson* (1824) 2 Bing. 86.
[123.] *Doe d Tilman v. Tarver* (1824) Ry. & M. 141.
[124.] (1859) 7 H.L. Cas. 633.
[125.] (1884) 13 Q.B.S.D. 818.
[126.] (1885) 18 L.R. Ir. 192, 194.

(4) Declarations of deceased as to public rights

The declaration must concern a public or general, and not a private, right. Public rights are rights of the public at large to use paths, highways, ferries or landing places. General rights are those common to a section of the public, such as inhabitants of a particular area or tenants of a manor.

A declaration as to general rights is only admissible if made by a person with some connection with, or knowledge of, the matter in question.[127] However, this limitation does not apply in the case of public rights.

In both cases, the declaration must relate to the reputed existence of that right rather than facts from which this right can be inferred. Again, the declaration must have been made before the dispute in which it is tendered had arisen.

In *Giant's Causeway Co. Ltd v. Attorney General*[128] the original 1832 Ordnance Survey map was held admissible to prove the existence of a public right-of-way. Chatterton V.-C. stated:

> "[T]he question we are dealing with is one of public, or at least of general, interest. On such questions evidence of reputation may consist of ancient documents which have been found in the custody of some person who is entitled to the property in question ... if a document is found in the custody of a person whose duty it was to have it and preserve it and to see that it was correct, it would stand upon the same principle and would therefore, come within these documents which are matters of reputation. This document is not to be received as having any effect on any conflict as to private rights. It is only received as a map, prepared by a captain of the Engineers, made sixty five years ago, who stated 'I made that map, and I saw those things' ... this document is produced from an office of safe custody, the department of which the gentleman was an officer, and it was the duty of that department to preserve those documents. It is a department of very great authority, and the officer of that department has produced this map, and therefore it is evidence of a document coming out of proper custody, and it is given as evidence of reputation, which, in my opinion, means that opinion of some person who has had an opportunity of acquiring knowledge on the spot, which on the cases may be acquired by hearsay from other people."[129]

(5) Testamentary declarations

Sugden v. Lord St Leonards[130] laid down the principle that "declarations made by a testator, both before and after the execution of his will, are, in the event of its loss, admissible as secondary evidence of its contents".

[127.] *Berkeley Peerage Case* (1811) 4 Camp. 401.
[128.] [1905] 5 New Ir. Jur. Rep. 301.
[129.] *Ibid.*, at 303.
[130.] (1876) 1 P.D. 154.

In *Re Ball*[131] a copy of the first page of the will in the testator's handwriting, bearing a statement by him that he had substituted the copy for the original, was admissible to prove the contents of the will.

Warren J. said that the rule applied whether the declarations were made before or after the execution of the will:

> "Declarations made by a testator, both before and after the execution of his will, are, in the event of its loss, admissible as secondary evidence of its contents...there is no distinction between this case, where the question is, what formed part of the will, and the case where the whole will is lost."[132]

(6) Declarations of deceased made in the course of a duty

Solicitors' notes of instructions taken from a client have been held admissible under this heading.[133]

The duty in pursuance of which the declarations were made must have been one owed to another to perform an act and then to make a report or record of having performed it. It must not be just a duty to perform an act but must involve an additional duty to record that act.[134] The act to which the declaration relates must be actually performed by the declarant prior to the making of the report.[135] The record must be contemporaneous.[136] In addition, there must be no motive to misrepresent.

This was how entries in marriage registers were originally admitted. *Malone v. L'Estrange*[137] was a civil case regarding the will of noted 19th century Irish lawyer Anthony Malone. It was held that books of Roman Catholic chapels containing entries of marriages were admissible under this exception. However, in *Miller v. Wheatley*[138] an entry in a marriage register was held inadmissible under this head on the ground that there was no duty to record stated, no proof of handwriting, nor of the official position of the writer.

In *Chambers v. Bernasconi*[139] a certificate prepared by a sheriff's officer stating the place of an arrest was inadmissible because he was under no duty to record it. However, it could be admitted to prove the fact and date of the arrest.

R. v. Worth Inhabitants[140] a master voluntarily kept a record of contracts with his servants; this could not amount to a declaration in the course of duty because the master had been under no duty to record.

---

131. (1890) 25 L.R. Ir. 556.
132. *Ibid.*, at 557-558.
133. *Somers v. Erskine* (No. 2) [1944] I.R. 368.
134. *Mercer v. Denne* [1905] 2 Ch. 538.
135. A record of letters to be posted is not sufficient: *Rowlands v. De Vecchi* (1882) Cab. & El. 10. However, in contrast to this, see *R. v. Buckley* (1873) 13 Cox C.C. 293: a police constable had declared that he was about to go and keep observation on the accused; this statement was held admissible as a declaration made in the course of a duty.
136. In *Henry Coxon* (1878) 3 P.D. 156 an entry in a ship's log book was made two days after the event and, therefore, was not admissible.
137. (1839) 2 I.R.. Eq. Rep. 16.
138. (1890) 28 L.R. Ir. 144.
139. (1834) 1 Cr. M. & R. 347.
140. (1843) 4 Q.B. 132.

In *Price v. Earl of Torrington*[141] the plaintiff, a brewer, brought an action against the Earl of Torrington who had failed to pay for his beer. Entries made by a deceased drayman in the plaintiff's delivery book were admissible in evidence to prove that beer had been delivered.

In *R. v. Mc Guire*[142] a trial for arson, a scientific officer's records of observations made by him at the scene of the fire were admitted, although his opinion as to where the fire started was not.

11.3.4   Statements in public documents

Phillimore J. in *Wilton & Co v. Philips* states:

> "A public document coming from the proper place or a certified copy of it is sufficient proof of every particular stated in it".[143]

Statements in public documents made by a public officer acting in the course of public duty to record documents of record to be retained indefinitely are admissible under an exception to the hearsay rule. This was first recognised by Parke B. in *Irish Society v. Bishop of Derry*[144] statements in a bishop's return to the Exchequer relating to advowsons in his diocese were held admissible.

The entries must have been made by someone under a public duty to inquire into and record the facts in question. *R. v. Halpin*[145] establishes that that person need not have personal knowledge of the matters recorded. Lane L.J. stated:

> "The common law as expressed in the earlier cases which have been cited was plainly designed to apply to an uncomplicated community where those charged with keeping registers would, more often than not, be personally acquainted with the person whose affairs they were recording and the vicar, as already indicated, would probably himself have officiated at the baptism, marriage or burial which he later recorded in the presence of the churchwardens on the register before putting it back in the coffers. But the common law should move with the times and should recognise the fact that the official charged with recording matters of public import can no longer in this highly complicated world, as like as not, have personal knowledge of their accuracy."[146]

The record must relate to a matter of public interest[147] and the documents must be meant for public inspection.[148] *R. v. Halpin* establishes that they need not be made immediately after the event.

[141.] (1703) 1 Salk 285.

[142.] (1985) 81 Cr. App. R. 323.

[143.] (1903) 19 T.L.R. 390.

[144.] (1846) 12 Cl. & Fin. 641.

[145.] [1975] Q.B. 907.

[146.] *Supra*, 914.

[147.] *Sturla v. Freccia* (1880) 5 App. Cas. 623.

[148.] *White v. Taylor* [1969] 1 Ch. 150: a draft document was not admissible. *Heyne v. Fischel & Co.* (1913) 30 T.L.R. 1190: records compiled by the post office showing the times at which telegrams were received were inadmissible as there was no intention to retain them.

In *Minister for Defence v. Buckley*[149] a map of the Curragh, outlining its divisions for the purposes of the Curragh of Kildare Act 1969, was held to be a public document and therefore evidence of those divisions.

11.3.5 Testimony of witnesses in former proceedings

Such testimony is only admissible if the witness is dead or unable to attend and had been subject to cross-examination in the former proceedings.

11.3.6 Works of reference

Authoritative published works of reference are admissible to prove facts of a public nature. As Lord Halsbury stated in *Read v. Bishop of Lincoln*:

"Where it is important to ascertain ancient facts of a public nature, the law does permit historical works to be referred to".[150]

In *East London Railway Co. v. Thames Conservators*[151] the report of an engineer who had constructed the Thames tunnel 60 years earlier was admissible to show the nature of the soil in this area. In *Malcolmson v. O'Dea* a book containing fishing leases granted by a predecessor in title of the plaintiff was held to be admissible evidence of the lessor's enjoyment of the fishing rights when the leases were granted.

11.3.7 New common law exception for hearsay statements of children

Eastern Health Board v. M.K.[152] arose before the Children Act 1997 came into force on January 1,1999,[153] and involved an *ex parte* application to make three children wards of court. Costello P. made an order on foot of an *ex parte* application by the Board, which authorised the Board to take the children into care pending the hearing of the matter. The *ex parte* application was based on affidavit evidence. One of the affidavits was sworn by a speech therapist, who stated that the child S. had told her that for a number of years his father had subjected him to serious sexual abuse on a regular basis. The Board did not call S. at the hearing of the matter but instead sought to give evidence as to what S. had said to the speech therapist and what he had said to a Mr. McGrath, a social worker. A video recording of this interview was made and shown to the court with the agreement of the children's parents. The parents denied sexual abuse had taken place and objected to the admission of hearsay evidence.

Costello P. held that if the hearsay evidence was excluded, the rest of the evidence would not justify the making of an order taking the children into care. The rule against the admission of hearsay was a judge-made rule, which

---

[149] Unreported, Case no 112/1974.
[150] [1892] A.C. 644 at 653.
[151] (1904) 90 L.T. 347.
[152] [1996] 1 I.L.R.M. 370 (H.C.); [1999] 2 I.R. 99 (S.C.). See O'Doherty [1996] I.L.T. 284.
[153] For further information on the new hearsay exception introduced by the Act, see para 11.3.10.

had never been applied strictly in wardship cases. The courts have an inherent jurisdiction to look after the children's welfare. In exercising its jurisdiction to admit an out-of-court statement by a child, the court must be satisfied of the necessity to do so, such as the fact that:

1. the child is not old enough to give sworn testimony in court;

2. the giving of evidence in a civil case would be too traumatic; at the time the concept of video evidence only applied in criminal cases.

He also held that the weight to be given to the hearsay evidence was a matter for the trial judge. The judge would have to determine the reliability of the testimony given by the witness who was narrating what the child had said, as the narrator may have been influenced by the out of court statement.

The Supreme Court held that the reported statements of S.K. had been improperly admitted. Denham J. and Keane J. felt that there was an exception allowing the admission of hearsay evidence in wardship cases but that the criteria for this exception had not been satisfied.

Keane J. laid emphasis on the special nature of wardship. It was not concerned with a *lis inter partes*. A judge exercising the wardship jurisdiction is not bound by the rules that apply to the adminstration of justice. He said that the trial judge had failed to consider whether the child was competent to give evidence. Evidence could only be admitted if the child was competent to give evidence. Also, there had been a failure to consider the reliability of the statements according to the criteria in *R. v. Khan*.[154]

McLachlin J. in *Khan* had said that hearsay evidence might be exceptionally admissible in wardship proceedings provided that it was reliable. Factors to take into account in deciding whether the statements were reliable were as follows: the timing, the demeanour, the personality of the child, the child's intelligence and understanding, and the possibility of fabrication.

Denham J. said that the hearsay rule had been adopted to protect fair trial process, but that new exceptions could be recognised. She said that the unique nature of wardship proceedings necessitated such an exception. However, in the circumstances the admission of the hearsay evidence had not been in accordance with fair procedures and due process. There should have been an adequate preliminary enquiry into whether S.K. could have given evidence.

Barrington J. and Lynch J. felt that hearsay evidence could be admitted in relation to non-contested matters. Barron J. felt that hearsay evidence could be received as expert opinion. The statement to the speech therapist, a non-expert, was admissible as source material for an expert opinion.

Southern Health Board v. C.H.[155] arose by way of a case stated to the High Court from the District Court. The Board sought to rely on hearsay evidence alleging sexual abuse by a father of his very young daughter. During the course of the hearing, the Health Board sought to introduce the evidence of a social worker, including video evidence of interviews with the child in respect

---

[154] [1990] 2 S.C.R. 531.
[155] [1996] 1 I.R. 219.

of allegations that the child had been sexually abused by his father. Objections were made to the admission of hearsay evidence. The issue raised was whether hearsay evidence is admissible in proceedings under section 58 of the Children Act 1990 to determine whether a parent is a fit person to care for the child.

It was argued that fit persons proceedings differ from wardship proceedings and that the rule against hearsay should continue to apply to fit persons proceedings. However, it was held that the nature of the proceedings under the 1980 Act were virtually the same as wardship applications made under sections 21, 24 and 58 of the Act. They relate to the welfare of the child and are not a *lis inter partes*. All such proceedings are governed by section 3 of the Guardianship of Infants act. The court must at all times be guided by the interests of the welfare of the child.

The High Court held that in fit persons proceedings, the court has a discretion to admit hearsay evidence, but that discretion should only be exercised in cases of necessity where either the child is too young to give evidence or where to do so would adversely affect the child's welfare. The Supreme Court took a different view and O Flaherty J., delivering the judgment of the court, held that it was not a case constituting an exception to the hearsay rule, but was rather a question of how to approach the evidence of an expert witness. The videotapes were admissible on the ground that they formed part of the material on which the social worker had based their expert evidence.

This judgment has been criticised.[156] The normal rule on opinion evidence is that while experts may draw on hearsay evidence as part of the process of arriving at their opinion, it is essential that the primary facts upon which their opinion is based are proven by admissible evidence. So under opinion evidence, the child's evidence must have been admissible by an exception to the hearsay rule in order for the expert to express an opinion on it.

11.3.8 Other common law exceptions

People (D.P.P.) v. Mc Ginley[157] states that the rule against hearsay applies with full force in criminal interlocutory proceedings. The applicant was charged with unlawful carnal knowledge of a girl. The Detective Sergeant gave evidence that the applicant had made threats to her. Keane J. in the Supreme Court held that this evidence was inadmissible. An applicant for bail is entitled to have the evidence tested by cross-examination. Keane J. held that there had been an error in allowing the evidence. However, Keane J. recognised that if there was a specific reason for not producing the author of the statement, *e.g.* preserving the anonymity of police informers, the evidence might be admitted.

---

[156] By D. McGrath writing in Byrne & Binchy "Annual Review of Irish Law 1996" (Round Hall, Dublin, 1996) at pp. 318-319, where he states that the decision "does not accord with established jurisprudence governing the admission of expert testimony.

[157] [1998] 2 I.R. 417.

In *Eastern Health Board v. M.K.*[158] Keane J. said that the admission of videotape evidence as an exception to the hearsay rule might be permissible. The court could see and hear the statement as it was actually made, and were in as good a position to assess the credibility of the maker of the statement as if he or she were giving evidence in court, subject to the principle that the maker is not subject to cross-examination. It was pointed out that the categories of exception to rule against hearsay must increase in line with technological progress. The judge should receive expert evidence to explain the video, such as the significance of body language, vocal inflections, the child's intellectual and verbal abilities, and any signs of fantasising on the part of the child.

11.3.9   Part II of the Criminal Evidence Act 1992

Section 5 of this Act allows the admission of evidence contained in a document, where the maker had personal knowledge of the matters recorded or was supplied information by someone who had personal knowledge of the matters recorded and the document was made in the course of business. Under section 8 the courts also have a residual discretion to exclude any documents covered in the interests of justice. Section 8 lists the factors that the court can take into account in deciding whether or not to exercise this discretion. This allows the admission of hearsay evidence in situations such as *Myers v. D.P.P.*,[159] but does not apply in civil proceedings.[160]

Section 5 also allows persons ordinarily resident outside the State to swear evidence before a District Court judge. That evidence will be admissible at the later trial. This may be relevant in relation to crimes against tourists.

In *People (D.P.P.) v. Byrne*[161] the accused was charged with handling a motor car, knowing or believing it to be stolen. The accused had sold a car and it was alleged by the prosecution that this car comprised the body shell of a stolen vehicle. The issue was whether hearsay evidence was admissible as to the engine number of the stolen car. It was argued that no certificate had been produced under section 6 of the Criminal Evidence Act 1992 in respect of this evidence.

The Court of Criminal Appeal held that a certificate under section 6 was not necessary. Each witness had identified a document that he had personally filled in or signed. The only documents in respect of which the makers were not available to testify were public documents. Therefore, even before the Criminal Evidence Act 1992, these documents would have been admissible.

At this point, it is worth referring to the recommendations of the Law Reform Commission regarding reform of the hearsay rule in civil proceedings. In the United Kingdom there has been wholesale reform of this rule in civil proceedings. Irish courts have never expressly followed *Myers v. D.P.P.* and

---

[158.] [1999] 2 I.R. 99.

[159.] [1999] 2 I.R. 99.

[160.] This gives effect to the recommendations of the Law Reform Commission in its 1987 Report on Receiving Stolen Property (LRC23-1987).

[161.] Unreported, Court of Criminal Appeal, June 7, 2000.

might opt instead to follow the decision of the Supreme of Canada in *Ares v. Venner*,[162] in which it was held that the hearsay rule needed to be restated to meet modern conditions. In two cases, *People v. Marley*[163] *and People v. Prunty*,[164] the Court of Criminal Appeal has reserved the question of whether *Myers* was correctly decided.

11.3.10 Sections 20-25 of Children Act 1997

These sections apply in relation to civil proceedings. Section 23 allows a statement made by a child to be admitted as evidence of any fact therein, where the court considers that (a) the child is unable to give evidence by reason of age; or (b) the giving of oral evidence would not be in the welfare of the child.

It should be noted that there is no requirement in section 23 that the child be capable of giving evidence. However, arguably, in the light of the judgment of Keane J. in *Eastern Health Board v. M(K)*[165] it is only in exceptional circumstances that the evidence of a child who is incompetent to testify should be admitted under section 23.

The judge also has a residual discretion to exclude such evidence if in his opinion it is not in the interests of justice that it should be admitted. One of the considerations that can be taken into account here is whether the admission would result in unfairness to any of the parties. Notice must be given to the other parties before this section can be exercised. The notice must include such particulars of the evidence as is reasonable and practicable in the circumstances to enable the other party to deal with any matter arising from it being hearsay.

Section 24 sets out the factors to be taken into account in estimating the weight to be attached to such a statement. Factors that are relevant under section 24 are as follows: whether the original statement was contemporaneous with the matters it deals with; whether the evidence involves multiple hearsay; any motives of the child to conceal or misrepresent; possibility of collaboration/editing; if the statement is being adduced in hearsay in an attempt to prevent proper evaluation of its weight. Denham J. in her judgment in *Eastern Health Board v. M(K)* lists a number of other factors: the child's age, intelligence, comprehension of the circumstances of the case, skill in communication and coherence; the content and consistency of the hearsay evidence; any subsequent inconsistent statements made by the child.

Evidence may be called in relation to the credibility of the child if such evidence would have been relevant had the child been called as a witness either in examination-in-chief or cross-examination.

[162.] [1970] S.C.R. 608. See Choo "Criminal Hearsay in Canada" [1993] C.L.J. 231.
[163.] [1985] I.L.R.M. 17.
[164.] [1986] I.L.R.M. 716.
[165.] [1999] 2 I.R. 99.

11.3.11 Pre-trial identification

Evidence of a pre-trial identification is also admissible in evidence under an exception to the hearsay rule. In *R. v. Burke*[166] a witness could not identify the accused in court as the man who had robbed him, but, nonetheless, evidence of a previous identification was admissible. *People (Attorney General) v. Casey (No. 1)*[167] held that evidence of pre-trial identification was admissible even where the person who made the identification did not testify.

11.3.12 Section 8 of the Proceeds of Crime Act 1996[168]

This section allows the opinion evidence of a member of the Gardaí in certain cases. McGuinness J. in *Gilligan v. Criminal Assets Bureau*[169] felt that orders should not be made under this provision without corroborating evidence.[170] Otherwise constitutional justice might be infringed.

In *Criminal Assets Bureau v. Craft*[171] it was argued that section 8 of the Proceeds of Crime Act 1996 was unconstitutional insofar as it deprived the defendant of the opportunity to cross-examine. The trial judge held that the evidence was inadmissible on other grounds and declined to deal with the constitutional point.

11.3.13 Bail

It was thought that the hearsay rule did not apply with full force in bail applications. However, this view was rejected by the Supreme Court in *People (D.P.P.) v. McGinley*[172] where Keane J. described the rule against hearsay as "an essential feature of our legal system".

He recognised that:

> "Where there is evidence which indicates as a matter of probability that the applicant, if granted bail, will not stand his trial or will interfere with witnesses, the right to liberty must yields to the public interest in the administration of justice. It is in that context that hearsay evidence may become admissible, where the court hearing the application is satisfied that there are sufficient grounds for not requiring that witness to give viva voce evidence. Here no specific reason had been given for not producing the author of the statement and therefore the hearsay evidence had been improperly admitted."

---

166. (1847) 2 Cox C.C. 225.
167. (1961) I.R. 264.
168. See McDermott (1999) Bar. Rev. 413.
169. [1998] 3 I.R. 185.
170. In this regard she mirrored the view of Moriarty J. in *M.M. v. D.D.*, unreported, High Court, December 10, 1998.
171. Unreported, High Court, O'Sullivan J., July 12.
172. [1998] 2 I.R. 417.

For an example of a case where hearsay evidence was admitted in a bail application, see *People (D.P.P.) v. McKeon.*[173]

11.3.14 Residual statutory provisions

(a) *Registration of Births and Deaths (Ireland) Act 1863*. This allows heasay evidence of the entries on the register of births and deaths.

(b) *Marriages (Ireland) Act 1844*. Hearsay evidence may be given of entries on the marriage register.

(c) *Bankers Books Evidence Act 1879 and 1959*.[174] Hearsay evidence of banker's books is permissible.

11.4 Hearsay rule in civil cases

The hearsay rule is generally applied less strictly in civil proceedings.[175] The Law Reform Commission in its Report on the Rule against Hearsay in Civil Cases[176] recognises that the courts freely allow hearsay evidence of probative value when tendered by the defence. This practice is also recognised by Order 40, Rule 4, of the Rules of the Superior Courts, which makes provision for the inclusion of hearsay in affidavits supporting interlocutory applications.

However, in *Smithkline Beecham v. Antigen Pharmaceuticals Ltd*[177] the dangers of relying on such evidence was recognised. In *Murphy v. GM PB PC Ltd*[178] it was argued that it would be unconstitutional to admit hearsay evidence in an application for an interlocutory freezing order under section 3 of the Proceeds of Crime Act 1996, as there was no requirement for an undertaking as to damages and the substantive hearing would not take place for seven years. O'Higgins J. said that the rule against hearsay was not a constitutional requirement.

The Law Reform Commission Report on Hearsay in Civil Cases 1998 states that, as a general principle, hearsay evidence in civil proceedings should be admissible, but that the judges should have a discretion to exclude out-of-court statements. The person who made the out-of-court statement should be called if he is available. Notice should be given to the other side of one's intention to call hearsay evidence.

---

173. Unreported, Supreme Court, October 12, 1995
174. A Dunne & Davies: The Bankers Books Evidence Act (1997) Bar Review,
175. However note *Maloney v. Jury's Hotel plc* unreported, November 12, 1999 where the Supreme Court set aside a decision in civil proceedings on the ground that the trial judge had erred in improperly taking hearsay evidence into account.
176. LRC 25-1990 p. 11.
177. [1999] 2 I.L.R.M. 190.
178. Unreported, O'Higgins J., High Court, June 1999.

Chapter 12

CHARACTER EVIDENCE

12.1 Introduction

Throughout this text the term "character evidence" is used in a broad sense to refer to any evidence of an individual's past conduct, disposition, or general reputation.[1] Whether such evidence is admissible depends on a number of factors:

1. The identity of the person whose character is in issue: is he the accused in a criminal case, a party in a civil case, or a mere witness?

2. The nature of the proceeding in which the evidence is raised: is it a criminal or a civil trial?

3. The nature of the evidence itself: does it indicate a good or bad character?

4. The purpose for which the evidence is sought to be adduced: is it relevant to a fact in issue or merely to the credibility of the individual in question?

Disputes regarding the admission of character evidence normally arise in relation to the character of the accused in criminal proceedings. Evidence of good character on the part of the defendant in a criminal trial is admissible, subject to certain qualifications. However, this is in contrast to the exclusionary rule which prohibits evidence of the accused's bad character being raised either in examination-in-chief or in cross-examination. The rule that a person should not be judged by his previous misconduct is one of the fundamental principles of criminal law. However, it may be departed from in certain situations.

This chapter begins by outlining the exclusionary rule that precludes evidence of the accused's bad character. It also looks at the rules relating to character evidence in civil proceedings and the situations in which the accused's good character and the character of witnesses may be put before the court in a criminal trial. The following two chapters set out the exceptional cases in which evidence of the accused's bad character may be admitted in criminal proceedings.

---

[1] The common law on occasion uses the term "character evidence" in a narrower sense so as to include only evidence of reputation and previous convictions. Evidence of past conduct is excluded from this definition. *R. v. Rowton* (1865) 34 L.J.M.C. 57; For criticism, see Munday [1997] Crim. L.R. 247. It should be noted that a cranky or sullen demeanour is not *per se* equivalent to bad character: *Attorney General v. Cornelius O'Leary and Hannah O'Leary* [1926] I.R. 445.

12.2 Criminal proceedings: Evidence of accused's bad character not usually admissible

The general rule in criminal trials is that evidence of the accused's bad character or previous misconduct cannot normally be put before the jury. However, in *Attorney General v. O'Leary*[2] the Irish Court of Criminal Appeal indicated that there was a distinction between evidence of bad character and evidence of demeanour. Questions about the accused's demeanour (*e.g.* "Was she cross or good tempered?") cannot in themselves be regarded as raising the issue of bad character and may be admitted if relevant, without further justification.

The rule was first developed in the early nineteenth century[3] and became established as a fundamental principle of criminal evidence by the end of that century by the judgment of the Privy Council in *Makin v. Attorney General for New South Wales*.[4] This rule was recently reaffirmed by Budd J. in *C.B. v. D.P.P.*[5] where he stated as follows:

> "[A]s a general rule it is not open to the Prosecution to adduce evidence of the bad character of the accused in any form. The exclusionary rule also precludes proof of the commission of discreditable acts which are not in themselves criminal and of any discreditable propensity which may make the accused appear more likely to have committed the act charged."[6]

The exclusionary rule has two consequences:

1. Evidence of the accused's bad character/previous misconduct cannot be introduced by the prosecution when trying to prove the accused's guilt in examination-in-chief.

2. Evidence of bad/character/previous misconduct cannot be raised by the prosecution when cross-examining the accused.

12.2.1 Constitutional status of the prohibition

The rule prohibiting evidence of the accused's bad character or previous misconduct has now been accorded constitutional status. McWilliam J. in *King v. Attorney General*[7] stated:

> "One of the concepts of justice which the Courts have always accepted is that evidence of character or of previous convictions shall not be given at a criminal

---

2. [1926] I.R. 445.
3. *R. v. Cole* unreported, 1910, noted by Lord Goddard in *Sims* [1946] K.B. 532 at 544. The rule was not always followed consistently at first; *R. v. Geering* (1849) 18 L.J.M.C. 215; *R. v. Winslow* (1860) 8 Cox C.C. 397. For an early Irish application of the rule, see *R. v. Flanagan and Higgins* (1884) 15 Cox C.C. 403 and see Stone (1933) 46 Harv. L.R. 954.
4. [1894] A.C. 57.
5. [1997] 3 I.R. 140.
6. Of course previous convictions or good or bad character may be taken into account by the judge after the verdict, where directly relevant to the question of sentence.
7. [1981] I.R. 233

> trial except at the instigation of the accused, as that could prejudice the fair trial of the issue of the guilt or innocence of the accused."

A prohibition on the admission of such evidence may be seen as an inevitable consequence of the constitutional presumption of innocence.

In *D.P.P. v. Keogh*[8] the accused was charged with failure to comply with a direction issued by a member of the Garda Síochána under section 8(1) of the Criminal Law (Sexual Offences) Act 1993. Section 8(1) provides that a garda who has reasonable cause to suspect that a person is loitering in a street in order to solicit persons for the purposes of prostitution, may direct that person to leave. Section 8(2) provides that it is an offence to fail to comply with such a direction.

In order to show that he had reasonable cause for giving the section 8(1) direction, the garda in question gave evidence that the area in question, Wilton Place, Dublin 2, was a well-known red-light district. He also stated that he had seen the accused approach cars on previous occasions for the purposes of prostitution. Endorsing the decision of McWilliam J. in *King v. Attorney General*, Kelly J. held that such reference to the accused's previous misconduct was in breach of her constitutional right to a fair trial.

The issue of the constitutionality of the admission of bad character evidence was also raised in the case of *D.P.P. (at the suit of Garda John Stratford) v. Alan O' Neill*.[9] The accused had been charged in the Children's Court with larceny of a bicycle. Section 5(1) of the Summary Jurisdiction Over Children (Ireland) Act 1884 provides that where a young person is charged before a court of summary jurisdiction with any indictable offence other than homicide, the court may deal summarily with the offence if the young person consents to waive his right to trial by jury, and if they think it expedient to do so, having regard to the character and antecedents of the person charged, the nature of the offence, and all the circumstances of the case.

The District Court Judge in this case referred a question to the High Court regarding the constitutionality of section 5(1). In particular, he was concerned that the tendering of evidence of character at this stage in the trial process might infringe the presumption of innocence contained in the Constitution. Smyth J. held that section 5(1) was constitutional, for two reasons. Firstly, the character and antecedents of the accused only arose to be considered if the young person himself consented to waive his right to trial by jury. Secondly, the young person's past character and antecedents were only admitted under section 5(1) in order to enable the District Court Judge to assess the quality of their consent to the summary proceedings.

12.2.2 Rationale for prohibition

There are a number of reasons why there is a prohibition on admitting evidence of the accused's bad character or past misconduct. Firstly, there is a

---

8. [1998] 4 I.R. 416.
9. Unreported, Smyth J., September 24, 1997.

concern that the admission of such evidence might distort the jury's reasoning process. The fear is that they might simply take the view that the evidence of previous misconduct shows the accused to be bad, that crimes are more often committed by the bad than the good, and hence the evidence tends to show the accused likely to be guilty.

If the previous misconduct is alleged rather than proven, the jury may mistakenly believe that their task is one of deciding whether the previous misconduct occurred, when they are actually supposed to be considering whether the accused committed the particular crime with which he is charged. Or, alternatively, the sheer volume of misconduct evidence may itself cause confusion[10].

Secondly, evidence of an accused's bad character or previous misconduct may lead the jury into error in a different respect. Such evidence may prompt a jury to conclude that the accused ought to be punished whether or not he is guilty of the particular crime with which he is charged. For instance, if the evidence shows that the accused has committed other crimes, which have gone undetected, the jury may feel that it is fair to convict him on the current charge whether or not they believe he is actually guilty. A less extreme version of such "moral prejudice" might be that the jury may be satisfied with a lower standard of proof for the offence charged because they feel that the accused deserves to go to prison in any case.

Thirdly, quite apart from the concern that it may lead the jury to engage in wrongful convictions, there are other problems attaching to the admission of evidence of bad character and previous misconduct. The argument has been made that increased admissibility of such evidence could hamper the process of police investigation. The police might unduly focus their inquiries on the past history of the accused and fail to give sufficient attention to the facts of the case. Equally, the prosecution, in presenting their case, might put excessive emphasis on the accused's previous misconduct.

Another practical problem is that the admission of such evidence leads to added expense and prolongation of the trial process. It also conflicts with the principle of offender rehabilitation, which is based on the fundamental belief that individuals are not limited by their past conduct[11] and that every offender should be given the opportunity to reform and turn over a new leaf. And, of

---

[10.] Lord Hewart C.J., *R. v. Bailey* [1924] 2 K.B. 300 at 305: "the risk, the danger, the logical fallacy is indeed quite manifest to those who are accustomed to thinking about such matters. It is so easy to derive from a series of unsatisfactory allegations, if there are enough of them, an accusation which at least appears satisfactory. It is so easy to collect from a mass of ingredients, not one of which is sufficient, a totality, which will appear to contain what is missing. That, of course, is only another way of saying that when a person is dealing with a considerable mass of facts, in particular if those facts are of such a nature as to invite reprobation, nothing is easier than confusion of mind and body. If such charges are to be brought in amass, it becomes essential that the methods upon which guilt is to be ascertained should be stated with a punctilious exactness."

[11.] Cardozo C.J. in *People v. Zackowitz*, 172 N.E. 466 (1930): "Fundamental hitherto has been the rule that character is never an issue in a criminal trial unless the defendant chooses to make it one. In a very real sense, a defendant starts his life afresh when he stands before a jury, a prisoner at the bar".

course, it contradicts other fundamental principles of criminal law, such as the presumption of innocence.

12.2.3 Effect of misconduct evidence being included

The wrongful admission of such evidence will in the vast majority of cases lead to a conviction being struck down. However, in very rare cases the conviction may be upheld.[12] In *People (D.P.P.) v. Kavanagh*[13] the appellant had killed his brother-in-law. The wives of the appellant and the victim were sisters. Evidence was put before the jury to the effect that the appellant had assaulted his wife, the victim's sister-in-law. This was inadmissible evidence of bad character. However, the court felt that it was inappropriate to discharge the jury in the circumstances.

12.2.4 Criminal proceedings: Exceptional situations where evidence of the accused's bad character is admissible

(a) Examination-in-chief

The common law recognises that there are some limited situations in which the prosecution must be allowed to adduce evidence of the bad character or previous misconduct of the accused. However, the common law has failed to define precisely when these limited situations exist. The current position is that evidence of bad character or previous misconduct is admissible in examination-in-chief where its probative effect can be said to outweigh its prejudicial value. This test was laid down by the House of Lords in *D.P.P. v. P.*[14] and was followed in Ireland by Budd J. in *C.B. v. D.P.P.*[15] and by the Court of Criminal Appeal in *D.P.P. v. Kelly.*[16]

In addition, if the accused has raised his good character or cast imputations on the character of the prosecution witnesses, the common law allows evidence of his previous convictions or bad reputation within the community to be put before the court by the prosecution.[17]

The situations in which evidence of the accused's bad character/previous misconduct can be admitted at the examination-in-chief stage will be discussed in more detail in the following chapter.

(b) Cross-examination

The normal rule is that a witness cannot be cross-examined about a matter unless that matter was admissible evidence in examination-in-chief.

---

12. *R. v. McKenzie* [1991] Crim. L.R. 767.
13. Unreported, Court of Criminal Appeal, *ex tempore*, July 7, 1999.
14. [1991] 2 A.C. 447.
15. [1997] 3 I.R. 140.
16. Unreported, Court of Criminal Appeal, December 13, 1999.
17. This rule also allows a co-accused to put evidence of an accused's reputation or previous convictions before the court where the accused has cast imputations on the character of the co-accused or has put his own good character in issue.

However, in the context of cross-examination of an accused, section 1(f) of the Criminal Justice (Evidence) Act 1924 sets out additional situations in which an accused can be cross-examined as to his misconduct or previous bad character. These situations are dealt with in more detail in Chapter 14.

In addition, where the accused has referred to his own good character or cast imputations on the character of the prosecution witnesses or a co-accused, the common law allows cross-examination of his witnesses in relation to his previous convictions or his bad character within the community.

12.3 Criminal proceedings: Evidence of accused's good character

In criminal proceedings, the accused is always allowed to adduce evidence of his good character. The courts do not normally require this to satisfy any test of relevance.

In theory, such evidence should relate to his general reputation among his acquaintances rather than any specific acts of good conduct that he may have performed. This rule was established in *R. v. Rowton*,[18] where Cockburn C.J. stated as follows:

> "The only way the [common] law allows of your getting at the disposition and tendency of [the defendant's] mind, is by evidence as to his general character founded upon the knowledge of those who know anything about him and his general conduc . No one pretends that...examination can be made as to a specific fact, though everyone would agree that evidence of one fact of honesty or dishonesty, as the case might be, would weigh infinitely more than the opinions of a man's friends or neighbours as to his general character. The truth is, this part of our law is an anomaly ... Evidence must be of [the defendant's] general reputation and not the individual opinion of the witness."[19]

However, in practice this limitation tends not to be observed.[20] In *R. v. Redgrave*[21] the prevailing judicial practice of ignoring *Rowton* and admitting evidence of specific acts of previous good conduct was recognised by the Court of Appeal. However, it was emphasised that this practice was an indulgence in favour of defendants and that an accused had no entitlement to have such evidence admitted if the judge decided against it.[22] The Court of Appeal, in this case, specifically refused to overrule *Rowton*.

---

18. *R. v. Rowton* (1865) Le. & Ca. 520.
19. *Supra*, n.1 at 530. Cockburn C.J.'s dictum was delivered in the context of an accused adducing evidence of good character and should be seen as limited to this context. For example, in the limited situations in which the prosecution is allowed to adduce evidence of the accused's bad character, the court takes a wider definition of character and allows evidence of specific acts of past misconduct by the accused.
20. See further Munday, "What Constitutes a Good Character" [1997] Crim. L.R 247 and *R. v. Samuel* (1956) 40 Cr. App. R. 8 discussed *supra* at para 14.3.2.
21. (1981) 74 Cr. App. R. 10.
22. The sole situation in which an accused is entitled to an indulgence from *Rowton* is where the co-accused has been allowed to give evidence of specific acts of good conduct; fair play dictates that both accused should be treated the same; *R. v. Bracewell* (1979) 68 Cr. App. R. 44.

Evidence of good character may be given by the accused himself or by other witnesses for the defence, or, alternatively, counsel for the accused may ask prosecution witnesses about his reputation.

12.3.1 Trial judge's obligations in relation to good character directions

Where good character evidence has been given, the judge is obliged to tell the jury in his summing up that, although good character cannot amount to a defence, it has a probative value in relation to guilt, in that a person of good character is less likely to have committed an offence.[23] In addition, where the accused has testified, or if any exculpatory statements made by him before the trial have been put before the court,[24] the judge must state that the evidence of his good character is relevant to his credibility.[25]

Sometimes, in addition to good character evidence, other evidence has been given which might be taken as indicia of bad character, *e.g.* previous misconduct on the part of the accused. In this situation the judge may have a discretion to decline to give a good character direction.[26] However, where the bad character evidence does not relate to previous convictions, then prima facie a direction, albeit a qualified one, should be given.[27] The judge should only refuse to give a direction in this case if the bad character evidence is such that it would be an insult to common sense to give any good character direction.[28]

Where the accused has pleaded guilty to another charge on the indictment, and the jury are unaware of this fact, the judge is precluded from giving a good character direction; but if the jury have been informed of the plea of guilty, it becomes a matter for the judge's discretion whether or not to give a direction.[29]

Where two accused are tried together and one of them adduces evidence of his good character but no character evidence of any sort is heard in respect of the other, the judge must give a good character direction in respect of the former. However, he then has the discretion to give a further direction to the effect thatH the jury must not take the absence of good character evidence by

---

[23] *R. v. Vye* [1993] 1 W.L.R. 471. For a strict application of this requirement, see *R. v. Marr* [1989] Crim. L.R. 743.

[24] The most common situation in which pre-trial exculpatory statements by the accused come before the court is where there are a number of charges against the accused and the prosecution puts in evidence a pre-trial statement made by him containing a confession in respect of one charge and a denial of liability in respect of another charge.

[25] *Supra*, n.5.

[26] *R. v. Aziz* [1995] 3 All E.R. 149; see also *R. v. H.* [2000] All E.R. (D.) 2289 as well as the slightly different approach taken in *R. v. Durbin* [1995] 2 Cr. App. R. 84, a Court of Appeal case which was not brought to the attention of the House of Lords in *Aziz*.

[27] *Ibid., R. v. Durbin.*

[28] *Ibid., R. v. Durbin.*

[29] *R. v. Challenger* [1994] Crim. L.R. 202; *R. v. Challenger* [1995] Crim. L.R. 153

the latter as evidence of his guilt.[30] No particular form of words need be used for any of the above directions.

12.3.2 Drawbacks of adducing good character

However, there is one drawback to the accused adducing evidence of good character, namely that the prosecution may become entitled to raise evidence to the contrary.[31] At common law, if the accused has drawn attention to his good character, the prosecution becomes entitled to call evidence in rebuttal or to ask the accused, or any of his witnesses, questions regarding his good character, and to rebut the answers to these questions by evidence as to his bad character.[32] However, it has been argued that the prosecution evidence given in rebuttal under this common law principle can only relate to previous convictions of the accused or his bad reputation among his acquaintances; it may not include evidence of specific acts of the accused nor the opinion evidence of witnesses as to his reputation.[33]

Under section 1(f)(ii) of the Criminal Justice (Evidence) Act 1924, if the accused has put his good character in issue, he may be asked questions in cross-examination about his previous convictions, charges, commissions of crimes, or bad character, and evidence may be adduced to rebut his answers to these questions. Section 1(f)(ii) allows for the admission of a wider variety of bad character evidence than the common law principle; however, it can only be used where an accused elects to testify.

12.4 Criminal proceedings: Evidence of good or bad character of witnesses

12.4.1 Good character of witnesses

Evidence as to the good character of the party's own witness is not strictly speaking admissible. The rule was summarised by Lawton L.J. in *R. v. Turner,*[34] where he said:

---

30. *R. v. Cain* [1994] 2 All E.R. 398. In *R. v. Aziz, supra,* n. 26 the House of Lords confirmed that a co-accused does not lose his right to a good character direction even if he raises a cut-throat defence incriminating the other defendant.

31. Evidence of bad character admitted in this way can only be taken into account in assessing the accused's credibility; the judge must direct the jury that it is not probative as to his guilt. For more information on s 1(f)(ii) see paras 14.3.2 and 14.3.3.

32. *R. v. Butterwasser* [1948] 1 K.B. 4; *R. v. de Vere* [1981] 3 All E.R. 473.

33. *R. v. Rowton* (1865) Le. & Ca. 520; however, the previous convictions/reputed bad behaviour do not have to be similar in nature to the offence with which the accused is charged. In *R. v. Winfield* (1939) 27 Cr. App. R. 139 an accused charged with indecent assault gave evidence of his sexual morality. It was held that the prosecution could adduce evidence as to his previous convictions for offences of dishonesty. See further Munday, [1997] Crim. L.R. 247. For a contrary view, see *Tapper & Cross on Evidence* (15th ed., 1999), p. 534, where it is argued that the *R. v. Rowton* limitation does not apply when cross-examining witnesses at common law to rebut an assertion of good character; in this case, the witness may be asked about specific acts of misconduct on the part of the accused; *R. v. Bracewell* (1978) 68 Cr. App. R. 44 is cited in support of this.

34. [1975] Q.B. 834.

"In general, evidence can be called to impugn the credibility of witnesses but not led in chief to bolster them up."[35]

However, introductory questioning in examination-in-chief about the witness's job and background often successfully operates to create the impression that he is of good character.

In *Attorney General v. O'Sullivan*[36] the accused was charged with attempted sodomy on a boy of 10 years. Counsel for the accused sought to impeach the character of the boy, saying that he had been expelled from a number of schools on account of his bad character. Kennedy C.J. held that the trial judge was entitled to allow evidence of the boy's good character to be given to contradict this.

It is necessary to be particularly careful in introductory questioning of the accused to avoid putting his good character in issue for the purposes of section 1(f)(ii) of the Criminal Justice (Evidence) Act 1924 since this will expose him to cross-examination by the prosecution in relation to his previous misconduct or bad reputation.

12.4.2 Bad character of witnesses or third parties

Evidence tending to show misconduct on the part of a third party or a witness will be admissible if relevant to the facts in issue.[37]

Quite apart from this, even where the witness's character is not relevant to a fact in issue and only goes to credibility, it is permissible to cross-examine witnesses for the other side about their bad character or previous acts of misconduct. However, such cross-examination is necessarily limited by the rule that it is not possible to adduce evidence to rebut the witness's denial. It is a fundamental principle of cross-examination that evidence may not be adduced to rebut a witness's answer to a collateral question. A collateral question is one which is not relevant to the issues in the case and which goes merely to the credibility of that witness.

However, in certain cases the character of a witness may be relevant to the facts in issue. For example, if the witness is the complainant in a rape case, her past sexual history may be relevant to the question of consent, and evidence may be adduced to rebut her answers to collateral questions.[38] In addition to

---

35. *Ibid.* at 842. In *R. v. Robinson* [1994] 3 All E.R. 346 it was stated that it is not possible *per se* for the prosecution to call a psychologist to give evidence as to their witness's reliability.

36. [1930] I.R. 532.

37. *R. v. Kracher* [1995] Crim. L.R. 819 under the general principle that all relevant evidence is admissible.

38. Subject to s. 3 of the Criminal Law (Rape) Act 1980 and section 13 of the Criminal Law (Rape) (Amendment) Act 1990. They state that where the accused pleads not guilty, no evidence may be adduced about the victim's previous sexual experience without the consent of the trial judge. The trial judge will grant leave to cross-examine on such matters if he feels that it is unfair to the accused to refuse. The concept of unfairness is defined in s. 3(2)(b), which states that it is unfair not to allow such questions or such evidence if they may raise a reasonable doubt as to the accused's guilt. An application for leave should be heard by the trial judge in the absence of the jury.

this, there are certain exceptional situations in which evidence may be adduced to rebut a witness's answer to collateral questions.

Firstly, previous inconsistent statements of a witness may be put in evidence. Sections 4 and 5 of the Criminal Procedure Act 1865 state that such statements are admissible. If a witness under cross-examination denies a previous oral or written statement, which is relevant to an issue in the case and inconsistent with his testimony, this statement may be proved against him. However, the witness must first be given the statement and asked if he has made it and then told about the circumstances in which the statement was made.[39]

Secondly, previous convictions of a witness may be put in evidence despite being collateral matters. Section 6 of the Criminal Procedure Act 1965 says that a witness may be questioned as to whether or not he committed a crime. If he denies this fact, evidence may be adduced in rebuttal.[40]

Thirdly, evidence may be adduced at common law to contradict a witness's denial of bias or partiality and to show that he is prejudiced. *R. v. Mendy*[41] involved a trial for assault. A man was observed taking notes at the trial. He left and spoke to a witness who was being kept outside. The witness denied that he talked to this man. It was held that evidence was admissible to contradict this on the ground that the witness's behaviour indicated bias or partiality.

Fourthly, evidence can be called as to a witness's reputation for untruthfulness. A party may call a witness to give evidence that in his opinion a witness for the other party is not to be believed. But the witness so called is merely allowed to state his belief, and cannot give evidence of any facts which form the basis for this belief.

Finally, evidence may be given of a physical or mental disability suffered by the witness which affects his reliability.

12.5 Conduct and character evidence in civil cases

12.5.1 Character of parties to proceedings

The character of the party in civil cases is admissible if it is a fact in issue. For example, in the law of defamation the character of the plaintiff will be admitted in order to determine whether the libel is true or a fair comment or

---

[39.] The witness should be asked whether he had on a different specified occasion made a contrary statement. If he denies this, he must stand down from the box while the previous statement is proved. He is then put back into the box and the statement is put to him for identification, with attention drawn to the section of the statement which is relied on for the purpose of contradicting him. If he admits the contradiction, the earlier statement is evidence of the facts contained in it. If he denies the contradiction, the earlier statement is evidence of facts going to credibility.

[40.] It should be noted that a defence counsel may be reluctant to use s. 6 because of fear of the accused losing his shield under section 1(f)(ii) of the Criminal Justice (Evidence) Act 1924 and becoming liable to be cross-examined about his bad character. See Chapter 4.

[41.] (1976) 64 Cr. App. Rep. 64.

whether it would lower him in the eyes of right-thinking persons.[42] It may also affect the quantum of damages.[43]

In *Bolton v. O'Brien*[44] other instances of libel were admitted to prove malice or deliberation. In *Campion v. Mooney*[45] previous instances of slander were admitted to show intention on the part of the defendant.

Smyth v. Tunney[46] indicates that the admission of past misconduct of a party in civil cases might be subject to the same restrictions as exist in relation to the admission of such evidence in criminal trials. The United Kingdom position is set out in *Mood Music Publishing Co. Ltd v. De Wolfe Publishing Ltd*,[47] where Lord Denning, having set out the rules regarding the admission of evidence of the accused's bad character in criminal proceedings, stated as follows:

> "In civil cases the courts have followed a similar line but have not been so chary of admitting it. In civil cases, the courts will admit evidence of similar facts[48] if it is logically probative, that is, if it is logically relevant in determining the matter which is in issue; provided that it is not oppressive or unfair to the other side: and also that the other side had fair notice of it and is able to deal with it."[49]

In *Smith v. National Union Bank*[50] a plaintiff who claimed in respect of the loss of a diamond, which he had deposited with the defendant bank, was held to be entitled to adduce evidence of another occasion when jewellery so deposited was found to be missing in order to show the negligence of the defendant bank.

Lord Denning seems to regard the test as slightly less onerous than that in criminal cases, simple relevance is sufficient unless the evidence is oppressive or unfair. However, in practice a strict approach has been taken. One example of this is *Thorpe v. Greater Manchester Chief Constable*,[51] a civil action against a policeman for misconduct. Evidence of previous acts of misconduct engaged in by him was not admissible.

[42.] *Cornwell v. Myskow* [1987] 2 All E.R. 504.

[43.] Subject to the rule in *Scott v. Sampson* (1882) 8 Q.B.D. 491, which states that evidence of rumours and suspicions about the plaintiff which are similar to the defamatory statement cannot be taken into account in assessing quantum. It should also be noted that any additional character evidence adduced in relation to quantum should relate to the plaintiff's general reputation in the community rather than specific acts of misconduct on his part. However, evidence of any previous criminal convictions on the part of the plaintiff may be taken into account in assessing quantum; see *Goody v. Odhams Press Ltd* [1967] 1 Q.B. 333.

[44.] (1883) 16 L.R. Ir. 97.

[45.] [1945] Ir. Jur. Rep. 72.

[46.] Unreported, Supreme Court, *ex tempore* April 8, 1997,

[47.] [1976] Ch. 119. See also *Hales v. Kerr* [1908] 2 K.B. 601; *Joy v. Philips, Mills & Co. Ltd* [1916] 1 K.B. 849; *Barrett v. Long* (1851) 3 H.L. Cas 395.

[48.] The phrase "evidence of similar facts" in this context is used by Lord Denning to refer to evidence of bad character or past misconduct on the part of the accused. For a discussion on the use of the phrase "similar fact" in relation to such evidence, see para 13.1.

[49.] [1976] Ch. 119, at 127.

[50.] (1978) 122 S.J. 367.

[51.] [1989] 2 All E.R. 827.

Also, note the judgment of Warner J. in *Berger v. Raymond & Son Ltd.*[52] Warner J. felt that Lord Denning had equated the test for evidence of bad character in criminal and civil proceedings; it was one of weighing probative force against prejucidical effect. However, the type of prejudice the courts had to beware of in civil proceedings was different.

However, the rules differ slightly as between civil and criminal cases in relation to (a) raising bad character in cross-examination, and (b) raising evidence of good character.

12.5.2 Raising party's bad character in cross-examination in civil proceedings

In relation to cross-examination of a party as to his bad character, sections 1(e) and 1(f) of the Criminal Justice Act 1924 do not apply in civil proceedings. In civil proceedings, the normal rule is that anyone who gives evidence may be asked about his character in order to assess his credibility. Therefore, a party to civil proceedings may be asked about his bad character. However, the rules of cross-examination preclude the cross-examiner from adducing evidence to contradict his answer if the question can be said to be on a collateral issue.[53]

Of course, if the bad character aspect would have been admissible in examination-in-chief,[54] evidence may be adduced to contradict the party's answer, as the question is relevant to a fact in issue and, therefore, more than just collateral.[55]

In addition, if a party has adduced evidence of his good character or has questioned the character of the other side or his witnesses, it appears that the other side is entitled to adduce evidence to rebut that party's answer to a question about his bad character. In addition, they are allowed to put questions to other witnesses as to that party's bad character and contradict their answers if necessary. However, such evidence can only be used in assessing that party's credibility.

12.5.3 Adducing evidence of party's good character in civil proceedings

In civil proceedings, the courts are reluctant to admit evidence of a party's good character. The probative effect of such evidence must be high in order for it to be admitted.[56]

12.5.4 Adducing evidence of bad character of non-parties in civil cases

Evidence of the bad character of non-parties in civil cases is admissible at any stage if it is a fact in issue or relevant to a fact in issue. In addition, to this any

---

[52.] (1984) 1 W.L.R. 625.

[53.] See para 7.31.1 for a discussion of the collateral issues rule. A collateral issue is one that is not relevant to a fact in issue and goes merely to the credibility of the witness.

[54.] *i.e.* if its relevance was so great as to outweigh any prejudice resulting from its admission.

[55.] Questions may also be put to other witnesses on the issue of his character if this issue would have been admissible in examination-in-chief and evidence adduced to rebut their answers if necessary.

[56.] *A.G. v. Bowman* (1791) 2 Bos. & P. 532n.

witness in civil proceedings may be cross-examined as to his bad character in order to assess his credibility. However, his answers to such questions cannot be contradicted by the other side unless one of the exceptions to the collateral issues rule[57] applies.

[57.] These exceptions are set out in para 7.3.1.

Chapter 13

ADDUCING EVIDENCE OF THE ACCUSED'S BAD CHARACTER IN EXAMINATION-IN-CHIEF

13.1 Introduction: Situations in which bad character evidence is admissible in examination-in-chief[1]

The criminal law contains a general prohibition on the admission of evidence of the accused's bad character or by the prosecution in examination-in-chief.[2] This prohibition originated at common law but is now enshrined in our Constitution. An outline of the exclusionary rule and its justifications is to be found in the preceding chapter, which also deals with evidence of good character, the character of witnesses, and the admissibility of character evidence in civil proceedings.

However, there are a number of exceptional situations in which evidence of the accused's bad character may legitimately be admitted. The following chapter deals with the role of this evidence in the cross-examination process and outlines when the prosecution have the power to cross-examine the accused or other witnesses on this point and to call evidence to rebut their answers, if necessary. This chapter outlines when such evidence may be adduced in their examination-in-chief. The situations in which the prosecution can adduce evidence-in-chief of the bad character of the defendant are regulated by the common law and fall into three categories.

Before moving on to consider these situations, however, it is necessary to clarify the term "similar fact evidence", which is most commonly used in relation to bad character evidence which is admissible in examination-in-chief.[3] However, it has been used on occasion in completely the opposite sense

---

[1.] See also Elliott "Young Person's Guide to Similar Fact Evidence" (1983) Crim. Lr. 284; Williams "The Problem of Similar Fact Evidence" (1979) 5 Dalhousie L.J. 283; Munday "Similar Fact Evidence: Identity cases and striking similarity" (1999) 58 C.L.J. 45; Pattenden "Similar fact evidence and proof of identity" (1996) 112 L.Q.R. 446; Tapper "The Probative Force of Similar Fact Evidence" (1992) 108 L.Q.R. 26; Law Commission: Evidence in Criminal Proceedings: Previous Misconduct of a Defandant, Consultation Paper no. 141, 1996; Lunt "Makin Out" [1987] C.L.J. 83; Zuckerman (1987) 103 L.Q.R. 187; Hoffman "Similar Fact after Boardman" (1975) 91 L.Q.R. 193; Carter "Forbidden Reasoning Permissible: Similar Fact Evidence – A Decade after Boardman" (1985) 48 M.L.R. 29; Allen "Similar Fact Evidence of Disposition: Law, Discretion and Admissibility (1988) M.L.R. 252. Ireland: Mee "Similar Fact Evidence: Still hazy after all these years" (1994) D.U.L.J. 83; Mee "Similar Fact Evidence: Accusation = Guilt" (1991) 1 I.C.L.J. 122.

[2.] The normal procedure if such evidence is admitted in a criminal case is to discharge the jury, *People (D.P.P.) v. Marley* [1985] I.L.R.M. 17. However, note *People v. Kavanagh*, unreported, Court of Criminal Appeal, *ex tempore*, July 7, 1997, where it was held that a trial judge was correct in directing the jury to disregard improperly admitted misconduct evidence.

– to refer to bad character evidence that is *not* so admissible. Furthermore, it has often been used in a third sense to include all bad character evidence, whether admissible or not.[4] Consequently the term has tended to create confusion and it has been avoided in this work.[5]

The four situations in which evidence of the accused's bad character is admissible in examination-in-chief are dealt with immediately below.

13.1.1   Where the bad character evidence is tendered by the accused himself

Bad character evidence may be tendered by the accused in order to show his previous misconduct or the misconduct of a co-accused. There is nothing to prevent the accused adducing evidence of his own misconduct. He may want to do so where the prosecution has the right to cross-examine him on this point, to pre-empt their raising the issue. The accused is, however, more likely to want to adduce evidence in relation to the misconduct of a co-accused. Such evidence is admissible whenever it is relevant to prove the innocence of the accused.[6]

Lowery v. R.[7] is an example of a case where the bad character of a co-accused was held to be relevant to the issue of innocence. Two accused were charged with murder. The facts were that one of them must have committed the crime. There was no motive for the crime other than sadism. One of the accused called psychological evidence to the effect that his co-accused had an aggressive personality and lacked self-control and, therefore, was the person most likely to have committed the offence. On appeal, the Privy Council held that this evidence had rightly been admitted

Lowery can be contrasted with the case of *R. v. Neale*.[8] Two individuals were charged with arson. One of the individuals claimed that he was not present at the time of the fire. He also sought to adduce evidence to the effect that the other accused had previously set fires in similar circumstances. The

---

3.   Keane, *The Modern Law of Evidence* (5th ed., Butterworths, London, 2000) uses the term in this sense at p. 458 where he states as follows: "in exceptional circumstances evidence of disposition towards wrongdoing is admitted as evidence relevant to the question of guilt on the charge before the court. Such evidence is known as 'similar fact evidence', a description which, as we shall see, is misleading". Lord Mackay has tended to use the term in this sense; see *R. v. H.* [1995] 2 All E.R. 865 at 877, where he talks about "an application to exclude evidence on the basis that it does not qualify as similar fact evidence".

4.   An example of the use of the term in this third sense is to be found in Elliott, "The Young Person's Guide to Similar Fact Evidence" [1983] Crim. L.R. 284 at 285, where he states that "similar fact evidence will not normally be allowed, because it is prejudicial to a person standing trial to have his earlier misdeeds exposed to the jury". Elliott later remarks at 288 that "the common rubric for the whole subject, Similar Fact Evidence, is misleading because it does not take account of this; we ought to be talking of Evidence of Misconduct on Former Occasions". Tapper, *Cross and Tapper on Evidence* (9th ed, Butterworths, London, 1999), p. 333 also uses the phrase in this broad sense when he describes it as "doubly misleading because it describes the exclusionary rule in a phrase more apt to describe one of the principal exceptions to it [namely striking similarity]".

5.   There is an increasing judicial tendency to discourage the use of this expression: *R. v. Wright* (1990) 90 Cr. App. R.325 at 329; *R. v. Ananthanarayanan* [1994] 2 All E.R. 847.

6.   *R. v. Miller* [1952] 2 All E.R. 667.

7.   [1974] A.C. 8.

8.   (1977) 65 Cr. App. R. 304.

court said that this was not relevant, because the accused was making the argument that he was not present. If the accused had been present, things might have been different.[9]

Another situation in which evidence of the bad character of a co-accused was sought to be raised was *R. v. Bracewell*.[10] The facts were similar to *Lowery*; a brutal murder was carried out and must have been committed by one of the co-accused. Bracewell wanted to call evidence as to the violent disposition of his co-accused. This was held to be insufficiently relevant to be admitted under the above principle.[11]

An accused may be reluctant to adduce evidence of the bad character of a co-accused if he plans to testify because of section 1(f)(iii) of the Criminal Justice (Evidence) Act 1924. This entitles a co-accused to cross-examine an accused who gives evidence about his past misconduct, if the accused has given evidence against him. The cross-examination goes to credibility and does not have to be relevant to the facts in issue. However if the accused elects not to testify, section 1(f)(iii) will be inapplicable.

13.1.2 Where the accused has put his good character in issue

The common law has always recognised a right on the part of the prosecution or a co-accused to call evidence of the accused's bad reputation or previous convictions wherever he has put his good character in issue. This principle was laid down in the case of *R. v. Rowton*.[12] However, the prosecution evidence given in rebuttal under this common law principle can only relate to previous convictions of the accused or his bad reputation among his acquaintances; it may not include evidence of specific acts of the accused or the opinion evidence of witnesses as to his reputation.[13]

There are a number of reasons why this ground is not invoked very often. Firstly, it does not allow evidence of specific acts of misconduct by the accused other than his previous convictions. Secondly, it only applies when the accused has put his good character in issue: the fact that the accused has cast

---

9. As stated at para 1.3 evidence is relevant if it tends to make the existence or non-existence of a fact in issue more likely. However, opinions may differ as to whether particular evidence is relevant, and on occasion the courts have given an artificially narrow meaning to the definition of relevance in order to exclude evidence which they feel should not be admissible or is of low weight.

10. (1979) 68 Cr. App. 44.

11. Despite the fact that the evidence in *Bracewell* was not relevant to guilt, it was ultimately admitted on an alternative ground. Bracewell's co-accused had given evidence as to his own good character. As set out above, when an accused gives evidence of his own good character, the prosecution or counsel for a co-accused may give evidence to contradict this. Such evidence goes to the credibility of the accused and is not meant to be probative as to guilt.

12. (1865) Le. & Ca. 520. See also *R. v. Butterwasser* [1948] 1 K.B. 4; *R. v. de Vere* [1981] 3 All E.R. 473.

13. *R. v. Rowton* (1865) Le. & Ca. 520; however, the previous convictions/reputed bad behaviour do not have to be similar in nature to the offence with which the accused is charged. In *R. v. Winfield* (1939) 27 Cr. App. R. 139 an accused charged with indecent assault gave evidence of his sexual morality. It was held that the prosecution could adduce evidence as to his previous convictions for offences of dishonesty. See further Munday [1997] Crim. L.R. 247.

imputations on the character of prosecution witnesses or a co-accused does not permit evidence of his bad character to be given under this principle.

Thirdly, if the accused gives evidence he can be cross-examined as to his bad character under section 1(f)(ii) or (iii) of the Criminal Justice (Evidence) Act 1924 and evidence can be adduced in reply to any incorrect or misleading answers given by him. Sections 1(f)(ii) and (iii) are not confined to situations where the accused has asserted his good character. They also include situations where the accused has cast imputations on the character of prosecution witnesses or given evidence against a co-accused. Where applicable, they allow evidence to be given of specific acts of misconduct on the part of the accused to be admitted. Section 1(f) has therefore largely superseded *R. v. Rowton*. However, in situations where the accused opts not to give evidence, the above common law rule retains some vitality.

13.1.3   *Where the bad character of the accused is a fact in issue*

Secondly, evidence of bad character will have to be adduced by the prosecution where bad character is a fact in issue, *i.e.* a matter which must be proved before the accused can be convicted of the particular offence. The offence of driving a motor vehicle while disqualified necessarily requires proof of previous misconduct. In order to convict, it must be shown that the accused previously committed a criminal offence which disqualified him from driving. Evidence of previous misconduct, therefore, is essential in order to convict the accused of this particular offence. This ground is rarely invoked because bad character is a fact in issue for very few offences.

13.1.4   *Where the bad character of the accused is relevant to a fact in issue*

In relation to most offences, previous misconduct or bad reputation does not have to be proved in order to convict. However, it may be sometimes be argued that, even though the accused's bad character is not in itself a fact in issue, it should be admitted on the alternative ground that it is relevant to a fact in issue. As outlined at para 1.2, evidence is relevant to a fact in issue if it tends to make the existence or non-existence of a fact in issue more likely.

R. v. Stratten[14] is a good example of a case in which bad character evidence could be said to be relevant to a fact in issue. The accused had been incarcerated in Broadmoor following a verdict of unfitness to plead to charges of strangling two young girls. Subsequently, he escaped from Broadmoor, and another young girl was strangled in the vicinity of the prison during the brief period of his four-hour escape. He was subsequently charged with her murder, and the prosecution sought to admit evidence of the previous murder charges brought against him.

There were strong similarities between the earlier murders and the one before the court. The victims were all young girls killed by the same method –

[14.] [1952] 2 Q.B. 911.

manual strangulation. They had not been sexually interfered with and the killings appeared to be motiveless. In none of the cases was there evidence of a struggle; nor had any attempt been made to conceal the bodies. Assuming that Straffen committed the earlier murders (and there was no attempt by the defence to contest this), this past behaviour, when combined with his presence in the area at the relevant time, significantly increased the likelihood that he was the person responsible for this subsequent crime.

As discussed at para 1.4, the normal rule in the law of evidence is that all relevant evidence is admissible. However, in a case such as *Straffen*, this rule comes into conflict with another important principle of evidence law, discussed in the previous chapter, which is the principle excluding evidence of the accused's bad character.[15] Once the jury hear that the accused committed previous crimes, their objectivity may become affected. They may attach a greater probative significance to the earlier crimes than they logically merit, failing to consider any countervailing factors in the case pointing to the innocence of the accused.[16] They may decide that Stratten deserves to be convicted of this crime because he committed the two earlier murders. Even if the jury do not fall into such errors, and reach their decision on logically correct grounds, this will not be apparent to the public, whose confidence in the integrity of the jury process may be undermined.[17]

On the other hand it could be argued that if evidence as probative as this were to be excluded, the jury would be left so blinkered as to deprive their decision of any real credibility or value.[18] This could result in public confidence in the jury system in general, and the criminal legal system as a whole, being undermined. The Irish law of evidence is, therefore, forced to strike a balance between these two arguments.[19]

The compromise reached is as follows: evidence of bad character on the part of the accused is *not* admissible just because it is relevant to a fact in issue. In order for such evidence to be admissible it must be highly relevant. A more accurate way of putting this would be to say that the probative value of

---

15. This conflict is identified by Professor Julius Stone, 46 Harv L. Rev. 954 (1932)

16. Lord Cross recognises this danger in *D.P.P. v. Boardman* [1975] A.C. 421 at 456, when he states that "the reason for this general rule [excluding evidence of bad character] is not that the law regards such evidence as inherently irrelevant but that it is believed that if it were generally admitted jurors would in many cases think that it was more relevant than it was."

17. See the comments of Zuckerman [1987] L.Q.R. 187 at 194, where he remarks that the admission of evidence of the accused's bad character "threatens two central principles of our criminal justice. The first is that in any criminal trial the accused stands to be tried, acquitted or convicted, only in respect of the offence with which he is charged. The second is that conviction must take place only if the jury are persuaded of the accused's guilt beyond reasonable doubt.... It is the risk to these cherished principles that accounts for the passion shown by judicial pronouncements on the subject, rather than the simple risk of over-estimation of probative value".

18. As Julius Stone, 46 *Harv L. Rev.* 954 (1932) points out: "There is a point in the ascending scale of probability when it is so near to certainty, that it is absurd to shy at the admission of the prejudicial evidence".

19. Lord Mustill in *R. v. H.* [1995] 2 All E.R. 865 at 885 stated that "the function of the trial judge is not to decide as an intellectual process whether the evidence satisfies prescribed conditions, but to strike as a matter of individual judgment, in the light of his experience and common sense, a balance between the probative value of the evidence and its potentially damaging effect".

the bad character evidence must be high enough to outweigh the drawbacks of admitting it. The precise formula used by the judiciary is as follows: the probative value of the evidence must outweigh its prejudicial effect. The rest of this chapter will be devoted to a discussion of this test, which is the ground most often invoked by the prosecution when they wish to admit bad character evidence in examination-in-chief.

13.2 Previous approaches to admission of bad character evidence relevant to fact in issue

Over the past century, a number of different approaches have been used to decide when evidence of bad character relevant to a fact in issue should be admitted in examination-in-chief. It is useful to compare these approaches.

The original principle governing the admission of such evidence was laid down in the case of *Makin v. Attorney General*[20] However, in the 1960s this was replaced by the *Boardman* approach which, as generally understood, required the bad character evidence to demonstrate "striking similarity" before it could be admitted. *D.P.P. v. Boardman*[21] has itself been supplanted by the test laid down in *D.P.P. v. P.*[22] of balancing prejudicial effect against probative value.

Irish judges have in turn subscribed to the *Makin*, the *Boardman*, and the *P.* approaches. It is likely that *D.P.P. v. P.* will not be the final pronoucement on this issue, and that there will be further judicial attempts to refine the circumstances in which evidence of bad character and previous misconduct on the part of the accused may be admitted in examination-in-chief.

13.2.1 Makin approach

The accused in *Makin v. Attorney General* were a married couple on trial for murder of a baby. The baby had previously been placed for adoption with them for a small sum. The baby disappeared, and when its mother tried to see it again, the accused tried to pass off another child as hers. The baby's bones were subsequently found buried in the back garden of the house in which it had last been seen. The Makins had moved from this house shortly after the disappearance. The police dug up the gardens of three other houses previously occupied by the Makins and found the dead bodies of no less than 13 infants. A number of these infants had also been left for adoption with the Makins and had subsequently disappeared. Meanwhile, criminal proceedings had been commenced against the Makins for the murder of the first baby.

The question was whether evidence of the discovery of the additional babies could be admitted at the trial for the murder of the first baby. The Makins' defence counsel objected to this evidence on the ground that it

---

[20]   [1894] A.C. 57.
[21]   [1975] A.C. 421.
[22]   [1991] 3 All E.R. 337.

breached the general principle that evidence of misconduct other than the misconduct for which the accused was on trial should not be admitted.

Lord Herschell, delivering the judgment of the Privy Council, stated as follows:

> "It is undoubtedly not competent for the prosecution to adduce evidence tending to show that the accused has been guilty of criminal acts other than those covered in the indictment, for the purpose of leading to the conclusion that the accused is a person likely from his criminal conduct or character to have committed the offence for which he is being tried.
>
> On the other hand, the mere fact that the evidence adduced tends to show the commission of other crimes does not render it inadmissible if it be relevant to an issue before the jury, and it may be so relevant if it bears upon the question whether the acts alleged to constitute the crime charged in the indictment were designed or accidental, or to rebut a defence which would otherwise be open to the accused."[23]

On the facts of *Makin*, it was held that the evidence was relevant in order to rebut the defence of inevitable accident in relation to the infant's death, which would otherwise have been open to the Makins. The application of Lord Herschell's dictum gave rise to the development of "categories of relevance". According to this approach, whether evidence of bad character could be admitted or not depended on the purpose for which it was sought to be admitted. If that purpose came within the two categories listed in the second half of the *Makin* test, *e.g.* to decide whether an act was by design or by accident, or to rebut a defence, then the evidence was admissible.

Lord Herschell had given no indication that the two categories of relevance expressly referred to in *Makin* were conclusive. A number of additional categories therefore sprang up; for example, evidence adduced for the purpose of proving identity or guilty knowledge was admissible.[24] Any evidence of bad character that did not fall into the recognised categories was inadmissible, no matter how relevant. The following are some examples of cases in which evidence of the accused's previous misconduct was admissible on the ground that it came within one of the permitted categories.

In *R. v. Ball*[25] a brother and sister were charged with incest. They were both living in the same house in which there was only one bed. Evidence showed that this bed had been shared by both the accused. They claimed that they had been sleeping together but not having sexual intercourse. Evidence that they had had sexual intercourse on previous occasions was admitted to show "guilty passion". The House of Lords applied the *Makin* test and recognised evidence adduced to show "guilty passion" as an additional category of admissible evidence under this test.

---

[23]. At p. 65.
[24]. For more examples, see Hoffman (1975) 91 L.Q.R. 193 and Mee [1994] D.U.L.J. 83.
[25]. [1911] A.C. 47.

The *Makin* approach was followed in Ireland in *People (Attorney General) v. Dempsey*.[26] The accused was charged with unlawful carnal knowledge of a girl between 15 and 17 years of age. It was held that evidence of his past bad behaviour was admissible to rebut the defence of chaste courtship. The defence was that the relationship between the defendant and the girl was completely innocent, never going beyond "cuddling and kissing". Maguire C.J. cited *R. v. Ball* and admitted the evidence of past misconduct "to establish the guilty relations between the parties and the fact that they had illicit connection".

Another Irish case that employed the categorisation approach was that of *A-G v. Kirwan*.[27] Kirwan was accused of murdering his brother. He had been found in possession of £200. His brother had had this sum in the house shortly before his death and it was now missing. The prosecution sought to adduce evidence that Kirwan had spent time in prison. The reasons for admitting this were two-fold. Firstly, the fact that Kirwan had recently been released from prison made it unlikely that he could have acquired the £200 himself. Secondly, Kirwan's stay in prison was relevant because, while there, he had learnt the trade of a butcher. His brother's body had been expertly dismembered. This evidence was allowed to the jury under the *Makin* test.

R. v. Bond[28] has similarly been explained as a situation in which the other evidence against the accused was strong. A doctor was convicted of unlawfully using instruments on his girlfriend and cohabitee with intent to procure an abortion. He claimed that he had merely been carrying out a medical examination for venereal disease with the assistance of these instruments when she miscarried spontaneously. Evidence was given by an old girlfriend and cohabitee, that he had performed an abortion on her some months earlier and had boasted about the number of abortions he had carried out. The Court for Crown Cases Reserved applied the *Makin* test and held that the evidence was admissible. However, all the judges differed as to the particular category under which the evidence should be held admissible. Some said it fell into the category of "negativing accident or mistake"; others preferred to describe it as "proof of system"; finally, some felt that it "negatived innocence of intent".

The purpose of the rule laid down in *Makin* was clear: to prevent juries ignoring the evidence in the case and jumping to the conclusion that the accused must have committed the particular crime in question merely because he had committed previous crimes or engaged in misconduct in the past. However, over the years, questions began to be asked as to whether the "categorisation" approach laid down in *Makin* was the most suitable one. According to its critics, this rule prevented the admission of vital evidence while at the same time allowing the admission of prejudicial, but not highly probative, evidence. As Zuckerman pointed out:

---

26. [1961] I.R. 288.
27. [1943] I.R. 279.
28. [1906] 2 K.B. 389.

> "The essence of the problem is that disclosure of the accused's criminal record could create prejudice irrespective of the purpose for which the prosecution calls the evidence."[29]

In addition, there was the unresolved question of the relationship between the two sentences in Lord Herschell's dictum in *Makin*. Did the second sentence lay down an exception to the rule set out in the first, or were the two principles mutually exclusive? It was argued that the common law rule against admitting evidence of bad character, as summarised in the first sentence of *Makin*, only excluded evidence of bad character which was admitted to show that because the accused had previously committed a crime of a particular type, he was more likely to commit other crimes of that type. This reasoning from propensity was known as the "forbidden chain of reasoning". According to some commentators, the situations in the second sentence did not involve the forbidden chain of reasoning and so were permitted. Rather than being an exception to the rule that evidence of misconduct should not be admitted, the situations contained in the second sentence did not breach the rule at all.

However, this analysis does not fit with the facts of *Makin* or subsequent cases such as *R. v. Stratten*.[30] As Mee[31] points out, some of situations permitted by the second sentence in *Makin* nonetheless involve the forbidden chain of reasoning:

> "While it was formerly argued, that evidence to rebut a suggestion of coincidence was relevant otherwise than via propensity, this seems now to be agreed to be false. Taking the example of Makin, while it is undoubtedly a coincidence that the bodies of so many children were found, the coincidence is based on the fact that the bodies were found on premises belonging to the same people. An essential part of the argument is that the Makins have systematically murdered children before and so are more likely to have done so on this occasion. Therefore the evidence is propensity evidence."[32]

A better view is that the common law prohibits all evidence of misconduct, irrespective of the purpose for which it has been admitted. The situations specified in the second sentence of *Makin* breach this rule but are held valid because of exceptional justifying circumstances.

The problem is that when the particular categories of admissibility developed under *Makin* are examined, it becomes somewhat difficult to identify the basis for their recognition. Gradually, criticism of the *Makin* approach began to surface and questions began to be asked as to whether it was the most suitable method for determining the exceptional cases in which evidence of bad character could be admitted. An alternative test came to the fore in the case of *Boardman v D.P.P.*[33]

[29.] (1987) 103 L.Q.R. 187, 189.
[30.] [1952] 2 Q.B. 911.
[31.] (1994) 16 D.U.L.J. 83 at 91-92.
[32.] Mee [1994] 16 D.U.L.J. 83, at pp. 92-93.
[33.] [1975] A.C. 421.

In *R. v. Lewis*[34] the judge tried to avoid applying the *Boardman* principle and to apply the *Makin* principle instead (under which the evidence was admissible) on the ground that the *Boardman* principle only applied to admit evidence that did not come within the *Makin* categories. On this view misconduct evidence could be admitted either when it came within *Makin* or when it came within *Boardman*. This confusion was caused by the dicta of some of the judges in *Boardman*.

13.2.2   Boardman approach

Boardman was the headmaster of a boarding school for boys, which specialised in language teaching for foreign pupils. In relation to one teenage pupil, Boardman was charged with the offence of attempted buggery. He was also charged with having incited another student to commit buggery. There were noticeable similarities between the allegations made by the two boys. They had been woken up in the dormitory and spoken to in a low voice, taken to the appellant's sitting room where they were invited to commit the offence, and requested to play the active role in the act of buggery. It was held by the House of Lords that the evidence of each boy in relation to the offence concerning him was admissible in deciding whether Boardman had committed the offence in relation to the other boy. The justification for this was that there were striking similarities between the two allegations of misconduct.

In the case of *Boardman v. D.P.P.* at least two members of the House of Lords, Lord Wilberforce and Lord Cross, demonstrated a willingness to depart from the categorisation approach when determining the circumstances in which evidence of the accused's bad character or previous misconduct might be admissible. In determining when such evidence might exceptionally be admitted, they put forward an approach based on degrees of relevance rather than categories of relevance.

Certain dicta of the House of Lords in *Boardman* indicate that the new test governing the admissibility of such evidence should involve balancing the probative value of the evidence against its prejudicial effect. Lord Wilberforce stated as follows:

> "The basic principle must be that the admission of similar fact evidence…is exceptional and requires a strong degree of probative force."[35]

However, Lord Wilberforce went on to add that probative force depended on the misconduct being strikingly similar in nature to the offence with which the accused is charged:

> "Probative force is derived, if at all, from the circumstance that the facts testified to by the several witnesses bear to each other such a striking similarity that they must, when judged by experience and common sense, either all be true, or have arisen from a cause common to the witnesses or from pure coincidence."[36]

[34.]   (1983) 76 Cr. App. R. 33.
[35.]   *supra*, at 444.

And Lord Salmon said:

> "If the crime charged is committed in a uniquely or strikingly similar manner to other crimes committed by the accused the manner in which the other crimes were committed may be evidence upon which a jury could reasonably conclude that the accused was guilty of the crime charged. The similarity would have to be so unique or striking that common sense makes it inexplicable on the basis of coincidence."[37]

Boardman therefore raised two slightly different tests – the striking similarity test and the prejudicial v. probative test, which would allow evidence to be admitted even where it was not strikingly similar so long as its prejudicial value outweighed its probative effect.[38]

After *Boardman* there were in fact three possible views as to how the exceptional circumstances in which evidence of misconduct was admissible should be defined. Some commentators believed that *Boardman* had not disposed of the *Makin* test. This was prompted by the fact that three of the judges in the case had endorsed the dictum of Lord Herschell in *Makin,* quoted above. Others interpreted *Boardman* as having abolished the *Makin* test and laid down an alternative test, namely that similar fact evidence was only admissible if striking similarity was present. The resemblances here were said to be striking. Other examples of cases in which there would be striking similarity were given by Lord Hailsham. These cases would probably be categorised today as situations in which probative effect outweighed prejudicial value.

> "While it would certainly not be enough to identify the culprit in a series of burglaries that he climbed in through a ground floor window, the fact that he left the same humorous limerick on the walls of the sitting room or an esoteric symbol written in lipstick on the mirror, might well be enough. In a sex case…while a repeated homosexual act by itself might be quite insufficient to admit the evidence as confirmatory of identity and design, the fact that it was alleged to have been performed wearing the ceremonial head-dress of a Red Indian chief or other eccentric garb might well in appropriate circumstances suffice."[39]

Athough the case of *R. v. Anderson*[40] was decided after *Boardman*, the striking similarity test was not the one used. This shows that even nowadays judges tend to pick and choose between the various tests to achieve the result they want. The evidence in this case would not have satisfied the striking similarity test, although it would have satisfied the prejudicial v. probative test. The

---

36. *Ibid.*, at 444.
37. Lord Morris said that the misconduct evidence must be "of close and striking similarity" (at. 441) and Lord Hailsham said that it must exhibit "a striking resemblance" (at 445). Lord Cross was the only member of the House of Lords to clearly state that probative value could exist through factors other than striking similarity.
38. For analysis see Hoffman (1975) 91 L.Q.R. 193; Ellish [1983] Crim L.R. 284; Lunt [1987] C.L.J. 83; Zuckermann (1987) 103 L.Q.R. 187; Carter (1985) 48 M.L.R. 29.
39. At p. 454.
40. [1988] 2 All E.R. 549.

prejudicial value of the evidence was slight, given that the defendant had already drawn to the jury's attention that she was involved in illegal I.R.A. activities. The precise offence for which she was wanted was not sought to be specified.

Thirdly, it was suggested that *Boardman* laid down a test of weighing probative value against prejucicial effect and the striking similarity situation was merely one example of a case in which probative value would exceed prejudicial effect.[41] Matters were clarified when the House of Lords in *D.P.P. v. P.*[42] opted for the third approach and decided that striking similarity was not absolutely necessary for similar fact evidence to be admissible. Applying this third approach, evidence of misconduct or bad character on the part of the accused will be admissible if there is striking similarity. It will also be allowed in other situations where its prejudicial effect exceeds its probative value. However, what these other situations will be is hard to say.

13.3 The current test laid down in *D.P.P. v. P.*[43]

The applicant was accused of rape and incest in relation to his two daughters. The question was whether the first daughter's evidence of abuse should be admitted as evidence to support the second daughter's story, and vice versa. It was demonstrated that although his behaviour in relation to the two daughters could not be said to be strikingly similar, there were some parallels in relation to the prolonged nature of the abuse, the father's domination over the abused child, and the fact that he paid for abortions for each daughter when they fell pregnant. In the circumstances it was held that the evidence given by daughter A. in relation to her abuse by the accused could be taken into account in deciding whether the accused abused daughter B. and vice versa.

The House of Lords in *D.P.P. v. P.* looked at situations in the case law in which evidence of misconduct had been admitted and said that these situations could not be explained by the *Makin* categorisation approach. Nor were they situations of striking similarity within the traditional interpretation of *Boardman*. Instead, they were situations in which the probative effect of the evidence outweighed its prejudicial value.

Lord Mackay stated as follows:

> "What has to be assessed is the probative force of the evidence in question, the infinite variety or circumstances in which the question arises, demonstrates that there is no single manner in which this can be achieved. Whether the evidence

---

41. This interpretation was supported by Lord Scarman L.J. in *R. v. Scarrott* [1978] Q.B. 1016 at 1022: "The phrase 'strikingly similar' is no more than a label...it is not to be confused with the substance of the law which it labels positive probative value is what the law requires, if similar fact evidence is to be admissible".

42. [1991] 3 All E.R. 337.

43. [1991] 2 A.C. 447. For analysis see Tapper (1992) 108 L.Q.R. 26; Pattenden (1996) 112 L.Q.R. 446; Munday (1999) 58 C.L.J. 58; Mee (1991) 1 I.C.L.J. 122.

has sufficient probative value to outweigh its prejudicial effect must in each case be a question of degree."[44]

He reinterpreted *Boardman* to mean that:

"the essential feature of evidence which is to be admitted is that its probative force in support of the allegation that an accused person committed a crime is sufficiently great to make it just to admit the evidence, notwithstanding that it is prejudicial to the accused in tending to show that he was guilty of another crime. Such probative force may be derived from striking similarities in the evidence about the manner in which the crime was committed and the authorities provide illustrations of that ... But restricting the circumstances in which there is sufficient probative force to overcome prejudice of evidence relating to another crime to cases in which there is some striking similarity between them is to restrict the operation of the principle in a way which gives too much effect to a particular manner of stating it, and is not justified in principle."

This test has been followed in a number of Irish cases.[45] In *C.B. v. D.P.P.*[46] the applicant was charged with indecent assault and rape of his three daughters between 1962 and 1974. He sought an order seeking separate trials in relation to each daughter's allegations. Budd J. redefined Irish law on the admission of evidence of the accused's bad character in examination-in-chief:

"[M]ore recently stress has been laid on the positive probative value of the evidence rather than the use of striking similarity as the test for admissibility in cases. This is because striking similarity is just one of the ways in which evidence may exhibit the exceptional degree of probative force required for admissibility, so that to insist upon it in an equal degree in all cases would be incorrect."[47]

In support of this Budd J. cited *D.P.P. v. P.*, quoting extensively from that case.

Budd J. went on to say that the allegations of the three complainants were "strikingly consistent and similar". All had been abused from a very young age in the absence of their mother, all had been subjected to acts of sexual self-gratification on the part of the father, and in all cases these acts had been accompanied by threats of violence.

He emphasised, however, that the test was now one of probative force rather than striking similarity:

"The mere existence of multiple accusations of similar offences does not mean that the evidence will be admissible as it is still essential that there should be a sufficient degree of probative force to overcome the prejudicial effect of such evidence. The probative value of multiple accusations may depend in part on their similarity, but also on the unlikelihood that the same person would find

---

44. [1975] A.C. 421.
45. In *Pfennig v. R.* (1995) 182 C.L.R. 461 the High Court of Australia stated that it also applied in Australia (citing *Hoch v. R.* (1988) 165 C.L.R. 292), Canada (citing *R. v. B* (C.R.) [1990] 1 S.C.R. 717) and New Zealand (citing *R. v. McIntosh* (1991) 8 C.R.N.Z. 514).
46. [1997] 3 I.R. 140.
47. At p. 154.

himself falsely accused on various occasions by different and independent individuals. The making of multiple accusations is a coincidence in itself, which has to be taken into account in deciding admissibility."[48]

In conclusion, Budd J. found that the evidence was admissible on the basis of the principles in *D.P.P. v. P.*

The test laid down in *D.P.P. v. P.* has subsequently been applied by the Irish courts in a number of other cases. In *People (D.P.P.) v. Kelly*[49] the appellant worked in a residential home for traveller children. He was charged with a number of sexual offences against three different individuals. In relation to two boys under his care, he was charged with the offence of attempted buggery. In relation to another boy, he was charged with indecent assault and buggery. One of the boys had allegedly been assaulted in a dormitory at night. However, the offences against the other two boys had been allegedly carried out while they were sharing a bed with the accused in a caravan. The accused applied to have each of the counts on the indictment tried separately.[50]

Barron J. cited *D.P.P. v. P.* as authority for the rule that

> "When the identity of the perpetrator is unknown some special feature is necessary before evidence is admissible to establish that it was the same perpetrator in each case. Where, however, the alleged perpetrator is not known it is not necessary to have that special feature because the issue is no longer was it done by the same person but was an offence committed on each occasion."[51]

In applying the rule, Barron J. began by stating that in deciding whether several counts should be heard together the real test was whether the evidence in respect of one count would be admissible in respect of the other, were they to be tried separately. He continued by confirming the applicability of *D.P.P. v. P.* in the Irish context, stating that where the probative value of the evidence outweighs its prejudicial effect it ought to be admitted. However, it should be noted that Barron J's judgment also referred back to the earlier *Makin* approach, with its reference to system evidence:

> "On the one hand, there is system evidence, which is so admissible, and on the other hand, there is similar fact evidence, which is inadmissible."[52]

---

48. At p. 157.

49. Unreported, Court of Criminal Appeal, December 13, 1999. See *McDermott* [2000] 10 I.C.L.J. 318.

50. The current rule is that offences can only be joined if the evidence of one of the offences would have been admissible at the trial of the other if they had been kept separate and vice versa. Otherwise, the judge should sever the indictment in exercise of his power under the Criminal Justice (Administration) Act 1924: *Conlon v. Kelly*, unreported, High Court, McGuinness J. December 14, 1999. As evidence of the other offences is misconduct evidence, the offences can only be joined if the probative value of one offence in relation to the other outweighs its prejudicial value and vice versa. In the past it was possible for offences to be joined even if this test was not satisfied; the trial judge would simply direct that evidence in respect of one count could not be considered in relation to the other – there was no need to separate them unless they were strikingly dissimilar: *R. v. Beggs* [1989] 90 Cr. App. Rep. 24.

51. At pp. 25-26.

52. At pp. 6-7.

He concluded by holding that the counts in relation to one of the boys should have been tried separately because his story was different. The counts relating to the other two boys were similar enough to be tried together. They are alleged to have been committed in unusual but identical circumstances, on a visit to the caravan, while the two were sleeping in a double bed, in the same furtive manner and by broadly similar actions.

In *People v. Byrne*[53] the applicants were charged with various offences in relation to drug importation. They were trying to smuggle in a large amount of drugs on a West of Ireland beach. Evidence was given that the Gardaí had prior knowledge of the applicants' involvement in criminal activities. The *D.P.P. v. P.* test was applied, and, in the circumstances, it was held that the probative value of this evidence outweighed its prejudicial effect.

13.3.1 The application of prejudicial value/probative effect test

The generality of the *D.P.P. v. P.* test represents both its strength and its weakness. This generality allows most of the cases prior to *D.P.P. v. P.* which did not fit within either the *Makin* or *Boardman* categories[54] to be re-explained as examples of the *P.* approach, thus bringing a much needed consistency into the law. However, such generality also makes the test difficult to apply, and gives an alarming amount of discretion to judges in this controversial area.

The test is a three-stage one. Firstly, it is necessary to assess the probative force that the evidence of bad character or previous misconduct carries. Secondly, it is necessary to assess the prejudicial effect of such evidence. Thirdly, it is necessary to weigh the prejudicial value of such evidence against its probative effect.

(1) Assessing probative force

Lord Mackay in *D.P.P. v. P.* explained the approach that should be taken:

> "... I would deduce the essential feature of evidence which is to be admitted is that its probative force in support of the allegation that an accused person committed a crime is sufficiently great to make it just to admit the evidence, notwithstanding that it is prejudicial to the accused in tending to show that he was guilty of another crime. Such probative force may be derived from striking similarities in evidence about the manner in which the crime was committed ... But restricting the circumstances in which there is sufficient probative force to overcome prejudice of evidence relating to another crime to cases in which there is some striking similarity between them is to restrict the operation of the principle in a way which gives too much effect to a particular manner of stating it, and is not justified in principle ... what has to be assessed is the probative force of the evidence in question ... there is no single manner in which this can

---

53. Unreported, Court of Criminal Appeal, December 17, 1997
54. Thus causing an enormous amount of trouble to commentators.

be achieved. Whether the evidence has sufficient probative value to outweigh its prejudicial effect must in each case be a question of degree."[55]

It has continually been emphasised that in assessing probative force the misconduct evidence should not be looked at in isolation. Instead, when assessing probative force, it has been stated that it is necessary to look at the misconduct evidence together with the other evidence in the case.[56]

(a) Looking at misconduct together with other evidence in case

If there is other strong evidence pointing to guilt, this taken together with the misconduct evidence has sufficient probative force to outweigh the prejudicial effect of the misconduct evidence.[57] In such a situation, the evidence of previous misconduct of the same type merely performs the function of the straw that breaks the camel's back, and does not have to have strikingly similar characteristics in order to be admitted.

For example in *R. v. Ball*[58] the misconduct evidence taken in isolation was not particularly strong. The fact that incest had been committed on a previous occasion did not mean that it had been committed during the particular time alleged. However, the fact that the couple were sharing a bed during that time made the evidence of the prior incest relevant. However, no matter how strong the other evidence, the previous misconduct must have some relevance in order to be admissible – the fact that the brother was a thief would not have been relevant to deciding whether he had committed incest.

R. v. Bond,[59] discussed above, has been explained as another situation in which the other evidence was strong. A doctor was convicted of unlawfully using instruments on his girlfriend/cohabitee with intent to procure an abortion. He claimed that he had merely been carrying out a medical examination for venereal disease with the assistance of these instruments when she miscarried spontaneously. Evidence was given by an old girlfriend and cohabitee, that he had performed an abortion on her some months earlier and boasted about the number of abortions he had carried out. The Court for Crown Cases Reserved applied the Makin test and held that the evidence was admissible. However, all the judges differed as to the particular category under which the evidence should be held admissible. Some said it fell into the category of "negativing accident or mistake"; others preferred to describe it as "proof of system"; finally, some felt that it "negatived innocence of intent". As with *R. v. Ball*, it is questionable whether the evidence in *R. v. Bond* would

---

[55.] [1991] 2 A.C. 447 at 460.

[56.] See Lord Cross in *Boardman v. D.P.P.* where he states that "the question must always be whether the similar fact evidence taken together with the other evidence would…point so strongly to his guilt that only an ultra-cautious jury, if they accepted it as true, would acquit…"

[57.] However, Zuckerman points out that "in some cases the strength of the rest of the evidence will count for the exclusion of [the bad character evidence] rather than its admission because a point will come at which the rest of the evidence is so strong that any evidence of past crime can add only little weight but much prejudice." (1987) L.Q.R. 187 at 192.

[58.] [1911] A.C. 47.

[59.] [1906] 2 K.B. 389.

satisfy the striking similarity test. However, according to commentators, it would satisfy the *P.* test.

Another example of the bad character evidence providing strong probative force without striking similarity is to be found in the Australian case of *Pfennig v. R.*[60] Pfennig was charged with the murder of a nine-year-old boy who had disappeared without trace. The boy's bike and clothes were found at a spot beside a river. If the boy had drowned in the river, it was most unlikely that his body would not have been recovered. The appellant admitted that he had been at the spot where the boy disappeared that day and had actually spoken to him. In the circumstances, evidence was permitted in relation to the previous abduction and rape of another boy by the appellant. The previous misconduct was not strikingly similar, but its probative force, when taken together with the other circumstantial evidence, was strong.

If there is no other evidence in the case pointing to the accused's guilt, the probative force of the misconduct evidence has to be very strong. Cases such as this may require striking similarities at least if their relevance depends on an argument from disposition. An example of a case where there was no direct evidence and the circumstantial evidence against the accused was very slight was *R. v. Stratten.*[61] The accused was charged with strangling a young girl. The death had occurred during the four hours while the accused had escaped from Broadmoor, where he was incarcerated after being found unfit to plead to charges of having killed two young girls. The accused had commented to the police, "I did not kill her", at a time when neither the police nor the newspapers had made reference to the death of a young girl.

Evidence was admitted here of two previous murders in relation to which Stratten had been held unfit to plead and committed, in order to identify him as the perpetrator in the case. The grounds of admission were firstly, that each of the victims was a young girl; secondly, each of the young girls was killed by manual strangulation; thirdly, no attempt was made at sexual interference, nor was there an apparent motive. Further, there was no evidence of a struggle, and no attempt was made to conceal the body. The test applied in this case was the *Makin* test. This would have satisfied the striking similarity test in *Boardman*. When applying the *D.P.P. v. P.* test, we see that, in this case, the other evidence was weak and, therefore, the evidence of misconduct had to do most of the work. It had to be, and was, highly probative in order to be effective.

Another case in which the high probative force was provided by similarities in relation to the misconduct was *R. v. Mullen.*[62] Mullen pleaded guilty to three cases of burglary in the Northeast of England, but not guilty to three other cases. In all the burglaries, the method of entry involved the use of a blow-torch to crack glass. Only six offenders from the Northeast were known to have used such a method. Evidence of the burglaries was held to have been properly admitted. Again, this case can easily be explained under *D.P.P. v. P.*

[60.] (1995) 182 C.L.R. 461
[61.] [1952] 2 Q.B. 911.
[62.] (1992) Crim. L.R. 735.

Although the other evidence was weak, the similarities were strong, giving the evidence high probative value.

However, in deciding whether striking similarity is present, it is not necessary for any one feature, which two offences have in common, to be "strikingly similar"; what matters is whether the overall effect is one of striking similarity. In *R. v. Julian* the New Zealand Court of Criminal Appeal stated:

> "The requisite standard of striking similarity may be attained not only by the presence of a singular striking reflection but by a combination of matters which taken together meet the same level of resemblance. They so far negative coincidence as to point to the same author..."[63]

This approach was followed by the Australian courts in *R. v. Fogarty*:

> "The question whether the evidence was or was not relevant... depends upon whether one can see in all these 14 thefts not only a similarity of procedure but such a marked similarity, such a connection between them, that one can detect in them, as a whole, a system and a technique which might well lead to the reasonable inference that it was the same person who had committed each of them."[64]

(b) Misconduct must be clearly linked to accused in order to have probative force

In assessing the probative force of the accused's misconduct and the degree to which it, taken together with the other evidence, points to the accused's guilt, it is important to note that the misconduct must be linked to the accused in some way in order to have probative value.[65]

This link failed to be satisfied in *Harris v. D.P.P.*,[66] where a policeman was charged on indictment of eight counts of larceny. He was acquitted on seven counts and convicted on the eighth. There were offences in May, June and July 1951. Evidence showed that, on each occasion, someone entered, the same method of entry being used, and only part of the money was stolen. On the first seven counts, the only evidence connecting the accused was that none occurred while he was on leave and that on each occasion he was on duty in the area. On the eighth occasion he was on duty and was found near the office shortly after the alarm. Stolen money was found in a nearby bin. His conviction was quashed because the trial judge had failed to warn the jury that the evidence of the first seven counts could not be relied upon in relation to the eighth.

---

63. [1981] 1 N.Z.L.R. 743 at 746.
64. [1959] V.R. 594 *per* O'Bryan J. at 597.
65. See *R. v. Downey* [1995] 1 Cr. App. R. 547 and *R. v. John (W)* [1998] 2 Cr. App. R. 289; Pattenden (1996) 112 L.Q.R. 446 provides a comprehensive discussion of this area.
66. [1952] 1 All E.R. 1044.

According to Viscount Simon L.C.:

> "Evidence of similar facts cannot in any case be admissible to support an accusation against the accused unless they are connected in some relevant way with the accused and with his participation in the crime...evidence of other occurrences which merely tend to deepen supicion does not go to prove guilt...evidence as to the thefts which occurred on the first seven occasions was not admissible for the purpose of the trial of the appellant on the eighth count, because the appellant was not proved to have been near the shop or even in the market at the time when these thefts occurred."[67]

Harris may be contrasted with the case of *R. v. Mansfield*.[68] Mansfield was convicted of arson for three offences. His application for separate trials in respect of each fire was rejected by the trial judge who held that the alleged similarities between them were sufficiently striking to warrant the admission of the evidence. The offences occurred within a period of three weeks. All occurred on his employer's premises. The similarities between the three charged offences were so great that, in each case, there was a similar method of starting the fire, M was acting suspiciously, and, when questioned by the police, told lies. Concerning the third fire, a waste-paper bin from his room was found near the site of the fire.

The Court of Appeal confirmed the convictions, distinguishing Harris on the grounds that, on each occasion, M was in the vicinity of the crime, had ample opportunity of committing the crime, and, subsequent to the offences, behaved suspiciously.

(c) Should cogency of misconduct evidence be taken into account in assessing its probative value?

Can the court take cogency of evidence, as well as its relevance, into account in assessing probative force? Out of the cases cited immediately above, we can see that in some cases other misconduct is proved to have been committed (*Stratten)* or admitted (*Mullen)* but in other cases such as *Bond* there is merely the word of one person that previous misconduct occurred.

It has been argued that the judge should take the possibility of collaboration between the victim and the witness into account in deciding the probative force of oral evidence of previous misconduct. However, in *D.P.P. v. H.*[69], H. was charged with sexual offences against his daughter and stepdaughter. The courts agreed that there existed a risk of collusion between the two complainants. Nonetheless, the evidence was admissible. Lord Mackay held that the judge should assume the truth of the testimony in assessing its probative force and leave the question of collaboration for the jury.

It was stated that the question of collusion went not only to the admissibility of similar fact evidence but also to its credibility, an issue for the jury, and it

---

[67] At p. 711.
[68] [1978] 1 All E.R. 134.
[69] [1995] 2 Cr. App. R. 437.

would be wrong for the judge to decide whether there is a risk of collusion, because he would inevitably be drawn into considering whether the evidence is untrue and, hence, whether there is a real possibility that the accused is innocent. The one exception is if it appears that no reasonable jury could accept the evidence as free from collusion, in which case the judge must withdraw the evidence. Where the question of collusion has been raised, the judge must draw the question of collusion to the attention of the jury.

The following extract from the judgment of Lord Mackay L.C., summarising the above principles, is worth quoting in full:

> "Where there is an application to exclude evidence [of bad character] ... and the submission raises a question of collusion (not only deliberate but including unconscious influence of one witness by another) the judge should approach the question of admissibility on the basis that the similar facts alleged are true and apply the test in ... *R v P* accordingly. It follows that generally collusion is not relevant at this stage.
>
> Secondly, if a submission is made raising a question of collusion in such a way as to cause the judge difficulty in applying the test referred to, he may be compelled to hold a voir dire. The situations in which collusion is relevant in the consideration of admissibility would arise only in a very exceptional case of which no illustration was afforded to the argument on this appeal, but I regard it as right to include this as a possibility, since it is difficult to foresee all the circumstances that might arise...
>
> Thirdly, if evidence of similar facts has been admitted and circumstances are adduced in the course of the trial which indicate that no reasonable jury could accept the evidence as free from collusion, the judge should direct the jury that it cannot be relied on as corroboration or indeed for any other purpose adverse to the defence.
>
> And fourthly, where this is not so but the question of collusion has been raised the judge must clearly draw the importance of collusion to the attention of the jury and leave it to them to decide whether, notwithstanding such evidence of collusion as may have been put before them, they are satisfied that the evidence can be relied upon as free from collusion and tell them that if they are not so satisfied they cannot properly rely upon it as corroboration or for any other purpose adverse to the defence."[70]

(2) Assessing prejudicial value

There are a number of different kinds of prejudice which may be caused by the admission of evidence of the accused's previous misconduct.

Firstly, the evidence may distort the jury's logical reasoning in a number of ways. They may conclude that, because he has committed a crime of this type on a previous occasion, he is more likely to have committed this one. Particularly if a number of counts are joined together, the jury may come to the

---

[70] At p. 451.

conclusion that with so many charges against the accused, he must be guilty. As McGuinness J. remarked in *Conlon v Kelly*:

> "A jury having to try an accused person for a number of quite distinctive offences may well be tempted to think that there cannot be smoke without fire, that the Accused would hardly be facing such a variety of charges unless he was guilty of some at least."[71]

In particular, if there is a question as to whether the accused committed the past misconduct or not, the jury may confuse the question of whether he committed the past misconduct with whether he committed the misconduct before them. In addition, the evidence may distort the jury's moral reasoning.

Furthermore, the police may focus inquiries on the accused's past and not look well enough into the facts of the case. There may be problems with prolonged trials and added expense, and damage may be caused to the principle of offender rehabilitation.

One question that has yet to be resolved is whether the prejudicial value varies in every case or whether it is a constant fixed value. Evidence of previous sexual offences may have prejudice beyond their relevance in the case of non-sexual offences. Also, evidence of a previous murder may cause unjustified prejudice in relation to other offences.

(3) Weighing prejudicial value against probative effect

In this context one commentator has remarked:

> "The application of the rule depends upon the precise balance between probative force and prejudicial effect. It is perhaps difficult to understand by what common criterion such balancing can be achieved ... the most serious deficiencies of the decision in *D.P.P. v P.* lay in its reluctance to emphasise the high standard which the evidence needs to achieve to overcome its inevitably prejudicial effect, or to explore very far the ways in which this could be achieved."[72]

However, some guidance may be achieved from the fact that the House of Lords in *D.P.P v. P.* did not see their test as a new one; rather they saw it as the only explanation of previous case law. Some guidance as to the application and scope of the *D.P.P v. P.* test may be achieved by looking at previous situations in which evidence of bad character and previous misconduct has been admitted.

[71.] Unreported, High Court, McGuinness J., December 14, 1999.
[72.] *Cross and Tapper on Evidence* (9th ed. Butterworths, London, 1999) pp. 341-345.

13.3.2 Examining existing case law in light of D.P.P. v. P. approach

(1) Cases where evidence of previous misconduct is relevant other than an argument from disposition

Firstly, there are cases where the relevance of the similar fact evidence does not depend on reasoning from the accused's disposition. Their relevance is not based on the fact that because an accused committed crime of this type in the past, he is more likely to have committed this one. Tapper[73] says that where evidence of the relevant discreditable conduct of the accused is relevant otherwise than by way of an argument involving a step relying upon his disposition, it is admissible without having to satisfy the prejudicial versus probative test. He uses *R. v. Mackie*[74] in support of this argument.

In this case, the appellant was convicted of the manslaughter of a three-year-old boy, to whom he stood *in loco parentis*. The boy fell downstairs when running away from the appellant and died as a result of his injuries. It was alleged that the boy was running away from the appellant because of his fear of ill-treatment, the appellant having disciplined the boy excessively on earlier occasions. It was held that such evidence was properly admitted to show the state of mind of the boy at the time, proof of which was an essential part of the prosecution case:

> "That they did not include evidence of the commission of offences similar to those with which the appellant was charged does not mean that they are not logically probative in determining the guilt of the appellant. Indeed we are of the opinion that taken as a whole they are inexplicable on the basis of coincidence and that they are of positive probative value in assisting to determine the truth of the charges against the appellant, in that they tended to show that he was guilty of the offences charged."[75]

It is difficult to explain *R. v. Mackie* as an example of the prejudicial versus probative test. The evidence was not particularly probative – there was no other evidence supporting the argument that the boy fell while running away from the accused. On the other hand, the evidence was highly prejudicial.

Cases such as *Mackie* involve a high risk of prejudice and distorted reasoning and, therefore, as a matter of policy, should be subject to the same scheme as cases where there is an argument from disposition. *R. v. Mackie* was after all a case decided prior to *D.P.P. v. P.*, and not all prior cases can be expected to be compatible with the prejudicial versus probative test. Despite Tapper's arguments,[76] the common law has traditionally treated these cases as being subject to the same test as other misconduct evidence and the ratio in *D.P.P. v. P.* applies equally to them. This is demonstrated by the following two cases. In both cases, the misconduct evidence was relevant other than by a

---

[73.] *Ibid.*, at p. 359.
[74.] (1973) 57 Cr. App. R. 4.
[75.] At p. 450
[76.] *Supra*, n. 72.

reasoning from disposition. In both cases, the standard test for misconduct evidence was applied.

In *R. v. Anderson* the accused was convicted of conspiracy to cause explosions. She had been found with false identification papers. She gave evidence that she knew nothing about any such conspiracy and claimed that she had the identification papers because she was involved in smuggling escaped I.R.A. prisoners out of the country. The question was whether the prosecution were entitled to draw the jury's attention to the fact that she was wanted by the police in Northern Ireland. The ostensible reason the prosecution wanted to mention this was because this fact would make it unlikely that the I.R.A. would have used her for smuggling purposes and therefore weakened her defence. It was held that the evidence was admissible under the categorisation approach in *Makin*; it went to rebut a defence. This case rebuts Tapper's arguments since it is an example of *Makin* being applied even though the relevance of the evidence does not depend on the forbidden reasoning. This case would achieve the same result under *D.P.P. v. P.* The prejudicial effect of the evidence was limited because she had already admitted to the jury that she was involved with an illegal organisation.

Attorney General v. Kirwan[77] has been discussed above. Again, the *Makin* test was applied. Kirwan was accused of murdering his brother. He had been found in possession of £200. His brother had had this sum in the house shortly before his death and it was now missing. The prosecution sought to adduce evidence that Kirwan had spent time in prison. The reasons for admitting this were two-fold. Firstly, the fact that Kirwan had recently been released from prison made it unlikely that he could have acquired the £200 himself. Secondly, Kirwan's stay in prison was relevant because, while there, he had learnt the trade of a butcher. His brother's body had been expertly dismembered. Despite the fact that the misconduct evidence was admissible other than by an argument from disposition, this evidence was subjected to the *Makin* test before being admitted. Today, the evidence would be admitted on the grounds that its probative value outweighs its prejudicial effect.

It is clear in cases where the relevance does not depend on a reasoning from disposition that the misconduct evidence does not have to be strikingly similar or indeed be the same type of misconduct as the misconduct charged, for example, as in *Kirwan* or *Anderson*.

(2) Cases where a crime has definitely been committed and it is argued that because accused has engaged in previous misconduct, he must be the offender

Another type of case is one where a crime has been committed and it is argued that because the accused has engaged in previous misconduct, he must be the offender. Because the relevance of the misconduct evidence depends on an argument from disposition to the effect that because the accused has engaged

---

77. [1943] I.R. 279.

in this misconduct before, he is likely to have done it again, the previous misconduct must at least be of the same type or a connected type.The degree to which the prior misconduct must be strikingly similar varies depending on the strength of the other evidence in the case. There must be some other evidence in the case – if not direct witness testimony, at least circumstantial evidence that the accused was in the vicinity of the crime scene. *Stratten*[78] and *Mullen*[79] mentioned above are good examples of this.

In addition, it must be shown that the previous misconduct was that of the accused. Otherwise, the probative force of the misconduct evidence is nil, as shown by *Harris v. D.P.P.*[80] Sometimes there may be a number of crimes and the prosecution wants to have both crimes tried together and add evidence from each together to identify the accused as the offender. This is not possible under the *Harris* approach, which takes the view that in order to bring in evidence of previous misconduct, it must be shown that the accused was the person who committed the previous misconduct. This may be contrasted with an alternative approach in *R. v. Downey*[81] which states that if it is clear that the same person committed both crimes, evidence, relevant to the issue of identity can be added together from each count (whether or not sufficient to settle the issue of identity on the count to which it relates) in order to establish the identity of that person.

The approach in *R. v. Downey* was followed in the case of *R. v. John (W.),*[82] in which it was stated:

> "Evidence tending to show that a defendant has committed an offence charged in count A may be used to reach a verdict on count B and vice versa, if: the circumstances of both offences...are such as to provide sufficient probative support for the conclusion that the defendant committed both offences and it would therefore be fair for the evidence to be used in this way notwithstanding the prejudicial effect of so doing."[83]

(3) Cases where the issue is whether a crime has been committed and it is argued that because the accused committed a crime of the type alleged in the past, he must have committed one here

Another type of case in which misconduct evidence may be sought is in order to show that a crime has been committed, for example where someone has

---

78. *R. v. Stratten* [1952] 2 Q.B. 911.
79. *R. v. Mullen* (1992) Crim. L.R. 735.
80. The *Harris* approach was approved by the Court of Criminal Appeal in *R. v. McGranaghan* [1995] 1 Cr. App. R. 559. Glidewell L.J. at 573 stated: "If it is sought to adduce similar fact evidence in order to prove that one of two or more offences was committed by the defendant, in our view such evidence may only be admitted if the jury are sure on evidence other than the similar fact evidence that the defendant is guilty of the other offence".
81. [1995] 1 Cr. App. R. 547.
82. [1998] 2 Cr. App. R. 289; *R. v. Black* [1995] Crim. L.R. 640 and *R. v. Barnes* [1995] 2 Cr. App. R. 491 also approved the *Downey* approach. For a comparison of the two approaches see Pattenden (1996) L.Q.R. 446.
83. At p. 299.

disappeared and the question is whether they have been murdered, or in a case of alleged rape where consent is in issue. The issue here is not one of identity: the issue is whether a crime has been committed at all. The relevance of the misconduct evidence here again depends on an argument from disposition; the fact that the accused has committed a crime of this type in the past makes it more likely that he has done so here. Whether the similar fact evidence is admissible here depends on the strength of the other evidence.

In this situation the danger is that a crime may be invented which has not actually occurred. For this reason, it is essential that there be other evidence either direct or circumstantial which indicates that the crime has been committed. Past misconduct on its own, no matter how similar, should not be enough to convict here.

The degree of similarity between the past misconduct and the crime alleged depends on the strength of the other evidence. The other evidence, looked at in conjunction with the evidence of previous misconduct, must have sufficient probative force to outweigh its prejudicial effect. If the other evidence is strong, the past misconduct does not have to be as similar.

(a) Murder

In murder cases where there were no witnesses to the killing, the only evidence that a crime has been committed is circumstantial. Striking similarity is particularly necessary in cases where there is no direct testimony of the commission of the crime. The *Makin* case was one case where there were striking similarities between the past misconduct and the crime charged. Another was the case of *R. v. Smith (George Joseph)*.[84]

Smith was accused of murdering his wife, whom he had recently married. He sought to explain her death by a supposed epileptic fit in the bath. Evidence was admitted of the subsequent deaths of two other women to whom he had been married. In each case, Smith stood to gain financially by their deaths. He had informed the doctor that each of them had epilepsy. The bathroom door was unlocked in each case. The woman was found drowned in the bath.

Smith was decided at a time when the *Makin* principle was still in operation. It was held in this case that the evidence was admissible because it fell into the category of showing system or design.

Lord Reading C.J. stated:

> "If you find an accident which benefits a person and you find that the person had been sufficiently fortunate to have that accident happen to him a number of times, benefiting him each time, you draw a very strong, frequently irresistible inference that the occurrence of so many accidents benefiting him is such a coincidence that it cannot have happened without design".[85]

[84.] (1915) 11 Cr. App. R. 229.

[85.] At p. 233.

This was a case cited in *Boardman* as having striking similarity. Now it would be defined as a case where the probative value of the evidence was so great as to outweigh its prejudicial effect.

Striking similarity was absent in *Attorney General v. Fleming*.[86] This is an example of a pre-*D.P.P. v. P.* case in which bad character evidence was admitted in the absence of any striking similarity between the earlier misconduct and that with which the accused was charged. It is worth noting, however, that, in this case, the other evidence against the accused was very strong. The appellant was charged with murdering his wife by hitting her on head with a heavy implement. The prosecution adduced evidence to show that over a year earlier he had tried to poison her with strychnine over an affair he was having with a young girl.

He had told the girl that his aunt had had a stroke and if she had another, it might kill her. There was further evidence that, prior to the wife's actual death, the girl had become pregnant and expected marriage. The girl did not know he was married and thought his wife was his aunt. Evidence of the accused's prior attempt to kill his wife was admitted to show intention on his part. In support of this conclusion, Fitzgibbon J. referred to *R. v. Bond*.[87] He also relied on an earlier Irish case, *Attorney General v. Joyce*.[88] In the latter case, the accused was charged with murder by poisoning, and evidence was allowed of an earlier attempt by the accused to poison the victim by putting guano in her milk. The evidence in this case was admitted "to prove malice".

In *R. v. Flanagan*[89] two sisters were charged with the murder of the husband of one of them. He had died after suffering agonising stomach pains. Butt J. admitted evidence to the effect that three other persons to whom the accused had access had died within the last year having exhibited the same symptoms, their exhumed bodies showing evidence of arsenical poisoning. He stated as follows:

> "[F]irst of all, and before any authority, I desire to say this, that I think, where the authorities are at all in conflict, the safest rule is to be guided by is one's common sense, and I cannot conceive that on a charge of this nature it is consistent with common sense to exclude such evidence."

He stated that he would admit evidence in order to show design:

> "It has been decided in some cases...in the case of poisoning by arsenic, that evidence of the deaths of people other than the deceased, whose death was the subject matter of the particular enquiry, might be given, with a view to showing, not that the prisoner had feloniously poisoned the deceased, but that the deceased had in fact died by poison administered by someone. That is the

---

86. [1934] I.R. 166.
87. [1906] 2 K.B. 389.
88. [1929] I.R. 526.
89. (1884) 15 Cox C.C. 403.

extent to which that authority went, and that is the extent to which I have no hesitation in saying I shall admit evidence as to the other deaths in this case." [90]

In *Attorney General v. McCabe*[91] the accused, a gardener, contacted the Civic Guard to tell them that the house where he worked was on fire. Six dead bodies were found in the house. At first they were thought to have died in the fire. The accused was subsequently charged with the murder of one of them. The prosecution case was that all the deceased had been killed by the accused before starting the fire. Evidence was given as to the position and condition of the other dead bodies and the fact that their examination had yielded evidence of arsenical poisoning. The accused appealed his conviction, arguing that this evidence was not relevant and that the jury should have been warned to ignore it.

Kennedy C.J. rejected the accused's argument, stating that the evidence was admissible under the *Makin* principle and quoting the following principle from *Taylor on Evidence*:

> "The mere fact that evidence adduced tends to show the commission of other crimes does not render it inadmissible if it bears upon the question of whether the acts alleged to constitute the crime charged in the indictment were designed or accidental, or to rebut a defence which would otherwise be open to the accused. Thus, where felonies are so connected together as to form part of one entire transaction, evidence of one may be given to show the character of the other."[92]

(b) Sexual offences

Case law in this area has been extremely confused. Arguably, the highly prejudicial character of evidence of past sexual misconduct has been underrated under the current test. In particular, the risk of collaboration in this area appears to have been given insufficient attention by the judiciary.

The only other evidence is the direct testimony of the victim. This is okay so long as there is no collaboration – of course there is no other evidence in sexual cases – but collaboration must be considered. Arguably, the present law is deficient on this.

D.P.P. v. Boardman,[93] discussed above, is of course the best known case on this issue. Boardman was the headmaster of a boarding school for boys, which specialised in language teaching for foreign pupils. In relation to one teenage pupil, Boardman was charged with the offence of attempted buggery. He was also charged with having incited another student to commit buggery. There were noticeable similarities between the allegations made by the two boys. They had been woken up in the dormitory and spoken to in a low voice, taken to the appellant's sitting room where they were invited to commit the offence,

---

90. At p. 408.
91. [1927] I.R. 129.
92. Taylor, *A Treatise on the Law of Evidence as Administered in England and Ireland* (11th ed., Sweet and Maxwell, London) Vol. 1, p. 242 sections 327. At p. 132.
93. [1975] A.C. 421.

and requested to play the active role in the act of buggery. It was held by the House of Lords that the evidence of each boy in relation to the offence concerning him was admissible in deciding whether Boardman had committed the offence in relation to the other boy. The justification for this was that there were striking similarities between the two allegations of misconduct. The House of Lords in *Boardman* recognised that the evidence of past misconduct in this case just scraped in as being admissible.

R. v. Sims[94] has been criticised as a case which should have fallen on the other side of the line. The accused was charged on three counts of buggery and one court of gross indecency. The question was whether the offences could be tried together. There were similarities between all the offences insofar as the offences were alleged to have been committed in the accused's house after the men had been invited in. The way in which the acts of indecency/buggery were performed was also similar. The courts held that the offences should be tried together. Evidence of previous acts of buggery or gross indecency with a male was admissible at the trial for sodomy and vice versa. After *Boardman*, the validity of *R. v. Sims* came into question because, arguably, the similarities in this case were not striking.

Another problem with *Sims* was that it appeared to indicate that the general rule prohibiting bad character evidence was not applicable at all in cases of sodomy. Lord Goddard C.J. stated:

> "Sodomy is a crime in a special category because ... persons who commit the offences seek the habitual gratification of a particular perverted lust, which not only takes them out of the class of ordinary men gone wrong, but stamps them with a hallmark of a special and extraordinary class as much as if they carried on their bodies some physical peculiarity."[95]

In *R. v. Shore*[96] a headmaster, was charged on several counts of indecently assaulting girls at his school The issue was whether it was permissible to admit evidence of the misconduct in relation to one girl at the trial for the misconduct in relation to another girl. It was held that the evidence of one victim was admissible at the trial of the other. All the incidents on the charge sheet concerned girls, all took place in certain locations, all involved a hand straying into the child's clothing and moving towards her genitalia.

The cases of *R. v. Novac*[97] and *R. v. Johannsen*[98] provide a useful contrast and illustrate the scope of judicial discretion in this area. In *R. v. Novac* the issue was whether evidence of a previous offence of buggery and gross indecency with a boy, allegedly committed by the accused after introducing

---

94. [1946] K.B. 532.
95. This dictum was strongly disapproved by the House of Lords in *Boardman*. Lord Cross stated that "the attitude of the ordinary man to homosexuality has changed very much even since *R. v. Sims* was decided and what was said on that subject in 1917 by Lord Summer in *Thompson v. R.* – from which the view that homosexual offences form a class apart appears to stem – sounds nowadays like a voice from another world": [1975] A.C. 421 at 458.
96. (1988) 89 Cr. App. R. 32.
97. (1976) 65 Cr. App. R. 11.
98. (1977) 65 Cr. App. R. 107.

himself to the boy in an amusement arcade, offering him a meal, and taking him to his home where the offence occurred, could be taken into account at a trial for the buggery of, and gross indecency with, another boy. The offence in relation to the second boy was again alleged to have been committed after meeting the boy in an amusement arcade, offering him a meal, and taking him to the beach where the offence occurred. This issue arose because it needed to be decided whether the offences could be tried together. On both occasions the accused was alleged to have introduced himself to the boys. It was held that the *Boardman* test rather than the *Makin* test was the one to be applied here and that the evidence was inadmissible because there was no striking similarity. Bridge L.J. stated:

> "We cannot think that two or more offences of buggery ... committed in bed at the residence of the alleged offender with boys to whom he had offered shelter can be said to have been committed in a uniquely or strikingly similar manner. If a man is going to commit buggery with a boy he picks up, it must surely be a commonplace feature of such an encounter that he will take the boy home with him and commit the offence in bed."[99]

R. v. Johannsen possessed very similar facts to *R. v. Novac*. However, in this case the Court of Appeal held that there was striking similarity:

> "We do not find it necessary to set out in much detail the sordid evidence given in this case.... The prosecution's case was that between May and December 1975 he made a practice of accosting boys in amusement arcades and similar places, offering them money or a meal or treating them to a game, taking them to his accommodation or on to the beach, and there committing the offences charged. His particular homosexual propensities were to handle the boys' penises and getting them to do the same with his, fellatio and buggery.... We have no hesitation in deciding that there were striking similarities about what happened to each of the boys – the accostings in the same kind of place, the enticements, the visits to his accommodation, his homosexual propensities and his ways of gratifying them."[100]

In *R. v. Barrington*[101] Barrington was accused of indecency offences in relation to three girls. The girls gave evidence that he had induced them to go into his house on the pretext that they were required as babysitters but that once inside he had shown them pornographic pictures, asked them to pose for photos in the nude, and committed the offences charged. The defence was that each of the girls had a private motive to tell lies and that they had put their heads together to concoct a false story against him.

Three other girls were allowed to give evidence that they had been induced to go into the house on the pretext of babysitting, and that they were shown porn pictures and asked to pose for photos in the nude. On appeal, it was argued that the evidence of these girls was inadmissible as similar fact

---

[99.] At p. 112.
[100.] (1975) 65 Cr. App. R. 101, 103.
[101.] [1981] 1 All E.R. 1132.

evidence because it included no evidence of indecent assault or of any other offence similar to those with which the appellant was charged. It was held that the evidence was properly admitted. The test applied was one of positive probative value.

Dunn L.J. in the Court of Criminal Appeal stated:

> "[I]t is well established that...evidence may in certain circumstances be led of similar facts tending to show that the accused is guilty of the offence charged. Such evidence has, it appears, hitherto only been admitted where it has disclosed the commission of similar offences though it has also included the surrounding circumstances. In some cases the similarity of the surrounding circumstances has been stressed more than the similarity of the mode of commission of the offences themselves. Surrounding circumstances include the preliminaries leading up to the offence, such as the mode and place of the initial approach and the inducement offered or words used.
>
> The various facts...in this case...were so similar to the facts of the surrounding circumstances in the evidence of the complainant that they can properly be described as "striking". That they did not include evidence of the commission of offences similar to those with which the appellant was charged does not mean that they are not logically probative in determining the guilt of the appellant. Indeed we are of opinion that taken as a whole they are inexplicable on the basis of coincidence and that they are of positive probative value in assisting to determine truth of the charges against the appellant, in that they tended to show that he was guilty of the offences with which he was charged."[102]

In *Reza v. General Medical Council*[103] R. was charged with making improper remarks and improper behaviour towards receptionists. Evidence of constant references to sex made by him to one receptionist was admissible in evidence at his disciplinary hearing in relation to the other receptionist.

In *R. v. Lewis*, the accused was convicted of indecent assault and indecency with the twin daughters of his girlfriend. He denied that one of the incidents had occurred and his defence in relation to the others was accident and innocent explanation. Evidence was admitted of his interest in and sympathy with paedophiles and possession of material from the paedophile society. His application for leave to appeal was refused.

In *Thompson v. R.*[104] the applicant was accused of gross indecency in a public toilet. His defence was "wrongful identification". After committing the offences the applicant had agreed to meet the two boys three days later at the same time and the same place. He met them and at the same time gave them money, although he said that this was to make them go away and also to pay for their faces to be washed. The police raided his flat and found photos of naked boys and powder puffs, which at the time were used in anal intercourse,

---

[102.] At p. 436.
[103.] [1991] 2 A.C. 182.
[104.] [1918] A.C. 221.

in his possession. This evidence was considered admissible similar fact evidence in identifying the accused as a homosexual and as the offender.

(c) Other offences

Past misconduct must also be adduced to show that a crime other than a murder or sexual offence has been committed. Again, the probative value it needs to possess in order to be admitted depends on the strength of the other evidence in the case.

In *People (D.P.P.) v. Wallace*[105] the accused were charged with stealing three leather jackets and suits in 1981. The three accused had gone into a store carrying a cardboard box with sellotape on it, giving the indication that it was closed, when in fact it was half open. The owner of the store watched them closely and they left without buying anything.

Evidence was given by the prosecution of a previous occasion on which two men had come into the shop, one of them carrying a cardboard box covered with sellotape. A third man came in and looked for a shirt. After a while both men left, followed by the third who had not purchased anything. After their departure a number of items were found to be missing. The accused were charged with attempted theft. The question was whether this evidence of previous misconduct had been rightly admitted. It was held that it had been because it tended to show that the box was used for purposes of stealing.

In *R. v. Rance*,[106] the accused was managing director of a building company and was convicted of corruptly procuring a payment to a local councillor. The payment was made on a certificate signed by R., which falsely described H. as a subcontractor. R.'s defence was that he must have signed the false authorisation and the cheque without knowing the true position, been tricked into signing the certificate. Evidence was admitted of two other corrupt payments, to M. and B., made on certificates that were signed by R. and containing false statements about work done by M. and B. The Court of Appeal admitted the evidence.

In *R. v. Taylor*[107] the evidence had insufficient probative value. Taylor's conviction for shopbreaking was quashed on the ground that evidence had been improperly admitted that a jemmy had been found in his possession – the evidence being that no jemmy had been used to break open the door in question, and Taylor's defence being that the door had been broken accidentally. The evidence was tendered for the sole purpose of showing him to be of a criminal disposition and likely not to have been in the doorway for an innocent purpose and was therefore inadmissible.

[105.] Unreported, Court of Criminal Appeal, November 22, 1982.
[106.] (1975) 62 Cr. App. R. 118.
[107.] (1923) 17 Cr. App. R. 109.

In *Topin v. Feron*,[108] a prosecution for wrongful picketing, Palles C.B. stated that antecedent instances of similar misconduct could be referred to in order to ascertain the intention of the accused.

13.3.3   Is the D.P.P. v. P. test a conclusive one?

(1) Application to identity cases?

The decision in *D.P.P. v. P.* left open whether or not the test should apply in identification cases – cases where a crime had been committed and the identity of the offender was in question. It was stated in *D.P.P. v. P.* that in such cases some special signature might be required in order for the evidence of bad character to be admissible.

D.P.P. v. P. was not a case involving identity. However, Lord Mackay stated *obiter* as follows:

> "Obviously in cases where the identity of the offender is in issue, evidence of a character sufficiently special reasonably to identify the perpetrator is required."[109]

He further remarked:

> "Where the identify of the perpetrator is in issue...obviously something in the nature of what has been called in the course of argument a signature or other special feature will be necessary."

The court in *R. v. West*[110] refused to apply the P. approach in an identification case and held that the old *Boardman* test of striking similarity was the appropriate one. In *R. v. West*, Rosemary West was convicted of ten murders allegedly committed by her in conjunction with her husband Frederick. The bodies of nine of her alleged victims were recovered from beneath their family home. Seven of the victims had been naked, tied up and gagged. They had been subjected to sustained sexual abuse, and their bodies had been mutilated/dismembered. Four surviving victims gave testimony at the trial – they showed that R. was a partner in the sexual abuse. It was argued that since no attempt had been made to murder the surviving victim there was no striking similarity. The Court of Appeal subscribed to the view that striking similarity was essential in identity cases, however, they felt such striking similarity was present on the facts.

However, in *R. v. John*[111] it was recognised by the Court of Appeal that striking similarities may provide sufficient probative support but are not a necessary pre-requisite to finding such support. It was stated that the special signature requirement was not necessary in all cases of identity. Where there is

---

[108.] (1996) 2 Cr. App. R. 374.
[109.] At p. 460.
[110.] (1996) 2 Cr. App. R. 374.
[111.] [1998] 2 Cr. App. R. 289, 296.

other evidence of substance before the court in identification cases, the misconduct evidence did not have to be strikingly similar.

R. v. John involved charges of false imprisonment and indecent assault on C. and of false imprisonment of S. Most of the descriptions of the attacker fitted the appellant; the descriptions of some of the attacker's clothes fitted the clothes that the appellant was known to be wearing; the appellant lived near both attacks, the attacks took place within a short time of one another and bore certain similarities. However, striking similarities could not be said to be present, although the evidence of the previous attacks, when taken together with the rest of the evidence in the case, was highly probative.

The Court of Criminal Appeal in *John* re-examined the dicta of Lord Mackay in *D.P.P. v. P.* and concluded as follows:

> "There are cases, albeit rare, where the only evidence on count A is the striking similarity of the circumstances of that alleged offence with the circumstances of another alleged offence with which the defendant is charged ... if the jury is sure in relation to the other offence, then the jury would be entitled to convict the defendant simply on the basis of the striking similarity ... That Lord Mackay did not intend the under lined passage to apply to cases like the present one when there is other evidence of substance peculiar to the relevant count, seems clear ..."[112]

The court continued:

> "To extract a simple test from Lord Mackay's speech has not always proved easy...to decide whether the evidence provides sufficient probative support so that it is fair to use it in this way, may require careful analysis...both the chronological relationship of the alleged offences and their circumstances may provide such support...sufficient probative support may be found more easily if the jury would be entitled to reach the conclusion that coincidence, collusion or contamination can be excluded...striking similarities may provide sufficient probative support but are not a necessary pre-requisite to finding such support."[113]

In this case the jury would be entitled to conclude that the previous attacks were carried out by the same person who committed the offence before the court and that the descriptions of the attacker in the previous attacks corresponded with the appellant.

(2) Background evidence[114]

R. v. T.M., P.M., P.A.M.[115] related to the trials of a number of male members of a family for offences against certain other members of that family. Because of

---

112. The Court of Criminal Appeal cited the cases of *Thompson v R.* [1918] A.C. 221, *R. v. Downey* [1995] Crim. L.R. 414, *R. v. Ruiz* [1995] Crim. L.R. 151 and *R. v. Lee* [1996] Crim. L.R. 825 in support of this conclusion.

113. At p. 298.

114. See further Birch [1995] Crim. L.R. 651.

115. [2000] 2 Cr. App R. 266.

the volume of the charges, it was deemed necessary to sever the indictment. The first trial dealt with offences committed by certain family members and one of their children in the 1960s. The second trial dealt with offences committed by those family members and three of their children in the 1980s. Appeals arising out of both trials were heard together.

In relation to the first trial, one of the defendants, T.M., appealed his conviction of sexual offence against his sister on the ground that the trial judge had allowed the prosecution to call evidence of previous offences committed by him against his other sisters. The prosecution's case was that the accused had been sexually abused by his father as a child and made to carry out similar acts of sexual abuse on his sisters. This practice was then continued by him in relation to the next generation.

The court stated that evidence of that defendant's previous misconduct was admissible against him, not because its probative effect outweighed its prejudicial value, but on the alternative ground that it was background evidence:

> "Background evidence, on the other hand, has a far less dramatic but no less important claim to be received. It is admitted in order to put the jury in the general picture about the characters involved in the action and the run-up to the alleged offence. It may or may not involve prior offences; if it does so this is because the account would be ... 'incomplete or incoherent' without them. It is not so much that it would be an affront to common sense to exclude the evidence, rather that it is helpful to have it and difficult for the jury to do their job if events are viewed in total isolation from their history."[116]

The court accepted as correct to the previous decision of Purchas L.J. in *R. v. Pettman*[117]:

> "Where it is necessary to place before the jury evidence of part of a continual background of history relevant to the offence charged in the indictment and without the totality of which the account placed before the jury would be incomplete or incomprehensible, then the fact that the whole account involves including evidence establishing the commission of an offence with which the accused is not charged is not of itself a ground for excluding the evidence."[118]

The court in *T.M., P.M.* and *P.A.M.* pointed out that "the evidence of [previous misconduct] was part of a continuous family history relevant to the offences charged".

In relation to the second trial, a number of T.M.'s brothers accused put forward a different ground of appeal against their convictions in the second generation trial, arguing that evidence of previous offences committed by their parents and co-accused G.M., E.M., and R.J. against the accused's sisters in the 1960s should not have been admitted. Even though the trial judge specifically stated that this was only relevant in assessing the guilt of these

---

[116.] At p. 270.
[117.] Unreported, CA (Crim Div), May 2, 1985 (U.K.).
[118.] At p. 460.

three accused, G.M., E.M. and R.J., in relation to the offences against their grandchildren, it was argued that the admission of this evidence prejudiced their children because the jury then knew that they were brought up in a home where sexual abuse was rife, which might explain why they came to be perpetrators of such abuse themselves. This argument was rejected and the evidence allowed, despite potential prejudice to the appellants, on the ground that its admission was essential to enable the jury to understand the background to the case.

Chapter 14

EVIDENCE OF THE ACCUSED'S BAD CHARACTER: CROSS-EXAMINATION

There are two ways in which evidence of the accused's bad character may be adduced by the prosecution in their cross-examination. Firstly, under section 1(f)(i), (ii) and (iii) of the Criminal Justice (Evidence) Act 1924 an accused who testifies may be asked questions about his bad character in certain situations. Secondly, even where an accused does not testify, other defence witnesses may be asked questions about the accused's character under *R. v. Rowton*,[1] where the accused has put that character in issue.

Most of this chapter will be devoted to an analysis of section 1(e) and (f) of the Criminal Justice (Evidence) Act 1924. *R. v. Rowton* is dealt with in a separate section at the end of this chapter.

14.1 Introduction: Relationship between section 1(e) and (f)

The Criminal Evidence Act 1898 allowed the accused to give evidence at his trial.[2] In order to facilitate the operation of this mechanism, the accused was denied the privilege against self-incrimination. Section 1(e) states that the accused may be asked any question even if it would tend to incriminate him.[3] This section was prompted by the concern that if the accused were to be able to invoke the privilege against self-incrimination possessed by ordinary witnesses, cross-examination of him would be rendered virtually worthless.

However, as a safeguard, and in line with the common law prohibition on bad character evidence, section 1(f) of the 1898 Act regulated the situations in which the prosecution could ask questions of the accused about his bad character. The provisions of the Criminal Evidence Act 1898 were reproduced in the Criminal Justice (Evidence) Act 1924, which has remained in force in this jurisdiction up to the present day.

Section 1(f) begins with a general prohibition on questions relating to the accused's bad character.[4] Such questions will only be allowed if they come within one of the four[5] exceptions set out in subsections (i), (ii) and (iii). Section 1(f)(i) allows questions about certain aspects of bad character where

---

[1.] (1865) 21 J.P. 149.

[2.] Section 1(f) provides the exclusive mechanism for cross-examining the accused as to his bad character. There is no common law right to cross-examine the accused about his bad character, because at common law the accused was not permitted to testify: *R. v. Weekes* (1983) 77 Cr. App. R. 207.

[3.] It should be noted that the accused is not obliged to testify. The justification for s.1(e) and the limitation it imposes on the right to silence is that testimony is at the option of the accused.

the subject-matter of the questions would have been admissible evidence in examination-in-chief. Answers to such questions may be taken into account in assessing the accused's guilt.

Furthermore, if the accused puts his good character in issue, questions the good character of the prosecution witnesses, or gives evidence against a co-accused, he may be asked about his bad character under subsection 1(f)(ii) or (iii). In theory, the responses given by him ought only to be taken into account in assessing his credibility. However, some juries may not understand the distinction between guilt and credibility and may incorrectly treat bad character evidence adduced under these subsections as being relevant as to guilt.

One of the most fraught issues in relation to section 1(f) has concerned its relationship with the preceding section 1(e). Section 1(e) states that the accused may be asked any question, notwithstanding that it may tend to incriminate him in relation to the offence charged. The previous chapter of this text gives many examples of situations in which evidence of the accused's bad character was highly relevant to the facts in issue in the case and therefore could be said to incriminate him in relation to the offence.

There is room for a potential clash between sections 1(e) and 1(f) insofar as questions about the accused's previous convictions or bad character may often incriminate him in relation to the crime. Section 1(e) appears to indicate that such questions are permissible; section 1(f), that they are not.

There are two different interpretations of the relationship between sections 1(e) and 1(f). The first interpretation sees section 1(f) as a limitation on the scope of section 1(e): on this analysis the prosecution has the right to ask the accused any question provided that it is not prohibited by section 1(f).

The second interpretation takes the view that sections 1(e) and 1(f) are mutually exclusive and that there is no overlap between them. Section 1(e) allows the accused to be asked any question that is relevant to his guilt. Section 1(f) prohibits questions about the accused's bad character being asked to impugn his credibility. On this analysis, if the question is permitted by section 1(e), it cannot be prohibited by section 1(f). These commentators interpret section 1(f) as only prohibiting questions about bad character where such question have no relevance to guilt.[6]

The problem with this second interpretation is that it allows questions about any aspect of bad character that can be said to be relevant to guilt. This is

---

4. This mirrors the general common law prohibition on evidence of bad character being adduced in examination-in-chief. However, although the exclusionary rules are identical, the exceptions to them are not necessarily the same. The evidence admissible under the exceptions in s.1(f)(i), (ii) and (iii) is not necessarily the same as that which can exceptionally be admitted in examination-in-chief under the rules set out in the preceding chapter.

5. Confusingly, subs.1(f)(ii) contains two distinct and separate exceptions.

6. An example of a case that applied this second interpretation was *R. v. Chitson* [1909] 2 K.B. 945. In this case bad character evidence was admitted even though none of the exceptions to s.1(f) were applicable, on the basis that such evidence was relevant to a fact in issue.

completely inconsistent with the approach of the courts to the admission of bad character evidence in examination-in-chief.

As outlined in the previous chapter, mere relevance is not enough to justify the admission of such evidence; it must be highly relevant, *i.e.* its probative effect must be so great as to outweigh the disadvantages that might result from its admission. The general exclusionary rule regarding the admission of bad character evidence in examination-in-chief would be deprived of practical effect if such evidence could be raised in the course of cross-examining an accused simply on the ground that it was relevant to guilt. It is not surprising, therefore, that the House of Lords in *Jones v. D.P.P.*[7] opted instead for the former approach.[8]

The accused was charged with the murder and rape of a girl guide. He raised an alibi defence, namely that he had been with a prostitute in London at the time. He gave an account of his return home and his subsequent conversation with his wife, in which he had assured her that his late return had nothing to do with the crime in question. The reason for his spouse's concerns was obvious in light of the fact that he had previously been convicted of the rape of a girl guide.

The prosecution counsel wished to cross-examine the accused about the virtually identical alibi he had given in the previous trial.[9] Such cross-examination could certainly be said to be relevant to the question of whether he was guilty of the offence charged. However, it also appeared to breach the prohibition in section 1(f) insofar as it related to an aspect of the accused's bad character. Prima facie there was a clash between section 1(e) and section 1(f): how ought this conflict be resolved?

In point of fact, the majority in *Jones* sidestepped the above question, saying that the evidence did not actually come within the prohibition in section 1(f). The precise wording of section 1(f) prohibits questions that "tend to show" that the accused had previously been charged with an offence. The House of Lords stated that the phrase "tend to show" should be taken as meaning "tend to show to the jury for the first time".[10] In *Jones* the accused had mentioned in examination-in-chief that he had been previously charged with a criminal offence. The jury already knew of this previous charge by the time the cross-examination stage was reached. Therefore, any cross examination on this previous charge was not prohibited by section 1(f). It did not "tend to show" that the accused had previously been charged with an offence because it did not introduce this fact to the jury for the first time; they knew it already.

---

7. [1962] A.C. 635.
8. Lord Reid in particular at 663 recognised that if s.1(f) were not taken as qualifying the generality of s.1(e), it would be rendered largely meaningless.
9. The prosecution did not ask him to give details of the previous crime.
10. This somewhat artificial interpretation has the advantage, from a common sense point of view, of ensuring that the accused can be cross-examined in relation to any matters raised in examination-in-chief.

On this interpretation of section 1(f), the questions asked did not come within the prohibition in section 1(f) and, therefore, on the facts of the case there was no conflict between section 1(e) and section 1(f). However, the House of Lords discussed *obiter* what the position would have been if the evidence had fallen within the prohibition in section 1(f), and came to the conclusion that in the case of a conflict between section 1(e) and section 1(f), section 1(f) would prevail and the question would be prohibited despite its relevance.

This view is consistent with the wary approach of the common law to evidence of the bad character of an accused. The previous chapter makes clear that evidence of bad character cannot be introduced in examination-in-chief merely because it incriminates the accused, *i.e.* is relevant in some way to showing his guilt. The justifications for this exclusionary rule, set out in para 12.2.2, are compelling ones.

It would be inconsistent for such evidence to be adduced indirectly through questions in cross-examination if it is not admissible directly as evidence-in-chief. Indeed the legislature in section 1(f) recognised the importance of the similar fact evidence rule in subsection (i), in which they recognised that the accused may be asked questions about his previous convictions in cross-examination if such evidence were admissible as evidence-in-chief under the similar fact evidence rule.

In light of the above, the majority interpretation of section 1(e) as subservient to section 1(f) seems the most appropriate solution. It is suggested that the rules laid down in *Jones* regarding the relationship between section 1(e) and section 1(f) are the ones applicable in this jurisdiction also.

Section 1(f) does more than narrow down section 1(e). In addition to a prohibitory function, section 1(f) also has a permissive function, allowing questions under section 1(f)(ii) or (iii) that go to the accused's credibility, even if they are not relevant to his guilt and therefore involve issues that could not have been raised in examination-in-chief. Such questions would not qualify as admissible under section 1(e). So, in one sense, section 1(f) narrows the range of questions that can be asked in cross-examination; in another sense, it extends it.

It should be noted, however, that *R. v. Butterwasser*[11] makes it clear that the permissive function of section 1(f) is dependent on the accused giving evidence. In this case, the defence cast imputations on the prosecution witnesses. The prosecution wanted to retaliate by putting forward evidence of the accused's bad character; however, section 1(f) was inapplicable because the accused chose not to testify.

14.2 Section 1(f): Prohibition on bad character

This part considers the scope of the prohibition in section 1(f). The exceptions specified in section 1(f)(i), (ii) and(iii) are considered below.

---

[11] [1948] 1 K.B. 4.

The prohibition in section 1(f) reads as follows:

> "A person charged and called as a witness in pursuance of this Act shall not be asked, and if asked shall not be required to answer, any question tending to show that he has committed or been convicted of or been charged with any offence other than that wherewith he is then charged, or is of bad character."

Section 1(f) prohibits questions which "tend to show" previous charges, previous convictions, previous commissions of offences, or bad character. A "charge" in this context refers to a charge in court. *Stirland v. D.P.P.*[12] established that a mere suspicion was not equivalent to a charge. Equally an out-of-court accusation cannot amount to a charge.[13] The question of whether suspicions or accusations can be prohibited on the alternative ground, that they are evidence of bad character, is discussed below. However, if an accused has been charged on a previous occasion but has been acquitted, evidence of the previous acquittal would be prohibited under section 1(f).[14]

The offence committed by the accused, or in relation to which he has been charged or convicted, does not have to have taken place before the offence charged.[15] In *R. v. Coltress*,[16] the term "offence" in section 1(f) was held to apply to offences committed 10 months after the offence charged.

The meaning of the term "bad character" in section 1(f) has been much debated. As already discussed, "character" has, on occasion, been given an artificially narrow meaning by the common law. *R. v. Rowton*[17] established that the common law right of an accused to prove his good character only extends to evidence of his reputation among his acquaintances. In addition, the same case stated that the common law right of the prosecution or a co-accused to adduce bad character evidence to rebut an accused who has put his good character in issue is similarly confined to adducing evidence of that accused's previous convictions or bad reputation.

In *R. v. Anderson*[18] evidence that the accused was wanted by the police was prima facie prohibited under section 1(f) because it pointed to her having committed a criminal offence. In *R. v. Coombes*[19] the defendant's conviction was quashed because the prosecution had been allowed to examine him about a previous conviction; this was clearly in breach of section 1(f).

There is no clear evidence as to the meaning the legislature intended to accord to the word "character" in the context of section 1(f). Judicial decisions have held that in this context it bears its ordinary meaning and includes evidence of the accused's disposition, his reputation in the general community,

---

12. [1944] A.C. 315.
13. (19780 68 Cr. App. Rep. 157.
14. It would probably have been prohibited in any case as irrelevant: *Maxwell v. D.P.P.* [1935] A.C. 309.
15. *R. v. Wood* [1920] 2 K.B. 179.
16. (1978) 68 Cr. App. R. 193.
17. (1865) 21 J.P. 149.
18. [1988] Q.B. 678.
19. (1960) 45 Cr. App. Rep. 36.

and any specific conduct performed by him.[20] It appears that previous out-of-court accusations, although not "charges", may be prohibited under section 1(f) on the basis that they constitute evidence of bad character.

The sole problem with this broad definition of character is that previous criminal charges, convictions, or conduct are necessarily included within it, which makes their separate legislative specification somewhat pointless. However, in opposition to this it could be argued that the operation of large parts of section 1(f), in particular the exception in 1(f)(ii) dealing with "imputations on the character of the prosecution", would be meaningless if the *Rowton* interpretation of character were to be followed, as the exception would then only apply in the unlikely eventuality that imputations on the "general reputation" of the prosecution witnesses were made.

It has been stated that section 1(f) does not prohibit the accused from giving evidence of his bad character or previous misconduct in examination-in-chief. Lord Reid in *Jones v. D.P.P.* was of the view that the wording of the section clearly indicated that it was to apply only to cross-examination by the prosecution or counsel for a co-accused:

> "The words 'shall not be required to answer' are quite inappropriate for examination-in-chief. The proviso is obviously intended to protect [the defendant]. It does not prevent him from volunteering evidence, and does not in my view prevent his counsel from asking questions tending to a disclosure of previous convictions or bad character, if such disclosure is thought to assist in his defence."[21]

If a question, truthfully answered, would oblige the accused to give evidence of his bad character, then the question is prohibited under section 1(f) as tending to show bad character.[22] This is subject to the particular definition that has been given by the House of Lords to the phrase "tending to show". In *Jones v. D.P.P.*[23] "tending to show" was interpreted as "tending to make the jury aware for the first time" of the accused's bad character or criminal past. This interpretation was instrumental in justifying the cross-examination in that case.

Jones was the case in which the accused, charged with the murder of a girl guide, claimed as an alibi that he had spent the evening with a prostitute and quarrelled with his wife when he returned home. He had raised a very similar alibi previously in a trial at which he was convicted of rape. The prosecution argued that he could be cross-examined as to the previous trial under section 1(e) as the issue of the prior alibi was relevant to his guilt.

[20.] This definition has been reaffirmed by the House of Lords in *Selvey v. D.P.P.* [1970] A.C. 304. In *R. v. Dunkley* [1927] 1 K.B. 323 at 325, Lord Hewart said that irrespective of its merits, it had become so well established as to be beyond question.

[21.] Questioning by the judge is presumably also covered by the prohibition: *R. v. Ratcliffe* (1919) 14 Cr. App. R. 95.

[22.] *R. v. Ellis* [1910] 2 K.B. 746 at 757.

[23.] [1962] A.C. 635.

The majority of the House of Lords rejected this argument and stated that section 1(e) could not be used to permit questions that were prohibited under section 1(f). Section 1(e) only applied to admit questions relevant to the question of guilt that did not "tend to show" the accused's bad character or previous convictions/charges/commissions. However, even on this narrow interpretation of section 1(e), evidence regarding the alibi in the previous trial was admissible. "Tending to show" was interpreted as "tending to reveal to the jury for the first time". Earlier in the trial, Mr Jones himself had mentioned that he had at one time in the past been in trouble with the police. Therefore, questioning about an alibi given by him in a previous trial was not prohibited by section 1(f).

The House of Lords were careful to emphasise that the prosecution questioning had avoided any details of the previous offence. The accused had simply been asked whether on a certain occasion he had answered questions in a certain way in court. It was stated that in order to avoid "tending to show" bad character, the cross-examination must not go significantly beyond the prior information provided by the accused so as to increase any prejudice against him.

R. v. Anderson[24] demonstrates a similar interpretation of the words "tending to show". As in *Jones,* this case shows a similar tendency on the part of the courts to sidestep the limitations placed on section 1(e). The accused in Anderson was charged with the bombing of the Conservative Party Conference in Brighton. She raised the defence that she had actually been engaged in smuggling I.R.A. prisoners out of the U.K. at the time the bombing occurred. The prosecution sought to cross-examine her about the fact that she was wanted by the Northern Ireland police in order to disprove this defence; they wanted to show that she was a high-up I.R.A. member and would not have been engaged in such a mundane task as smuggling prisoners.

The cross-examination sought in *Anderson* was relevant under section 1(e) but prima facie prohibited under section 1(f). However, the court produced two solutions which allowed the accused to be cross-examined under section 1(e). They said that her cross-examination fell outside the prohibition in section 1(f) for two reasons:

1. The questions did not "tend to show" previous commissions as they did not create any additional prejudice in the mind of the jury. She had already admitted in her defence that she was a member of the I.R.A. and was in possession of false documentation, either of which would have qualified her as a potential wanted person.

2. The questions were admissible under exception (i) to section 1(f): the similar fact evidence exception. Under the principle in vogue at the time, similar fact evidence was admissible to disprove a defence raised by the accused.

[24.] [1988] Q.B. 678.

This somewhat artificial interpretation in *Jones* and *Anderson* of the words "tending to show" has the advantage, from a common sense point of view, of ensuring that the accused can be cross-examined in relation to any matters that have been raised in examination-in-chief. This includes any evidence of the accused's bad character adduced by the prosecution in examination-in-chief under an exception to the exclusionary rule. At first glance it might be thought that section 1(f)(i) automatically permits such cross-examination but, as outlined below, there are some problems with its wording.

14.3 Section 1(f)(i), (ii) and (iii): Exceptional situations in which cross-examination about previous misconduct or bad character is permitted

There are four exceptions to the protection accorded by section 1(f), and if an accused comes within them, he may find himself being cross-examined about aspects of his bad character which are irrelevant to the facts in issue. It has been held that if an accused falls within the exceptions in section 1(f)(ii) and (iii), he may be asked any questions relevant to his credibility as a witness. These questions are not confined to such matters as are admissible in examination-in-chief, nor do they have to be relevant to the issue of the accused's guilt.[25] As stated already, section 1(f) has a permissive as well as a prohibitory function in relation to evidence of the accused's bad character.

To avail of this permission the questions must first come within section 1(f) generally, in that they must tend to introduce to the jury for the first time the accused's charges, commission, conviction, or bad character. In this regard, a wide definition of the prohibition in section 1(f) may actually benefit the prosecution, allowing them to adduce significant amounts of bad character evidence where an accused has lost his shield despite the fact that such evidence is relevant only to credibility. It has been held that a mere suspicion of bad character is not enough to come within section 1(f) and can only be admitted if relevant to guilt under section 1(e).

In addition, one of the following four exceptions to the prohibition in section 1(f) must be applicable:

1. Evidence of the commission or conviction of other offences is admissible similar fact evidence in examination-in-chief (section 1(f)(i)).

2. The accused has put his own good character in issue (section 1(f)(ii), part 1).

3. The accused has cast imputations on prosecution witnesses (section 1(f)(ii), part 2).

4. The accused has given evidence against a co-accused (section 1(f)(iii)).

These exceptions are discussed further on in this part.

---

25. In this regard cross-examination under ss. 1(f)(ii) and (iii) may be contrasted with questioning pursuant to section 1(f)(i).

Thirdly, the question asked must at least be relevant to the accused's credibility and, if asked pursuant to section 1(f)(i), must be relevant to his guilt. In *Maxwell v. D.P.P.*[26] the accused was charged with manslaughter by performing an illegal abortion. He testified that he was of good moral character. He was cross-examined to show that he had been charged with, but acquitted of, a similar offence. It was held that he could not be asked questions about this as it was not relevant to either his guilt or his credibility. It could not be viewed as a rebuttal of the statement made by him about his moral character.[27]

In R. v. McLeod[28] the Court of Criminal Appeal laid down guidelines for determining whether evidence was relevant as to the accused's credibility:

> "It is undesirable that there should be prolonged or extensive cross-examination in relation to previous offences, because it will divert the jury from the principal issue in the case, the guilt of the accused on the instant offence, and not the details of earlier ones. Unless the earlier offences are admissible as similar fact evidence, prosecuting counsel should not seek to probe or emphasise differences between the underlying facts of previous offences and the instant offence.... Similarities of defences which have been rejected by juries on previous occasions, for example, false alibis or the defence that the incriminating substance has been planted and whether or not the accused pleaded guilty or was disbelieved having given evidence on oath, may be a legitimate matter for questions. These matters do not show a disposition to commit the offence in question but are clearly relevant to credibility. Underlying facts that show particularly bad character over and above the bare facts of the case are not necessarily to be excluded. However, the judge should be careful to balance the gravity of the attack on the prosecution with the degree of prejudice to the defence which will arise from the disclosure of the facts in question."[29]

In *Stirland v. D.P.P.*[30] the accused was charged with forgery and gave evidence of his good character. It was held that questions as to whether his previous employer had suspected him of a similar forgery were not relevant either to guilt or credibility; they did not show that he was of bad character and could not be permitted under section 1(f) because they were not questions regarding his bad character. Viscount Simon stated:

> "The most virtuous may be suspected, and an unproved accusation proves nothing against the accused, but the questions, while irrelevant both to the charge which was being tried and the issue of good character, were calculated to injure the appellant in the eyes of the jury by suggesting that he had been in trouble before and were therefore not fair to him."[31]

---

26. [1935] A.C. 309.
27. *R. v. Maxwell* may be contrasted with *R. v. Waldman* (1934) 24 Cr. App. R. 204, where the cross-examination of an accused about a previous acquittal was upheld.
28. [1994] 1 W.L.R. 1500.
29. *Ibid.* pp. 1512-1513.
30. [1944] A.C. 315.
31. At p. 325.

Finally, it appears that counsel must get the leave of the court before asking any questions under the exceptions to section 1(f).[32] This is because the court has a discretion in relation to matters coming within section 1(ii) and (iii),[33] to refuse cross-examination even where the strict requirements of those sections are fulfilled.

14.3.1 Section 1(f)(i): Evidence admissible in examination-in-chief

Section 1(f)(i) provides that the accused may be cross-examined as to past offences which he has committed or in relation to which he has been convicted, if the proof that he has committed or been convicted of such other offences would have been admissible in examination-in-chief to show that he was guilty of the offence wherewith he is charged.

There are serious problems with the wording of this exception.[34] It only permits questioning on certain aspects of the accused's bad character. It does not allow questions relating to his non-criminal misconduct, his bad reputation or disposition, or previous charges brought against him, even where evidence of these matters would have been admissible in examination-in-chief. By some oversight the wording of the section excludes these matters.

It is worth noting that the High Court of Australia has refused to adopt a literal construction of the section. However, in the United Kingdom, the importance of section 1(f)(i) has been significantly reduced by the interpretation of the words "tending to show" adopted by the court in *Jones*. If the matters have already been raised in examination-in-chief, they do not fall within the prohibition and, therefore, can be admitted under section 1(e).[35]

Evidence that is admissible under section 1(f)(i) goes to prove the accused's guilt. However,because of the wording of section 1(f)(i), such evidence is not relevant to the accused's credibility.[36] This is in contrast to questions allowed under section 1(f)(ii) and (iii). Questioning under these two latter subsections is only relevant to the credibility of the accused, *i.e.* whether his testimony was truthful or not. It cannot be taken into account in deciding his guilt.

---

[32] *R. v. McLean* (1926) 19 Cr. App. Rep. 104.

[33] The discretion does not exist in relation to questions admissible under section 1(f)(i); such questions are automatically admissible.

[34] [1960] 2 Q.B. 207.

[35] A situation in which the prosecution wishes to rely on evidence of previous misconduct which would have been admissible in examination-in-chief but which was not admitted would be very rare. In addition, it is arguable that the prosecution should be prohibited from adducing such issues for the first time in cross-examination because this would be to deprive the accused of the opportunity to cross-examine prosecution witnesses: *R. v. Coombes* (1960) 45 Cr. App. R. 36.

[36] *Jones v. D.P.P.* [1962] A.C. 635.

14.3.2 Section 1(f)(ii): Part 1 Good character[37]

Section 1(f)(ii), part 1, provides that the accused may be asked[38] about his bad character or commissions/convictions/charges if he has personally, or by his advocate, asked questions of the witnesses for the prosecution with a view to establishing his own good character. The word "character" here is given the same meaning as earlier in the section; it includes evidence of actual disposition and evidence of reputation.

An accused may put his character in issue when he gives evidence of situations in which he has behaved in a good way, *e.g.* giving back lost property. A mere assertion of innocence by the accused or any of his witnesses, or cross-examination by the defence with this aim in mind, will not be enough to put good character in issue.

In *R. v. Samuel*[39] the defendant was accused of the theft of a camera from a young girl in the National History Museum. He called evidence to show that on two previous occasions he had found property, and instead of keeping it for himself, had returned it to its owner. It was held that he had adduced evidence of his good character and, therefore, could be cross-examined as to his bad character under section 1(f)(ii).

In *R. v. Ferguson*[40] the defendant adduced evidence that he was a regular churchgoer. Again, this was held to be putting his good character in issue. However a contrasting result was achieved in the case of *R. v. Malindi*.[41] The defendant to a charge of conspiracy called evidence to show that at a meeting where violence was discussed, he had advised against it. It was held that he had not made an independent assertion of good character and, therefore, could not be cross-examined under section 1(f). The evidence he had referred to was directly relevant to the matters in issue in the trial.

Even though the section does not appear to include cases where evidence of good character has been given not by the accused, but by witnesses for the defence, case law has interpreted the section to include such situations, at least where the evidence of good character by the defence witnesses was known to the accused or his counsel in advance. In other words, section 1(f)(ii), part 1, is to be interpreted purposively as covering all situations where the defence deliberately puts the accused's good character in issue. If a witness spontaneously volunteers a statement as to the accused's good character, which he has not been asked to make, the shield is not lost.[42]

The reasoning behind the good character exception is as follows: if the accused brings his own good character into play, it is regarded as correct that

---

[37] Munday "What constitutes a Good Character" [1997] Crim. L. R. 247.
[38] A possible deficiency of this exception is that, unlike the casting imputations exception, it does not specifically provide for the recall of the accused where one of his own witnesses puts his good character in issue after he has given testimony.
[39] (1956) 40 Cr. App. Rep. 8
[40] (1909) 2 Cr. App. Rep. 250.
[41] [1967] 1 A.C. 439.
[42] *R. v. Redd* [1923] 1 K.B. 104.

he be required to answer questions about his bad character or previous offences.

However, if the accused is trapped by prosecuting counsel into asserting his good character, it may be unfair to apply the exception.[43] Alternatively, this may be an appropriate case for the exercise of the trial judge's discretion to prohibit questioning that is admissible under section 1(f).

An accused who falls within section 1(f)(ii) may be questioned about his bad character in order to impugn his credibility. However, there is always the risk that the jury may treat evidence of bad character as meaning the accused is guilty, even though the evidence does not come within the similar fact evidence rule. For this reason, it must be expressly stated by the judge that such questions asked under section 1(f)(ii) or (iii) go to credibility only. In *People (Attorney General) v. Bond*[44] a retrial was ordered because the judge gave an inadequate direction on this point. It is up to the judge to point out the distinction between taking the answers to the questions in relation to guilt and taking them in relation to credibility, and to make it clear that any evidence admitted under section 1(f)(ii) goes to credibility only.

In addition, it is open to the judge to refuse permission if he feels that the jury is incapable of distinguishing between guilt and credibility.[45] He also has a discretion to refuse to allow cross-examination where the prejudicial effect of the questions asked would outweigh their probative value. Most of the case law on these discretions relates to the exception in the second limb of section 1(f)(ii), and is discussed later under that head. However, there is no reason why these discretions should not apply to cross-examination under the first limb. It should be noted, though, that the scope of these discretions has been interpreted narrowly by recent courts.[46]

14.3.3 Section 1(f)(ii): Part 2 Casting imputations on the prosecution[47]

Section 1(f)(ii), part 2, provides that the accused may be cross-examined as to bad character or previous commissions/convictions or acquittals if the nature or conduct of the defence is such as to involve imputations on the character of the prosecutor or the witnesses for the prosecution.[48] In *R. v. Britzman*[49] Lawton L.J. stated:

> "When allegations of the fabrication of evidence are made against prosecution witnesses...juries are entitled to know about the characters of those making them."

[43.] *R. v. Beecham* (1921) 16 Cr. App. R. 26.
[44.] [1966] I.R. 214.
[45.] *Maxwell v. D.P.P.*, [1935] A.C. 309.
[46.] *R. v. McLeod* [1984] 3 All E.R. 254.
[47.] Munday [1986] Crim. L.R. 511; Munday 7 *Legal Studies* 187; Newman (1993) 3 I.S.L.R. 96.
[48.] In the U.K., s.31 of the Criminal Justice and Public Order Act 1994 provides that the casting of imputations on deceased victims of the crime will also lose the accused his shield under s.1(f)(ii). However, in Ireland, casting imputations on a deceased victim does not come within s.1(f)(ii): *R. v. Biggin* [1920] 1 Q.B. 213.
[49.] [1983] 1 All E.R. 369.

The imputations must be created by "the nature or conduct of the defence". In *R. v. Jones*[50] it was stated by the Court of Criminal Appeal that if an accused makes imputations in the course of cross-examination by the prosecution, these cannot be said to be made by the defence because cross-examination is the prosecutor's case.[51] However, this view was rejected *obiter in R. v. Britzman.* Nonetheless, *Britzman* has been departed from on another point, and it is submitted that Irish judges are free to consider this issue for themselves.

There is a specific provision for the accused to be recalled if the imputations are made after he has given testimony. This was applied in *R. v. Seigley.*[52]

The imputations must relate to the character of the prosecution or their witnesses. As stated already, the term "character" is given a broad meaning throughout the section. Casting imputations on character could be created by references to the previous acts of misconduct, bad disposition and bad reputation of the prosecution witnesses. Imputations on the character of the victim do not result in the loss of the shield unless the victim has given evidence. This means that the accused in a murder trial may make imputations against the character of the victim without having to worry about his own bad character being dragged in.

There is considerable case law relating to the question of what amounts to casting imputations on the character of the prosecution or witnesses for the prosecution. In *R. v. Bishop*[53] the defendant was charged with burgling a house. His fingerprints had been found in the house and he tried to explain this by saying that he had been having an affair with the man who was living in it.

Irish and United Kingdom case law differs radically on this point. In the United Kingdom, a mere denial of the prosecution case is permissible, but anything more risks losing the shield.[54] Any attack on the veracity of a prosecution witness will allow the accused's past misconduct to be put in issue. This is so, even where the attack is absolutely essential for the defence case. *R. v.Owen*[55] established that it is immaterial that the accused had done his best to avoid such imputations. Owen was accused of stealing a purse. Two officers said that they saw him stealing the purse. Owen said that the officers must have been mistaken. The court held that he had lost his shield because even though his counsel talked about the officers being mistaken, this was not a feasible possibility in the circumstances, and what counsel was really saying was that the officers were lying.

---

[50]. (1909) 3 Cr. App. R. 67.
[51]. Also see *R. v. Baldwin* (1925) 18 Cr. App. R. 175.
[52]. (1911) 6 Cr. App. R. 106.
[53]. [1975] Q.B. 274.
[54]. It is unclear whether a mere denial simply does not come within s.1(f)(ii), part 2, or whether it comes within s.1(f)(ii) but is saved by the trial judge exercising his discretion.
[55]. (1986) 83 Cr. App. R. 100.

In *Selvey v. D.P.P.*[56] the accused was charged with buggery. He alleged that the complainant had also committed buggery and had planted indecent photos on the accused. This was regarded as casting imputations on a prosecution witness and resulted in the loss of the accused's shield. It was held as follows:

Section 1(f)(ii) allows cross-examination even when the imputations in question are an integral part of the accused's defence. However, an allegation of consent in a rape case will not result in loss of the shield. Nor will a denial of the prosecution case, even if made in improper language. .An assertion of mistake, rather than dishonesty, on the part of the prosecution, is permissible.

The rule that the shield is lost even where the imputations in question are an integral part of the defence raises particular problems where the defence rests on allegations of police misconduct. In *R. v. Britzman and Hall*[57] the accused was charged with burglary. Police officers gave evidence of admissions made by the accused during a shouting match in the cells with his co-accused. The accused denied that this shouting match had taken place. He didn't actually state in so many words that the police officers had fabricated their account of the incident. However, the Court of Appeal said that his defence carried an implied allegation of fabrication in that he contradicted the prosecution evidence but made no allegation of mistake or misunderstanding on their part. This was sufficient to lose him his shield.

It has been argued that the judge should give a warning to the accused if he looks to be in danger of losing his shield, but more recent decisions have held that a warning is not strictly necessary.[58] Also, it has been argued that there is a discretion in the trial judge to refuse questions, even if they come within section 1(f)(ii), if their prejudicial value would outweigh their probative effect., or if the jury would be misled into thinking that the answers to such questions went to guilt as opposed to credibility. However, *D.P.P. v. Selvey* takes a narrow approach to the first discretion; the second discretion was also construed narrowly in *R. v. Powell*[59] and *R. v. McLeod.*[60]

The position in Ireland is now radically different as a result of the decision of the Court of Criminal Appeal in *D.P.P. v. McGrail.*[61]. In *McGrail* the defendant alleged that Gardaí prosecution witnesses had fabricated evidence. They had said that he had made statements which he had not in fact made. The trial judge said that the accused had lost his shield and allowed him to be cross-examined as to misconduct.

On appeal, the Court of Criminal Appeal said that the trial judge was incorrect. The judgment of the Court was given by Hederman J. He held that the constitutional rules of fair procedure require that the accused be given an opportunity to make a case. The United Kingdom interpretation of section

56. [1968] 2 All E.R. 497.
57. [1983] 1 All E.R. 369.
58. *R. v. McGee and Cassidy* (1970) 70 Cr. App. R. 247.
59. [1986] 1 All E.R. 193.
60. [1984] 3 All E.R. 254.
61. [1990] 2 I.R. 38. Newman (1993) 3 I.S.L.R. 96.

1(f)(ii) meant that the accused could not do this if he had a bad record. This interpretation is unfair and should not be followed. The accused should be allowed to say that particular policemen fabricated evidence, although he may lose his shield if he goes beyond individuals to cast imputations on the police force generally, *i.e.* to say that it was the general practice of the Gardaí to fabricate evidence in this way.

The effect of *McGrail* is that the accused can make imputations against the character of the prosecution witnesses if these imputations are relevant to proving his innocence. However, imputations which are not relevant (which relate to matters unconnected with the proofs of the case) may result in the accused losing his shield.[62]

Prior to *McGrail* there was one Irish decision, *People (Attorney General) v. Coleman*,[63] in which the accused was held to have cast imputations on the prosecution. It is worth considering whether this decision would have been decided differently after *McGrail*. Coleman was charged with carrying out an abortion on a young woman. In his defence, he made general allegations relating to the immorality of the young woman, pointing out the fact that she had used contraceptives prior to marriage and that she had only married the father of the child he was alleged to have aborted in order to defeat justice. It is suggested that the accused in *Coleman* would have lost his shield even under the *McGrail* principle insofar as some of the imputations he cast on prosecution witnesses were not strictly relevant to his defence and were merely intended to blacken such witnesses and reduce their credibility.

Again, if questions are admissible under the second limb of section 1(f)(ii), answers received to them go only to the credibility of the accused, and cannot directly be taken into account in deciding his guilt, and it is up to the trial judge to make this point clear.[64].

Finally, even if the accused has lost his shield under section 1(f)(ii) (*e.g.*, through irrelevant imputations or assertions of good character), the trial judge still has a discretion to refuse leave to cross-examine where he regards such cross-examination as unfair in all the circumstances.[65]

It is worth noting that even in the United Kingdom a defence of lack of consent in a rape case does not cause the accused to lose his shield.[66] Neither does accusing prosecution witnesses of giving false evidence. In *R. v. Rouse*[67] it was stated by Darling J.:

> "Merely to deny a fact alleged by the prosecution is not necessarily to make an attack on the character of the prosecutor or his witnesses...to add in cross-

---

62. The interpretation taken in *McGrail* can be seen as supported by a line of early cases on the interpretation of this section: *R. v. Sheean* (1908) 21 Cox C.C. 561; *R. v. Preston* [1909] 1 K.B. 568; *R. v. Westfall* (1912) 7 Cr. App. R. 176.

63. [1945] I.R. 237.

64. *R. v. McLeod* [1994] 1 W.L.R. 1500.

65. This indicates that Irish courts will take a much broader approach to the trial judge's discretions than U.K. courts.

66. *R. v. Turner* [1944] K.B. 463; *Selvey v. D.P.P.* [1970] A.C. 304.

67. [1904] 1 K.B. 184.

examination that the prosecutor is a liar is merely an emphatic form of denial and does not affect its essential quality."

14.3.4 Section 1(f)(iii): Giving evidence against a co-accused[68]

Section 1(f)(iii) provides that the accused may be questioned as to bad character/previous commissions/convictions/charges if he has given evidence against any other person charged with the same offence.[69] If the accused gives evidence against a co-accused, he loses the shield. However, evidence admissible under section 1(f)(iii) goes only to credibility and not to guilt. The trial judge must give a direction to that effect.

The key question in deciding whether section 1(f)(iii) is fulfilled is whether the accused's evidence is *against* the co-accused or not? The general principle was laid down in the case of *R. v. Murdoch and Taylor*.[70] Here, two individuals were charged with receiving stolen goods. M. gave evidence that his co-accused had been the person who owned and controlled the box in which the property was found. It was held that Murdoch had given evidence against a co-accused and had lost his shield.

Lord Morris said that an accused would be regarded as having given evidence against a co-accused in the following situation:

> "If, while ignoring anything trivial or casual, the positive evidence given by the witness would rationally have to be included in any survey or summary of the evidence in the case which, if accepted, would warrant the conviction of the [co-defendant] then the witness would have given evidence against such other person".[71]

Lord Donovan stated:

> "What kind of evidence is ... 'evidence against' a co-accused is perhaps the most difficult part of the case. At one end of the scale is evidence which does no more than contradict something which a co-accused has said, without further advancing the prosecution case in any significant degree ... this is not the kind of evidence contemplated by [s.1(f)(iii)] .... At the other end of the scale is evidence which, if the jury believes it, would establish the co-accused's guilt, for example in a case of theft "I saw him steal the purse" or in a case of assault "I saw him strike the blow". It is this kind of evidence which alone, so the appellant contends, will satisfy the words "has given evidence against". Again, I regret I cannot share that view... the test prescribed by the Court of Appeal in Stannard was whether the evidence in question tended to support the prosecution's case in a material respect or to undermine the defence. I have no substantial quarrel with this definition. I would, however, observe that some danger may lurk in the use of the expression "tended to". There will probably be occasions when it could be said that evidence given by the accused "tended

---

68. Tapper 36 M.L.R. 167.
69. In the U.K., the phrase "charged with the same offence" has been amended to read "charged in the same proceedings".
70. [1965] 1 All E.R. 406
71. At p. 584.

to" support the prosecution's case, simply because it differed from the evidence of his co-accused; and the addition of the words "in a material respect" might not wholly remove the danger.... I myself would omit the words "tended to" and simply say that "evidence against" means evidence which supports the prosecution's case in a material respect or which undermines the evidence of the co-accused."[72]

As with section 1(f)(ii), there is no need for a hostile intent on the part of the accused in order for section 1(f)(iii) to swing into play. It was irrelevant whether the evidence was "the product of pained reluctance or of malevolent eagerness". In order for evidence to be against the co-accused, it must either support the prosecution case in some material respect or undermine a defence of the co-accused.

Contradicting the evidence of the co-accused may be enough to count as evidence against him. However, some contradictions may not amount to evidence against the co-accused because they neither materially support the prosecution case nor undermine a co-accused's defence.

The guidelines were laid down by the Court of Appeal in *R. v. Varley*:

"(1) If it is established that a person jointly charged has given evidence against the co-defendant that defendant has a right to cross-examine the other as to previous convictions and the trial judge has no discretion to refuse an application (2) Such evidence may be given either in chief or during cross examination. (3) It has to be objectively decided whether the evidence either supports the prosecution case in a material respect or undermines the defence of the co-accused. A hostile intent is irrelevant. (4) If consideration has to be given to the undermining of the other's defence care must be taken to see that the evidence clearly undermines the defence. Inconvenience to or inconstancy with the other's defence is not of itself sufficient.(5) Mere denial of participation in a joint venture is not of itself sufficient to rank as evidence against the co-defendant. For the proviso to apply, such denial must lead to the conclusion that if the witness did not participate then it must have been the other who did. (6) Where the one defendant asserts or in due course would assert one view of the joint venture which is directly contradicted by the other, such contradiction may be evidence against the co-accused."[73]

The distinction can be difficult to draw. This is shown by the contrasting cases of *R. v. Bruce*[74] and *R. v. Varley*. In *R. v. Bruce* B. was accused of robbery. M. said that there was a plan, but he was not involved. B. said that there was no plan. It was held that B.'s statement that there was no plan was not evidence against M. It merely contradicted M.'s evidence but didn't advance the prosecution case. Its effect, if believed, was to make it more likely that M. would be acquitted. Stephenson L.J. said that "the fact that Bruce's defence

72. At p. 591.
73. [1982] 2 All E.R. 519.
74. [1975] 3 All E.R. 277.

undermined McGuinness's defence by supplying him with another does not make it evidence given against him".[75]

In *R. v. Varley,* V. was accused of robbery. Q. claimed that he had participated in the robbery because of threats from V. V. said that he had no part in the robbery. It was held that V. could be cross-examined. His evidence suggested that Q. had committed the robbery. Kilner Brown J. stated that:

> "this evidence was against [the co-accused], because it mounted to saying not only that [the co-accused] was telling lies, but that he would be left as a participant on his own, and not acting under duress It rebutted a defence".[76]

R. v. Bruce can also be contrasted with the case of *R. v. Davies.*[77] In this case, D. and O. were jointly charged with theft. In the circumstances of the case, one or other of them must have stolen the items. D. denied the theft of one of the items. It was held that he could be cross-examined under section 1(f)(iii). A mere denial did not normally amount to giving evidence against a co-accused but in the circumstances, where only D. or O. could have committed the robbery, a mere denial by D. amounted to an assertion that O. had committed the robbery.

14.4 Cross-examination of other witnesses about the accused's bad character

The common law has always recognised a right on the part of the prosecution or a co-accused to call evidence of the accused's bad reputation or previous convictions wherever he has put his good character in issue. This principle was laid down in the case of *R. v. Rowton.*[78] This principle also allows the cross-examination of defence witnesses in order to obtain such evidence. Evidence may be called to rebut their answers if incorrect.

However, *R. v. Rowton* itself indicates that the questions asked can only relate to previous convictions of the accused or his bad reputation among his acquaintances; they may not seek to obtain evidence of specific acts of the accused nor the opinion evidence of witnesses as to his reputation.[79] However, Colin Tapper has argued that the *R. v. Rowton* limitation does not apply when cross-examining witnesses at common law to rebut an assertion of good character.[80]

---

75. At p. 127.
76. (1982) 75 Cr. App. R. 242, 246.
77. [1975] 1 W.L.R. 345.
78. *R. v. Rowton* (1865) Le. & Ca. 520; *R. v. Butterwasser* [1948] 1 K.B. 4; *R. v. de Vere* [1981] 3 All E.R. 473. See also para 13.1.2.
79. *R. v. Rowton* (1865) Le. & Ca. 520; however, the previous convictions/reputed bad behaviour do not have to be similar in nature to the offence with which the accused is charged. In *R. v. Winfield* (1939) 27 Cr. App. R. 139 an accused charged with indecent assault gave evidence of his sexual morality. It was held that the prosecution could adduce evidence as to his previous convictions for offences of dishonesty. See further Munday [1997] Crim L.R. 247.
80. *Cross and Tapper on Evidence* (15th ed, Butterworths, London 1999), p.534.

In support of his argument, *Tapper cites R. v. Bracewell*,[81] where an accused was allowed to cross-examine witnesses about disposition and specific acts of misconduct by a co-accused who had put his good character in issue. However, *Bracewell* could alternatively be explained on the more limited ground that because the co-accused had been granted an indulgence from Rowton and allowed to give evidence of specific acts of good conduct,[82] fair play dictated that both accused should be treated the same. The question of whether evidence of specific acts of misconduct or disposition of an accused could be admitted in situations where he had put his good character in issue was left open by the Irish Court of Criminal Appeal in *Attorney General v. Cornelius O'Leary and Hannah O'Leary*.[83]

In conclusion, *R. v. Rowton* is inferior to the mechanism in the Criminal Justice (Evidence) Act in a number of ways. Firstly, there is uncertainty as to whether or not it allows questions about specific acts of misconduct by the accused. Secondly, it only applies when the accused has put his good character in issue: the fact that the accused has cast imputations on the character of prosecution witnesses or a co-accused does not permit the cross-examination of other witnesses as to his bad character.[84] However, it may prove a useful method of obtaining information in cross-examination where an accused opts not to give evidence.

At first sight these provisions may seem like a reasonable solution to the problems caused by the accused testifying. However, there are serious problems with the wording and interpretation of the Criminal Justice Act 1924. Certain parts of the sections are ambiguous; other parts contain gaps. The constitutional right to a trial in due course of law may be invoked again by courts in this context.

Lord Lane in *Anderson*[85] described the almost identical United Kingdom provisions contained in the Criminal Evidence Act 1898 as "a nightmare of construction". Proposals for reform have been drawn up by both the U.K. Law Commission and the Australian Law Commission. The recent U.K. Law Commission consultation paper[86] is well worth looking at. It points out the flaws in the statutory provisions, criticising the assumption that the jury can

---

81. (1979) 68 Cr. App. R. 44.
82. As outlined at para 14.3.2, the issue before the court in *Rowton* was whether evidence of bad character of an accused who had put their character in issue could be admitted. However, the court also stated, *obiter,* that the accused's common law power to adduce evidence of good character was similarly limited to evidence of general reputation and previous convictions and excluded evidence of disposition or specific acts of misconduct. However, in practice the courts grant indulgences to defendants to allow them to adduce evidence of specific acts of good character and disposition: *R. v. Redgrave* (1981) 74 Cr. App. Rep. 10.
83. [1926] I.R. 445.
84. *R. v. Butterwasser* [1948] 1 K.B. 4; *R. v. Rowton* (1865) Le. & Ca. 520.
85. [1988] Q.B. 678.
86. Consultation Paper No. 1: *Evidence in Criminal Proceedings: Previous Misconduct of a Defendant.*

distinguish between credibility and guilt, and the uncertain role of judicial discretion in this area.[87]

Chapter 15

UNLAWFULLY OBTAINED EVIDENCE

Unlawfully obtained evidence may be divided into two types. On the one hand, there is evidence obtained in breach of the Constitution. Such evidence is normally inadmissible. On the other hand, there is evidence obtained in breach of statute or the common law. Such evidence is normally admissible, subject to a discretion on the part of the trial judge to exclude it.

15.1 Unconstitutionally obtained evidence[1]

Evidence obtained as a result of a direct and conscious breach of constitutional rights is automatically excluded under Irish law in the absence of extraordinary excusing circumstances. This rule was first developed in the context of real evidence in *People (Attorney General) v. O'Brien*.[2] In the course of the applicant's trial for the Gardaí sought to adduce evidence of stolen property which they had found in his house. However, it transpired that the Gardaí had entered the property pursuant to an invalid search warrant. An error had been made in filling out the address of the applicant's house on the warrant, which referred to "Captain's Road" instead of "Cashel Road".

The majority of the Supreme Court stated that where there had been a deliberate and conscious violation of constitutional rights by the State or its agents, evidence obtained by such violation should be excluded unless extraordinary excusing circumstances were present. However, in the case in hand, the violation had been accidental and unintentional rather than deliberate and conscious and should not prevent the evidence being admitted.

The principle in *O'Brien* was extended to confessions in *People (D.P.P.) v. Madden*.[3] The applicant had been detained for questioning under section 30 of the Offences Against the State Act 1939 and this detention was extended beyond the period permitted by law. A confession completed by him during this extended detention was held to be inadmissible on the grounds that there had been a deliberate and conscious breach of his constitutional rights.

---

[1] O'Connor "The Admissibility of Unconstitutionally Obtained Evidence in Irish Law" (1982) Ir. Jur. 257; Hogan "The Law of Confessions in the United States and Ireland" (1988) 10 D.U.L.J. 43; Kelly "The Irish Constitution" (4th ed., Butterworths, 2001); Casey "Constitutional Law in Ireland" (3rd. ed., Dublin, Round Hall, 2000) pp. 530-535; Charleton "Confessions – An Overview of the Law", Lecture to the Bar, May 7, 1991; McGuckian "Recent Developments in the Law Governing the Adminissibility of Confessions in Ireland" (1999) 9 I.C.L.J. 8.

[2] [1965] I.R. 42.

[3] [1977] I.R. 336.

15.1.1 Deliberate and conscious breach

Initial difficulties were encountered when it came to defining a deliberate and conscious breach of constitutional rights. In *People (D.P.P.) v. Shaw*[3] Griffin J. was of the view that conduct should not constitute a deliberate or conscious breach of constitutional rights unless the person engaging in the conduct knew of the unconstitutionality. According to this view, some *mala fides* was necessary.

However, a contrasting line of authority, originating in the judgment of Walsh J. in the above case, indicated that so long as the act in question was a deliberate and conscious act, that was sufficient. There was no requirement that the maker of the act know that it was in breach of constitutional rights.

The decisions of *People (D.P.P.) v. Healy*[4] and *People (D.P.P.) v. Kenny*[5] were important in clarifying this issue. The particular unconstitutionality in *People (D.P.P.) v. Healy* involved a refusal to allow the accused to consult a solicitor. McCarthy J. stated that so long as the particular act in question was an intentional one, there was no need for the perpetrator to be actually aware of its unconstitutionality:

> "A violation of constitutional rights is not to be excused by the ignorance of the violator no more than ignorance of the law can ensure to the benefit of a person who is presumed to have intended the nature and probable consequences of his conduct."[6]

The decision in *Healy* is of further importance insofar as it confirmed beyond doubt that the doctrine in People *(D.P.P.) v. O'Brien*[7] extended to unconstitutionally obtained confessions.

In *People (D.P.P.) v. Kenny* a search warrant was, unbeknownst to the garda who executed it, invalid. The Peace Commissioner who granted the warrant under section 26 of the Misuse of Drugs Act 1977 had failed to exercise the independent judicial discretion required by that section. He had simply acted on the opinion of the garda seeking the warrant.

The majority of the Supreme Court felt that evidence obtained as a result of the search ought to be excluded. The view was taken that, given the duty imposed on the courts to protect the constitutional rights of the individual, the term "deliberate and conscious breach" ought to be interpreted widely so as to include situations where the individual concerned was not aware of the unconstitutionality. The majority judgment of Finlay C.J. is particularly noteworthy insofar as it favoured the absolute protection of constitutional rights. On this view, the rule preventing the admission of unconstitutionally obtained evidence is more than just a deterrent against misconduct by the Gardaí; it also has the function of upholding individual rights.

---

4. [1990] 2 I.R. 73.
5. [1990] I.L.R.M. 569.
6. At p. 89.
7. [1965] I.R. 142.

There were strong dissents from Griffin and Lynch JJ. in *People (D.P.P.) v. Kenny*. Lynch J. in particular felt that there should be some element of culpability (such as negligence) on the part of the police before the evidence could be excluded.

Given the extremely wide approach taken in *Healy* and *Kenny*, is there a continuing role for the requirement of deliberate and conscious breach, or should it simply be abolished? Judges have consistently reaffirmed that there was no deliberate and conscious breach in *People (D.P.P.) v. O'Brien* and that, therefore, the admission of the evidence in that case was justified. Finlay C.J. in *People (D.P.P.) v. Kenny* indicated that if the particular actions were unintentional or accidental, there would be no deliberate and conscious breach.

However, in the light of cases continually widening the concept of deliberate and conscious breach, the finding that the breach in *O'Brien* was not deliberate and conscious becomes more and more anomalous. In *D.P.P. v. O'Connell*[8] the unconstitutionality involved a failure to grant the accused's request to be allowed access to his solicitor. The garda in charge was mistakenly told that such access had already been granted and, therefore, the solicitor was not contacted. This was an inadvertent mistake similar to that in *O'Brien* and yet, in this case, it was regarded as a deliberate and conscious violation of constitutional rights.

15.1.2 Causation[9]

It appears that even if a deliberate and conscious breach of constitutional rights has occurred, it may still be possible to admit evidence obtained subsequent to the breach, on the ground that it was not made as a result of the breach.

In *Walsh v. O'Buachalla*[10] the appellant had been arrested on a suspicion of drunk driving contrary to section 49 of the Road Traffic Act 1961 and brought to a garda station. When asked to provide a sample of blood or urine, he requested to see a solicitor. The garda in charge refused to grant this request. The appellant argued that the subsequent sample provided by him should be held inadmissible on the ground that his constitutional right of access to a solicitor had been infringed.

Blayney J. rejected this argument on the ground that there was no causal connection between the infringement of the appellant's constitutional rights and the obtaining of the sample. The sample had been obtained after the violation but not as a result of the violation. The appellant had been obliged by statute to give a specimen of blood or urine. According to Blayney J., a solicitor could not have done anything other than confirm that fact. He could not have advised the appellant to commit an offence by refusing to give the samples.

8. [1995] I.R. 244.
9. Butler and Ong "Breach of the Constitutional Right of Access to a Lawyer and the Exclusion of Evidence – the Causative Link" (1995) 5 I.C.L.J. 156.
10. [1991] 1 I.R. 56.

A similar issue arose in *D.P.P. v. Spratt*,[11] again involving an accused arrested under the Road Traffic Act 1961. In this case, the accused had not been informed of his right of access to a solicitor. O'Hanlon J. held that there was no constitutional right in this jurisdiction to be informed of one's right to a solicitor. Furthermore, he followed the approach of Blayney J. in *Walsh v. O'Buachalla* in holding that even if the accused had been told of his right and spoken to a solicitor, the sample would have been obtained anyway. The approach taken in Spratt was affirmed recently in another section 49 case, *D.P.P. v. Jamie Cullen*.[12]

In a similarly named case, *People (D.P.P.) v. Cullen*,[13] the appellant had been arrested under the Offences Against the State Act 1939. On his arrival at the garda station, he asked for a solicitor. Neither this solicitor, nor another one subsequently nominated by the appellant, could be contacted. The Gardaí asked the appellant to remove his clothes under powers contained in section 7(1) of the Criminal Law Act 1976. The appellant initially objected but, subsequently, handed over his clothes. He subsequently claimed that fibres obtained from these clothes had been unconstitutionally admitted in evidence.

It was argued that there had been a breach of the appellant's constitutional right to a solicitor and that he had been prejudiced thereby. If a solicitor had been present, he might have advised the appellant not to hand in his clothing and to suffer the consequence of the less serious offence under section 7(2) of refusing or obstructing the Gardaí from exercising their powers.

However, the Court of Criminal Appeal rejected this argument, stating that no person could have a constitutional right to seek legal advice urging him to commit a criminal offence. Consequently, there was no causative link between the absence of legal advice and the obtaining of the fibres from the appellant's clothes.

The above cases on the causation requirement all involve the admissibility of particular pieces of real evidence, which the accused had been under a statutory obligation to provide. However, in relation to a confession made after an accused had been unconstitutionally refused access to his lawyer, it would be extremely difficult for the prosecution to prove that this confession had not been influenced by the unconstitutionality.

However, on this point attention should be drawn to the recent decision of Herbert J. in *People (D.P.P.) v. Cleary*.[14] The applicant made a confession during a period of illegal detention in his sister's house. A short time afterwards his detention became a legal one, and he made further statements expanding on his earlier confession. It was held that the statements made by the applicant while in his sister's house were inadmissible, but the statements made subsequently in the police station were admitted on the ground that they could not have been caused by the earlier unconstitutionality.

---

11. [1995] 2 I.L.R.M. 117.
12. Unreported, O'Caoimh J., February 7, 2001.
13. Unreported, March 30, 1993.
14. Unreported, Herbert J., December 7, 2001.

Finally, it is worth noting that not all the cases show such a restrictive approach to the issue of causation. In *People (D.P.P.) v. Madden*[15] a confession completed during a period of unlawfully extended detention was held inadmissible. Part of the confession had been made during the lawful detention period and, therefore, could not have been caused by the unconstitutionality; nonetheless the entire confession was excluded.

In *People (D.P.P.) v. Finnegan*[16] it was held that a breach of a detainee's right of access to a solicitor would have the effect of making all subsequent detention illegal. The consequence of this would be that all statements made by an accused after that point would be automatically illegal without the need to decide whether or not they were caused by the failure to provide the solicitor or not. It is worth noting that this dictum, which is in direct contrast with the approach taken in *D.P.P. v. Spratt* and *Walsh v. O'Buachalla,* appears to have been adopted obiter by the Supreme Court in *Lavery v. Member-in-Charge, Carrickmacross Garda Station.*[17]

15.1.3 Extraordinary excusing circumstances

Once a deliberate and conscious breach of constitutional rights is shown, the onus shifts to the prosecution to establish either absence of causation or extraordinary excusing circumstances. Although the phrase "extraordinary excusing circumstances" is part of the original *O'Brien* test, it has yet to be fully considered by the courts.

Some examples of extraordinary excusing circumstances were given by Walsh J. in *O'Brien*:

1. where there is a risk of imminent destruction of vital evidence;

2. where there is the need to rescue a victim in peril; and

3. where evidence is obtained by a search incidental to and contemporaneous with a lawful arrest, although made without a valid search warrant

The situation in *People (Attorney General) v. Shaw* came within the victim in peril example. The accused was detained for an excessive period in order to ascertain the whereabouts of a girl he had abducted, and whom the Gardaí believed to be still alive. A confession made by him during this unconstitutional detention was held admissible.

In *People (D.P.P.) v. Delany,*[18] it was argued by the Gardaí that the presence of persons outside a dwelling who threatened to harm persons within it was an extraordinary excusing circumstance justifying a forcible entry by the Gardaí without warrant.

---

15. [1977] I.R. 336.
16. Unreported, Court of Criminal Appeal, July 15, 1997. See Breen 5(1) 1999 Bar Rev. 6.
17. [1999] 2 I.R. 390.
18. [1996] 1 I.L.R.M. 236.

People (D.P.P.) v. Lawless[19] held that the need to prevent the imminent destruction of vital evidence was an extraordinary excusing circumstance.

In *Freeman v. Director of Public Prosecutions*[20] the accused had been observed unloading goods from a van and carrying them into his house. He saw the Gardaí and ran into the house. The Gardaí followed him, without waiting to obtain a search warrant, and found stolen goods in the house. Carney J. stated that the entry by the Gardaí was unconstitutional and the only question was whether there were extraordinary excusing circumstances present. He emphasised that the presence of extraordinary excusing circumstances would not stop the behaviour of the Gardaí from being unconstitutional, but might allow evidence obtained as a result of such behaviour to be admitted.

In the circumstances, Carney J. felt that the admission of the evidence in question was justified despite the unconstitutionality. The accused had been caught *in flagrante delicto* and would have destroyed the evidence in question before the issue of the warrant.

In conclusion, there is now a large amount of case law fleshing out the principle of inadmissibility first established by Walsh J. in *People (Attorney General) v. O'Brien.*[21] There are four issues, which are relevant in deciding whether evidence will be held inadmissible on this ground.

Firstly, there must be a breach of constitutional rights. Secondly, the breach must be a deliberate and conscious one. Thirdly, the evidence may still be allowed in if it is possible to regard it as not having been obtained as a result of the breach. Fourthly, the evidence may also be admitted despite the unconstitutionality if there are extraordinary excusing circumstances.

15.2 Examples of constitutional rights, breach of which may render evidence inadmissible

15.2.1 Constitutional right to liberty: Unlawful arrest[22]

The accused has a right under Articles 40.4.1 and 40.5 not to be detained save in accordance with law. In order for detention to be in accordance with law, the initial arrest must be lawful. An arrest may be an arrest under a warrant or an arrest without warrant.

Section 5 of the Criminal Law Act 1997 provides that, in the case of an arrest under warrant, the warrant does not have to be in the possession of the arresting officer. However, it must be shown to the accused as soon as possible. If an arrest with warrant is in respect of a charge other than that in respect of which the warrant has been issued, the arrest is unlawful.

Traditionally, it was possible to arrest without warrant at common law in certain situations. At common law, a garda could arrest without warrant once

---

[19.] Unreported, Court of Criminal Appeal, November 20, 1985.
[20.] Unreported, High Court, Carney J., November 18, 1996.
[21.] [1965] I.R. 142.
[22.] Ryan "Arrest and Detention: A Review of the Law" (2000) 10(1) I.C.L.J. 2.

he had a reasonable suspicion that a felony had occurred and that the arrestee had committed it. A reasonable suspicion might be based on hearsay evidence, including evidence given by an informer, or be a suspicion created by a false alibi.

A citizen could arrest without warrant at common law once a felony had been committed and he had a reasonable suspicion that the person arrested had committed it. However, powers of arrest without warrant at common law are now of historical interest since the enactment of the Criminal Law Act 1997, which abolished the distinction between a felony and a misdemeanour and stated that, except where the Act specifically provides otherwise, the law applicable to misdemeanours shall apply.

Under the Criminal Law Act 1997 specific powers of arrest without warrant have been given in respect of an arrestable offence. An arrestable offence is defined as an offence for which a person of full capacity and not previously convicted may be punished by imprisonment for a term of five years or a more severe penalty. The definition of arrestable offence includes an attempt to commit such an offence.

Section 4 of the 1997 Act allows members of the Gardaí to arrest without warrant once an arrestable offence has been committed, or they have reasonable cause to suspect that such an offence has been committed, provided that they have reasonable cause to suspect that the person they are arresting is guilty of the offence.

Members of the public have power to arrest under the 1997 Act only if an arrestable offence has actually been committed or if they suspect the arrestee to be in the very act of committing an arrestable offence. In addition, they must have reasonable cause to believe both that the arrestee is guilty of the offence in question, and that he is attempting to avoid arrest. Members of the public must transfer any person arrested by them under the 1997 Act into the custody of the Gardaí as soon as possible.

This is a general principle in relation to arrest: no matter who is carrying out the arrest, the arrested person must be brought to a garda station with reasonable expedition and without undue delay. This principle, originally laid down by O'Higgins C.J. in *People (D.P.P.) v. Walsh*,[23] was recently reaffirmed by Herbert J. in *People (D.P.P.) v. Cleary*.[24] The applicant had been arrested at 8.20 a.m. in his sister's house. He was kept in the house for 10 minutes after his arrest. During these 10 minutes, he admitted to the killing. It was held that the statements made by the accused in his sister's house were not admissible in evidence.

However, subsequent statements made by him in the garda station were admissible except for one that was made in response to a reminder about his previous admission. It was held that these subsequent statements could not be said to have been caused by the earlier unconstitutional confession and that the accused could have changed his mind.

---

[23] [1980] I.R. 294.
[24] Unreported, High Court, December 7, 2001.

A number of other statutes give a power of arrest without warrant for certain offences. Section 30(1) of the Offences Against the State Act 1939 allows a member of the Gardaí to arrest without warrant if he has a suspicion that the arrestee has committed or intends to commit a scheduled offence, or that he is in possession of information relating to the commission or intended commission of any scheduled offence, or that he is carrying a document relating to the commission or intended commission of such an offence. *D.P.P. v. Howley* indicates that such suspicions must be reasonable.

The following are scheduled offences within the meaning of the Offences Against the State Act 1939: offences under the Malicious Damage Act 1861, the Explosive Substances Act 1883, the Firearms Acts 1925-1971, the Conspiracy and Protection of Property Act 1875, and the Offences Against the State Act 1939.

The Supreme Court in *People (D.P.P.) v. Quilligan & O'Reilly (No. 3)*[25] established that the powers of arrest and detention under section 30 can be used irrespective of whether the scheduled offence in question is subversive or not. In addition, in this case it was stated that an arrest for a scheduled offence would be lawful even where the arrestee was suspected of being involved in a more serious unscheduled offence, such as murder, provided that there was a genuine suspicion on the part of the arresting garda that the accused had also been involved in the scheduled offence and that the arrest and interrogation were genuinely directed towards the investigation of that scheduled offence.

This principle had been applied in *People v. Howley*,[26] where an arrestee was purportedly arrested for the scheduled offence of cattle maiming but in fact was arrested in order to be interrogated about a murder. Walsh J. in the Supreme Court stated that, so long as there was a genuine desire and intent to pursue the investigation of the scheduled offence and so long as the arrest was not a colourful device to enable a person to be detained in pursuit of some other alleged offence, there was nothing to stop the Gardaí putting questions to the person in custody about the other offence.

Howley can usefully be contrasted with the *State (Bowes) v. Fitzpatrick*.[27] Here, an individual had been killed with a knife, which had been damaged in the murder by contact with the victim's bone. The accused, one of the murder suspects, was arrested under section 30 of the Offences Against the State Act 1939 on the ground of having caused malicious damage to the knife. The arrest was declared unlawful.

Similarly, in the recent case of *Criminal Assets Bureau v. Craft*[28] it was stated *obiter* that if an arrest under the Criminal Law (Drug Trafficking) Act 1996 was a sham or cover for the purpose of eliciting information exclusively in relation to revenue offences, then it ought to be treated as unlawful.

---

25. [1993] 2 I.R. 305.
26. [1989] I.L.R.M. 629.
27. [1978] I.L.R.M. 195.
28. Unreported, July 12, 2000.

Finally, it is worth noting that *Re O Laighleis*[29] establishes that everyone is entitled to be told the reason for his arrest. However, even if the initial arrest was invalid, the subsequent detention of the accused may be validated once he is told the reason for his arrest.

In *Madigan v. Devally*[30] a garda told the appellant that he was being arrested under a particular section of the Road Traffic Act 1994. In actual fact, that particular section was not the one applicable. It was held that the arrest and consequent taking of a blood sample was unlawful, on the ground that:

> "[a]n arrest is a very serious intrusion on a person's liberty and should only be done in strict accordance with the law."

A recent decision on the issue of arrest was *O'Mahony v. Ballagh*.[31] Here, the garda did not identify the specific offence for which the accused was being arrested. Under *Brennan v. D.P.P.*[32] the arresting garda must identify the particular section of the Road Traffic Act 1994 under which the accused is being arrested. It was argued in *O'Mahony* that the arrest was unlawful and that the evidence subsequently obtained was in breach of the accused's constitutional right to liberty. It was held by the High Court that the accused must have been aware of the reason for his arrest. However, on appeal, this finding was rejected and the arrest held invalid.

15.2.2   Constitutional right to liberty: Unlawful detention[33]

Even if the initial arrest is valid, subsequent unlawful detention of the accused may breach his constitutional right to liberty. At common law, an arrestee must be brought before a court at the first possible opportunity. This could allow detention of the accused overnight pending the next court sitting. However, in *Doherty v. Liddane*[34] detention of an arrestee for 26 hours pending the next court sitting was held to be excessive.

Statute has amended the common law to allow for lawful detention without charge in certain situations. Section 30 of the Offences Against the State Act 1939 allows detention without charge on suspicion of a scheduled offence for a period of 24 hours, which may be extended by a further period of 24 hours on the direction of a Chief Superintendent or higher officer. The Supreme Court in *People (D.P.P.) v. Quilligan*[35] upheld the constitutionality of this section.

[29.]   [1960] I.R. 93.
[30.]   [1999] 2 I.L.R.M. 141.
[31.]   High Court, O'Caoimh J., January 23, 2001; Supreme Court, December 13, 2001.
[32.]   [1996] 1 I.L.R.M. 267.
[33.]   Costello "Detention for Questioning and Oppressive Interrogation" (2001) 11(1) 1 C.L.J. 12; Keane "Detention Without Charge and the Criminal Justice (Drug Trafficking) Act 1996 (1997) 7(1) I.C.L.J. 1; White "The Confessional State – Police Interrogation in the Irish Republic" (2000) 10(1) I.C.L.J. 17.
[34.]   [1940] Ir. Jur. Rep. 58.
[35.]   [1986] I.R. 495.

The Criminal Justice Act 1984 gives a power of detention in relation to an accused who has been validly arrested on a reasonable suspicion of having committed or attempting to commit an offence punishable by five years' imprisonment or more. It authorises detention for up to 12 hours without charge. The initial period of detention is six hours. After this period has expired, a Superintendent or higher officer may direct that detention be extended for another six hours.

The Criminal Justice (Drug Trafficking) Act 1996 allows for the prolonged detention of a person arrested without warrant on reasonable suspicion that he has committed a drug trafficking offence. The maximum initial period of detention is six hours, but this may be extended by a further 18 hours if a Chief Superintendent so directs and has reasonable grounds for so directing. The detention may then be extended by a further 24 hours to 48 hours in total by further direction of a Chief Superintendent.

A further extension of up to 72 hours is possible by obtaining a warrant from a District or Circuit Court judge. The judge may subsequently be applied to for an additional 24 hours detention, thus bringing the maximum detention time under this Act up to almost seven days.

A drug trafficking offence for the purposes of this legislation is that of producing, supplying transporting, storing, importing, or exporting a controlled drug under section 3(1) of the Criminal Justice Act 1994.

Detention without charge is also possible for the purposes of search under the Misuse of Drugs Acts 1977 and 1984 and for taking a blood or urine sample under the Road Traffic Acts.

15.2.3 Constitutional right of reasonable access to legal advisers[36]

While in detention, the accused has a constitutional right of access to a lawyer on request. This has been established since *People (D.P.P.) v. Healy.*[37] In this case, the Supreme Court affirmed that:

> "such an important and fundamental standard of fairness in the administration of justice as the right of access to a lawyer must be deemed to be constitutional in its origin".[38]

The effect of this is that if the accused requests a lawyer while in detention, and is refused, any evidence obtained as a result will be inadmissible. *Healy* indicates that, unlike its counterpart in the United States, the Irish constitutional right to legal access is not simply a facet of the right against self-incrimination. Rather, it is important in its own right in securing a balance between the accused and the interrogators.

---

36. Butler "The Right to Be Informed of the Right to a Lawyer – the Consitutional Dimension" (1993) 3 I.C.L.J. 173; Butler and Ong "Breach of the Constitutional Right of Access to a Lawyer and the Exclusion of Evidence – the Causative Link" (1995) 5 I.C.L.J. 156.
37. [1990] I.L.R.M. 313.
38. *Ibid.* Finlay CJ. at p. 81.

This is what occurred in *People (D.P.P.) v. Connell.*[39] A confession made by an accused was declared inadmissible on the ground that he had not had access to a solicitor. The applicant asked a relative to contact a solicitor on his behalf. Gardaí incorrectly informed this individual that a solicitor had in fact already been found. Consequently, the applicant was not attended by a solicitor prior to making his confession.

Despite the emphatic statements made in *Healy* and *Connell* regarding the importance of the right to legal access, subsequent decisions have failed to take practical steps to protect the substance of that right. It may be argued that if someone is being detained at a garda station, his constitutional right to legal access requires that he be expressly informed of such a right.

In fact, section 5 of the Criminal Justice Act 1984 and regulation 8(1)(b) of the Criminal Justice Act 1984 (Treatment of Persons in Custody) Regulations 1987 require the right to legal access to be brought to the attention of a detainee. However, breach of these provisions (as opposed to breach of the Constitution) does not make evidence obtained as a result automatically inadmissible but rather gives the trial judge a discretion to exclude.

In order for evidence to be automatically inadmissible on the ground that the detainee was not told of his right of access to a lawyer, it would have to be shown that he had a constitutional right to be given this information. However, the judgment of O'Hanlon J. in *D.P.P. v. Spratt*[40] unequivocally indicates that there is no constitutional right to be told of your right to a solicitor. In this regard, the right of a detainee to legal access may be contrasted with the right to free legal aid. *State (Healy) v. O'Donoghue*[41] established that in order to ensure full and adequate protection of the right to free legal aid, an accused must be expressly told of it.

The accused, however, does have the right to speak to his solicitor in private. In *People (D.P.P.) v. Finnegan*[42] the appellant was arrested on suspicion of larceny. He asked to speak to his solicitor. and was allowed to telephone him; however members of the Gardaí remained in the room while he made the call. The Court of Criminal Appeal stated that:

> "the right to consult a solicitor would usually be of little value unless it carried with it, as a necessary concomitant, the right to consult him in private".

There was no need for the appellant to expressly request private legal access; it was inherent in all legal access that it be private.

In this context, it is worth noting that the right to a solicitor is one of reasonable access only. Carney J. in *Barry v. Waldron*[43] states that the accused has no right to have his solicitor present during questioning. This may be

---

[39.] [1995] 1 I.R. 244.
[40.] [1995] 2 I.L.R.M. 117.
[41.] [1976] I.R. 325.
[42.] Unreported, Court of Criminal Appeal, July 15, 1997.
[43.] Unreported, High Court, *ex tempore*, May 23, 1996.

contrasted with the judgment of the United States Supreme Court case in *Miranda v. Arizona,*[44] in which the contrary conclusion was reached.

The issue of reasonable access was further elaborated on in *Lavery v. Member-in-Charge, Carrickmacross Garda Station.*[45] The applicant had been arrested under section 30 of the Offences Against the State Act 1939 on suspicion of belonging to an unlawful organisation. In light of the fact that sections 2 and 5 of the Offences Against the State (Amendment) Act 1998 allow inferences to be drawn from the failure of the accused to answer certain questions put to him by the Gardaí, the applicant's solicitor requested that the interviews be recorded audiovisually and/or that complete notes be taken and made available to him.

The Supreme Court held that the right of access to a solicitor was one of reasonable access. In this they differed from the ruling of McGuinness J. in the High Court. There was no obligation on the Gardaí to give the solicitor regular updates. The solicitor was not entitled to be present at the interviews, nor was he entitled to prescribe the manner in which the interviews would be conducted.

The question of reasonable access was further considered in *People (D.P.P.) v. Darcy.*[46] The applicant, aged 16 years at the time, was arrested in the early hours of the morning. The applicant's uncle was brought in, and he requested a solicitor. Unsuccessful attempts were made to contact three solicitors. A fourth solicitor finally arrived at 12.15 p.m., by which time the accused had already been questioned. Upon arrival of the solicitor, the applicant refused to answer any further questions and argued that earlier statements made by him were inadmissible.

The Court of Criminal Appeal stated that, in the circumstances, the accused's right to legal access had not been infringed. The Gardaí had made reasonable attempts to contact a solicitor. Given the limited time period during which the accused could be detained, it was not necessary to delay questioning him until the arrival of the fourth solicitor. It is worth noting that the Gardaí, in this case, refrained from asking the accused to sign his confession until his solicitor arrived – something which made a positive impression on the court.

In *People (D.P.P.) v. Holland*[47] the applicant was arrested on suspicion of possession of a controlled drug. His lawyer was arrested shortly afterwards. The applicant argued that this was done as part of a conspiracy. It was held that no such conspiracy existed. The Gardaí had made reasonable and genuine attempts to contact a nominated solicitor. The applicant had eventually succeeded in getting the services of another solicitor. The court stated that if the applicant could have shown that the Gardaí had deliberately sought to deprive him of this particular solicitor, things would have been different.

---

44. 384 U.S. 436 (1966).
45. [1999] 2 I.R. 390.
46. Unreported, Court of Criminal Appeal, July 29, 1997.
47. Unreported, Court of Criminal Appeal, June 15, 1998.

15.2.4 *Constitutional right to medical assistance*

In addition to the right of reasonable legal access, *Re The Emergency Powers Bill 1976*[48] recognised that a detainee has a constitutional right to medical assistance.

15.2.5 *Constitutional right to inviolability of the dwelling*[49]

Breaches of the constitutional right to inviolability of the dwelling have tended to feature in cases where the admissibility of real evidence, rather than confessions, is at issue. However, a breach of this right could also render a confession inadmissible if the confession was obtained as a result of the breach.

The right to inviolability of the dwelling is the right not to have one's dwelling entered without one's consent except in accordance with law.

As a rule, private property can only lawfully be entered under a warrant. However, *D.P.P. v. Owens*[50] recognises that members of the Gardaí are entitled to go onto private property without a warrant, when carrying out an arrest.

This common law power appears to have been limited to some extent by the Criminal Law Act 1997. Section 5 provides that a garda can only enter a dwelling house for the purpose of an arrest under that Act if he or another member of the Gardaí has observed the person entering the dwelling; or if he, with reasonable cause, suspects that before a warrant of arrest could be obtained, the person will have absconded; or if he, with reasonable cause, suspects that before a warrant of arrest could be obtained, the person would commit an arrestable offence; or if the person ordinarily resides at that dwelling.

In order for an unlawful entry onto private property to be unconstitutional, the property in question must be a dwelling. The Constitution only recognises the inviolability of the dwelling. If the property is not a dwelling house, unlawful entry by the Gardaí breaches the occupier's legal rights, and gives the trial judge a discretion to exclude evidence obtained as a result, but does not make such evidence automatically inadmissible.

In *D.P.P. v. McMahon McMeel and Wright*[51] the Gardaí entered on licensed premises without a search warrant and without identifying themselves as Gardaí. Because of their failure to identify themselves, and because of the absence of statutory sanction for their activities, they were regarded as being on the premises without the owners' permission. However, even though their entry on the premises was unlawful, it did not constitute a breach of constitutional rights because the property was not a dwelling house.

---

[48] [1977] I.R. 159.
[49] McDermott, P.A. "Search Warrants" (2000) 10(2) I.C.L.J. 16.
[50] Unreported, Supreme Court, February 16, 1999.
[51] [1986] I.R. 393.

15.2.6   Constitutional right to fair procedures

When referring to constitutional rights, breaches of which may render evidence inadmissible, attention should be drawn to the amorphous constitutional right to fair procedures. This is an undefined right, which has been judicially referred to in other areas of evidence law, such as identification evidence. It is likely to become more important in the future, after being successfully invoked in *People (D.P.P.) v. Ward.*[52]

15.2.7   Fundamental fairness

Finally, it appears that a new ground for automatically excluding confession evidence is being recognised. If the way in which the evidence has been obtained breaches principles of fundamental fairness, it may be inadmissible.

Ironically, the concept of fundamental fairness originally developed as an alternative principle to the automatic exclusion on unconstitutionally obtained evidence. Its origins are to be found in the dissenting judgment of Griffin J. in *People (D.P.P.) v. Shaw.*[53]. Griffin J. was of the view that even if a confession was technically voluntary, a judge should have a discretion to exclude it if by reason of the manner or the circumstances in which it was obtained, it falls below the required standards of fairness.

As originally envisaged, the test of fundamental fairness did not impose a policy of absolute exclusion, but left matters up to the discretion of the trial judge.

However, more recent cases such as *People (D.P.P.) v. Ward*[54] have treated it as a ground for automatically excluding voluntary confessions. It may also be seen in the judgment of Walsh J. in *People (D.P.P.) v. Conroy.*[55] Walsh J. refers to the need for:

> "Observance of basic or fundamental fairness or procedures during interrogation by members of the Garda Síochána. If such basic fairness of procedures is not observed by members of the Garda Síochána, then it is the duty of the courts to implement constitutional guarantees by excluding the evidence so obtained."[56]

Given that basic fairness of procedures is a constitutional right, this exclusionary ground could possibly be seen as a subset of the rule preventing the admissibility of unconstitutionally obtained evidence.

Alternatively, it could be accommodated by extending the concept of oppression. When Walsh J. in *People (D.P.P.) v. Quilligan*[57] stated that a person held under section 30 of the Offences Against the State Act 1939 must not be subject to any form of questioning which the courts would regard as unfair or

---

[52.]   Special Criminal Court, November 27, 1998. See para 17.2.5.
[53.]   [1982] I.R. 1.
[54.]   Unreported, November 27, 1998. See para 17.2.5.
[55.]   [1986] I.R. 460.
[56.]   *Ibid.* at pp. 478-479
[57.]   [1986] I.R. 495, 508.

oppressive, he appears to be using the terms "unfairness" and "oppression" interchangeably.

15.3 Illegally obtained but not unconstitutionally obtained evidence[58]

Evidence which is obtained illegally but not unconstitutionally is not automatically prohibited. Evidence may be obtained illegally, either in breach of the common law or in breach of statute. If the source of law making the procedure illegal specifically says that evidence obtained as a result shall be inadmissible, then the evidence will be excluded. However, if statute or common law does not specifically provide that evidence obtained as a result of the breach is inadmissible, then the normal rule is that the evidence may be admitted.

D.P.P. v. Spratt[59] involved an accused arrested under the Road Traffic Act 1961. In this case, the accused had not been informed of his right of access to a solicitor. O'Hanlon J. held that there was no constitutional right in this jurisdiction to be informed of one's right to a solicitor, only a right under section 5 of the Criminal Justice Act 1984 and the Criminal Justice Act 1984 (Treatment of Persons in Custody) Regulations 1987, which require the right to legal access to be brought to the attention of a detainee. Breach of these provisions (as opposed to breach of the Constitution) does not make evidence obtained as a result automatically inadmissible.

However, the trial judge has an arguable discretion to exclude illegally but not unconstitutionally obtained evidence. This discretion was recognised by Kingsmill Moore J. in *People (D.P.P.) v. O'Brien*.[60] In the course of the applicant's trial for housebreaking, the Gardaí sought to adduce evidence of stolen property that they had found in his house. However, it transpired that the Gardaí had entered the property pursuant to an invalid search warrant. An error had been made in filling out the address of the applicant's house on the warrant, which referred to "Captain's Road" instead of "Cashel Road".

Kingsmill Moore J. stated that:

> "...the presiding judge has a discretion to exclude evidence of facts ascertained by illegal means where it appears to him that public policy, based on a balancing of public interests, requires exclusion".

It appears that this discretion is peculiarly subject to review by higher courts:

> "If he decides to admit the evidence an appeal against his decision should lie to a superior court which will decide the question according to its own views and will not be bound to affirm the decision of the trial judge if it disagrees with the

---

58. Pattenden (1980) 29 I.C.L.Q. 664; Martin "The Rationale of the Exclusionary Rule of Evidence Revisited" (1992) 2 I.C.L.J. 1; Ashworth "Excluding Evidence as Protecting Rights" (1977) Crim. L.R. 723; Choo "Improperly Obtained Evidence: A Reconsideration" (1989) Legal Studies 261.
59. [1995] 2 I.L.R.M. 117.
60. [1965] I.R. 142.

manner in which the discretion has been exercised, even if it does not appear that such discretion was exercised on wrong principles." [61]

In the circumstances, there was no deliberate treachery, deceit or illegality, no policy to disregard the provisions of the Constitution or to conduct searches without warrant. The misconduct was insufficient to outweigh the public interest in having crime detected and punished, and the evidence was admitted.

However, Walsh J., in the same case, failed to approve such a discretion:

"In my judgment the law in this country has been that the evidence in this particular case is not rendered inadmissible and that there is no discretion to rule it out by reason only of the fact that it was obtained by means of an illegal as distinct from an unconstitutional seizure."

He referred to:

"the anomalies which might be produced by the many varying ways in which that discretion might be exercised by individual judges".[62]

and preferred:

"absolute exclusion rather than a rule which might appear to lend itself to expediency rather than to principle".

However, arguably, the Supreme Court in *D.P.P. v. Mc Mahon McMeel & Wright*[63] have preferred the approach of Kingsmill Moore J. to that of Walsh J. and recognised a general discretion to exclude illegally obtained evidence. In this case the Gardaí had made a search of licensed premises without a warrant and without identifying themselves as Gardaí. This was contrary to legislation. However, the premises was not a dwelling, so there was no breach of constitutional rights. The Supreme Court said that they were dealing with a situation of evidence that had been obtained illegally but not in breach of constitutional rights, and they applied the judgment of Kingsmill Moore J., in *O'Brien*. They balanced the public interest in the detection of crime against the undesirability of using improper police methods.

In *McKenna v. Deery*[64] undercover Gardaí gave evidence at the trial of the applicant for providing facilities for unlawful gaming. The Supreme Court stated, *obiter,* that even if the Gardaí had acted unlawfully, the decision as to whether or not to exclude their evidence was a matter for the discretion of the trial judge. It was up to the trial judge to balance the public interest in obtaining such evidence against the prejudice to the applicant in admitting it. This approach appears to conflate the two discretions.

In addition, there have been a large number of cases in which the court has recognised a discretion to admit real evidence which does not comply with the custody regulations. However, this discretion, rather than arising from

---

[61.] *Ibid.* at 161.
[62.] *Ibid.* at p. 168.
[63.] [1986] I.R. 393.
[64.] [1998] 1 I.R. 62.

common law, appears to have been granted by the terms of the regulations themselves. Section 7(3) of the Criminal Justice Act 1984 provides:

> "A failure on the part of any member of the Garda Síochána to observe any provision of the Regulations shall not of itself render that person liable to any criminal or civil proceedings or of itself affect the lawfulness of the custody of the detained person or the admissibility in evidence of any statement made by him."

In *D.P.P. v. Spratt*[65] O'Hanlon J. said that section 7(3) leaves it to the court of trial to adjudicate on the question of whether or not the evidence could be admitted. Subsequent cases have laid down guidelines on the exercise of this discretion. In *People (D.P.P.) v. Darcy*[66] it was stated that there must be something in the circumstances of the case that would render the admission of the evidence unfair. The discretion to exclude in the case of unlawfully but not unconstitutionally obtained evidence was affirmed by Laffoy J. in *Universal City Studios v. Mulligan.*[67]

It appears that this discretion may primarily operate against the prosecution. United Kingdom case law indicates that the trial judge has no discretion to exclude admissible evidence tendered by an accused, even where it operates against a co-accused.[68]. Separate trials are the solution in this case.

In recognising a general discretion on the part of the trial judge to exclude illegally obtained evidence Irish judges have avoided the path of the United Kingdom courts in *R. v. Sang.*[69] The accused was charged with conspiracy to issue forged banknotes. He argued that he had been entrapped by an agent provocateur. In that case, it was held that the trial judge's discretion at common law to exclude illegally obtained evidence was regarded as founded on the privilege against self-incrimination, *nemo debet se ipsum prodere,* and only applied in the case of evidence obtained from the accused after the commission of the offence.[70] Lord Diplock stated as follows:

> "Save with regard to admissions and confessions and generally with regard to evidence obtained from the accused after commission of the offence [the judge] has no discretion to refuse to admit relevant admissible evidence on the ground that it was obtained by improper or unfair means. The court is not concerned with how it was obtained."[71]

This case went against the dicta of Lord Goddard in *Kuruma v. R.*[72] The accused was charged with unlawful possession of ammunition during a period

---

[65] [1995] 1 I.R. 585.
[66] Unreported, Court of Criminal Appeal, July 29, 1997.
[67] Unrepealed, High Court, Laffoy J., March 25, 1998.
[68] Devlin J. in *R. v. Miller* [1952] 2 All E.R. 667; Privy Council in *Lobban v. R.* [1995] 1 W.L.R. 877.
[69] [1980] A.C. 402.
[70] However, arguably, *R. v. Sang* was wrongly decided. It has been much criticised: [1979] Crim. Lr. 656; [1979] 30 N.I.L.Q.; Pattenden, "*Judicial Discretion and Criminal Litigation*" (2nd ed., Oxford University Press, 1990).
[71] At p. 436.
[72] [1955] A.C. 197.

of emergency in Kenya. The ammunition was found during an unlawful search. Lord Goddard stated:

> "In a criminal case the judge always has a discretion to disallow evidence if the strict rules of admissibility would operate unfairly against the accused."

Kuruma was approved by Davitt P. in *People (Attorney General)* and *O'Brien v. McGrath*.[73]

Also, in *Jones v. Owens*[74] a constable unlawfully searched the accused and found young salmon. Mellor J. said that if such evidence could not be used against the accused, it would be "a dangerous obstacle to the administration of justice".[75]

In *Jeffrey v. Black*[76] the accused was charged with the theft of a sandwich from a public house, and the police conducted a search of his room that was conducted without his consent. The Court of Appeal refused to admit evidence that cannabis had been discovered in the rooms. Lord Widgery C.J. recognised that the exercise of the discretion would be comparatively rare:

> "But if the case is exceptional, if the case is such that not only have the police officers entered without authority, but they have been guilty of trickery or they have misled someone, or they have been oppressive or they have been unfair, or in other respects they have behaved in a manner which is morally reprehensible, then it is open to the justices to apply their discretion and decline to allow the particular evidence to be let in as part of the trial ... if the case is such that not only have the police officers entered without authority, but they have been guilty of trickery, or they have misled someone, or they have been oppressive or they have been unfair or in other respects they have behaved in a manner which is morally reprehensible then it is open to the justices to apply their discretion and decline to allow the particular evidence to be let in as part of the trial."[77]

In *Callis v. Gunn*[78] Lord Parker C.J. said that fingerprint evidence was admissible in law, subject to the overriding discretion to exclude:

> "That discretion...would certainly be exercised by excluding the evidence if there was any suggestion of it having been obtained oppressively, by false representations, by a trick, by threats, by bribes, anything of that sort."

Arguably, *R. v. Sang* was wrongly decided insofar as it ignored the above authority. In any case, Irish judges have consistently recognised the existence of the discretion[79].

---

73. 99 I.L.T.R. 59.
74. (1870) 34 J.P. 759.
75. However, in contrast to this, in *R. v. Leatham* (1861) 8 Cox C.C. 498, a letter was found because of inadmissible confessions. Crompton J. held that "if you steal it even, it would be admissible".
76. [1978] Q.B. 490.
77. At p. 497.
78. [1964] 1 Q.B. 495, 502.
79. In the U.K., the courts have a statutory discretion to exclude under section 78 of the Police and Criminal Evidence Act if, having regard to all the circumstances, the admission of the evidence would have such an adverse effect on the fairness of the proceedings that the court ought not to admit it.

The approach in *R. v. Sang* has not been followed in other jurisdictions. In Australia, unlawfully obtained evidence may be excluded on grounds of public policy. *Bunning v. Cross*[80] outlined the basis of this exclusionary discretion:

> "It is not fair play that is called into question in such cases but rather society's right to insist that those who enforce the law themselves respect it."[81]

In Scotland, the position is directly the opposite to that of Ireland and Australia; here, illegally obtained evidence is automatically excluded, subject to an inclusionary discretion.[82]

Possibly the judgment of Morris P. in *Director of Public Prosecutions v. Lennon*[83] most closely accords with the Scottish approach. The accused had been deprived of her statutory right to provide a urine sample in preference to a blood sample because of lack of privacy in the toilets. Morris P. appeared to think that deprivation of a statutory right automatically rendered evidence obtained as a result inadmissible.

15.4 Civil cases

Unconstitutionally obtained evidence is automatically excluded in civil as well as in criminal cases. This was recognised by Laffoy J. in *Universal City Studios v. Mulligan.*[84] The action here was one for breach of copyright. Video cassettes that had been seized from the defendant's vehicle were important evidence for the plaintiff. However, the search warrant pursuant to which this evidence was obtained had been lost. Laffoy J. was forced to operate on the assumption that it had been invalid. She found that the unlawfulness had not amounted to breach of the accused's constitutional rights. However, she said obiter that if there had been such a breach, then the same rule would apply as in criminal cases, and the evidence would have been automatically excluded.

In relation to illegally but not unconstitutionally obtained evidence, it appears that the discretion referred to by Kingsmill Moore J. in *People (Attorney General) v. O'Brien* operates in this situation as well. Indeed, this was expressly recognised by Laffoy J. in *Universal City Studios v. Mulligan*, where she stated that the discretion to exclude unlawfully obtained evidence in criminal cases applied to civil cases also.

This can be contrasted with the United Kingdom decision of *Ibrahim v. R.*,[85] in which it was denied that such a discretion existed in civil proceedings.[86] However, in *ITC Film Distributors Ltd v. Video Exchange Ltd*[87] the defendant had obtained certain papers from the plaintiffs by a trick after they had been

---

80. (1978) 141 C.L.R. 54.
81. *Ibid.* at p. 75
82. *Lawrie v. Muir* (1950) J.C. 19.
83. Unreported, High Court, Morris J., June 26, 1998.
84. Unreported, High Court, Laffoy J., March 25, 1998.
85. [1914] A.C. 599.
86. See also *Helliwell v. Piggott-Sims* [1980] F.S.R. 356.
87. [1982] Ch. 436.

brought into court to use during the trial. The judge held that such an action was a contempt of court and that the documents should not be used in evidence. Warner J. said that the exclusion of the documents was necessitated in "the interests of the proper administration of justice".

However, in *Goddard v. Nationwide Building Society*[88] Nourse L.J. said that the decision of Warner J. "proceeded not on an exercise of the court's discretion, but on the grounds of public policy" and disapproved a general discretion in civil cases. Similarly, in *Rank Film Distributors v. Video Information Centre*[89] Lord Denning said that there was no exclusionary discretion in civil cases.

[88.] [1987] Q.B. 670.
[89.] [1982] A.C. 380.

Chapter 16

PRIVILEGE

16.1 Introduction[1]

Where applicable, the doctrine of privilege allows individuals or the State to avoid having to disclose relevant documents to a court. It also allows individuals or State officials to refuse to answer questions about privileged matters, even where such questions are relevant to the facts in issue. In the case of *Wentworth v. Lloyd*[2] it was stated that no adverse inference should be drawn against the side claiming the privilege.

By excluding relevant matters, the doctrine of privilege restricts the right to a fair trial and, therefore, requires constitutional justification. In order for the right to a fair trial to operate, it is necessary that a court should have all relevant evidence before it. This can be seen as a component of the administration of justice and also as a crucial part of the individual's right to a fair trial and right of access to the courts. This was recognised by Finlay C.J. in *Smurfit Paribas Bank Ltd v. AAB Export Finance*,[3] where he stated as follows:

> "The existence of a privilege or exemption from disclosure for communications made between a person and his lawyer clearly constitutes a potential restriction and diminution of the full disclosure both prior to and during the course of legal proceedings which in the interests of the common good is desirable for the purpose of ascertaining the truth and rendering justice. Such privilege should, therefore...only be granted by the courts in instances which have been identified as securing an objective which in the public interest in the proper conduct of the administration of justice can be said to outweigh the disadvantage arising from the restriction of disclosure of all the facts."

16.1.1 Types of privilege

There are two main types of privilege. Private privilege applies to individuals. Public interest privilege applies to the State. Public interest privilege will be dealt with in the final part of this chapter. The earlier parts of this chapter relate to instances of private privilege.

[1.] See generally: Delaney and McGrath "*Civil Procedure in the Superior Court*" (Round Hall Sweet & Maxwell, Dublin 2001) Ch. 8; McNichol "*Law of Privilege*" (Law Book Company, Sydney, 1992); Arbour, Lourie "Exposing truth while keeping secrets: publicity, privacy and privilege" XXXV (2000) *Ir. Jur.* 17.

[2.] (1864) 10 H.L. Cas. 589.

[3.] [1990] 1 I.R. 469.

Both public and private privilege are based on the idea of balancing the importance of ensuring truth against the public interest. However, it has been argued that, in the case of a private privilege, the judge does not engage in overt balancing in the same way that he does in relation to public privilege. Lord Taylor C.J. in *R. v. Derby Magistrates' Court, ex parte B.*[4] stated:

> "[I]f a balancing exercise was ever required in the case of legal professional privilege, it was performed once and for all in the sixteenth century, and since then has applied across the board in every case, irrespective of the client's individual merits."

Lord Lloyd in that case said that there could not be a balancing exercise in such cases – it would risk destroying the basis of the solicitor/client confidence. Lord Nicholls referred to the practical difficulties of a balancing test.[5]

There are a number of grounds on which an individual can claim private privilege. Private privilege applies to certain relationships, which are respected by the courts. Legal professional privilege allows an individual to prevent the disclosure of communications between himself and his legal adviser. It also allows him to prevent disclosure of communications between himself and/or his legal adviser and third parties, where such communications relate to contemplated litigation. The privilege against self-incrimination allows an individual to avoid disclosing documents or answering questions, which may implicate him in criminal proceedings. Sacerdotal privilege applies to priests and allows them to avoid disclosing matters of the confessional.

16.1.2 Duration of privilege

In *Quinlivan v. Tuohy*,[6] a case on legal professional privilege, Barron J. indicated that where a party to legal proceedings is entitled to claim privilege in those proceedings in relation to particular medical reports, that privilege is not lost in subsequent proceedings where the same reports are relevant.

The plaintiff instituted proceedings claiming damages for personal injuries out of a car accident. She had been involved in a previous accident in which she had suffered similar injuries. They sought the medical reports from those proceedings but this was rejected on the ground that they were privileged.[7]

16.1.3 Extent of privilege

Even if a document is privileged, this only means that the person who has the privilege does not have to disclose it or answer questions about it. If a third party has seen the document, then they can give evidence about it.

---

4. [1996] A.C. 487.
5. Comparison with Canadian courts in *R. v. Dunbar* (1983) 138 D.L.R. (3d) 221; *Smith v. Jones* [1999] 1 S.C.R. 565.
6. High Court, Barron J., July 29, 1992. See Conlon [1995] I.L.T. 56.
7. Contrast with *Kerry C.C. v. Liverpool Salvage Association* (1904) 38 I.L.T.R. 7.

In *Calcraft v. Guest*[8] the originals of privileged documents had been seen by witnesses and they had made notes on them. They were allowed to give evidence of the documents.

16.1.4 Waiver of privilege

It is possible for an individual to waive private privilege expressly or impliedly. Waiver may be implied from the failure of the individual to assert privilege. In Ireland, public privilege may be waived also.[9]

Waiver may be implied by the supply of privileged material to an expert who gives testimony about this material, or when the side claiming privilege uses the privileged material in cross-examination or to refresh a witness's memory.

Disclosure of the information to the public[10] or to the other side amounts to a waiver because it breaches confidentiality. If a privileged document is offered to an opponent to read, this waives the privilege whether or not he reads it. However, in the case of accidental disclosure, where it is obvious that the material must have been disclosed in error, then the privilege will not necessarily be taken as having been waived and an injunction may be obtained to stop the other side disclosing the information in evidence.[11]

There is an implied waiver of privilege in the context of a joint retainer. Communications between a solicitor and one of his clients will not be privileged against the other client but will be protected against outsiders. The institution of proceedings by a client against his solicitor also constitutes an implied waiver of privilege.

McMullen v. Carty[12] involved proceedings against solicitors for negligence in earlier proceedings. Evidence was given by the senior counsel briefed in the previous proceedings, and the plaintiff argued that this was in breach of his legal professional privilege. However, Lynch J., delivering the judgment of the Supreme Court, held:

> "When a client sues his solicitor for damages for alleged negligence arising out of the conduct of previous litigation against third parties and especially as in this case arising out of the settlement of such previous litigation, the client thereby puts in issue all the communications as between the solicitor and the client and the barrister and the client and also as between the barrister and the solicitor relevant to the settlement of the case and thereby impliedly waives the privilege of confidentiality."[13]

---

8. [1898] 1 Q.B. 759.
9. *McDonald v. RTE* [2001] 2 I.L.R.M. 1.
10. However, in *Bula v. Crowley*, unreported, High Court, March 8, 1991, Murphy J. held that privilege will not be lost where the communication was disseminated to third parties who share a common interest in the communication with the client.
11. *Lord Ashburton v. Pape* [1913] 2 Ch 469.
12. Unreported, Supreme Court, January 27, 1998.
13. *Ibid.* at p. 9.

A waiver of privilege is taken as only applying to the particular proceedings in respect of which the waiver was made and does not prevent the privilege being asserted in subsequent proceedings. In *British Coal Corp v. Dennis Rye Ltd (No. 2)*[14] the plaintiff in a civil suit handed a legally privileged document over to the police for the purposes of prosecuting the defendant. However, they were entitled to claim privilege in respect of the documents in the civil action.

If a document is privileged, is it possible to waive privilege in respect of part only of that document? It appears that the part waived must be capable of severance in order for the waiver to apply in respect of that part only. In *Great Atlantic Insurance Co. v. Home Insurance Co.*[15] part of a privileged document was introduced into a case. This was treated as being a waiver in respect of the entire document.

16.1.5 Privilege in civil and criminal proceedings

All heads of privilege apply equally to both civil and criminal proceedings. However, in criminal trials, private privilege is liable to be overridden in the interest of protecting the innocent from conviction.

16.1.6 Effect of failure to recognise privilege

A party may not necessarily be entitled to have his conviction overturned or get an appeal simply because a claim of privilege by a witness has been wrongly rejected or accepted.[16] It appears that it has been only where there has been an error in relation to a privilege belonging to that party, that decisions have been reversed.

16.2 Legal professional privilege[17]

Mellish L.J. in *Anderson v. Bank of British Columbia*[18] identified two heads of legal professional privilege. Legal advice privilege prevents the disclosure of any communications between lawyer and client made for the purpose of securing legal advice without the consent of the client. Litigation privilege prevents the disclosure of communications between the lawyer/client and third

---

14. [1988] 3 All E.R. 816.
15. [1981] 1 W.L.R. 529.
16. *R v. Kinglake* (1870) 11 Cox C.C. 499.
17. See also Conlon "Once Privileged Always Privileged: *Quinlivan v. Touhy*" 1995 I.L.T. 56; McGrath "Legal Professional Privilege and the Identity of a Client" 2001 6 Bar Rev. 268; McGrath, "Legal Professional Privilege" XXXVI (2001) I.R. Jur. 126; Collins, "Community Law and its impact on the Law of Provilege" (1997) I.C.L.R. 2-9; Hunt "Professional Privilege – on update" 15 (2002) *Irish Tax Review* 391; Fennelly "Legal Professional Privilege in Community Law" 1997, I.C.L.R. 2-1; Hunt "Whither professional privilege in Ireland" 15 (2002) Irish Tax Review 278; Noctor "Legal professional privilege and the public safety exception" (1999) I.L.T. 230; Fennelly "Lawyer and employed lawyers; the application of legal professional privilege" (1998) Irish Business Law 2; Matthews "Breach of Confidence and Legal Privilege" (1981) 1 L.S. 77; C. Passmore "The Future of Legal Professional Privilege (1999) 3 E. & P. 71; Nokes "Professional Privilege" (1950) 66 L.Q.R. 88.
18. (1876) 2 Ch. D. 644 at 649-650.

parties made in respect of pending or contemplated litigation without the consent of the client.

In both cases, legal professional privilege belongs to the client, rather than to the legal adviser or the third party. The client is the only person who can waive the privilege. If he decides to assert the privilege, he can stop his lawyers, communicating agents, or any third parties involved in the privileged communication from disclosing it.

The modern rationale behind this head of private privilege is to encourage people to seek legal advice. Legal advice can only be accurate if it is made after the consideration of all relevant facts. It is therefore necessary to encourage clients to disclose all facts to their lawyers without the fear that these facts will subsequently be used against them in court. The privilege has been described by Browne Wilkinson V.-C. in *English and American Insurance v. Herbert Smith*[19] as

> "...an important safeguard of a man's legal rights. It is the basis on which he and his advisers are free to speak as to matters in issue in litigation and otherwise without fear that it will subsequently be used against him."

In R. v. Derby Magistrates' Court, ex parte B.[20] Lord Taylor L.C.J. stated:

> "[T]he principle which runs through all these cases is that a man must be able to consult his lawyer in confidence, since otherwise he might hold back half the truth...legal professional privilege is thus much more than an ordinary rule of evidence...it is a fundamental condition on which the administration of justice as a whole rests."

Lord Taylor L.C.J. viewed the right to legal professional privilege as being a fundamental human right protected by the European Convention on Human Rights.

Finlay C.J. in *Smurfit Paribas Bank Ltd v. AAB Export Finance Ltd*[21] said that the rationale of this privilege was:

> "the requirement of the superior interest of the common good in the proper conduct of litigation which justified the immunity of communications from discovery insofar as they were made for the purpose of litigation as being the desirability in that goal of the correct and efficient trial of actions by the courts".

McCarthy J., in the same case, said that the justification lay in the need for candour between clients and solicitors.

Originally, the justification for legal professional privilege was based on respect for the position and honour of the lawyer. However, subsequently the basis of the privilege shifted to the importance of confidentiality in the lawyer-client relationship, on the basis that, as it is necessary for people to employ lawyers, they ought to be able to have confidence in them.

---

[19]   [1988] F.S.R. 232.
[20]   [1996] 1 A.C. 487.
[21]   [1990] 1 I.R. 469.

Legal professional privilege requires more extensive justification now that it has been recognised as infringing the constitutional right to a fair trial; this may be found in the argument that the privilege on balance operates to aid the administration of justice, and that it is in the interests of justice that a client should be legally represented. Indeed, this is recognised in criminal cases by the constitutional right to free legal advice.

In *Gallagher v. Stanley*[22] O'Flaherty J. demonstrated a restrictive approach to legal professional privilege. He stated that the purpose of such privilege was "to aid the administration of justice, not to impede it" and that "justice will be best served where there is the greatest candour and where all relevant documentary evidence is available".[23]

In this jurisdiction it appears that legal professional privilege has constitutional status. In *Miley v. Flood*[24] Kelly J. stated:

> "Legal professional privilege is more than a mere rule of evidence. It is a fundamental condition on which the administration of justice as a whole rests."

16.2.1 Legal advice privilege

Legal advice privilege can be asserted by the client who sought the advice or the solicitor. It can also be asserted by a third party who shares a common interest in the litigation with the client whether or not the third party is joined in the proceedings.[25]

Firstly, all communications between client and solicitor in the course of a legal relationship are privileged. However, a solicitor has to disclose the identity of his client.[26]

(1) The matter must be a communication

In the context of legal professional privilege, the term "communication" includes both oral and written communications. A solicitor cannot be asked questions about, or asked to provide notes of, oral communications with his client.

In the United Kingdom case of *R. v. R.*[27] the term "communication" was also held to include a blood sample sent by the client to a third party for the purposes of testing for pending litigation. This case was decided on the wording of section 10(1) of the Police and Criminal Evidence Act 1984 which defines legal professional privilege as applying to any items enclosed which have been made in connection with the giving of legal advice or in connection with or in contemplation of legal proceedings. However, it should be noted that

---

22. [1998] 2 I.R. 267.
23. *Ibid.* at p. 271.
24. [2001] 1 I.L.R.M. 489.
25. *Bula v. Crowley* [1990] I.L.R.M. 756.
26. *Burstill v. Tanner* (1885) 16 Q.B.D., recently reaffirmed in *Miley v. Flood* [2001] 1 I.L.R.M. 489. This is perhaps based on the rationale that a disclosure of identity is not necessary for the purpose of giving legal advice.
27. [1995] 1 Cr. App. R. 183.

this section was stated by Lord Goff in *R. v. Central Criminal Court, ex parte Francis*[28] to replicate the common law.

However, facts which have been inadvertently noticed by the legal adviser, are not regarded as communications and the legal adviser may be compelled to disclose them. In *Brown v. Foster*[29] a barrister saw a book at the preliminary examination of his client and was permitted to testify to the contents of this book at the trial of the charge. In *R v. Jack*[30] a husband was tried for his wife's murder. It was held that the wife's attitude to her husband as observed by her solicitor at the separation proceedings could be given in evidence by the solicitor.

The term "communication" includes any documents the originals of which were brought into existence for the purpose of instructing the lawyer and obtaining his advice. It also contains a selection of pre-existing documents, whether obtained from the client or a third party, which are not in themselves privileged, but which have been copied or assembled by a solicitor and betray the trend of the advice that he is giving. This term includes drafts of letters giving legal advice and notes made for the purpose of preparing such a letter.[31] A document cannot be made privileged simply because it is attached to a privileged communication, unless it is prepared for the privileged purpose. Otherwise, it would be easy to make all documents privileged. Therefore, it has been held that if a client deposits evidence of his crime with his solicitor, this is not covered by the privilege. In *R v. King*[32] a forged document was entrusted to a solicitor. This was held not to be privileged. In *R v. Justices of the Peace for Peterborough, ex parte Hicks*[33] a client sent pre-existing documents to a solicitor for the purpose of gaining legal advice. It was held that since the documents were not privileged in the hands of the client, they couldn't become so by being sent to a third party. This principle was reaffirmed in *Tromso Sparebank v. Beirne*.[34]

(2) The communication must be between a legal adviser and his client

The term "legal adviser" in this context includes someone who is mistakenly believed to be a lawyer.[35] It includes solicitors.[36] It also includes barristers: in *Bristol Corporation v. Cox*[37] a counsel's opinion, sent to the client via a solicitor, was held to be privileged. However, it does not extend to

---

[28.] [1989] A.C. 346.

[29.] (1857) 1 H. & N. 736.

[30.] (1992) 70 C.C.C. (301) 67.

[31.] *Hustridge Finance Ltd v. Lismore Homes Ltd*, unreported, High Court, Costello J., February 15, 1991.

[32.] [1983] 1 All E.R. 929.

[33.] [1978] 1 All E.R. 225.

[34.] [1989] I.L.R.M. 257.

[35.] *Calley v. Richards* (1854) 19 Beav. 401.

[36.] *Wheeler v. Le Marchant* (1881) 7 Ch. D. 675.

[37.] (1884) 26 Ch. D. 678.

communications with legal aid officers[38] or probation officers. It has been recognised also that the term includes in-house lawyers.[39]

A communication made to or from an agent of the legal adviser, such as his secretary or assistant, is regarded as a communication to or from the legal adviser. In *Wheeler v. Le Marchant*[40] Jessel M.R. stated that a communication was protected whether it was made by the client or an agent, and whether it was made to the solicitor or a clerk or subordinate who acts in his place and under his direction.

A communication made to an agent of the client is regarded as being a communication to the client, provided that the agent is employed for the purposes of giving advice on the part of the client.

Legal advice privilege does not protect communications between opposing parties or their advisers. Such communications can only be privileged on the alternative ground that they are without prejudice settlement negotiations.

(3) The communication must be referable to the relationship of client and solicitor

It is not necessary that there be a lawyer/client relationship in existence at the time of the communication. The privilege also extends to communications made to a solicitor with the aim of retaining his services.[41] However, the communication must be made in the course of a professional legal relationship or with the intention of establishing one. In *Buckley v. Incorporated Law Society*[42] correspondence with solicitors in the law society regarding the misconduct of a solicitor was not privileged because the Law Society was not being consulted as legal adviser.

However, the privilege does not extend to a solicitor who is consulted as a friend and not in a legal capacity,[43] even if that person is a solicitor.

(4) The communication must be for the purpose of seeking or giving legal advice

These communications must be for the purpose of seeking and giving legal advice. Originally, it was thought that these communications had to be in anticipation of prospective litigation; however this was rejected in 1833 in *Greenough v. Gaskell*[44] when Lord Brougham said that there is no need for litigation to be in contemplation in order for client-solicitor communications to be privileged.

---

38. *R. v. Umoh* (1986) 84 Cr. App. R. 138.
39. *Geraghty v. Minister for Local Government* [1975] I.R. 300 at 312 and *Attorney General, Quinlivan v. Governor of Portlaoise Prison*, unreported, Supreme Court, March 5, 1997 and *Duncan v. Governor of Portlaoise Prison (No. 2)* [1998] 1 I.R. 433.
40. (1881) 17 Ch. D. 675.
41. *Minter v. Priest* [1930] A.C. 558.
42. [1994] 2 I.R. 44.
43. *Smith v. Daniel* (1874) L.R. 18 Eq. 649.
44. [1824-34] All E.R. Rep. 767.

Conveyancing documents are not privileged because they do not come under the heading of legal advice. However, correspondence associated with a conveyance for the purpose of seeking or giving legal advice does constitute legal advice. In *Balabel v. Air India*[45] the privilege extended to communications between the appellants and their solicitors, such as drafts, working papers, attendance notes, and memoranda. Where information is passed between solicitor and client as part of a continuum of information to keep both informed, privilege will attach.

The dominant purpose of the communication must be legal advice: this can cause problems for in-house lawyers or civil servants where a mixture of political-legal advice or financial-legal advice may be looked for. In *Nederlandse Reassurantie Groep Holding NV v. Bacon & Woodrow (a firm)*[46] the solicitor in question provided both commercial and legal advice in relation to a particular transaction. It was held that communications in relation to this transaction would be privileged even if they didn't contain legal advice on matters of law, provided that they could be related to the performance by the solicitor of his professional duty as legal adviser.

It is irrelevant that the legal advice may not have related to the transaction which was before the court. In *Calcraft v. Guest*[47] the documents had been brought into existence for the purpose of a particular claim, which had been concluded – but they were still privileged. However, there may be a long-stop point. In *Schneider v. Leigh*[48] the plaintiff was claiming damages for personal injuries. The defendants in the proceedings had obtained a medical report from a doctor. The plaintiff viewed the doctor's report as defamatory and sought disclosure of it. It was held that the doctor was not entitled to rely on the defendants' privilege. This case also illustrates that legal professional privilege belongs to the client rather than to the third party who provides the information.

The leading Irish case on legal advice privilege is *Smurfit Paribas Bank Ltd v. AAB Export Finance Ltd.*[49] The defendant had a floating charge and had corresponded with its solicitor in relation to this charge. It claimed privilege in relation to the correspondence. The correspondence did not request legal advice but dealt with the drafting of documents in relation to the floating charge. Costello J. in the High Court said that these documents were not privileged because they did not request or contain legal advice and did not contain confidential information.

Finlay C.J. in the Supreme Court drew a distinction between communications made for the purpose of obtaining legal assistance and communications made for the purpose of obtaining legal advice. In the case of communications made for the purpose of obtaining legal assistance, there was

---

45. [1988] Ch. 317.
46. [1995] 1 All E.R. 976.
47. [1898] 1 Q.B. 759.
48. [1955] 2 Q.B. 195.
49. [1990] 1 I.R. 469.

no public interest stopping their disclosure. The documents in question were for the purpose of obtaining legal assistance rather than legal advice.

McCarthy J. in the above case further held that:

> "[a] communication of fact leading to the drafting of legal documents and requests for the preparation of such, albeit made to a solicior, unless and until the same results in the provision of legal advice, is not privileged from disclosure."[50]

(5) The communication must be confidential

Legal advice privilege only applies if the communication is confidential. In *Bord na gCon v. Murphy*[51] Murphy was charged with breach of the Greyhound Industry Act 1858. Bord na gCon wished to put in evidence a letter written to them by Murphy's solicitor. It was held that this letter was not confidential in nature and, therefore, was not protected by the privilege. However, it was held to be inadmissible because it was hearsay.

(6) The person claiming privilege must be client

Legal advice privilege belongs to the client rather than the lawyer, and the client can choose to waive or not to waive it as he sees fit. If the document is privileged in the hands of the solicitor, it is privileged in the hands of the client and vice versa. The privilege survives the death of a client and vests in the person entitled to his estate. However, in probate cases, a solicitor can give evidence as to the execution, validity, or interpretation of a will.

16.2.2   Litigation privilege

The second element of legal professional privilege excludes communications between clients and third parties or between legal advisers and third parties, which are made for the purpose of pending or contemplated litigation. This form of the privilege has been justified by reference to the adversarial system. James L.J. in *Anderson v. Bank of British Columbia* stated:

> "As you have no right to see your adversary's brief, you have no right to see that which comes into existence merely as the materials for the brief."[52]

(1) The matter must have formed part of a communication

The meaning of the term "communication" has been defined above in the context of legal advice privilege. Unlike legal advice privilege, the communication does not have to be between lawyer and client. It may be between the lawyer and a third party, or the client and a third party. Neither

---

[50.] See also *Hurstridge Finance Ltd v. Lismore Homes Ltd*, unreported, High Court, Costello J., February 15, 1991.
[51.] [1970] I.R. 301.
[52.] (1876) 2 Ch. D. 644.

does the communication have to be referable to a present or contemplated legal relationship.

There is a degree of overlap between litigation and legal advice privilege. In *Silver Hill Duckling Ltd v. Minister for Agriculture*[53] O'Hanlon J. felt that communications between client and lawyer while litigation is pending are best dealt with under legal advice privilege, but this point has yet to be definitively decided.

Communications with the other side will not attract privilege. In *Tobakin v. Dublin Southern District Tramways Co.*[54] a statement obtained from the plaintiff by an inspector of the tram company three days after the accident was not privileged.

(2) There must have been pending or contemplated litigation

In order for litigation to be pending or contemplated, there must be some definite proposal of litigation.

In *Wheeler v. Le Marchant*,[55] Jessel M.R. stated that letters passing between a surveyor and the defendant's solicitor in respect of property were not privileged under this head because they had been sent before litigation was contemplated in respect of this property.

Similarly, in *Kerry County Council v. Liverpool Salvage Association*[56] a claim of litigation privilege failed because no litigation had been contemplated at the time. This principle was affirmed in *Mc Mahon v. Great Northern Railway Co.*[57] in which it was stated that litigation must have commenced or be anticipated. This approach was affirmed by the courts of the Irish Free State in *Rushbrooke v. O'Sullivan*[58] and by the Supreme Court in *Gallagher v. Stanley.*[59]

(3) The dominant purpose of communication must have been use in pending or contemplated litigation

The dominant purpose for which the document was prepared must have been that of the pending or contemplated litigation. In *Waugh v. British Railways Board*[60] the plaintiff's husband, a railway worker, had been killed in a railway accident. She sought discovery of internal reports regarding his accident. The defendant claimed privilege in respect of these reports. The court held that litigation privilege was not appropriate in the circumstances and required disclosure of the documents. The dominant purpose of these reports was not to

---

53. [1987] 1 I.R. 289.
54. [1905] 2 I.R. 58. However, note *Horgan v. Murray* [1999] 1 I.L.R.M. 257.
55. 17 Ch.D. 675.
56. (1903) 38 I.L.T.R. 7.
57. (1906) 40 I.L.T.R. 72.
58. [1926] I.R. 500.
59. [1998] 2 I.R. 267.
60. [1980] A.C. 521.

counteract pending litigation but rather to increase employee safety in the future and to prevent such accidents recurring.

In *Neilson v. Laugharne*[61] it was held that statements obtained in the course of investigating a complaint against the police were not privileged. They had been prepared as part of a statutory duty under section 49 of the Police Act 1964 to investigate the complaint.

However, litigation does not have to be the sole purpose of the document in order for the privilege to be availed of. In *Bula Ltd v. Crowley*[62] it was alleged that if documents are created for two different purposes, it must be shown that the dominant purpose was the one attracting privilege. It was held that this had been satisfied here – there was only one purpose and there was no need for the person swearing the affidavit of discovery to assert that this was the dominant purpose unless it was a duality of purpose situation.

Murphy J. stated:

"It seems to me that the principle is material only where it appears that a document or documents came into existence for a duality of reasons one of which would attract the privilege and the other not. In the present case... the defendant has sworn that all the purposes for which the documents came into existence were privileged and hence it would be neither necessary nor appropriate to assert that there was a particular dominant purpose."

In *Re Highgrade Traders Ltd*[63] the Court of Appeal held that a report procured by an insurance company from a fire investigations firm was privileged because its dominant purpose had been the obtaining of legal advice.

In *Guinness Peat Properties Ltd v. Fitzroy Robinson Partnership (a firm)*[64] the plaintiffs were building developers who had notified the defendants, their architects, of a design fault. The defendants wrote to their insurance company in satisfaction of their obligation to notify of claims. The question was whether the document was privileged. It was held that it was. The purpose behind the insurance company's requirement of immediate notification of claims was to enable them to defend a future claim. *Re Barings*[65] criticised Re Highgrade Traders and Guinness Peat Properties as unduly lax applications of the dominant purpose test.

In *Power City Ltd. v. Monahan*[66] a letter was written by solicitors who were acting on behalf of people being sued for damages on the ground that a consignment of hi-fi equipment was in their custody when it was stolen. The owner of the equipment was suing them for its loss. The letter had been written by the defendants' solicitor to the superintendent of Store Street Garda Station. The defendants claimed privilege in respect of the letter. Kinlen J. said that this

---

61. [1981] 1 Q.B. 736.
62. [1991] I.R. 220.
63. [1984] B.C.L.C. 151.
64. [1987] 2 All E.R. 716.
65. Also known as *Secretary of State for Trade and Industry v. Baker* [1998] Ch. 356.
66. Unreported, High Court, Kinlen J., October 14, 1996.

document was privileged because its dominant purpose was preparation for apprehended or threatened litigation.

In *Silver Hill Duckling v. Minister for Agriculture*[67] it was held that in deciding the purpose of a communication, the courts will look at the content of a document and the surrounding circumstances, and not just at the heading put at the top of the document. In this case, the plaintiffs sought damages for loss caused to them by the slaughter of their ducks because of a contagious illness. The defendants claimed privilege in respect of a number of documents. O'Hanlon J. said that litigation could be regarded as threatened at the time these documents were made and, therefore, their dominant purpose was probably use in the litigation.

In *P.J. Carrigan Ltd. v. Norwich Union Fire Society Ltd*[68] a premises was destroyed by fire. The insurers commissioned a report because they were suspicious of the claim, and it was held that the report was privileged. It had been commissioned to deal with future litigation.

In *Davis v. St Michael's House*[69] the plaintiff, who was mentally handicapped, was injured in a fall at the defendants' school. The defendants claimed privilege in respect of an accident report form, which they had compiled as part of their duty to inform their insurer of all accidents. The purpose of this report form was to prepare the insurers for a claim. It was held that the dominant purpose of the form was to deal with the prospect of future litigation. It was consequently held to be privileged.

Gallagher v. Stanley[70] related to an action in respect of an infant who had been born severely disabled. The defendant hospital claimed privilege in respect of statements made by the nurses on duty at the birth to the Matron on the day following the birth. The matron gave evidence that she had requested these statements because she anticipated litigation. O'Flaherty J. refused to hold the statements privileged, being of the view that this was not the main reason behind the request for the statements. The actual reason the Matron had requested the statements was in order to be in a position to account for the events of the night in question and to prevent such events happening again.

16.2.3 Loss of legal professional privilege

There are certain recognised situations where legal professional privilege may be lost.

However, the recent approach of the House of Lords in *R. v. Derby Magistrates Court, ex parte B.*[71] has been to interpret these situations restrictively. As Lord Taylor L.C.J. stated in that case:

---

[67] [1987] I.R. 289.
[68] [1987] I.R. 619.
[69] Unreported, High Court, Lynch J., November 25, 1993.
[70] [1998] 2 I.R. 267.
[71] [1996] 1 A.C. 487.

"Once any exception to the general rule [of privilege] is allowed, the client's confidence is necessarily lost. The solicitor, instead of being able to tell his client that anything which the client might say would never in any circumstances be revealed without his consent, would have to qualify his assurance. He would have to tell the client that his confidence might be broken if in some future case the court were to hold that he no longer had any recognisable interest in asserting the privilege."[72]

On a contrary note it has been argued by some commentators that there should be a general exception to legal professional privilege where the public interest in disclosure clearly outweighs the public interest in the privilege. These commentators refer to the constitutional role in the administration of justice and argue that if legal professional privilege causes unjustified damage to the administration of justice, it may be curtailed.

As against this, the decision of Finlay C.J. in *Bula Ltd v. Crowley (No. 2)*[73] may be noted. In this case, the Chief Justice refused to extend one of the exceptions to the doctrine of legal professional privilege on the ground that this would lead to:

"a massive undermining...of the important confidence in relation to communications between lawyers and their clients which is a fundamental part of our administration of justice."[74]

(1) Where the privileged document accidentally comes into possession of prosecution

If the document comes into the possession of the prosecution, it may be admitted in evidence. This rule may be limited to documents rather than oral communications. In *R. v. Uljee*[75] it was held that a policeman could not testify to a conversation accidentally overheard by a solicitor and his client.

Documents may be admitted in evidence even though they were obtained in breach of confidence or even if they were mistakenly disclosed. In *Calcraft v. Guest*[76] the Court of Appeal allowed the use of privileged material where the originals had accidentally fallen into the defendant's hands.

R. v. Tomkins[77] involved a prosecution for handling stolen goods. The goods which were recorded as being stolen included a stereo with a loose button. (unclear?) The accused denied that his stereo was the one registered as stolen, saying that the button had never been loose on it. However, he ran into difficulty when confronted by a note from him to his counsel in which he stated that the button on his stereo had been loose and that he had glued it back on. Counsel for the prosecution had found this note on the floor of the court. It was held that the note was admissible in evidence.

---

72. At p. 507.
73. [1994] 2 I.R. 54.
74. *Ibid.* at p. 59.
75. [1982] 1 N.Z.L.R. 561.
76. [1898] 1 Q.B. 759.
77. (1977) 67 Cr. App. R. 1.

However, in contrast to the principle in the above cases, the equitable decision of *Ashburton v. Pape*[78] stated that the court of Equity will grant an injunction to restrain the use of confidential documents which have not yet been used in the relevant litigation, where such documents have been obtained by trickery. In *Ashburton v. Pape,* Pape, a party to bankruptcy proceedings, obtained by a trick copies of confidential and privileged correspondence between Ashburton and his legal advisers. Lord Ashburton obtained an unqualified injunction against any use being made of these copies, on the ground that Equity acts to restrain a breach of confidence. The principle is not confined to copies but would apply equally to prevent Pape from disclosing the original documents.[79]

In *English and American Insurance Co Ltd v. Herbert Smith,* Browne Wilkinson V.-C. stated that if documents merely escaped by mischance, it would be unfair to allow them in evidence. This case also established that the scope of the *Ashburton v. Pape* principle depends on how soon proceedings for the equitable injunction are initiated. They must be initiated before the document is sought to be adduced in evidence.

Guinness Peat Properties v. Fitzroy Robinson Partnership[80] held that this principle could apply even where confidential documents were not disclosed by trickery, but were produced as a result of inadvertence. One party to litigation mistakenly gave discovery of documents, which were clearly privilege. It was stated that if the other party should have realised on inspection that he had been permitted to see the document only by a mistake, then the court could grant an injunction to prevent him using it.[81]

This case also held, quite independently of *Ashburton,* that documents adduced by mistake may be taken back at any time before they have been inspected. However, once the other party has inspected the document, it is too late, unless the *Ashburton* principle applies.

Again, quite apart from the *Ashburton* principle, in *ITC Film Distributors v. Video Exchange Ltd*[82] it was held that policy precluded the use by parties of any privileged documents inadvertently left in court by their opponents. The public interest that litigants should be able to bring their documents into court without fear that they might be filched required that the documents not be disclosed. This was not an injunctive relief case as such; as the trial had already started, there would be difficulties in getting an injunction under *Ashburton*, but the documents were precluded in any case.

---

[78]   [1913] 2 Ch. 469.
[79]   However, note the limitation placed on *Ashburton v. Pape* by *Butler v. Board of Trade* [1971] Ch. 80; analysed by Tapper (1972) 35 M.L.R. 83; Heydon (1974) 37 M.L.R. 601. Quare whether this decision would be followed in this jurisdiction.
[80]   [1987] 2 All E.R. 716.
[81]   In this situation, the court has a discretion to grant an injunction against disclosure of the document and will normally exercise such discretion. This was stated by the Court of Appeal in *Derby v. Weldon & Co. (No 8)* [1991] 1 W.L.R. 73.
[82]   [1982] Ch. 431.

(2) In relation to proceedings under the Guardianship of Infants Act 1964

Special rules may apply in relation to proceedings under the Guardianship of Infants Act 1964. Section 3 of this Act requires a court to have regard to the welfare of the child as the paramount consideration and this requirement has been recognised as constitutionally mandated. In *L.(T.) v. L.(V.)*[83] McGuinness J. followed English authority on this matter[84] and held that where the welfare of the child required it, legal professional privilege must be departed from in such proceedings. However, a balancing approach had to be carried out in each individual case in order to decide this:

> "[T]he desirability of disclosure must on the facts of the case be weighed against the desirability of maintaining the privilege and a decision taken in the light of the interests of the child concerned."[85]

On the facts of the particular case she decided to allow the legal professional privilege to stand.

(3) In relation to testamentary dispositions

Legal professional privilege can be departed from where necessary to ascertain the intention of a testator. This exception has been recognised since the case of *Russell v. Jackson*.[86]. In *Re Fuld's Estate (No. 2)*[87] Scarman J. stated the rationale for this exception as follows: if there is a clash between the right of court to know everything necessary and the right of a party to claim privilege, the court is entitled to look for the truth of the matter; the whole purpose of such proceedings is to ascertain the truth:

> "[I]f the court comes to the conclusion that the truth can be discovered only byasking a witness to produce earlier statements that he may have made in writing concerning execution, the court is entitled to insist on seeing those statements."[88]

The recognition of this exception is no doubt also influenced by the fact that the original client is dead and has no real interest in maintaining privilege[89]. Arguably the solicitor-client relationship is not harmed but rather enhanced by disclosure in such a situation.

[83.] [1996] F.L.R. 126.
[84.] In *Re. L. (a minor)* [1996] 2 All E.R. 78 a report was prepared by a pathologist at the request of solicitors acting for the child's mother. The purpose of the report was to establish how the child had suffered an overdose of methadone. The report went against the mother, and the question was whether it should be admitted in proceedings relating to the welfare of the child under the Children Act 1989. In the circumstances, given that the proceedings were inquisitorial rather than adversarial, it was held to be permissible to disclose the report in the interests of the child.
[85.] *Ibid.* at p. 137.
[86.] (1851) 9 Hare 387.
[87.] [1965] 2 All E.R. 657.
[88.] *Ibid.*, p. 659.
[89.] Although, in theory, the privilege has passed on to his descendant.

Crawford v. Treacy[90] was a probate case where the wife of deceased was claiming her legal right share in respect of his estate. The testator's executors claimed legal professional privilege in respect of certain documents. The wife challenged this and argued that discovery of the documents should be allowed as the proceedings were not truly inter partes. However, O'Sullivan J, refused to ignore the privilege, stating that in this case the truth could be discovered in other ways. His judgment, however indicated that things might be different if the interests of justice could only be served by disclosing the documents.

(4) Where the communication exculpates an innocent person

The privilege may also be departed from in criminal proceedings where the communication in question exculpates the accused. In *R v. Barton*[91] the accused was charged with fraudulent conversion. He sought to obtain documents from a solicitor who pleaded legal professional privilege. Caulfield J. stated that:

> "if there are documents in the possession or control of the solicitor which, on production, help to further the defence of an accused man, then in my judgment no privilege attaches".

In *R. v. Ataou*[92] the question was whether a defendant in a criminal trial could compel disclosure of a statement made to a solicitor by one of his co-defendants, who had subsequently pleaded guilty and testified for the prosecution. The Court of Appeal held that it was up to the person seeking to exclude the privilege on this ground to show that it could not be sustained. The judge had to determine whether the legitimate interest of the defendant in seeking to breach the privilege outweighed that of the client in seeking to maintain it. French J. stated:

> "The resolution of the problem in each individual case involves balancing the competing interests of the public in the due and orderly administration of justice, on the one hand, and of the public and the accused, in ensuring that all evidence supportive of his case is before the court, on the other hand."[93]

However, this should be contrasted with a recent House of Lords decision in *R. v. Derby Magistrates Court, ex parte B.*[94] in which the House of Lords overruled *Barton* and *Ataou* and stated that legal professional privilege was absolute.

Derby Magistrates involved a prosecution for murder. One of the accused was acquitted. The second was charged with the murder and sought access to his co-defendant's communications with his lawyer before his trial. The House of Lords refused to recognise this right.

---

[90] Unreported, High Court, O'Sullivan J., November 4, 1998.
[91] [1972] 2 All E.R. 1192.
[92] [1988] Q.B. 709.
[93] At p. 807.
[94] [1996] 1 A.C. 487.

There are no Irish decisions on this point; however, the need to avoid convicting innocent persons has been taken into account in relation to the public interest immunity.[95]

(5) Where the communications were made for the furtherance of criminal offence or fraud

Also, communications made for the furtherance of a criminal offence, a crime or a fraud are excluded from legal professional privilege. The legal adviser does not have to be aware of the fraud.[96] It is merely necessary for the party seeking to obtain disclosure to establish a prima facie case of an intention to obtain advice in furtherance of a criminal or fraudulent purpose.

An early example is the case of *Annesley v. Earl of Anglesea*.[97] The plaintiff, James Annesley, brought ejectment proceedings against his uncle. The plaintiff had previously killed a gamekeeper and been acquitted of his murder. The defendant engaged a solicitor to start a private prosecution against the prosecution for murder, saying that he would give £10,000 if he could get the plaintiff hanged. This statement was held by the Irish Court of Exchequer not to be privileged and the solicitor could give evidence of it. It was:

> "so highly criminal that…whoever it was made to, attorney or not attorney, lies under an obligation to society in general, prior and superior to any obligation he can lie under to a particular individual, to make it known".[98]

In *People (Attorney General) v. Coleman*[99] it was held that a document attempting to procure the subornation of witnesses was not privileged because it contemplated the commission of a crime. In *R. v. Cox and Railton*[100] the case which established the rule, communications with solicitors made for the purpose of drawing up an allegedly fraudulent bill of sale were held not to be privileged. The *Derby Magistrates* case affirmed this exception.

This exception has been extended beyond crime or fraud to include other conduct injurious to the interest of justice. In *Murphy v. Kirwan*[101] the plaintiff sought an order of specific performance against the defendant in respect of an alleged agreement for the sale of shares. In his defence, the defendant alleged that the plaintiff had deliberately tried to stall the sale by the defendant of properties connected with the shares to a third party.

When the plaintiff's case was dismissed, the defendants pursued their counterclaim and sought discovery of all documents relating to legal advice sought and obtained by the plaintiff. The plaintiff claimed legal privilege but this was rejected. Costello J. ordered discovery on the grounds that the

---

[95]. *Director of Consumer Affairs v. Sugar Distributors* [1991] 1 I.R. 225; *Goodman International v. Hamilton (No. 3)* [1993] 3 I.R. 320.
[96]. *R. v. Cox and Railton* (1884) 14 Q.B.D. 153; *Tichborne v. Lushington* (1872) 22 Digest (Rep.) 409.
[97]. (1734) 17 How S. & Tr 1139.
[98]. *Ibid.*, p. 1243.
[99]. [1945] I.R. 237.
[100]. (1884) 14 Q.B.D. 153.
[101]. [1993] 3 I.R. 501.

plaintiffs could not hide their misconduct behind legal privilege. They had engaged in vexatious and frivolous proceedings. This was upheld in the Supreme Court.

Finlay C.J. stated:

> "[P]rofessional privilege cannot and must not be applied so as to be injurious to the interests of justice and to those in the administration of justice where persons have been guilty of conduct of moral turpitude or of dishonest conduct even though it may not be fraud.... Nothing could be more injurious to the administration of justice nor to the interests of justice than that a person should falsely and maliciously bring an action, and should abuse for an ulterior or improper purpose the processes of the court."[102]

In *Crescent Farm (Sidcup) Sports Ltd v. Sterling Offices Ltd*[103] there was a conveyance of land which was allegedly in breach of the plaintiff's right of pre-emption. The plaintiff sought discovery of an opinion prepared by the defendant's counsel prior to the conveyance. Goff J. held this to be privileged on the ground that committing the tort of inducing a breach of contract was not equivalent to fraud or dishonesty:

> "Parties must be at liberty to take advice as to the ambit of their contractual obligations and liabilities in tort and what liability they will incur whether in contract or tort by a proposed course of action without thereby in every case losing professional privilege."[104]

Similarly, in *Bula Ltd v. Crowley (No. 2)*[105] the plaintiffs brought proceedings claiming negligence on the part of the first-named defendant. They sought discovery of documents containing legal advice given to the defendant by his legal advisers. The Supreme Court said that this exception was restricted to conduct which contained an element of fraud, dishonesty, or moral turpitude.

Horgan v. Murray[106] involved a petition under section 205 of the Companies Act 1963. The petitioner claimed privilege in relation to advice obtained by him in the course of negotiations with the other side. It was argued that the advice had been obtained for the purpose of avoiding litigation and was, therefore, not privileged. O'Sullivan J. rejected this argument, stating that "[t]he policy of courts is to encourage settlement...the purposes of litigation include attempting to compromise it".[107]

It was irrelevant that the document in question had been drafted to be handed over to the other side but that the negotiations broke down before this could happen. O'Sullivan J. stated:

---

102. *Ibid.*, p. 511.
103. [1972] Ch. 553.
104. *Ibid.* at p. 565.
105. [1994] 2 I.R. 54.
106. [1999] 1 I.L.R.M. 257.
107. *Ibid.*, at 260.

"[T]his document came into being for the purposes of litigation, albeit for the specific purpose being presented to the other side as part of an effort to avoid litigation by compromise."[108]

(6) Where there has been a waiver of the privilege

The final way in which legal professional privilege can be lost is if it is waived by the client. Waiver can be express or implied. The issue of waiver is common to all types of privilege and is dealt with above at para 16.1.4.

16.3 Without prejudice communications

Communications which aim at settling a legal dispute, and which are intended to be immune from disclosure if the negotiations fail, are privileged from disclosure in such circumstances. The rationale behind this head of private privilege is to encourage the settlement of disputes.

In order to qualify for privilege, it is necessary to show that the communication was made in an attempt to settle a legal dispute. The case of *O'Flanagan v. Ray-Ger Ltd*[109] demonstrates that it is not enough to show that the communication was made in the context of a legal dispute; it must actually aim at settling that dispute. It is also necessary to show that it was the intention of the parties that if the negotiations failed, the communication would not be disclosed. In deciding these questions the court will not be unduly influenced by the fact that the communication is headed "without prejudice" and will examine the entire background to the making of the particular document before coming to a conclusion.

These principles were applied in *Ryan v. Connolly*,[110] where letters headed "without prejudice" were nonetheless held not to be privileged. This case also emphasised that the privilege may be departed from where the administration of justice requires this. Kelly J. stated:

"The rule, although firmly based on considerations of public policy, should not be applied in so inflexible a manner as to produce injustice."[111]

In addition, this privilege cannot be used as a cloak for an illegality or impropriety.

16.4 Informer privilege

It has been established since *Attorney General v. Briant*[112] that privilege can be claimed in respect of the identities of informers and documents disclosing their identities. This was affirmed in Ireland in *Director of Consumer Affairs v. Sugar Distributors Ltd*[113] in respect of a complaint made by a company to the

---

[108.] *Ibid.,* at 260.
[109.] Unreported, High Court, Costello J., April 28, 1983.
[110.] [2001] 2 I.L.R.M. 174.
[111.] *Ibid.*, p. 181.
[112.] (1846) 15 M. & W. 169.
[113.] [1991] 1 I.R. 225.

Director of Consumer Affairs that Sugar Distributors had breached restrictive practice legislations. In *D. v. N.S.P.C.C.*[114] it was established that communications to the National Society for the Protection of Children in relation to the abuse of children are also protected by this privilege.

However, informer privilege could not be claimed in *Buckley v. Incorporated Law Society*[115] in respect of an individual who had made a complaint to the Law Society because the complaint did not relate to a breach of criminal law. The only possible claim was one of public interest privilege. The court balanced the relevant public interests and found in favour of disclosure. This decision can be contrasted with the case of *Goodman International (No. 3) v. Hamilton*[116] in which a T.D. was allowed to refuse to disclose his sources. In this case, the importance of public matters being brought to the attention of political representatives was emphasised.

In *Ward v. Special Criminal Court*[117] O'Flaherty J. emphasised that informer privilege is not absolute and may be set aside where the disclosure of the identity of an informer might tend to show the innocence of an accused. This limitation on informer privilege has long been recognised.[118]

In this case the accused sought disclosure of 40 statements made to Gardaí in the course of the investigation into the murder of crime journalist Veronica Guerin. The prosecution refused to disclose the identities of the individuals who had made the statements. The accused argued that the defence could not assess the information without being aware of the identities of the informants.

In the High Court, Carney J. said that the decision regarding disclosure ought to be made by the judiciary rather than by the Gardaí or by the legal team for the prosecution. The Special Criminal Court had stated that the accused's legal advisers could look at the documents so long as they did not disclose their contents to the accused. Carney J said that this was incorrect. He said that the Special Criminal Court had to look at the documents and decide whether any of them might be useful to the accused. If they were of use in proving his innocence, then they should be disclosed. In the Supreme Court, O'Flaherty J. endorsed this conclusion. However, he declined to give a direction to the Special Criminal Court to examine the documents and left this up to their discretion.

16.5 Journalistic privilege

It appears that despite the decision in *Re Kevin O'Kelly*[119] stating that journalists were not entitled to refuse to disclose their sources, a journalist may be able to claim privilege in extreme circumstances. In *Burke v. Central Independent Television plc*[120] the plaintiffs instituted proceedings against the

---

[114]. [1978] A.C. 171.
[115]. [1994] 2 I.R. 44.
[116]. [1993] 3 I.R. 320.
[117]. [1998] 2 I.L.R. 493.
[118]. *Marks v. Beyfus* (1890) 25 Q.B.D. 494.
[119]. (1974) 109 I.L.T.R. 97.
[120]. [1994] 2 I.R. 61.

defendant for libel. The defendants refused to disclose certain documents on the grounds that to do so would put their sources' lives at risk. The court refused to order disclosure, holding that the right of the sources to bodily integrity must be given precedence.

16.6 Sacerdotal and counselling privileges[121]

In Cook v. Carroll[122] a priest refused to testify regarding the contents of a conversation he had had with the defendant in the action. Gavan Duffy J. refused to hold him in contempt of court and held that he was entitled to claim privilege in respect of the conversation.

Gavan Duffy J. said that in order for a privilege to arise, the following must apply:

1. the communications must be confidential;

2. the confidentiality must be essential to the full and satisfactory maintenance of the relation;

3. the relation must be one which, in the opinion of the community, ought to be fostered; and

4. the injury which would ensue by the disclosure of the communications must be greater than the benefit gained for the litigation.

He concluded that priests should be entitled to claim privilege in respect of matters confided to them in the confessional.

In *E.R. v. J.R.*[123] Carroll J. extended the above privilege to cover communications made with a religious officer acting as a marriage counsellor. However, she regarded the privilege as belonging to the spouses rather than the officer and could be waived by their consent. Gavan Duffy J., on the other hand, had regarded the privilege as belonging to the priest rather than to the person who had confided in him.

These decisions were reviewed by Geoghegan J. in *Johnston v. Church of Scientology.*[124] The plaintiff was arguing that she had been brainwashed by the defendants. She sought disclosure of "counselling notes" which had been made during "auditing" and "training", part of the spiritual practices of scientology. The defendants explained that these were one-to-one confidential sessions and that an "auditor" was under compuslsion not to disclose details of them.

Geoghegan J. was of the view that Gavan Duffy J. in *Cook v. Carroll*[125] had confused "sacerdotal privilege" and "counselling privilege". The concept of a "sacerdotal privilege" belonging to religious officers appears to have been

---

121. Callahan "Historical Enquiry into the Priest Privilege" (1976) 36 *Jurist* 328; Foley-Friel, "Privilege for Marriage Counsellors" (1994) I.L.T. 193.
122. [1945] I.R. 515.
123. [1981] I.L.R.M. 125.
124. Unreported, High Court, Geoghegan J., April 30, 1999.
125. [1945] I.R. 515.

upheld by Geoghegan J.; however, he viewed it as a *sui juris* construct of the pre-reformation common law. In the context of the case before him, he felt that no analogy could be drawn between "auditing" and "training" on the one hand, and the confessional on the other. In addition, there was the vexed question of whether Scientology actually qualified as a religion.

Counselling privilege, on the other hand, did not belong to the counsellor, but rather to the person being counselled, who could choose to waive it, as in this case. Geoghegan J. indicated that the counselling privilege could extend to secular counselling and made a specific reference to marriage counselling in this context.

16.7 The privilege against self-incrimination[126]

16.7.1 Definition of the privilege

The privilege against self-incrimination was defined by Shanley J. in *Re National Irish Bank*[127] as a right on the part of an individual to refuse to answer a question or to produce a document when to do so would tend to expose such an individual to a real risk of criminal prosecution or penalty.

This mirrors the dictum of Lord Goddard C.J. in *Blunt v. Park Lane Hotel*:

> "No one is bound to answer any question if the answer thereto would, in the opinion of the judge, have a tendency to expose the deponent to any criminal charge, penalty or forfeiture."[128]

16.7.2 Privilege allows refusal to answer question/produce document/comply with search order

The privilege applies to allow a person to refuse to produce documents in court or to answer requests for further information. It also permits refusal to comply with search orders, or to answer questions either in or out of court.[129]

The privilege does not prevent questions being asked of a witness, although it does allow him to refuse to answer those questions. When a witness is asked questions which might incriminate him, the judge should let the witness know that he is entitled to claim the privilege against self-incrimination.

---

126. Redmond "The Privilege against self-incrimination in the context of the 1990 Companies Act" (1993) 3 I.C.L.J. 118; Dillon-Malone "The privilege against self-incrimination in the light of *Saunders v. United Kingdom*" 2(4) 1997 Bar Rev. 132; Ring, "The Right to Silence: *Rock v. Ireland and Others*" 3 (5) 1997 Bar Rev. 225; Davies "Prohibition against adverse inferences from silence: a rule without reason" (2000) 74 A.L.J. 26, 99; McDermott "Silence as a Criminal Offence" (2001) 11(1) 1 C.L.J. 9; Keane "Privilege Against Self-Incrimination – Implied Statutory Abrogation and Human Rights" (2000) *Crime Online Commentary Archive* F19.14; New Zealand Law Commission Preliminary Paper 25 "The Privilege Against Self Incrimination" (1996); O'Connor and Cooney "Criminal Due Process, the Pre-Trial Stage and Self Incrimination" (1980) 15 Ir. Jur. (n.s.) 219; Dennis "Instrumental Protection, Human Right or Functional Necessity? Reassessing the Privilege Against Self Incrimination" (1995) C.L.J. 342.
127. [1999] 3 I.R. 145.
128. [1942] K.B. 253.
129. *Tate Access Floors v. Boswell* [1991] Ch. 512.

16.7.3 Criminal charge, penalty or forfeiture

The privilege against self-incrimination allows a witness to avoid answering questions which might tend to expose him to a criminal charge, penalty or forfeiture. Penalty in this context includes a revenue penalty. *RTZ Corporation v. Westinghouse Electric Corporation*[130] also established that this expression included any fine, which might become due to the E.U. Commission. However, exposure to an order for damages in civil proceedings or a divorce suit does not amount to a penalty for the purposes of the privilege against self-incrimination and a witness is not entitled to refuse to answer a question put to them on this ground.

16.7.4 Tendency to expose

The precise words used by Lord Goddard in *Blunt v. Park Lane Hotel*[131] are that the penalty must have "a tendency to expose" the witness to the charge, penalty, etc.

In *R. v. Boyes*[132] it was stated that the expression "tendency to expose" means that there must be a reasonable ground to apprehend that the criminal charge will be brought or that the charge will be levied or that the forfeiture will be carried out. The danger must not be of an imaginary and unsubstantial character. In this case, a witness was handed a pardon in order to encourage him to testify. It was held that, in the light of this pardon, his answers would not tend to expose him to criminal liability.

In *State (Magee) v. O'Rourke*[133] O'Dalaigh C.J. held that before a person could allege that he might be incriminated under foreign law there would have to be a reasonable possibility of his extradition to the country in question. This contemplates that liability to conviction in a different jurisdiction may on occasion be sufficient to justify a witness invoking the privilege.[134]

16.7.5 The deponent

The person incriminated must be the witness himself. A witness cannot refuse to answer questions on the ground that his answers might incriminate strangers,[135] or even on the ground that he might incriminate a spouse. The privilege is, after all, described as a privilege against self-incrimination.

The Law Reform Commission has suggested that the privilege against self-incrimination should be extended to cover answers tending to incriminate the

---

[130.] [1978] A.C. 547.

[131.] [1942] 2 K.B. 359.

[132.] 9 Cox. C.C. 32.

[133.] [1971] 1 I.R. 205.

[134.] In the United Kingdom, liability to conviction in a different jurisdiction was not sufficient to entitle a witness to invoke the privilege against self-incrimination at common law: *Brannigan v. Davison* [1996] 3 W.L.R. 859.

[135.] *R v. Minahane* [1921] 16 Cr. App. R. 38.

spouse of a witness. *R. v. All Saints Worcester Inhabitants*[136] contains a statement that the privilege may extend to matters incriminating a spouse. However, in contrast to this, in *R. v. Pitt*[137] it was held that if a spouse chose to testify for the prosecution, she would be treated like any other witness; this implied that she was not able to claim a privilege against incriminating her spouse.

16.7.6 Purpose of the privilege

The privilege against self-incrimination is based on the Latin maxim *Nemo tenebatur prodere seipsum,* namely that a man should not be his own accuser. The purpose of the privilege may be located in the need to encourage people to come forward and testify. This rationale for the privilege regards it as assisting the administration of justice.

An alternative rationale for the privilege against self-incrimination sees it as located in the right to privacy and personal autonomy.

16.7.7 Application in relation to the accused in criminal proceedings

Originally, the privilege against self-incrimination applied only to an accused, and operated to stop him from giving any testimony in criminal proceedings. It was based on the principle that no one should jeopardize his own life or liberty by answering questions on oath. The privilege came to be applied to all witnesses in all proceedings in the seventeenth century.

Nowadays, the accused is permitted to testify in criminal proceedings, and the privilege against self-incrimination has been modified in its operation in relation to his testimony. Section 1(e) of the Criminal Justice (Evidence) Act 1924 provides that the accused may be asked any question in cross-examination notwithstanding that it might tend to incriminate him. However, if the accused's answers would tend to reveal his guilt in relation to offences for which he has not yet stood trial, he should be able to claim the privilege in the same way as other witnesses.

However, section 1(e) only applies to cross-examination. The privilege against self-incrimination applies in full to any pre-trial questioning of an accused and prevents him from being penalized for failing to answer such questions.

16.7.8 Application in civil proceedings

The privilege applies to all witnesses in civil proceedings, parties and non-parties alike. It also applies to pre-trial situations such as *Anton Piller* discovery orders.

[136.] [1817] 6 M. & S. 194.
[137.] [1983] Q.B. 25.

In *Rank Film Distributors v. Video Information Centre*[138] the House of Lords held that the privilege could be invoked at common law by defendants to a civil action for copyright infringement who had been served with an interlocutory mandatory injunction known as an *Anton Piller* order requiring them to disclose records and materials. The defendants were held entitled to refuse to comply with such an order on the ground that such compliance might tend to expose them to criminal charges for a conspiracy to defraud.

Cross has remarked of the privilege against self-incrimination:

"One area of pressure has been to extend the privilege further and further before the occasion of testifying."[139]

The application of the privilege to pre-trial procedures in civil proceedings has been criticized by Lord Templeman in *AT & T Istel v. Tully.*[140] In the United Kingdom, the Lord Chancellor's Department has published a consultation paper recommending the withdrawal of the privilege in civil proceedings subject to a secondary privilege to the effect that information so divulged could not be used in subsequent civil proceedings.

16.7.9 Relationship between the privilege against self-incrimination and the right to silence

The right to silence was defined by Lord Mustill in *R. v. Director of Serious Fraud Office ex parte Smith*[141] as being any one or more of a disparate group of six protections. The constituents of the right to silence are as follows:

1. The accused cannot be compelled to testify.

2. The prosecution cannot comment on the accused's failure to testify, and the judge can only do so subject to constraints.

3. The accused cannot be compelled to say anything prior to his trial.

4. No inferences may be drawn in court from an accused's failure to answer questions or tell his story prior to the trial.

5. A witness or a party in a civil case cannot be compelled to provide a document or answer a question at the trial if it may incriminate him.

6. A witness or a party in civil case is also allowed immunity from providing documents or answering questions prior to the trial if this may incriminate him.

On the above analysis the privilege against self-incrimination constitutes a subset of the right to silence. However, a number of Irish decisions such as *Rock v. Ireland*[142] and the judgment of Barrington J. in *Re National Irish Bank*[143] have tended to use the two terms interchangeably. The judgment of the

---

[138]. [1982] A.C. 380.
[139]. *Cross and Tapper on Evidence* (4th ed., London, Butterworths 1999), p. 488.
[140]. [1993] A.C. 45.
[141]. [1993] A.C. 1.
[142]. [1991] 3 I.R. 484.

European Court of Justice in *Saunders v. United Kingdom*[144] recognizes the
overlap between the two rights, stating that "the right not to incriminate
oneself is primarily concerned with respecting the will of an accused person to
remain silent."

In this work, the privilege against self-incrimination is used to refer to the
accused's right not to be penalized for refusing to answer questions which
might incriminate him. The right to silence is given a broader meaning so as to
include not only the privilege against self-incrimination but also the right of
the accused in a criminal trial not to have adverse inferences drawn from his
silence to such questions or from his failure to testify.

Finally, both the right to silence and the privilege against self-incrimination
have been seen as connected with the presumption of innocence.

16.7.10 The constitutional status of privilege against self-incrimination

In the United Kingdom, statutes have been passed which interfere with the
privilege against self-incrimination. However, the courts have held substituted
protection to exist in these circumstances, namely, the concept of secondary
privilege, which provides that information obtained subject to such statutes
cannot be used against the person who has been compelled to provide it in any
subsequent proceedings.

In Ireland, statutes have been introduced which compel an accused to reply
to pre-trial questioning and either penalize him if he fails to do so or provide
that his failure to speak can be used in evidence against him at the trial. It has
been argued that these statutes are unconstitutional and, indeed, in this
jurisdiction it appears that the privilege against self-incrimination has been
given constitutional status as a facet of the right to silence.

16.7.11 Statutory interference with the privilege against self-incrimination

Heaney and McGuinness v. Ireland[145] involved a constitutional challenge to
section 52 of the Offences Against the State Act 1939. Section 52 provides that
whenever a person is detained under Part IV of the Offences Against the State
Act 1939, any member of the Gardaí can demand of that person a full account
of all his movements and actions during any specified period and all
information in his possession in relation to the commission or intended
commission by another person of any offence under any section or subsection
of this Act or any scheduled offence. Failure on the part of the person arrested
to give such an account on request amounts to an offence, which carries a
liability to imprisonment for up to six months.

The plaintiffs were arrested under section 30 of the Offences Against the
State Act 1939, on suspicion of being members of the I.R.A. While in
detention, they were asked to account for their movements. They refused to do

---

143. [1999] 3 I.R. 145.
144. (1996) 23 E.H.R.R. 313.
145. [1996] I.R. 580.

so and were consequently convicted under section 52 of the Offences Against the State Act 1939.

In this case, O'Flaherty J., delivering the judgment of the Supreme Court, held that the right to silence/privilege against self-incrimination was prima facie breached by this provision. O'Flaherty J. viewed the right to silence, which included the privilege against self-incrimination, as a corollary of the right to freedom of expression conferred by Article 40 of the Constitution. However, the right to freedom of expression could be limited by public order and morality. The State was entitled to encroach on the right to remain silent in order to maintain peace and order, provided that such encroachment was proportionate. He concluded that this particular encroachment had been proportionate.

As stated above, the privilege against self-incrimination prevents the accused from being penalized for failure to speak. The right to silence is arguably wider and prevents inferences to be drawn from the accused's silence in cases where he is not penalized for failure to speak. *Rock v. Ireland* involved a constitutional challenge to a statutory provision which allowed inferences to be drawn from the accused's failure to speak. Although, strictly speaking, this provision did not involve a breach of the privilege against self-incrimination, this case is worth examining in this context as the principles laid down in it could equally apply to statutes which infringe the principle against self-incrimination.

In *Rock v. Ireland* the accused was charged with the offence of being in possession of forged banknotes, knowing them to be forged, contrary to section 8 of the Forgery Act 1913. He had been found in a toilet cubicle with a bag filled with stolen banknotes on the floor beside him. The accused was detained under section 4 of the Criminal Justice Act 1984 and the provisions of sections 18 and 19 were explained to him.

These provisions stated that the accused's a failure to account for a mark or presence at a particular place would allow the court to draw such inferences as might appear proper. The court could treat the accused's failure to answer as corroboration of any other evidence, but the accused could not be convicted of an offence solely on an inference drawn from such failure or refusal. Rock argued that these sections were unconstitutional, arguing that the right to silence, as well as the presumption of innocence had been infringed.

The Supreme Court upheld the constitutionality of these sections, stating that they did not infringe the principle that the burden of proof rests on the prosecution in a criminal trial. Neither did the provisions infringe the right to silence.

In contrast to the earlier decision in *Heaney, Rock v. Ireland* appears to view the right to silence as being a component part of the right to a fair trial. However, this right had not been breached in the instant case. It was recognized that the trial court when deciding what inferences can be drawn from an accused's failure to account must act in accordance with the accused's right to a fair trial and the presumption of innocence. The Supreme Court in

Rock held that there was a right to silence under the Constitution but that the restrictions imposed on it in this case were proportionate.

The court did not automatically accept the State's argument that sections 18 and 19 were less restrictive than section 52 and were therefore more justifiable. They pointed out that the Criminal Justice Act 1984 was of much wider application then the Offences Against the State Act 1939 and that, in addition, it could be potentially more dangerous to allow inferences be drawn at the main trial rather to prosecute the accused separately for remaining silent. They drew attention to the fact that, although the accused is liable to imprisonment for failure to comply with section 52 of the Offences Against the State Act, no adverse inferences can be drawn from his silence at the trial of the scheduled offence for which he had been arrested.

Hamilton C.J. said that in enacting sections 18 and 19, the legislature was seeking to balance the individual's right to avoid self-incrimination against the right and duty of the State to defend and protect the life, person and property of its citizens. In this context, the task of the Supreme Court was not to decide whether a perfect balance had been achieved, but rather to decide whether in restricting individual constitutional rights the legislature had acted within the range of permissible options. In this case, the legislature had done so. In coming to this conclusion the Supreme Court drew attention to certain safeguards in sections 18 and 19. A person could not be convicted solely on the basis of an inference under these sections, and, secondly, the sections only allowed an adverse inference to be drawn where the court was of the opinion that such an inference was proper. The court viewed these as sufficient safeguards.

In *Gilligan v. Criminal Assets Bureau*[146] the accused argued that the Proceeds of Crime Act 1996 infringed the privilege against self-incrimination. In particular, he claimed that sections 2 and 3 of the Act required him to give evidence or risk losing his property. However, McGuinness J. came to the conclusion that these sections did not involve any direct or indirect compulsion to provide information. It may be noted, however, that the doctrine of compulsion in contract law, which allows contracts to be set aside where entered into under duress, regards threats to a person's property or business as amounting to sufficient compulsion.

In addition, McGuinness J. considered whether or not section 9 of the Act infringed the privilege against self-incrimination. Section 9 provides that at any time the court may, by order, direct a respondent to file an affidavit in the Central Office specifying the property which he owns and its income. In *M.(M.) v. D.(D.)*,[147] Moriarty J. applied the concept of secondary privilege and held that no disclosure made in compliance with the order could be used as evidence in the prosecution of an offence alleged to have been committed by the person who had been required to make that declaration or by his or her spouse. An undertaking must be given by the Director of Public Prosecutions

---

146. [1998] 3 I.R. 185.
147. [1998] 3 I.R. 175.

to this effect. McGuinness J. felt that the type of undertaking required by Moriarty J. in the above case should be required in every case where an order under section 9 was granted.

It is also worth noting in this context that section 7(1) of the Criminal Justice (Drug Trafficking) Act 1996 provides that where, in any proceedings against a person for a drug trafficking offence, evidence is given that the accused, on being questioned, charged or informed that he or she might be prosecuted, failed to mention any fact relied on in his or her defence, being a fact which in the circumstances existing at the time he or she could reasonably have been expected to mention, the court, in determining whether the accused is guilty of the offence charged, may draw such inferences from it as appear proper. Such failure may be treated as corroboration, but no one can be convicted of an offence solely on an inference to be drawn from such failure. The effect of this section must also be made known to the accused. It appears that this section would be found to be constitutional under the principles laid down in *Rock v. Ireland.*

In *Re National Irish Bank (No. 1)*[148] a constitutional challenge was brought in relation to questions asked by inspectors under section 10 of the Companies Act 1990. Inspectors were appointed by the High Court under section 8(1) of the Companies Act 1990 to examine the affairs of National Irish Bank. Section 10 of the Companies Act 1990 places a duty on officers and agents of a company being investigated and other persons in possession of relevant information to co-operate with the inspectors and to produce documents and answer questions. Section 18 provides that an answer given by a person "may be used in evidence against him".

Both the High Court and the Supreme Court recognized that the requirement to provide information infringed the right to silence. In this case it was recognized that the privilege against self-incrimination was a component part of the right to silence; that it applied to documents as well as testimonial statements, and that it could be applied in non-judicial proceedings. However, applying the principles laid down in *Heaney and McGuinness v. Ireland,*[149] it was held that this restriction was proportionate.

Shanley J. in the High Court stated:

"[I]t is, of course, a legitimate objective of the State, and entirely in the public interest, to lay bare frauds and dishonest stratagems, and where the only means of effectively achieving such an objective is to provide an investigative procedure without a right to silence one can properly assert that the restrictions imposed by section 10 on the right to silence are no greater than are necessary."[150]

However, a slightly different approach was taken by Barrington J. in the Supreme Court regarding the question of the admissibility in a subsequent

---

[148.] [1999] 3 I.R. 145.
[149.] [1996] 1 I.R. 580.
[150.] *Ibid.*, p. 166.

criminal trial of evidence obtained under section 10. He felt that the admissibility of such evidence would breach the right to a fair trial contained in Article 38.1. Applying the presumption of constitutionality, he said that section 10 did not allow evidence obtained under it to be admitted in a subsequent criminal trial where the voluntariness of such evidence could be said to be suspect.

It was a matter for the trial judge to decide if the evidence was voluntary or not. If it was not voluntary, it should not be admitted. However, it was emphasized that all of the circumstances in which the statement was made have to be looked at in deciding this question. Barrington J. stated:

> "[T]he fact that Inspectors are armed with statutory powers or may even have invoked them does not necessarily mean that a statement made in reply to their questions is not voluntary".[151]

McGrath has stated:

> "[I]t would appear in the aftermath of the decision [in Re National Irish Bank] that there is a constitutional division of labour in the protection of the privilege between Articles 40.6.1 and Article 38.1 based on a distinction between the extraction and use of compelled testimonial statements. Provisions which seek to compel testimonial statements will be considered under Article 40.6.1. I while the issue of the use to be made of such statements falls to be examined under the rubric of article 38.1 and the newly constitutionalised voluntariness rule."[152]

He also says:

> "[I]t would appear that the net effect of the decision may be that the Legislature may readily abridge the privilege but if the statute in question does not make provision for substituted protection by sterilizing any compelled answers then the courts will achieve the same result by applying the voluntariness test."[153]

Sections 2 and 5 of the Offences Against the State (Amendment) Act 1998 allow inferences to be drawn from the failure of an accused to mention facts later relied on in his defence when being questioned or charged by the Gardaí. Section 5(2) is very similar to section 7 of the Criminal Justice (Drug Trafficking) Act 1996. Section 9 makes it an offence for a person to stay silent without a reasonable cause when he has information which he knows or believes might be of material assistance to the Gardaí. This section is similar to section 52 of the Offences Against the State Act 1939.

These sections provide for a warning to be given to the accused by the Gardaí in ordinary language about the risks of a failure to refer to the facts or to provide the information in question. However no guidance is given as to how to deliver this warning. In *Lavery v. Member-in-Charge, Carrickmacross*

[151.] *Ibid.*, p. 180.
[152.] Byrne and Binchy *Annual Review of Irish Law* 1998 (Round Hall Sweet & Maxwell, Dublin, 1998), p. 403.
[153.] At p. 404.

Garda Station[154] it was held that the solicitors of persons in custody under the Offences Against the State Act 1998 had no right to see the notes of their interviews with the Gardaí.

It has been argued that, in the case of detention under the Offences Against the State Act 1998, such access is necessary in order to make an informed legal assessment of the information the accused person is obliged to provide under that Act. This was the view taken by McGuinness J. in the High Court in *Lavery* but it was not followed by the Supreme Court in that case. The Supreme Court decision conflicts with the decision of the European Court of Human Rights in *Murray v. United Kingdom,*[155] in which the view was taken that when the right to silence is infringed, there must be adequate legal advice given.

At common law, it is not permissible for the prosecution to refer to the accused's silence at any stage of the criminal process. In *People (D.P.P.) v. Finnerty*[156] the accused was tried by the Central Criminal Court for the offence of rape. During cross-examination, counsel for the prosecution put to the accused that his version of the events of the night in question had not been given by him to the Gardaí during questioning. In his address to the jury, the trial judge made no reference to this remark.

The accused appealed his conviction on the ground that his silence while in detention had been brought to the attention of the jury in an adverse way. He argued that the trial judge had erred in permitting the prosecutor to adduce evidence before the jury of a positive nature to the effect that he had refused to answer any questions put to him by the Gardaí during his period of detention and in asking him why not. The Court of Criminal Appeal held that the accused's right to silence had not been infringed but the Supreme Court came to a different conclusion.

The Supreme Court in *Finnerty* stated that there was a tension between two competing principles – the right of the police and the community to discover whether a crime had been committed and the right of a suspect not to be compelled to answer questions and to be informed of his right in this regard. The Supreme Court said that the Criminal Justice Act 1984 did not modify in any way either the right of a person whom the Gardaí suspect of having committed a crime to refuse to answer questions put to him by the Gardaí or his entitlement under the Judge's Rules to be reminded of the right before any questioning begins.

According to the Supreme Court, to allow the jury to draw inferences from the accused's failure to give evidence would be to render this right meaningless. The Oireachtas had specifically legislated in sections 18 and 19 of the Criminal Justice Act 1984 to erode the accused's right to silence in certain limited circumstances. However, even this provision states that no person may be convicted of an offence solely on the basis of these inferences.

---

154. [1992] 2 I.R. 390.
155. (1993) 16 E.H.R.R. 29.
156. [1999] 4 I.R. 364.

The Supreme Court recognised that the right to silence was a constitutional right and may only be modified or abridged by legislation if such abridgment is proportionate to the objects intended to be achieved by such legislation. Here, however, there had been no statutory abridgment.

If no information is obtained by detention, the court should simply be informed that the defendant was detained but that nothing of probative value emerged. The prosecution should, under no circumstances, be allowed to refer to the accused's failure to answer questions and the trial judge should, in general, make no reference to the fact that the accused had refused to answer questions during his detention.

This case reaffirms *People (Attorney General) v. Quinn,*[157] in which it was held that because the trial judge said they could take into account the silence of the accused during questioning, the accused's conviction must be quashed.

16.7.12 European Court of Human Rights decisions

In the circumstances, some reference should be made to a number of European Court of Human Rights decisions on the right to silence. In *Funke v. France*[158] the accused was convicted of a failure to produce a blood sample; this was held to be a violation of Article 6(1) of the Convention. In this case the right to silence was regarded as inherent in the right to a fair trial.

Customs officers had searched the applicant's house and seized documents relating to his overseas assets. The applicant was convicted of failing to provide statements of his overseas bank accounts and ordered to produce them. He complained that the conviction breached Article 6(1). The European Court of Human Rights found in his favour, on the ground that the customs officers were trying to compel someone to provide evidence of his criminal offences, which breached the privilege against self-incrimination.

Saunders v. United Kingdom[159] arose out of a trial for fraud. In this case, it was held that statements or evidence obtained under a legal compulsion could consequently be held inadmissible. The European Court of Human Rights saw the right to silence/the privilege against self-incrimination as linked to the presumption of innocence contained in Article 6(2) of the Convention. It defined the right not to incriminate oneself as concerned with respecting the will of an accused person to remain silent. The right precluded the obtaining of documents by compulsion.

In this case, there had been a violation of the privilege against self-incrimination. The interviews in question were a significant part of the prosecution case. The complexity of corporate fraud and the public interest in its investigation were insufficient justifications for admitting the evidence.

Murray v. United Kingdom related to a conviction under the Criminal Evidence (N.I.) Ordnance 1998. In this case, the European Court of Human

---

[157.] Unreported, Court of Criminal Appeal, *ex tempore*, March 23, 1998.
[158.] (1993) 16 E.H.R.R. 29.
[159.] (1996) 22 E.H.R.R. 29; McDermott 11(1) I.C.L.J. 9.

Rights held that the drawing of inferences from the accused's silence might be prohibited. However,

> "[w]hether the drawing of adverse inferences from an accused's silence infringes Article 6 is a matter to be determined in the light of all the circumstances of the case, having particular regard to the situations in which inferences may be drawn, the weight attached to them by the national courts, and the degree of compulsion inherent in the situation."[160]

In *Heaney and McGuinness v. Ireland*[161] and *Quinn v. Ireland,*[162] section 52 of the Offences against the State Act and its practice of making silence a criminal offence was held to be in violation of the Convention. The applicant in *Quinn* had been arrested under section 30 of the Offences Against the State Act on suspicion of being a member of the I.R.A. He was requested to account for his movements during certain periods of time around the time a police officer had been killed. He refused to give an account. He was charged with three counts of refusing to give an account of his movements and was sentenced to six months' imprisonment. He argued that section 52 breached Articles 6 and 10 of the Convention.

The courts said that the right to silence and the principle against self-incrimination were generally recognized international standards, which were part of the right to fair procedures contained in Article 6. The Court referred back to its decision in *Saunders* in which it concluded that the public interest could not be invoked to justify the use of answers obtained in breach of the right to self-incrimination.

16.8 Public interest privilege[163]

This occurs when privilege is claimed by the State from disclosing information or documents on the ground of the public interest. Public interest privilege, formerly known as executive privilege, is based on the principle that the State must not be put in jeopardy by producing documents that may injure it. The categories of public interest privilege are not closed. Its application in criminal trials is limited, as it can be overridden if disclosure is necessary to enable the accused to prove his innocence.

This class of privilege was applied in the case of *Duncan v. Cammell Laird & Co Ltd.*[164] A claim was brought against the defendants that they had negligently constructed a submarine. The Admiralty objected to the production of certain documents by the defendants. The defendants were government contractors and World War II was being fought at the time. It was held that the structure of the submarines was a matter of national security and

---

[160.] *Ibid.*at p. 60.
[161.] Unreported, E.C.H.R. December 21, 2000.
[162.] *Ibid.*
[163.] McGrath "Public Interest Privilege" 22 D.U.L.J. 74.
[164.] [1942] A.C. 624.

should be kept secret. The documents were, therefore, privileged and could not be disclosed.

Leen v. President of the Executive Council (No. 1)[165] held that the concept of executive privilege had been carried over into the Irish Free State. Meredith J. described the privilege as "broad-based upon the public interest" and stated that:

> "the principle has roots in the general conception of State interests and the functions of the courts of justice, which make it independent of the particular type of constitution under which the body of law which recognises that principle is administered".[166]

A claim for State privilege becomes more controversial when it is a class claim: namely, that the document belongs to a certain class of documents which should never be made public. Lord Reid in *Conway v. Rimmer*[167] recognised that "there are certain classes of documents which ought not to be revealed whatever their content".

It was assumed in this jurisdiction that the doctrine of public interest privilege existing in Ireland was identical to that in the United Kingdom.[168] Following the approach of the United Kingdom courts in *Conway v. Rimmer*, the Irish courts refused to go behind ministerial certificates which stated that, in the opinion of the minister, certain classes of documents ought to be privileged on the ground of the public interest.

The issue of class claims was raised in Ireland in *Murphy v. Dublin Corporation*.[169] The plaintiff, Murphy, wanted discovery of an inspector's report in relation to a compulsory purchase order made against him by Dublin Corporation. The defendants pleaded public interest privilege and provided a ministerial certificate saying that disclosure would be against the public interest. They asked the court to take this certificate at face value and to come to its decision without reading the document.

Following previous Irish High Court authority, Kenny J. applied the principles in *Conway v. Rimmer*, which said that if the Minister decided not to disclose a document on the ground that it belonged to a class that as a matter of policy ought not to be published, the court should normally endorse this decision without looking at the documents:

> "There are certain classes of documents which ought not to be produced under any circumstances: in these cases the court will not inspect them. Minutes of government meetings, documents relating to military and diplomatic matters, memoranda dealing with proposed legislation and letters between departments

---

[165] [1926] I.R. 456.

[166] *Ibid.*, p. 463.

[167] [1968] A.C. 910.

[168] For a summary of the U.K. approach, see Eagles "Public Interest Immunity and Statutory Privilege" (1983) 42 C.L.J. 118; Kharam "Crown Privilege in Criminal Cases [1971] Crim. L.R. 675; Allen "Public Interest Immunity and Ministers Responsibilities" (1993) Crim. L.R. 660; Scott "The Acceptable and Unacceptable Use of Public Interest Immunity" (1996) Ph. 427.

[169] [1972] I.R. 215.

relating to policy formation are examples of the type of document the non-disclosure of which is necessary for the proper functioning of the State.... In addition where the minister feels that documents outside this class should be withheld the court should normally accept this view."[170]

The Supreme Court took a different view, rejecting the idea of class claims, and stating that the decision as to the public interest must be made by the court, rather than the Minister, after disclosure of the particular document. The courts must be entitled to look at the document and come to their own decision on whether or not it should be refused. In addition, "there can be no documents which may be withheld from production simply because they belong to a particular class of documents. The court must be allowed to examine the document.

Walsh J. in the Supreme Court stated:

"Under the Constitution the administration of justice is committed solely to the judiciary in the exercise of their powers in the courts set up under the Constitution. Power to compel the attendance of witnesses and the production of evidence is an inherent part of the judicial power of government of the State and is the ultimate safeguard of justice in the State. The proper exercise of the functions of the three powers of government is in the public interest. There may be occasions where the different aspects of the public interest "pull in contrary directions" to use the words of Lord Morris of Borth-y-gest in Conway v Rimmer. If the conflict arises during the exercise of the judicial power, then, in my view, it is the judicial power which will decide which public interest shall prevail."[171]

Walsh J. continued:

"Where documents come into existence in the course of carrying out the executive powers of the State, their production may be adverse to the public interest in one sphere of government in particular circumstances. On the other hand, their non-production may be adverse to the public interest in the administration of justice. As such documents may be anywhere in the range from the trivial to the vitally important, somebody or some authority must decide which course is calculated to do the least injury to the public interest, namely, the production of the document or the possibility of the denial of right in the administration of justice. It is self evident that this is a matter which falls into the sphere of the judicial power for determination. In a particular case the court may be able to determine this matter having regard to the evidence available on the subject and without examining the document in question, but in other cases it may be necessary, as the court may think, to produce the document to the court itself for the purpose of inspecting it and making the decision having regard to the conflicting claims made with reference to the document."

The decision of the Supreme Court in *Murphy v. Dublin Corporation* was upheld in *Ambiorix v. Minister for the Environment*.[172] The plaintiffs in this

---

[170.] *Ibid.*, p. 226.
[171.] *Ibid.*, p. 233-235.

case were challenging a decision of the Minister for the Environment to designate certain building sites for the purposes of the Urban Renewal Act 1986. It was argued that a class or category of documents consisting of documents emanating at a level not below that of assistant secretary and for the ultimate consideration of government ministers should be absolutely exempt from production and should not be examined by a judge. The Supreme Court affirmed the dicta of Walsh J. in *Murphy* to the effect that:

> "power to compel the production of evidence is an inherent part of [the] judicial power and is part of the ultimate safeguard of justice in the State.The judicial power must have the authority to decide all conflicts of public interest."[173]

Finlay C.J. stated that the Constitution had given the judiciary powers relating to the administration of justice. Power to compel evidence was an essential part of the administration of justice. Where the admission of particular evidence brings two aspects of the public interest into conflict, it was the judicial power who was responsible for resolving that conflict. This did not mean that the judicial power will automatically disclose the documents; the judicial power would not automatically favour the administration of justice and ignore the competing interest.

Per Finlay C.J., there was no obligation on the judicial power to examine the contested documents and judges could uphold a claim of privilege simply on a basis of the description of the document given by the Minister. However, the judiciary reserved the right to choose on a case-by-case basis whether the documents should be disclosed or whether they should be withheld with or without examination.

It is worth noting that Finlay C.J. also recognised in *Ambiorix* that the need for efficient discharge of the functions of the executive organ of the Government could sometimes be a public interest consideration militating against disclosure. This demonstrated that state security was not the only ground for invoking public interest privilege.[174] International relations is also a factor which may be raised as a ground for asserting public interest privilege.

In *Walker v. Ireland*[175] the plaintiff had been a victim of sexual offences and claimed that she had suffered personal injury as a result of the State's negligent delay in extraditing the offender from Northern Ireland for trial. The State claimed public interest immunity in respect of a particular document that had

---

[172] [1992] 1 I.R. 277.

[173] *Murphy v. Dublin Corporation* [1972] 1 I.R. 215 at 233.

[174] *Attorney General v. Hamilton (No. 1)* [1993] 2 I.R. 250, may be seen as backtracking to some extent from the approach in *Ambiorix*. In this case, the Chairman of the Tribunal of Inquiry into the Beef Industry sought to question a Government Minister about whether a particular decision had been taken at a cabinet meeting. The Supreme Court held that cabinet discussions were confidential because of the collective responsibility provisions of Article 28.4.2 of the Constitution. The tribunal was not exercising judicial powers and Finlay C.J. left the issue open as to whether the same principles would have applied if the Minister had been questioned in a court. Article 28.4.3 of the Constitution now provides for the disclosure of such discussions. For commentary on this case see Hogan & Morgan "*Administrative Law in Ireland*" 3rd ed. (Round Hall Sweet & Maxwell, 1998) at pp. 939-942 and Hogan "The Cabinet Confidentiality Case" (1993) 8 *Irish Political Studies* 131.

[175] [1997] 1 I.L.R.M. 363.

been sent to the then Attorney-General by the Attorney-General of the United Kingdom and Northern Ireland.

Geoghegan J. said there could be no absolute privilege in relation to communications between states. He recognised that there was a public interest in maintaining the confidentiality of inter-state communications in relation to extradition requests. However, he found that the public interest in favour of the administration of justice prevailed in this case and he ordered disclosure. He pointed out that there had been no objection by the United Kingdom's Attorney-General to the production of this document.

In the United Kingdom, communications between police officers made in the course of duty are automatically privileged from disclosure. In *D.P.P. (Hanley) v. Holly*[176] Keane J. stated that the adoption of a policy of exclusion in relation to such documents by Irish judges would run counter to *Murphy v. Dublin Corporation.* He confirmed this in *Breathnach v. Ireland (No. 3),*[177] where he stated that in relation to such documents it was necessary in each individual case for the courts to weigh the public interest in the proper administration of justice against the public interest "in the prevention and prosecution of crime".

In this case, the plaintiff sought discovery of all documents relating to his arrest, detention and interrogation. The Director of Public Prosecutions claimed public interest privilege. Keane J. said that grounds put forward in favour of the privilege (confidentiality, the need for full disclosure by the Gardaí) could be applied so as to preclude disclosure in any criminal prosecution, which was clearly not permissible. He allowed disclosure of the documents.

In *Hughes v. Commissioner of An Garda Síochána*[178] a member of the Gardaí challenged disciplinary sanctions that had been taken against him. He sought discovery of a number of documents. Laffoy J. permitted the disclosure of certain documents, which had been compiled by the Gardaí in the course of investigating criminal and subversive activities, in addition to internal communications by high-ranking Gardaí relating to the conduct of subordinates. She felt that the documents were so relevant to the issues in the case as to necessitate their disclosure.

In *Corbett v. D.P.P.*[179] public interest privilege was successfully claimed. The applicant had been charged with assault. He brought an application for judicial review, claiming that his prosecution had not been in accordance with law. O'Sullivan J. held that, in criminal proceedings, the confidentiality of communications between Gardaí and the Director of Public Prosecutions must be respected:

> "The public interest in the prevention and prosecution of crime must be given due weight."

[176.] [1984] I.L.R.M. 149.
[177.] [1993] 2 I.R. 458.
[178.] Unreported, High Court, Laffoy J., January 20, 1998.
[179.] [1999] 2 I.R. 179.

Chapter 17

CONFESSIONS AND ADMISSIONS

17.1 Introduction[1]

A confession is an oral or written[2] statement made by an accused in a criminal case to a person in authority, which is adverse to his or her interest. Because of the particular vulnerability of an accused in the criminal investigatory process, special rules govern the admissibility of confessions.

17.1.1 Distinction between confessions and admissions

Statements made by a party in a civil case which are adverse to his or her interest are known as admissions. It appears that some of the same admissibility principles may apply to admissions as to confessions. However, the law on admissions and confessions is not by any means identical, and, therefore, the admissibility of adverse statements made by a party in a civil case is dealt with separately at para 17.4.

What about statements made by an accused in a criminal case which are adverse to his or her interest, but which are not made to a person in authority? Technically speaking, these are not confessions, but rather admissions, and the rules applicable to these are outlined at para 17.3, after the rules on confessions proper have been set out and explained.

17.1.2 No writing requirement for confessions

Firstly, some general rules in relation to the use of confessions in criminal proceedings will be considered. A confession does not have to be in writing in order to be valid. It need not be signed. Although an out-of-court statement, it is admissible in court as proof of the truth of its contents under an exception to the hearsay rule.

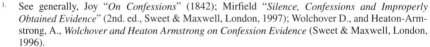

[1.] See generally, Joy "*On Confessions*" (1842); Mirfield "*Silence, Confessions and Improperly Obtained Evidence*" (2nd. ed., Sweet & Maxwell, London, 1997); Wolchover D., and Heaton-Armstrong, A., *Wolchover and Heaton Armstrong on Confession Evidence* (Sweet & Maxwell, London, 1996).

[2.] It is also theoretically possible to infer confessions from conduct. However, the situations in which such an inference may constitute a confession are rare, because of the requirement that a confession be made to someone in authority. However, one example of a confession made partly by conduct was *Moriarty v. London, Chatham, & Dover Railway Co.* (1870) L.R. 5 Q.B. 314; also *Li-Shu-Ling v. R.* [1989] A.C. 270, where the Privy Council upheld admissibility of a video-taped re-enactment of the killing of the victim made by the accused at the request of police officers.

17.1.3 Confessions or admissions by third parties

The normal rule is that any confessions or admission by third parties to the case are inadmissible hearsay. This can produce unfair results. Even if the maker of the confession or admission dies before trial or revokes, it it is still inadmissible. Examples of the hearsay rule being applied to such statements are to be found in the case of *R. v. Blastland*,[3] where the accused could not call police officers to give evidence that a third party had confessed to the crime, and *R. v. Gray*,[4] where the deathbed confession of a third party to the crime with which the accused was being charged could not be admitted in evidence.

17.1.4 The confession of one co-accused cannot be used in evidence against the other

Special rules apply in relation to confessions where a number of accused are tried jointly. *People v. Keane*[5] establishes that if one of the accused has made a confession, that confession cannot be used as evidence against his co-accused. If the confession indicates in any way that the co-accused may be guilty, *People (D.P.P.) v. Sherlock*[6] obliges the judge to tell the jury that they cannot take the confession into account when assessing the guilt of the co-accused.

17.1.5 Corroboration of confessions

There are also special rules relating to corroboration of confessions. In *Braddish v. D.P.P.* Hardiman J. stated:

> "A confession should if possible be corroborated...relatively recent history both here and in the neighbouring jurisdiction has unfortunate examples of the risks of excessive reliance on confession evidence."[7]

Section 10 of the Criminal Procedure Act 1993 currently embodies this principle by providing that where a confession is not corroborated by other evidence, the judge should direct the jury's attention to that fact.

17.1.6 Admissibility of confessions

The main legal issue in relation to confessions in criminal cases is that of admissibility. Often the accused at trial will deny he ever made the confession, or will, alternatively, argue that it should be held inadmissible because of some flaw in the circumstances in which it was made. The grounds on which such statements can be held inadmissible make up the greater part of this chapter.

---

3. [1986] A.C. 41.
4. (1841) I.R.C.I. Rep. 76.
5. (1976) 110 I.L.T.R. 1.
6. (1975) 1 Frewen 383.
7. Unreported, Supreme Court, May 18, 2001.

17.1.7 *Rationales for restricting admissibility of confessions*

The best-known rationale for restricting the admissibility of confessions is the reliability principle, which takes the view that confessions should not be admitted if there are factors present which cast doubt on their accuracy.

In addition, according to Lord Hailsham in *D.P.P. v. Ping Lin*,[8] the law on confessions is underlaid by a protectionist/protective principle. The rules governing the admissibility of confessions were developed:

> "at a time when the savage code of the 18th century was in full force. At that time almost every serious crime was punished by death or transportation. The law enforcement officers formed no disciplined police force and were not subject to effective control...there was no legal aid. There was no system of appeal. To crown it all the accused was unable to give evidence on his own behalf and was therefore largely at the mercy of any evidence, either perjured or oppressively obtained, that might be brought against him. The judiciary were therefore compelled to devise artificial rules designed to protect him against dangers now avoided by other and more rational means."

Lord Griffiths in *Lam Chi Ming v. R.*[9] gave two further justifications for judicial intervention in the area of confessions. Firstly, there is the principle that an accused should not be compelled to incriminate himself. Secondly, there is the disciplinary principle, which emphasises the importance of proper police behaviour in a civilised society. This principle opposes the admission of any confessions obtained by police misconduct, irrespective of their accuracy. Connected with this is the principle of fairness, which states that society has a right to insist that those who enforce the law themselves respect it. This principle is embodied in the Australian case of *Bunning v. Cross*.[10]

In Ireland, a common rationale for judicial intervention in the area of confessions is that of the protection of constitutional rights. This approach is exemplified by the following dicta of Egan J. in *State (Trimbole) v. Governor of Mountjoy Prison*:

> "Courts have no higher duty to perform than that involving the protection of constitutional rights and if at any time the protection of these rights should delay, or even defeat, the ends of justice in a particular case, it is better for the public good that this should happen rather than that constitutional rights should be nullified."[11]

17.1.8 *Dangers in challenging admissibility of confessions*

It is worth noting that an accused who attempts to deny or challenge the validity of a confession may come up against section 1(f)(ii) of the Criminal Justice (Evidence) Act 1924 if he then decides to give evidence. Despite the

---

8.   [1976] A.C. 574.
9.   [1991] 2 A.C. 212.
10. (1978) 141 C.L.R. 54.
11. [1985] I.R. 550.

general rule that the prior misdeeds of an accused should not be brought up at trial, section 1(f)(ii) provides that an accused may be cross-examined as to previous misconduct if he has cast aspersions on the character of the prosecution or its witnesses.

In the United Kingdom, an accused who contradicts police evidence will be regarded as having lost his shield and, if he takes the stand, may be cross-examined on previous misconduct. The position in Ireland is different. *People (D.P.P.) v. McGrail*[12] establishes that the accused may contradict the prosecution case and indeed accuse police officers of misconduct and lying if this accusation is relevant to proving his innocence. The effect of this is that an accused in Ireland can challenge the fact or the validity of a confession without being put at risk of cross-examination as to his or her past misconduct.

17.2 Grounds for holding confessions inadmissible

17.2.1 Involuntariness[13]

An involuntary confession is automatically inadmissible. Two factors must be present before a confession will be held to be involuntary. Firstly, the confession must have been made as a result of a threat, inducement or oppression. Secondly, this threat, inducement or oppression must have come from somebody in authority.

In *Ibrahim v. R.*[14] it was stated that no statement by an accused is admissible in evidence against him unless shown by the prosecution to have been a voluntary statement, in the sense that it was not obtained from him either "by fear of prejudice or hope of advantage held out by a person in authority". This dicta mirrors an earlier formulation in *R. v. Warickshall*:

> "A confession forced from the mind by the flattery of hope, or by the torture of fear, comes in so questionable a shape when it is to be considered as the evidence of guilt, that no credit ought to be given to it, and therefore it is rejected."[15]

A confession induced by threats or inducements is, therefore, prohibited. To this restriction has been added the modern requirement, first officially recognised in the United Kingdom in the case of *Callis v. Gunn*,[16] that a confession cannot be obtained as a result of oppression. As Lord Parker L.C.J. declared in that case, it is:

> "a fundamental principle of law that no answer to a question and no statement is admissible unless it is shown by the prosecution not to have been obtained in

---

12. [1990] 2 I.R. 38.
13. See generally, O'Connor "Observations on the Voluntariness Test in Irish Law" (1980) 74 *Gazette* 198; White "The Confessional State – police interrogation in the Irish Republic" (2000) I.C.L.J. 17 and Costelloe "Detention for Questioning and Oppressive Interrogation" (2001) 11(1) I.C.L.J. 12.
14. [1914] A.C. 599.
15. (1783) 1 Leach 263.
16. [1964] 1 Q.B. 495.

an oppressive manner and to have been voluntary in the sense that it has not been obtained by threats or inducements".[17]

State v. Treanor[18] was the first decision to recognise that these common law principles had been carried over into the Irish legal system. A confession made under the influence of a promise or threat held out by a person in authority was stated to be inadmissible unless it could be shown that the confession was not caused by the promise or threat. There was no reference at this stage to the doctrine of involuntariness having any wider application.

However, in *People (D.P.P.) v. McNally and Breathnach*[19] the Court of Criminal Appeal accepted the concept of oppression as a factor vitiating a confession at common law, and this was affirmed by the Supreme Court in *People (D.P.P.) v. Lynch*.[20] Since then, there have been many Irish decisions recognising oppression as an alternative ground for declaring a statement involuntary at common law.

The judicial definition of oppression will be dealt with later. First of all it is necessary to consider the meaning of a threat or inducement for the purposes of this doctrine.

(1) Threat

The following are examples of cases in which a threat by someone in authority vitiated a confession. In *Attorney General v. Cleary*[21] the accused was suspected of infanticide. She was threatened with a medical examination to see if she had recently given birth. Her subsequent confession was held involuntary and inadmissible.

In a subsequent case, *People (D.P.P.) v. Hoey*,[22] firearms were found in a house at 78 Rossmore Avenue. The son of the house was taken in for questioning. The Detective Inspector asked him:

> "Will I have to get some member to go up to your family and find out from them if anybody at 78 Rossmore Avenue is going to take responsibility for the property in the house?"

The accused understood this to mean that the police would blame his family if he didn't own up. The Supreme Court held his subsequent confession to be involuntary. Walsh J. stated as follows:

> "The effect of the words used by the Inspector, irrespective of what he intended to mean, was calculated to convey that the appellant's family would be left undisturbed and free from further investigation by the Garda Síochána if the appellant admitted responsibility…in the particular circumstances of this case that amounted to an improper inducement which did produce a confession."[23]

---

17. *Ibid.* at 501.
18. [1924] 2 I.R. 193.
19. (1981) 2 Frewen 43.
20. [1982] I.R. 64
21. (1934) 1 Frewen 14.
22. [1988] I.L.R.M. 666.

In *R. v. Smith*[24] a soldier was stabbed in a fight. His company were put on parade and told by the Sergeant-Major that they would be kept on parade until one of them made a confession. This was held to be a threat, which made the accused's subsequent confession inadmissible.

The above case may be contrasted with that of *People (Attorney General) v. Galvin*.[25] At 12.10 a.m., while interrogating the accused, a garda officer said to him "You should not be keeping us here all night – tell the truth and be finished with it". These words were held to be neither an inducement nor a threat, even though they might have been taken to mean that the interrogation would continue indefinitely until a confession was produced.

In order for a threat to render a confession involuntary, it must be shown that the threat caused the confession. In *People (D.P.P.) v. Pringle*[26] the applicant was informed that his girlfriend Eva Curtin might be called as a witness or charged as an accessory to the offence of which he was suspected. He was further told that if he gave an account of his movements on the day of the murder, this problem would not arise. However, rather than making an immediate confession, the applicant consulted his solicitor, who told him that there was no risk of Mrs Curtin being charged as an accessory. The applicant showed every sign of being reassured by this. Consequently, it could not be said that his subsequent confession had been induced by the threat.

(2) Inducement

An inducement may be distinguished from a threat insofar as its effect is based on hope rather than fear.

In *People (Attorney General) v. Flynn*[27] the applicant had remained silent throughout two hours of questioning. The Garda Sergeant brought him his lunch and had a chat with him. After lunch the accused made a confession. It was thought by the judge that the confession must have been made as a result of some advice made by the Sergeant over lunch to the effect that it would be better for the applicant to make a confession. Such advice constituted an inducement and rendered the subsequent confession invalid (although this case is perhaps more appropriately explained as one of oppression).

People (Attorney General) v. Murphy[28] was a similar case. It was held that the statement "You're all right – come along with me" should be understood as "You will be alright" and as such constituted an improper inducement to co-operate.

In *R. v. Northam*[29] the accused was being interrogated in relation to a housebreaking offence. He asked a police officer if he could have this

---

23. *Ibid.* per Walsh J. at 671.
24. (1963) 48 Cr. App. R. 116.
25. [1964] I.R. 325.
26. (1981) 2 Frewen 57.
27. [1963] I.R. 255.
28. [1947] I.R. 236.
29. (1968) 52 Cr. App. Rep. 97.

particular offence taken into consideration at a pending trial for other housebreaking offences. The officer said that the police would have no objection. The accused then confessed. In fact he was tried separately for this particular offence. His conviction was set aside on the ground that the police officer's reply to his question constituted an inducement.

The appellant in *R. v. Zavekas*[30] asked an officer during questioning: "If I make a statement, will I be given bail now?" He was told yes. His conviction was quashed on the ground that the subsequent confession was made in response to an inducement. *R. v. Zavekas* and *R. v. Northam* may be contrasted with the case of *D.P.P. v. Ping Lin.*[31] Here, an accused had confessed that he had been dealing in heroin. The police officer then told him that if he disclosed the name of his supplier, the judge would bear it in mind when sentencing him. This statement, although amounting to an inducement, could not vitiate the appellant's confession. The confession, having been made prior to the inducement, could not have been caused by it.

D.P.P. v. Ping Lin mirrors *People (D.P.P.) v. Pringle*. In neither case could the confession have been caused by the threat or inducement. This reflects the requirement, first articulated in this jurisdiction in *State v. Treanor,*[32] that the threat or inducement influence the confession. It further appears from *Treanor* that, once a threat or inducement has been shown to exist, the onus shifts to the prosecution to prove that this threat or inducement did not influence the confession.

It does not matter whether the inducement or the threat is true or false. Neither does it matter whether the person making the threat or inducement intended his statement to be taken as such. As shown by *People (D.P.P.) v. Hoey,*[33] the test of whether a threat or inducement exists is an objective one. The question is whether the statement is likely to be understood as a threat or inducement. This objective test was recently affirmed in *People (D.P.P.) v. McCann.*[34]

However, in answering this question the particular vulnerability of persons in custody must be taken into account. As stated by Lord Reid in *Commissioners of Customs and Excise v. Harz:*[35]

> "It is true that many of the so-called inducements have been so vague that no reasonable man would have been influenced by them, but one must remember that not all accused are reasonable men and women: they may be very ignorant and terrified by the predicament in which they find themselves. So it may have been right to err on the safe side"

---

[30]   [1970] 1 All E.R. 413.
[31]   [1976] A.C. 574.
[32]   [1924] 2 I.R. 193.
[33]   [1988] I.L.R.M. 666.
[34]   [1984] 4 I.R. 397.
[35]   [1967] 1 All E.R. 177.

The accused in *People (D.P.P.) v. McCann*[36] was suspected of starting a fire at his home in which his family had died. He was convicted of murder. He was arrested under section 30 of the Offences Against the State Act 1939. After being detained for two days his brothers came to visit him and the accused decided to make a statement. It was argued that the statement was made under the influence of a promise or threat held out by a person in authority. It was held that it was not. In order to influence a statement, the words must not only be objectively capable of amounting to a threat or a promise, they must also be seen as a threat or a promise by the accused and they must lead him to make the confession.

(3) Oppression[37]

As stated above, the concept of oppression appears to have been identified as an alternative ground of involuntariness by United Kingdom courts in the 1960s and this approach has subsequently been followed here.

Oppression was defined in the case of *R. v. Prager*[38] (following a description given by Lord McDermott L.C.J. in an extra-judicial address to the Bentham Club), as:

> "questioning, which by its nature, duration or other attendant circumstances (including the fact of custody) excites hopes (such as the hope of release) or fears or so affects the mind of the suspect that the will crumbles and he speaks when otherwise he would have remained silent".

There is, however, no reason to believe that oppression is confined to oppressive questioning. Other definitions are wide enough to include other forms of oppressive behaviour, such as torture and physical abuse. In *R. v. Priestly*[39] Sachs J. defined oppression as:

> "something which tends to sap, and has sapped, that free will which must exist before a confession is voluntary".

In *People (D.P.P.) v. McNally and Breathnach*[40] the Court of Criminal Appeal recognised the concept of oppression as a factor making a confession involuntary and accepted both of the above definitions of oppression as being correct.

The applicant had been kept in custody and constantly interrogated for 40 hours, while being denied access to his legal advisers (the denial of legal access is now recognised as unconstitutional). He had been allowed very little sleep. Having been awakened from a brief rest, he made a confession at 4 a.m. in the course of an interrogation in a passageway of the Bridewell Garda Station in Dublin. In the circumstances it was held that the treatment and

---

[36] [1998] 4 I.R. 397.
[37] Costelloe "Detention for Questioning and Oppressive Interrogation" (2001) 11(1) I.C.L.J. 12.
[38] [1972] 56 Cr. App. R.
[39] [1967] 51 Cr. App. R.1.
[40] (1981) 2 Frewen 43.

questioning of the accused had been oppressive so as to sap his will and make his confession involuntary.

In *People (D.P.P.) v. Shaw*[41] Griffin J. defined behaviour which might sap the will and qualify as oppressive. He defined the use of physical or psychological pressure, promises or threats, drugs, hypnosis, alcohol, or prolonged interrogation as oppressive.

The Supreme Court further pronounced on the issue of oppression in *People (D.P.P.) v. Lynch*,[42] when Walsh J. stated that:

> "all the circumstances surrounding the taking of any...statement or circumstances which go to create the atmosphere in which a written or non-written admission is made must be examined with a view to ascertaining whether or not any such statement may be regarded as the free and voluntary act or admission of the person making it".

Lynch had spent almost 22 hours in custody and under constant surveillance without being able either to sleep or to communicate with his family or friends. In the circumstances, it was held that oppression had occurred. Walsh J. was also influenced by the fact that parts of Lynch's confession had subsequently turned out to be untrue, saying that this raised a grave doubt as to the validity of the confession as a whole.

It is not relevant whether the person engaging in the oppressive behaviour intended it to be oppressive. What has to be looked at is the effect his conduct had on the mind of the detainee. With this in consideration, it must be remembered that the effect of particular behaviour varies from person to person. What would sap the will of one person might not affect another. The court takes into account the particular circumstances and characteristics of the accused in deciding whether their will has been oppressed.

In *People (D.P.P.) v. Pringle*[43] the accused had been interviewed for a long period during detention of 40 hours under the Offences Against the State Act. He was suffering from sleep deprivation, having had only two five-hour rest periods during this time. His girlfriend had been brought into the interview room and questioned in his presence. Generally speaking, the circumstances were similar to those in *People (D.P.P.) v. McNally and Breathnach*.[44]

However, taking particular characteristics of the accused into account, the Court of Criminal Appeal held that the interrogation had not been such as to sap Pringle's will and make his confession involuntary. He was 42 years old, a tough character, a fisherman in good health and used to roughing it, "an experienced man of the world not unused to conditions of physical hardship". The court emphasised that what might constitute oppression in relation to one person might not in relation to another. It is worth noting one difference

---

41. [1982] I.R. 1.
42. [1982] I.R. 64.
43. (1981) 2 Frewen 57.
44. (1981) 2 Frewen 43.

between this case and *People (D.P.P.) v. Mc Nally and Breathnach*: Pringle had received five visits from a solicitor during his detention.

People (D.P.P.) v. Flynn[45] has been mentioned above. Although traditionally classified as a case of inducement, this decision could perhaps be more accurately explained as one of oppression, decided before that vitiating factor had officially been adopted in this jurisdiction.

Flynn was charged with unlawful carnal knowledge of his niece. He appealed his conviction to the Court of Criminal Appeal. They had to consider whether or not a statement he had made to the Gardaí before being cautioned was admissible. The court was of the view that a Garda Sergeant interviewing him had advised that it would be better for him to make a statement. The Court of Criminal Appeal concluded as follows:

> "Having regard to this probability, and to the undoubted fact that the purpose of arresting the applicant and bringing him to the station was to get a statement from him; that, though interviewed for nearly two hours in the morning he persisted in denying all his niece's allegations; that he was kept nearly seven hours in custody, and that he was released only when he had made a statement admitting nearly all of her allegations, we consider that notwithstanding the evidence of the guards in question it is impossible to be sure that the statement was voluntarily made."[46]

People (D.P.P.) v. Ward[47] is one of the most recent cases on confessions, and also one of the most important. Paul Ward was tried before the Special Criminal Court for the murder of journalist Veronica Guerin. Part of the case against him depended on a confession made by him while in custody under section 30 of the Offences Against the State Act 1939. He claimed that this confession was inadmissible.

While in custody, Ward had sat silently through 14½ hours of interrogation. Then two visitors were brought to see him. It is important to note that Ward had not requested these visits. Firstly, he saw his girlfriend, Vanessa Meehan. Ms Meehan was showing the effects of severe psychological pressure that she had earlier been subjected to by Gardaí. Secondly, his 74-year-old mother was brought in. In *People (D.P.P.) v. Pringle*, Pringle's girlfriend had been brought in to see him but her visit did not particularly distress Pringle. Unlike Pringle, Ward was upset and made a confession after the two visits. Furthermore, Ward had sustained an unexplained neck injury while in custody.

In the circumstances, the Special Criminal Court held that Ward's confession was inadmissible. Barr J. stated that both visits were in disregard of the constitutional right to fair procedures and rendered the admissions involuntary. He was of the view that the visits were a deliberate ploy devised by the police to soften up Ward and cause him to incriminate himself in the murder. In the circumstances:

---

45. [1963] I.R. 255.
46. *Ibid.* at pp. 261-262.
47. Unreported, Special Criminal Court, November 27, 1998. This decision was subsequently overturned by the Court of Criminal Appeal on a different ground.

"[b]oth meetings amounted to a conscious and deliberate disregard of the accused's basic constitutional right to fair procedures and treatment while in custody and constituted deliberate gross violations of the fundamental obligation which the interrogators and their superiors had of conducting their dealings with the accused in accordance with the principles of basic fairness and justice".[48]

The precise ground on which the Special Criminal Court excluded Ward's confession was not clearly specified by them. The terms involuntariness and oppression were used. However, the judgment could equally be explained as the operation of the nascent ground of fundamental unfairness.

In contrast, in two recent decisions, no oppression was found to be present. In *People (D.P.P.) v. McCann*[49] the accused was arrested on suspicion of starting a fire at his home in which his wife and child had died. After he had been detained, for two days his brothers came to visit him and he decided to make a statement. It was held that the statement had not been made as a result of oppression, despite the fact that the accused had been subject to aggressive interrogation. It was emphasised that he had had five visits from solicitors, and two visits from doctors, as well as ample opportunity to sleep, eat and drink. In this context, aggressive interrogation did not amount to oppression. It was emphasised that interrogation must by its nature involve a certain degree of aggressiveness.

In *People (D.P.P.) v. C.*[50] the issue of oppression and involuntariness was also considered. The accused had been attending a party at his neighbour's house when the alleged crime occurred. The complainant and her boyfriend were also friends of the neighbour and had been attending the same party, although they were not previously known to the accused. They had made arrangements to stay in the house that night, sharing the same bedroom.

The accused, who had been drinking heavily, went upstairs to look for cigarettes at 4-5 a.m. and went into a bedroom to lie down. The complainant was asleep in the bed. He lay down beside her and they had sexual intercourse. The complainant was initially under the belief that he was her boyfriend. Subsequently, there was a row between the girl's boyfriend and the accused.

The accused went back home and not surprisingly, was only able to manage one hour of sleep that night. He was arrested the following day and made a statement admitting sexual intercourse with the complainant. The admissibility of this statement was challenged on the ground that, at the time when it was made, the accused had only had one hour's sleep in the past 30 hours and had consumed a significant amount of alcohol.

However, the court pointed out that, prior to making the statement, the accused had been examined by a doctor, who said that he appeared normal. The Gardaí said that the accused had been sober. The court held that there had been no oppression or misuse of fair procedures.

---

48. *Ibid.* at p. 14.
49. [1998] 4 I.R. 397.
50. [2001] 3 I.R. 345.

It appears that the causation requirement applies to oppression as well as to threats and inducements. In order for the confession to be excluded, it must have been caused to some extent by the oppression. Otherwise, it cannot be said to be involuntary. However, it appears that once oppression is present, the burden shifts to the prosecution to prove that the confession was not due to the oppression. In most situations of oppression, it will be very difficult for the prosecution to prove that the confession was not due to the oppression.

Finally, *People (D.P.P.) v. Hoey*[51] has already been mentioned under the heading of threats. It is worth mentioning again at this stage, because, like *People (D.P.P.) v. Flynn,*[52] it demonstrates a degree of overlap between the three categories of involuntariness. In this case, there had been a threat, which, coupled with some degree of oppression (questioning for a prolonged period), was sufficient to make the statement involuntary.

(4) Person in authority

It is not sufficient to show that the statement is involuntary because of a threat, inducement or oppressive behaviour. In order to exclude the confession on this ground, it is necessary to go further and show that the threat/inducement/ oppression has come from somebody in authority, whether or not that person was the person to whom the confession was actually made.

The term "person in authority" has been defined as someone who may reasonably be supposed to be in a position to influence the prosecution. In *Sullivan v. Robinson*[53] it was held that a doctor, called in by the Gardaí to examine a person suspected of being drunk, may be a person in authority. *R. v. McLintock*[54] stated that a headmistress could constitute a person in authority in relation to schoolgirls.

In *Deokinian v. R.*[55] it was held that a person "known to be close to the police" qualified as a person in authority. However, if that person was also a trusted friend of the accused, he was not a person in authority. In *People (D.P.P.) v. McCann*[56] it was held that the accused's brothers were not persons in authority. A person in authority was "someone engaged in the arrest, detention, examination or prosecution of the accused or someone acting on behalf of the prosecution".

A person in authority may by his silence adopt a threat, an inducement or oppressive behaviour made in his presence by somebody not in authority. In *R. v. Cleary*[57] the father of the accused told him in the presence of the police:

> "Put your cards on the table. Tell them the lot. If you didn't hit him they cannot hang you."

[51.] [1988] I.L.R.M. 666.
[52.] [1963] I.R. 255.
[53.] [1954] I.R. 161.
[54.] [1962] Crim. L.R. 549.
[55.] [1969] 1 A.C. 20.
[56.] [1998] 4 I.R. 397.
[57.] [1963] 48 Cr. App. R. 116.

The police were held to have adopted the father's inducement by their silence.

It has been argued that the requirement that the involuntariness be created by a person in authority, should be abolished. Viscount Dilhorne in *Deokinian v. R.* pointed out:

> "If the ground on which confessions induced by promises held out by persons in authority are held to be inadmissible is that they may not be true, then it may be that there is a similar risk that in some circumstances the confession may not be true if induced by a promise held out by a person not in authority, for instance if such a person offers a bribe in return for a confession."[58]

In the United Kingdom, the requirement that the threat, inducement or oppressive behaviour come from a person in authority, has been abolished. It is sufficient if the involuntariness is such as to make the confession unreliable.

The test of whether someone is a person in authority is a mixed objective and subjective one: Did the accused reasonably believe that this individual was a person in authority? However, even the subjective component in this test can create problems, as shown by the case of *Rothman v. R.*[59] In this case, the court admitted statements made by the accused to a police officer in disguise, who was put into the same cell as the accused and whom the accused thought to be a fellow prisoner. The rationale was that the accused did not believe that this individual was a person in authority; therefore, inducements held out by him were insufficient to make the confession inadmissible.

Finally, it is worth noting that the effect of a threat/inducement/oppression may not just invalidate an immediately subsequent statement, it may carry on to vitiate a later statement made by the accused.

Finlay C.J. in *People (D.P.P.) v. Buckley*[60] stated that if an accused has previously been induced to make an inadmissible statement, "the court must, in respect of a latter statement, even though no immediate circumstances of oppression, threat or inducement surround it, have regard to the possibility that the threat or inducement remains so as to affect the free will of the party concerned and therefore the voluntary nature of the statement".

This dictum was recently applied by the Special Criminal Court in *People (D.P.P.) v. Ward.*[61]

(5) Reliability

Given that the concept of involuntariness has been extended beyond threat or inducement to include oppression, it might be asked whether it should be extended further to include non-oppressive factors which may nonetheless vitiate the accused's free consent and cast doubt on the reliability of the confession.

---

[58]. [1969] 1 A.C. 20.
[59]. [1981] 1 S.C.R. 640.
[60]. [1990] I.R. 14.
[61]. Unreported, Superior Criminal Court, November 27, 1998.

The difficulty with this lies in the requirement that the involuntariness be traced to a person in authority. A person in authority can hardly be said to be responsible for mental disability, drunkenness or youth on the part of the accused. It could however be argued that to question someone who is weakened in this way is arguably oppressive behaviour. Nonetheless, the courts have generally found such factors go to weight rather than inadmissibility.

In *D.P.P. v. McCormack*[62] the accused was charged with drink driving. He admitted driving the car. It was held that his admission was admissible. O'Flaherty J., in an *ex tempore* judgment of the Supreme Court stated that "any admission said by a person, drunk or sober, is prima facie admissible in evidence".[63]

Similarly in *People (Attorney General) v. Sherlock*[64] it was held that drunkenness was not a ground for excluding the accused's confession. The Court of Criminal Appeal said that:

> "the fact that his debilitated condition may have either prompted him or not restrained him from making his statements which incriminated himself either because of carelessness for his own safety or perhaps because of feelings of remorse does not make the statements involuntary."[65]

In *People v. Connolly*[66] the Court of Criminal Appeal held that there was no reason to exclude a statement from evidence simply because the person who made it was upset.

In *D.P.P. v. Murphy*[67] the appellant challenged his conviction for burglary. He argued that his confession could not be relied upon, as it was made when he was under the influence of drugs. The court accepted the statement of the Garda Sergeant to the effect that Murphy appeared perfectly normal.

It is possible that such cases could be dealt with under the trial judge's discretion to exclude confession evidence from the jury in order to prevent a wrongful conviction. This discretion is presumably a subset of the general discretion to exclude evidence if its prejudicial effect outweighs its probative value.

In *People (D.P.P.) v. Quinn*[68] the applicant was 13 years old at the time of being arrested but had a mental age of only eight to nine years. He was interviewed at a garda station with his mother and made two statements. Unfortunately, the protection of having his mother there was limited by the fact that the mother was also functioning at a low intellectual level. There were inconsistencies between the two statements, and further inconsistencies between the statements and the testimony of the complainant in the case. The

---

62. [1999] 1 I.L.R.M. 398.
63. *Ibid.*, at 400.
64. (1975) 1 Frewen 383.
65. *Ibid.*, at 391.
66. Unreported, Court of Criminal Appeal, *ex tempore*, April 14, 1997.
67. Unreported, Supreme Court, July 12, 2001.
68. Unreported, Court of Criminal Appeal, *ex tempore*, March 23, 1998.

trial judge admitted the statement on the ground that there had been no oppression or breach. However, the Court of Criminal Appeal quashed the conviction on the ground that the trial judge should have exercised his discretion to exclude.

(6) Fundamental fairness

It appears that a new ground for automatically excluding confession evidence is being recognised. If the way in which the confession has been obtained breaches principles of fundamental fairness, it may be inadmissible.

Ironically, the concept of fundamental fairness originally developed as an alternative principle to the automatic exclusion of unconstitutionally obtained evidence. Its origins are to be found in the dissenting judgment of Griffin J. in *People (D.P.P.) v. Shaw.*[69] Griffin J. was of the view that, even if a confession was technically voluntary, a judge should have a discretion to exclude it if, by reason of the manner or the circumstances in which it was obtained, it falls below the required standards of fairness.

As originally envisaged, the test of fundamental fairness did not impose a policy of absolute exclusion, but left matters up to the discretion of the trial judge.

However, more recent cases such as *People (D.P.P.) v. Ward,*[70] have treated it as a ground for automatically excluding voluntary confessions. It may also be seen in the judgment of Walsh J. in *People (D.P.P.) v. Conroy.*[71] Walsh J. refers to the need for:

> "observance of basic or fundamental fairness or procedures during interrogation by members of the Garda Síochána. If such basic fairness of procedures is not observed by members of the Garda Síochána, then it is the duty of the courts to implement constitutional guarantees by excluding the evidence so obtained."[72]

Given that basic fairness of procedures is a constitutional right, this exclusionary ground could possibly be seen as a subset of the rule preventing the admissibility of unconstitutionally obtained evidence.

Alternatively, it could be accommodated by extending the concept of oppression. When Walsh J. in *People (D.P.P.) v. Quilligan*[73] stated that a person held under section 30 of the Offences Against the State Act 1939 must not be subject to any form of questioning which the courts would regard as unfair or oppressive, he appears to be using the terms "unfairness" and "oppression" interchangeably.

However, there may still be a role for this separate test in situations where the oppressive behaviour could not be said to have caused the confession but

---

[69] [1982] I.R. 1.
[70] Unreported, Supreme Criminal Court, November 27, 1998.
[71] [1986] I.R. 460.
[72] *Ibid.* at pp. 478–479.
[73] [1986] I.R. 495.

the behaviour was so reprehensible that the confession would be excluded anyway.

For a possible example of such behaviour, see *People (D.P.P.) v. C.*,[74] where it was stated that if investigating Gardaí had resorted to sleep deprivation tactics, statements so obtained would be excluded on the ground of public policy and breach of fair procedures by the State, by reason of the use of such methods independent of any question concerning the voluntariness of the statement.

In addition, in *People (D.P.P.) v. Kelly*[75] it was again stated *obiter* that if the removal of a person from one garda station to another was mala fides or done for the purposes either of harassment or of isolating him from assistance or access to that which he could properly be entitled, then that fact itself would clearly render his detention unlawful.

17.2.2 Breach of constitutional rights

Confessions obtained as a result of a breach of constitutional rights are also automatically admissible. See generally in para 15.1.[76] The issue of unconstitutionally obtained evidence in general is discussed in more detail at para 15.1. However, because of the importance of this issue in relation to confessions in particular it is also outlined here with particular focus on its application in the context of confessions.

The rule excluding evidence obtained in breach of constitutional rights was first developed in context of real evidence in *People (Attorney General) v. O'Brien*.[77] The majority of the Supreme Court stated that where there had been a deliberate and conscious violation of constitutional rights by the State or its agents, evidence obtained by such violation should be excluded unless extraordinary excusing circumstances were present. However, in the case in hand, the violation had been accidental and unintentional rather than deliberate and conscious and should not prevent the evidence being admitted.

O'Brien was a case involving unconstitutionally obtained real evidence and did not relate to confessions. The *O'Brien* principle was first extended to confessions in *People (D.P.P.) v. Madden*.[78] The applicant had been detained for questioning under section 30 of the Offences Against the State Act 1939 and this detention was extended beyond the period permitted by law. A confession completed by him during this extended detention was held to be inadmissible on the grounds that there had been a deliberate and conscious breach of his constitutional rights.

[74.] Unreported, Count of Criminal Appeal, July 31, 2001.

[75.] [1983] 1 I.L.R.M. 271.

[76.] Relevant material: O'Connor "The Admissibility of Unconstitutionally Obtained Evidence in Irish Law" (1982) Ir. Jur. 257; Kelly "*The Irish Constitution*" 4th ed. (2001); Casey "*Constitutional Laws in Ireland*", (3rd ed., Round Hall, Dublin, 2000), pp. 530-535.

[77.] [1965] I.R. 142.

[78.] [1977] I.R. 336.

The decision in *People (D.P.P.) v. Healy*[79] is of further importance insofar as it confirmed beyond doubt that the doctrine in *People (D.P.P.) v. O'Brien* extended to unconstitutionally obtained confessions.

The rule prohibiting the admission of unconstitutionally obtained confessions has four main components:

1. There must have been a breach of the accused's constitutional rights.

2. The breach must have been deliberate and conscious.

3. This breach must have caused the confession.

4. There must be no extraordinary excusing circumstances.

(1) There must have been a breach of the accused's constitutional rights

There are a significant number of constitutional rights which may have been breached in the context of obtaining a confession.

(a) The constitutional right to liberty is breached if the accused's arrest or detention is unlawful[80]

In particular a confession obtained in consequence of an unlawful arrest is invalid as being in contravention of the accused's constitutional right to liberty. The accused has a right under Articles 40.4.1 and 40.5 of the Constitution not to be detained save in accordance with law. In order for detention to be in accordance with law, the initial arrest must be lawful.

The arrest may be unlawful because the warrant was improperly completed or because a warrant never issued.

It is worth noting that arrest without warrant may be legal in certain circumstances. The current law governing arrest without warrant is the Criminal Law Act 1997, which gives specific powers of arrest without warrant in respect of an arrestable offence. An arrestable offence is defined as an offence for which a person of full capacity and not previously convicted may be punished by imprisonment for a term of five years or a more severe penalty. The definition of arrestable offence includes an attempt to commit such an offence.

Section 4 of the 1997 Act allows members of the Gardaí to arrest without warrant once an arrestable offence has been committed, or if they have reasonable cause to suspect that such an offence has been committed, provided that they have reasonable cause to suspect that the person they are arresting is guilty of the offence.

---

[79] [1990] I.L.R.M. 313.

[80] See para 15.2.1 for more detail on this. Also note Ryan "Arrest and Detention: A Review of the Law" (2000) 10(1) I.C.L.J. 2; Costelloe "Detention for Questioning and Oppressive Interrogation" (2001) 11(1) I.C.L.J. 12; Keane "Detention Without Charge and the Criminal Justice (Drug Trafficking) Act 1996" (1997) 7(1C) I.C.L.J. 1.

Members of the public have power to arrest under the 1997 Act only if an arrestable offence has actually been committed or if they suspect the arrestee to be in the very act of committing an arrestable offence. In addition, they must have reasonable cause to believe both that the arrestee is guilty of the offence in question, and that he is attempting to avoid arrest. Members of the public must transfer any person arrested by them under the 1997 Act into the custody of the Gardaí as soon as possible.

A number of other statutes give a power of arrest without warrant for certain offences.[81] Section 30(1) of the Offences Against the State Act 1939 allows a member of the Gardaí to arrest without warrant if he has a suspicion that the arrestee has committed or intends to commit a scheduled offence, or that he is in possession of information relating to the commission or intended commission of any scheduled offence, or that he is carrying a document relating to the commission or intended commission of such an offence. *People (D.P.P.) v. Howley*[82] indicates that such suspicions must be reasonable.

The following are scheduled offences within the meaning of the Offences Against the State Act 1939: offences under the Malicious Damage Act 1861, the Explosive Substances Act 1883, the Firearms Acts 1925-1971, the Conspiracy and Protection of Property Act 1875, and the Offences Against the State Act 1939. The advantage of arresting an accused under these provisions is that he or she can be detained for a longer period.

Even if the initial arrest is valid, subsequent unlawful detention of the accused may breach his constitutional right to liberty. Statute has amended the common law to allow for lawful detention without charge in certain situations. The Criminal Justice Act 1984 gives a power of detention in relation to an accused who has been validly arrested on a reasonable suspicion of having committed or attempting to commit an offence punishable by five years imprisonment or more. It authorises detention for up to 12 hours without charge. The initial period of detention is six hours. After this period has expired, a Superintendent or higher officer may direct that detention be extended for another six hours.

Section 30 of the Offences Against the State Act 1939 allows detention without charge on suspicion of a scheduled offence for a period of 24 hours, which may be extended by a further period of 24 hours on the direction of a Chief Superintendent or higher officer.

The Criminal Justice (Drug Trafficking) Act 1996 allows for the prolonged detention of a person arrested without warrant on reasonable suspicion that he

---

81. The Supreme Court in *People (D.P.P.) v. Quilligan and O'Reilly* [1993] 2 I.R. 305 established that the powers of arrest and detention under section 30 can be used irrespective of whether the scheduled offence in question is subversive or not. In addition, in this case it was stated that an arrest for a scheduled offence would be lawful even where the arrestee was suspected of being involved in a more serious unscheduled offence, such as murder, provided that there was a genuine suspicion on the part of the arresting garda that the accused had also been involved in the scheduled offence and that the arrest and interrogation was genuinely directed towards the investigation of that scheduled offence.

82. [1989] I.L.R.M. 629.

has committed a drug trafficking offence.[83] The maximum initial period of detention is six hours, but this may be extended by a further 18 hours if a Chief Superintendent so directs and has reasonable grounds for so directing. The detention may then be extended by a further 24 hours to 48 hours in total by further direction of a Chief Superintendent. A further extension of up to 72 hours is possible by obtaining a warrant from a District or Circuit Court judge. The judge may subsequently be applied to for an additional 24 hours' detention, thus bringing the maximum detention time under this Act up to almost seven days.

Detention without charge is also possible for the purposes of search under the Misuse of Drugs Acts 1977 and 1984 and for taking a blood or urine sample under the Road Traffic Acts. However, it is important, in order to avail of the detention provisions under these sections, that the police be genuinely investigating an offence covered by the sections.[84]

---

[83]　A drug trafficking offence for the purposes of this legislation is that of producing, supplying, transporting, storing, importing or exporting a controlled drug under section 3(1) of the Criminal Justice Act 1994.

[84]　In *People (D.P.P.) v. Howley* [1989] I.L.R.M. 629, an arrestee was purportedly arrested for the scheduled offence of cattle maiming so that he could be detained for the extended period permitted by the Offences Against the State Act 1939 but, in fact, was arrested in order to be interrogated about a murder. He argued that his detention under the Offences Against the State Act 1939 was invalid. Walsh J. in the Supreme Court stated that so long as there was a genuine desire and intent to pursue the investigation of the scheduled offence and so long as the arrest was not a colourful device to enable a person to be detained in pursuit of some other alleged offence, there was nothing to stop the Gardaí putting questions to the person in custody about the other offence. *Howley* can usefully be contrasted with *State (Bowes) v. Fitzpatrick* [1978] I.L.R.M. 195. Here, an individual had been killed with a knife, which had been damaged in the murder by contact with the victim's bone. The accused, one of the murder suspects, was arrested under s. 30 of the Offences Against the State Act 1939 on the ground of having caused malicious damage to the knife. The arrest was declared unlawful. Similarly, in the recent case of *Criminal Assets Bureau v. Craft*, unreported, July 12, 2000, it was stated *obiter* that if an arrest under the Criminal Law (Drug Trafficking) Act 1996 was a sham or cover for the purpose of eliciting information exclusively in relation to revenue offences, then it ought to be treated as unlawful.

Finally, it is worth noting that *Re O'Laighleis*[85] establishes that everyone is entitled to be told the reason for his arrest.[86] Another general principle in relation to arrest is as follows: no matter who is carrying out the arrest, the arrested person must be brought to a garda station with reasonable expedition and without undue delay.[87]

(b) The accused has constitutional right of access to legal advisers when in police custody[88]

While in detention, the accused has a constitutional right of access to a lawyer on request. This has been established since *People (D.P.P.) v. Healy*.[89] In this case, the Supreme Court affirmed that:

> "such an important and fundamental standard of fairness in the administration of justice as the right of access to a lawyer must be deemed to be constitutional in its origin".[90]

This is what occurred in *People (D.P.P.) v. Connell*.[91] A confession made by an accused was declared inadmissible on the ground that he had not had access to a solicitor. The applicant asked a relative to contact a solicitor on his behalf. Gardaí incorrectly informed this individual that a solicitor had in fact already been found. Consequently, the applicant was not attended by a solicitor prior to making his confession. The confession was therefore obtained in breach of O'Connell's constitutional rights.

---

85. [1960] I.R. 93.

86. However, even if the initial arrest was invalid, the subsequent detention of the accused may be validated once he is told the reason for his arrest. In *Madigan v. Devally* [1999] 2 I.L.R.M. 141, a garda told the appellant that he was being arrested under a particular section of the Road Traffic Act 1994. In actual fact, that particular section was not the one applicable. It was held that the arrest and consequent taking of a blood sample was unlawful, on the ground that "[a]n arrest is a very serious intrusion on a person's liberty and should only be done in strict accordance with the law."This was recently affirmed by the Supreme Court in *O'Mahony v. Ballagh*, unreported, Supreme Court, December 12, 2001. Here, the garda did not identify the specific offence for which the accused was being arrested. Under *Brennan v. D.P.P.* [1996] 1 I.L.R.M. 267, the arresting garda must identify the particular section of the Road Traffic Act 1994 under which the accused is being arrested. It was argued that the arrest was unlawful and that the evidence subsequently obtained was in breach of the accused's constitutional right to liberty. However, it was held by the High Court that the accused must have been aware of the reason for his arrest. On appeal, this decision was overturned.

87. This principle, originally laid down by O'Higgins C.J. in *People v. Walsh* [1980] I.R. 294, was recently reaffirmed by Herbert J. in *People (D.P.P.) v. Cleary*, unreported, December 7, 2001. The applicant had been arrested at 8.20 a.m. in his sister's house. He was kept in the house for 10 minutes after his arrest. During these 10 minutes, he admitted to the killing. It was held that the statements made by the accused in his sister's house were not admissible in evidence. However, subsequent statements made by him in the garda station were admissible except for one, made in response to a reminder about his previous admission. It was held that these subsequent statements could not be said to have been caused by the earlier unconstitutional confession and that the accused could have changed his mind.

88. See para 15.2.3. for more detail. Also note Butler (1993) 3 I.C.L.J. 173 and Butler and Ong (1995) 5 I.C.L.J. 156.

89. [1990] I.L.R.M. 73.

90. Finlay C.J. at p. 81.

91. [1995] 1 I.R. 244.

There is no constitutional right for the accused to be informed of his right to a solicitor.[92] The accused however does have the right to speak to his solicitor in private. In *People (D.P.P.) v. Finnegan*[93] the appellant was arrested on suspicion of larceny. He asked to speak to his solicitor and was allowed to telephone him; however, members of the Gardaí remained in the room while he made the call. The Court of Criminal Appeal stated that the right to consult a solicitor would usually be of little value unless it carried with it, as a necessary concomitant, the right to consult him in private.

There was no need for the appellant to expressly request private legal access; it was inherent in all legal access that it be private.

A number of cases have limited the right to a solicitor to one of reasonable access only. Carney J. in *Barry v. Waldron*[94] states that the accused has no right to have his solicitor present during questioning. This may be contrasted with the judgment of the United States Supreme Court in *Miranda v. Arizona*,[95] in which the contrary conclusion was reached.

The issue of reasonable access was further elaborated on in *Lavery v. Member-in-Charge, Carrickmacross Garda Station*.[96] The applicant had been arrested under section 30 of the Offences Against the State Act 1939 on suspicion of belonging to an unlawful organisation. In light of the fact that sections 2 and 5 of the Offences Against the State (Amendment) Act 1998 allowed inferences to be drawn from the failure of the accused to answer certain questions put to him by the Gardaí, the applicant's solicitor requested that the interviews be recorded audiovisually and/or that complete notes be taken and made available to him.

The Supreme Court held that the right of access to a solicitor was one of reasonable access. In this, they differed from the ruling of McGuinness J. in the High Court. There was no obligation on the Gardaí to give the solicitor regular updates. The solicitor was not entitled to be present at the interviews, nor was he entitled to prescribe the manner by which the interviews would be conducted.

The question of reasonable access was further considered in *People (D.P.P.) v. Darcy*.[97] The applicant, aged 16 years at the time, was arrested in the early hours of the morning. The applicant's uncle was brought in and requested a solicitor. Unsuccessful attempts were made to contact three solicitors. A fourth solicitor finally arrived at 12.15 p.m., by which time the accused had already been questioned. Upon arrival of the solicitor the applicant refused to answer any further questions and argued that earlier statements made by him were inadmissible.

[92.] *D.P.P. v. Spratt* [1995] 1 I.R. 585.
[93.] Unreported, Court of Criminal Appeal, July 15, 1997.
[94.] Unreported, High Court, *ex tempore*, May 23, 1996.
[95.] 384 U.S. 436 (1966).
[96.] [1999] 2 I.R. 390.
[97.] Unreported, Court of Criminal Appeal, July 29, 1997.

The Court of Criminal Appeal stated that in the circumstances the accused's right to legal access had not been infringed. The Gardaí had made reasonable attempts to contact a solicitor. Given the limited time period during which the accused could be detained, it was not necessary to delay questioning him until the arrival of the fourth solicitor. It is worth noting that the Gardaí in this case refrained from asking the accused to sign his confession until his solicitor arrived – something which made a positive impression on the court.

In *People (D.P.P.) v. Holland*[98] the applicant was arrested on suspicion of possession of a controlled drug. His lawyer was arrested shortly afterwards. The applicant argued that this was done as part of a conspiracy. It was held that no such conspiracy existed. The Gardaí had made reasonable and genuine attempts to contact a nominated solicitor. The applicant had eventually succeeded in getting the services of another solicitor. The court stated that if the applicant could have shown that the Gardaí had deliberately sought to deprive him of this particular solicitor, things would have been different.

(c) Other constitutional rights

Finally, in addition to the right of reasonable legal access, *In Re Emergency Powers Bill 1976*[99] recognised that a detainee has a constitutional right to medical assistance.

Breaches of the constitutional right to inviolability of the dwelling[100] have tended to feature in cases where the admissibility of real evidence, rather than confessions, is at issue. However, a breach of this right could also render a confession inadmissible, if the confession was obtained as a result of the breach.

Finally, when referring to constitutional rights, breaches of which may render evidence inadmissible, attention should be drawn to the amorphous constitutional right to fair procedures. This is an undefined right, which has been judicially referred to in other areas of evidence law such as identification evidence. It is likely to become more important in the future, after being successfully invoked in *People (D.P.P.) v. Ward*,[101] which has already been referred in the context of involuntariness.

(2) The breach of constitutional rights must be a deliberate and conscious breach

Initial difficulties were encountered when it came to defining a deliberate and conscious breach of constitutional rights. The current position, originating in the judgment of Walsh J. in *People (D.P.P.) v. Shaw*, indicated that so long as the act in question was a deliberate and conscious act, that was sufficient.

[98.] Unreported, Court of Criminal Appeal, June 15, 1998.
[99.] [1977] I.R. 159.
[100.] The right to inviolability of the dwelling is the right not to have one's dwelling entered without one's consent except in accordance with law.
[101.] Unreported, Special Criminal Court, November 27, 1998.

There was no requirement that the maker of the act know that it was in breach of constitutional rights.

The decisions of *People (D.P.P.) v. Healy*[102] and *People (D.P.P.) v. Kenny*[103] were important in clarifying this issue.

Given the extremely wide approach taken in *Healy* and *Kenny*, is there a continuing role for the requirement of deliberate and conscious breach, or should it simply be abolished? Judges have consistently reaffirmed that there was no deliberate and conscious breach in *People (D.P.P.) v. O'Brien* and that, therefore, the admission of the evidence in that case was justified. Finlay C.J. in *People (D.P.P.) v. Kenny* indicated that if the particular actions were unintentional or accidental, there would be no deliberate and conscious breach.

(3) The unconstitutionality must have caused the confession

It appears that, even if a deliberate and conscious breach of constitutional rights has occurred, it may still be possible to admit evidence obtained subsequent to the breach on the ground that it was not made as a result of the breach. In particular, urine samples obtained in denial of the constitutional right to legal advice have been held not to have been obtained as a result of legal advice.

The cases on the causation requirement all involve the admissibility of particular pieces of real evidence, which the accused had been under a statutory obligation to provide. However, in relation to a confession made after an accused had been unconstitutionally refused access to his lawyer, it would be extremely difficult for the prosecution to prove that this confession had not been influenced by the unconstitutionality.

However, on this point, attention should be drawn to the recent decision of Herbert J. in *People (D.P.P.) v. Cleary*.[104] The applicant made a confession during a period of illegal detention in his sister's house. A short time afterwards his detention became legal, and he made further statements expanding on his earlier confession. It was held that the statements made by the applicant while in his sister's house were inadmissible, but the statements made subsequently in the police station were admitted on the ground that they could not have been caused by the earlier unconstitutionality.

Finally, it is worth noting that not all the cases show such a restrictive approach to the issue of causation. In *D.P.P. v. Madden*[105] a confession completed during a period of unlawfully extended detention was held inadmissible. Some of the confession had been made during the lawful detention period and, therefore, could not have been caused by the unconstitutionality; nonetheless the entire confession was excluded.

---

[102] [1990] 2 I.R. 73.
[103] [1990] 2 I.R. 110.
[104] Unreported, Court of Criminal Appeal, July 15, 1997.
[105] [1977] I.R. 336.

In *People (D.P.P.) v. Finnegan*[106] it was held that a breach of a detainee's right of access to a solicitor would have the effect of making all subsequent detention illegal. The consequence of this would be that all statements made by an accused after that point would be automatically illegal without the need to decide whether or not they were caused by the failure to provide the solicitor. It is worth noting that this dictum, which is in direct contrast with the approach taken in *D.P.P. v. Spratt*[107] and *Walsh v. O'Buachalla,*[108] appears to have been adopted *obiter* by the Supreme Court in *Lavery v. Member-in-Charge, Carrickmacross Garda Station.*[109]

(4) There must be no extraordinary excusing circumstances

Once a deliberate and conscious breach of constitutional rights is shown, the onus shifts to the prosecution to establish either absence of causation or extraordinary excusing circumstances. Although the phrase "extraordinary excusing circumstances" is part of the original *O'Brien* test, it has yet to be fully considered by the courts.

Some examples of extraordinary excusing circumstances were given by Walsh J. in *O'Brien* as follows:

1. where there is a risk of the imminent destruction of vital evidence;

2. where there is the need to rescue a victim in peril; and

3. where evidence is obtained by a search incidental to and contemporaneous with a lawful arrest, although made without a valid search warrant

The situation in *People (Attorney General) v. Shaw*[110] came within the victim in peril example. The accused was detained for an excessive period in order to ascertain the whereabouts of a girl he had abducted, and whom the Gardaí believed to be still alive. A confession made by him during this unconstitutional detention was held admissible.

17.2.3 *Trial judge's discretion to exclude confessions*[111]

Even where the confession is not automatically inadmissible under one or other of the above grounds, the trial judge may have a discretion to exclude it. A trial judge has a general discretion at common law to exclude evidence if it would threaten the accused's right to a fair trial. As stated by Lord Goddard when delivering the judgment of the Privy Council in *Kuruma v. R.*:

> "In a criminal case the judge always has a discretion to disallow evidence if the strict rules of admissibility would operate unfairly against the accused."[112]

[106.] Unreported, Court of Criminal Appeal, July 15, 1997.
[107.] [1995] 2 I.L.R.M. 117.
[108.] [1991] 1 I.R. 56.
[109.] [1999] 2 I.R. 390.
[110.] [1982] I.R. 1.
[111.] See Sharpe *"Judicial Discretion and Criminal Investigation"* (Sweet & Maxwell, London, 1997).
[112.] [1955] A.C. 197.

This principle may be broken down into two parts. Firstly, the trial judge has a general discretion to exclude evidence obtained by improper or unfair means. Secondly, the judge has a discretion to exclude evidence if its prejudical effect outweighs its probative value.

(1) Discretion to exclude if prejudicial effect outweighs probative value

The discretion to exclude evidence if its prejudicial effect outweighs its probative value is commonly used to exclude evidence of the accused's previous misconduct or bad character in situations where such evidence is not automatically prohibited. However, it could also have application in the context of confessions the reliability of which is suspect. The Supreme Court in *People (D.P.P.) v. Quilligan and O'Reilly*[113] referred to the trial judge's discretion to withdraw a confession from the jury in order to prevent a wrongful conviction. In *People (D.P.P.) v. Quinn*[114] the Court of Criminal Appeal stated that the trial judge should have exercised this discretion to exclude two confession statements made by a 13-year-old of low intelligence. There were inconsistencies between the two statements, and further inconsistencies between the statements and the testimony of the complainant in the case.

(2) Discretion to exclude confessions obtained by improper or unfair means

The discretion to exclude evidence obtained by improper or unfair means gives the trial judge the power to exclude illegally obtained evidence. He is entitled to exclude such evidence, but is not obliged to do so. In *People (Attorney General) v. O'Brien*[115] Kingsmill Moore J. recognised a discretion to exclude evidence which has been unlawfully obtained. Such evidence should be excluded if public policy requires it. This discretion arguably also extends to allow the trial judge to exclude evidence, which, although not illegally obtained, can be said to have been obtained improperly or unfairly.

This discretion was exercised by the Supreme Court in *D.P.P. v. McMahon McMeel and Wright*[116] in order to decide whether or not evidence obtained by an unlawful (although not unconstitutional) search of licensed premises could be admitted. In the event, the Supreme Court decided that public policy did not require the exclusion of the evidence in question. Although these cases relate to illegally obtained real evidence, the principles contained in them equally extend to unlawfully obtained confessions.

---

[113] [1993] 2 I.R. 305.
[114] Unreported, Court of Criminal Appeal, *ex tempore*, March 23, 1998.
[115] [1965] I.R. 142.
[116] [1986] I.R. 393.

In the context of confessions, the issue of the discretion to exclude evidence obtained by illegal or unfair means has tended to arise in two situations: firstly, in the case of confessions obtained by a breach of the Judges' Rules,[117] and, secondly, in relation to confessions obtained in breach of the Criminal Justice Act 1984 (Treatment of Persons in Custody) Regulations 1987.[118] It is now proposed to look in more detail at the exercise of the discretion in these particular contexts. It should be noted, however that these situations are mere examples of the more general discretion of a trial judge to exclude any evidence obtained by illegal or unfair means. It is possible that a confession may be excluded in the future for some illegality other than non-compliance with the Judges' Rules or the Custody Regulations. For example, if a confession failed to comply with the Criminal Justice Act 1984 (Electronic Recording of Interviews) Regulations 1997,[119] the trial judge would be entitled to exercise this discretion to exclude it.

(3) Discretion to exclude for breach of Judges' Rules

As stated above, the discretion to exclude confessions for breach of the Judges' Rules is a subset of the discretion to exclude evidence that has been obtained by illegal or unfair means. The Judges' Rules were established in 1912 when the then government asked the judiciary to clarify the circumstances in which one could be questioned by the police. *People (D.P.P.) v. Darcy*[120] established that the existence of the Criminal Justice Act 1984 (Treatment of Persons in Custody) Regulations 1987 does not affect the operation of the Judges' Rules.

The Judges' Rules are set out in the case of *People (Attorney General) v. Cummins*[121] and may be summarised as follows: firstly, it is possible for the Gardaí to ask anyone to participate in voluntary questioning and put questions to them without a caution; secondly, once a garda has made up his mind to charge someone, he should caution them first.

In the case of *Moore v. Martin*[122] the applicant had been convicted of drunk driving. The applicant had left the scene of the accident on foot. A garda caught up with the applicant, asked him questions, formed the opinion that he was intoxicated, and arrested him. The applicant argued that the garda had acted in breach of the Rules. However, it was held that there was no need for the garda to have cautioned the applicant before he spoke to him. The garda had not made up his mind to charge the applicant and was only trying to find out if an offence had been committed.

[117.] As set out in *People (Attorney General) v. Cummins*; for commentary see (1974) *Journal of Criminal Law* 234 and (1974) 107 I.L.T. & S.J. 125.

[118.] S.I. No. 119/87.

[119.] S.I. No. 74/97.

[120.] Unreported, Court of Criminal Appeal, July 29, 1997.

[121.] [1972] I.R. 312.

[122.] Unreported, High Court, Finnegan J., May 29, 2000.

It is a facet of the Judges' Rules that persons who have been arrested should not be questioned without being cautioned. In *Re Gunner Buckley*[123] the individual being questioned had been called to the interview room as part of a military disciplinary procedure and would not have been entitled to leave. He was, therefore, in an equivalent position to someone who was in custody and should have been cautioned before being questioned.

In *People (D.P.P.) v. Morgan*[124] the accused was cautioned in accordance with the Judges' Rules. An identification parade was held and after the parade he was re-interviewed. He claimed that he had not been cautioned again. He had, however, been told by a police officer that the caution still applied. It was held that there was no breach of the Rules; there is no need for the garda to repeat the caution on every occasion so long as the accused knows it still applies.

In addition, the Judges' Rules state that if a person in custody volunteers a statement without being cautioned, he should be cautioned before continuing. Furthermore, there should be no cross-examination on a voluntary statement. In *People (D.P.P.) v. O'Driscoll*[125] the applicant challenged the admissibility of a statement made by him as a result of a question and answer session in which inconsistencies in his original statement had been pointed out. It was held that this session could not be regarded as cross-examination and, therefore, was not in breach of the Rules.

In addition, the Rules provide that when two or more persons are questioned about the same offence, statements of each should be provided to the other. Any statements made should be taken down and read back to the individual who made them, who should then be asked to sign these statements.

Finally, young persons should not be questioned in the absence of their parents. This requirement was not originally contained in the Rules, but was added by the case of *Travers v. Ryan*.[126]

As the case of *People (D.P.P.) v. Farrell*[127] makes clear, non-compliance with the Rules does not mean that the confession obtained is automatically inadmissible, merely that the trial judge has a discretion to exclude it. Two examples of the exercise of this discretion are the cases of *R. v. Voisin*[128] *and R. v. Purcell*.[129]

In *R. v. Purcell* the plaintiff had been on the run from the police on a charge of rape. He was picked up on a suspicion of burglary and, after being cautioned in relation to the burglaries, said, "I am Purcell...I have done something bad", and went on to talk about the rape. It was held that there was no breach of the Judges' Rules here, or if there was, it was not such as to make the evidence inadmissible. There was effectively no time to question Purcell

---

123. [1998] 2 I.R. 454.
124. Unreported, Court of Criminal Appeal, *ex tempore*, July 28, 1997.
125. Unreported, Court of Criminal Appeal, July 19, 1999.
126. [1918] 1 K.B. 531.
127. [1978] I.R. 13.
128. [1918] 1 K.B. 531
129. [1992] Crim. L.R. 806.

before he made the statement about the rape. The Gardaí should have cautioned him about the burglaries and did so. His evidence could be accepted.

In *R. v. Voisin,*[130] a murder case, a paper in which the victim's body was wrapped had "blady belgium" written on it. The police took Voisin in for questioning and asked him to write "bloody belgian": he wrote "blady belgium". It was argued that this evidence was inadmissible at trial because he should have been cautioned first. The court refused to interfere with the trial judge's exercise of his discretion.

In *People (D.P.P.) v. Murray*[131] Murray had been convicted of rape. The doctor examined him for the purpose of taking semen samples. The doctor was asked to examine the applicant again in relation to a mark on his lip to ascertainwhether it was a cold sore. The complainant had said she had bitten her attacker on the lip. The complainant was not cautioned before this second examination. However, even though there was a breach of the Judges' Rules, the trial judge admitted the evidence. This case is also significant because it is the first example of the Judges' Rules being applied outside the context of confession evidence.

(4) Discretion to exclude for breach of Custody Regulations

The Criminal Justice Act 1984 gave the authority to make regulations regarding the treatment of persons in custody. These were enacted in the 1987 (Treatment of Persons in Custody) Regulations.[132]

Section 7(3) of the Criminal Justice Act 1984 provides that a failure on the part of any member of the Gardaí to observe any provision of the Regulations shall not of itself affect the lawfulness of the custody of the detained person or the admissibility in evidence of any statement made by him.

It would be possible for statute to specifically provide that a breach of the Regulations would make evidence obtained as a result automatically inadmissible. Although the common law rule is that evidence obtained contrary to a statute or statutory instrument is admissible subject to the trial judge's discretion to exclude, like all common law rules, this could be overturned by statute.

However, section 7(3) of the Criminal Justice Act does not do this. It merely recognises the trial judge's discretion to decide whether to admit a confession obtained in breach of the Regulations. This is made clear by the wording of section 7(3), which states as follows:

> "A failure on the part of Gardaí to abide by the regulations shall not of itself affect the admissibility of a statement made by the accused."

The crucial words here are of course the phrase "not of itself". The meaning of this phrase was discussed in *People (D.P.P.) v. Connell.*[133] This case involved a

---

[130.] [1918] 1 K.B. 531.

[131.] Unreported, Court of Criminal Appeal, April 12, 1999.

[132.] S.I. No. 119/87.

[133.] [1995] I.R. 244.

breach of the Custody Regulations. The accused was interrogated for more than four hours without adjournment. He did not get any sleep. The next day his statement was taken after adjourning an interrogation of more than four hours. He had been offered the opportunity of adjournment earlier in the interrogation but did not take it. However, the Regulations do not provide for any power to waive the right to adjournment. In addition, the accused's constitutional rights had been breached insofar as he had been denied access to a solicitor.

The statement made by the accused was held inadmissible because of the breach of constitutional rights and the breach of the Custody Regulations. It was stated that section 7 gave the trial judge a discretion to decide whether to admit a statement in breach of the Regulations:

> "A statement of itself could not be held inadmissible by virtue of the fact that it was taken in the course of an interview of more than 4 hours…however if combined with additional factors, e.g. lack of sleep…the judge has a discretion not to admit it."[134]

It is unclear whether this discretion is a facet of the general common law discretion to exclude evidence obtained by unfair means or whether it is a statutory discretion created by section 7.

The following cases provide examples of how the discretion is exercised in practice. In *People (D.P.P.) v. Darcy*[135] there had been a breach of regulation 12(3) of the Regulations, which provides that not more than two members should question an accused person at any one time. In this situation, the court refused to exclude the evidence. It stated that, in addition to a breach of the Regulations, there must be something in the circumstances of the case which would render the admission of the evidence unfair. In this case, even though the Custody Regulations were breached, the questioning was not otherwise oppressive or unfair.

In *People (D.P.P.) v. Devlin*[136] it was held that in order for a breach of the Custody Regulations to make the evidence of the accused inadmissible, it must be shown that the evidence in question was obtained as a result of the breach.

The respondent was arrested under section 49 of the Road Traffic Act 1961 for drunk driving. The arresting garda acted as Member-in-Charge. This was in breach of regulation 4(3) of the Custody Regulations, which states that the Member-in-Charge shall not be a garda involved in the arrest. The garda handed the respondent a statement informing him of his rights to consult a solicitor but did not orally inform him of the rights as required by regulation 8. Despite these breaches of the Regulations, Budd J. stated that evidence obtained in breach of the Regulations could only be excluded if it could be shown that the non-compliance with the Regulations had an impact on the

---

[134.] *Ibid.*, Egan J., p. 252.
[135.] Unreported, Court of Criminal Appeal, July 29, 1997.
[136.] Unreported, High Court, Budd J., September 9, 1997.

prosecution case, *i.e.* caused inculpatory evidence to be obtained. Otherwise, the applicant would not have been prejudiced in any way by the breach.

This case mirrors the approach taken in *D.P.P. v. Spratt.*[137] In this case, regulation 8 had been breached insofar as the accused had not been informed of his right to consult a solicitor. The evidence was admitted on the basis that it could not be said to have been obtained as a result of the breach. This approach was recently followed by O'Caoimh J. in the case of *D.P.P. v. Jamie Cullen*[138] and was approved by the Supreme Court in *People (D.P.P.) v. Murphy.*[139]

The applicant's argument in *Murphy* for overturning his conviction was based on regulation 12(11) of the Custody Regulations, which states that a record shall be made of each interview. This failed to happen here. However, there was no evidence that this breach had prejudiced the applicant in any way. No case was made that there occurred any event to influence or affect the applicant's position. The Supreme Court held that this was a matter for the determination of the trial judge. The appropriate question to ask was whether the accused was prejudiced by the breach. It stated that it is only when there was a causal connection between the breach and the prejudice that the District Court could conclude that it would be legitimate to consider dismissing the charge.

In *People (D.P.P.) v. Smith*[140] the applicant said that three Gardaí had asked him questions at the one time. This was in breach of regulation 12(3) of the Regulations, which provides that no more than two Gardaí can question a suspect at any one time. In the circumstances, even though there had been a breach of the rules, the statement had been properly admitted.

17.3 Admissions made by an accused in a criminal case

As stated above, a statement made by the accused in a criminal case to a person in authority is known as a confession. However, a statement made other than to a person in authority is not a confession; it is an admission and is subject to slightly different rules.

17.3.1 Distinguishing between a confession and an admission in criminal cases

It becomes important to decide who is a person in authority for the purpose of distinguishing between confessions and admissions in criminal cases. The term "person in authority" has been defined in the context of confessions in deciding whether a threat, inducement or oppression came from a person in authority; this is a necessary requirement of the confession being involuntary.

It is worth looking at the definition of the term "person in authority" in this context, where it has been defined as someone who may reasonably be

---

[137.] Unreported, High Court, February 8, 1995.
[138.] Unreported, O'Caoimh J., 7 February, 2001.
[139.] Unreported, Supreme Court, July 12, 2001.
[140.] Unreported, Court of Criminal Appeal, November 22, 1999.

supposed to be in a position to influence the prosecution. The test appears to be a mixed objective and subjective one: did the accused reasonably believe that this individual was a person in authority?[141]

17.3.2 Rules applicable to admissions in criminal cases

Like a confession, an admission does not have to be in writing. In *Rumping v. E.P.P.*[142] an informal admission made by the accused to his wife was admitted in evidence. The admission may be made in a diary.[143] Conduct may, on occasion, amount to an admission.[144] The accused may later lead evidence at his trial to reveal the circumstances under which his admission was made in order to reduce its prejudicial effect.

Normally, admissions by one co-accused or party cannot be used against another unless they are acts or declarations made in furtherance of a common design. In *R. v. Blake and Tye*[145] the accused were charged with a conspiracy to pass goods through customs without paying tax. Entries made in books by one of the co-accused that incriminated both of them were held admissible where the making of such entries had been a necessary part of the fraud.

17.3.3 Admissibility of admissions

It is possible that an admission made by the accused in a criminal case to an individual not a person in authority could be struck down as being involuntary if the confession had been induced by a threat, inducement, or oppression from a third party who qualified as a person in authority. Fitzgibbon J. in the *State v. Treanor*[146] stated that:

> "A confession made to any person under the influence of a promise or threat held out by a person in authority, calculated to induce the confession, is inadmissible."

In the United Kingdom, the requirement, that the threat, inducement or oppressive behaviour come from a person in authority, has been abolished. It is

---

[141.] In *Sullivan v. Robinson* [1954] I.R. 161, a doctor, called in by the Gardaí to examine a person suspected of being drunk, may be a person in authority. *R. v. McLintock* [1962] Crim. L.R. 549 stated that a headmistress could constitute a person in authority in relation to schoolgirls.

In *Deokinian v. R.* [1969] A.C. 20 it was held that a person "known to be close to the police" qualified as a person in authority. However, if that person was also a trusted friend of the accused, he was not a person in authority In *People (D.P.P.) v. McCann* [1998] 4 I.R. 397 it was held that the accused's brothers were not persons in authority. A person in authority was "someone engaged in the arrest, detention, examination or prosecution of the accused or someone acting on behalf of the prosecution".

[142.] [1964] A.C. 814.

[143.] *Bruce v. Garden* (1869) 18 W.R. 384.

[144.] *O'Sullivan v. Robinson* [1954] I.R. 161: submission to a test for drunkenness was treated as a species of admission; *Powell v. McGlynn* [1902] 2 I.R. 154; *Vandeleur v. Glynn* [1905] 1 I.R. 483 at 506; *Tait v. Beggs* [1905] 2 I.R. 525.

[145.] (1844) 6 Q.B. 126.

[146.] [1924] 2 I.R. 193.

sufficient if the involuntariness is such as to make the confession or admission unreliable.

It appears also that an admission made by an accused in a criminal case to a third party could be struck down if it was obtained in breach of the individual's constitutional rights. Where the breach of constitutional rights has been committed not by the State but by a private individual, however, questions arise as to whether the principle should also apply in this situation.

17.4 Admissions by one of the parties in a civil case

There is a special category of admission in a civil case known as a formal admission. The inclusion of information in pleadings or in a letter sent to the other party's legal adviser constitutes a formal admission of that information in a civil case. Once made, a formal admission cannot subsequently be contradicted by the person who has made it. Formal admissions, however, are binding only for the purposes of the case in which they are made. The concept of a formal admission is not recognised in criminal proceedings in this jurisdiction.[147]

In respect of admissions other than formal admissions, the rules regarding the admissibility of such admissions in civil cases are the same as for admissions in criminal cases.

In criminal cases, the accused's right to silence precludes silence from amounting to an admission at common law. However, the right to silence is modified in civil cases and a party's silence may amount to an admission in circumstances where it would be reasonable to expect some explanation.[148]

As with admissions in criminal cases, an admission in a civil case may be inferred from a party's conduct,[149] and an admission by one party in a case is not normally evidence against his co-defendant.[150]

17.4.1 Third-party admissions and confessions

The normal rule is that any confession or admission by third parties to the case are inadmissible hearsay. This can produce unfair results. Even if the maker of

---

[147.] *R. v. Riley* (1896) 18 Cox C.C.285.

[148.] *Bessela v. Stern* (1877) 2 C.P.D. 265 involved an action for breach of promise; the defendant's silence by way of answer to the plaintiff's assertion that he had always promised to marry her amounted to an admission. See also *Cleland v. McCune* [1908] 42 I.L.T.R. 201; *Morrissey v. Boyle* [1942] I.R. 514; *O'Shea v. Roche* [1952] Ir. Jur. Rep. 1; *People (Attorney General) v. Quinn* [1955] I.R. 57.

[149.] This was recognised in *Powell v. McGlynn and Bradlaw* [1902] 2 I.R. 154; however, the conduct in this case did not amount to an admission. See also *Moriarty v. London, Chatham and Dover Railway* (1870) L.R. 5 Q.B. 314, where evidence of the plaintiff having suborned witnesses was admitted as evidence of the weakness of his claim, and *Tait v. Beggs* [1905] 2 I.R. 525, where a husband and wife were jointly sued for slander. An offer by the husband to the plaintiff of a sum of money if she would abandon her claim, coupled with a threat to bring witnesses and other charges, was held to be an admission against both defendants.

[150.] However, note *Tait v. Beggs*, [1905] 2 I.R. 525.

the confession or admission dies before trial or revokes it, it is still inadmissible.

However, in some situations the admissions of third parties may be admitted in evidence on the basis that they are, in effect, the admission of a party in a civil case. The situations in which this may occur are set out below.

(1) Vicarious admissions and confessions

In order for the statement of a third party to be treated as being that of the party, there must be a relationship of privity between them, *i.e.* some identity of interest in the litigation or in the subject-matter of the litigation, which suggests that an admission from the maker of the statement is tantamount to an admission by the party himself.

(2) Agents

The admission of a party's agent may sometimes be treated as that party's admission. However, in order for this to occur, the admission must have been made at the time when the agency existed, and must have been expressly or impliedly authorised by, or must have formed part of, a communication authorised by the principal. It must be made to a third party: an admission by an agent to the party himself is not sufficient.[151]

In *Bord na gCon v. Murphy*[152] the court refused to treat a statement by a party's solicitor as being an admission by that party. There was no evidence that the solicitor had been authorised to write this letter. In *Johnson v. Lindsay*[153] it was held that an admission by a servant in relation to a tort, for which his master was being sued, could not be treated as an admission by the master because the servant had no express or implied authority to make such a statement.

In *Swan v. Miller, Son and Torrance Ltd*,[154] O'Connor L.J. stated that a solicitor has an implied authority in civil cases to make statements on behalf of his client. However, the solicitor must have express authority if he is to make statements on behalf of his client in criminal cases.[155] In criminal cases, statements by an accused's counsel in open court may be admitted against him, though only for the purposes of that particular case.

(3) Predecessors in title

An admission made by a party's predecessor in title may bind him in proceedings relating to ownership of the particular property. In *Smith v. Smith*,[156] in relation to the administration of an intestate's estate, a previous

---

[151.] *Re Devala Provident Gold Mining Co.* (1883) 22 Ch. D. 593.
[152.] [1970] I.R. 301.
[153.] (1889) 53 J.P. 599.
[154.] [1919] 1 I.R. 151.
[155.] *R. v. Downer* (1880) 14 Cox C.C. 486.
[156.] (1836) 3 Bing N.C. 29

admission by the intestate regarding ownership of a particular watch in his possession was admitted against his administrator. In *MacKenna v. Earl of Howth*[157] maps made by a predecessor in title of a landlord were admissible against that landlord and any person claiming through him.

(4) Partners

Books executed by one of the partners in a firm can be used in evidence against the other partner; the admissions of one partner are attributable to the other in relation to litigation about that partnership.[158] They count as an admission by that partner.

However, an admission made by one joint tenant cannot bind his fellow joint tenants.[159]

(5) Referees

Williams v. Innes[160] established that if a party in the case has referred individuals to a third party for further information any admissions made by that third party may be put in evidence against him.[161]

(6) Actions arising out of fatal injuries

In an action arising out of a fatal injury, any statements made by the deceased person before his death are treated as being admissions by the party in the case and may be admitted in evidence.[162]

(7) Admissions in affidavits previously relied on by party in another case

Any admissions in affidavits previously relied on by the party in question in another case are regarded as admissions by that party and may be put in evidence.[163]

Finally, it should be noted that a party is not bound by admissions made by his spouse.[164]

[157.] (1893) 27 I.L.T.R. 48

[158.] *Corporation of Waterford v. Price* (1846) 9 Ir. L.R. 310.

[159.] *Turner v. Attorney General* (1847) I.R. 10 Eq. 386.

[160.] (1808) 1 Camp 364.

[161.] *R. v. Mallory* (1884) 13 Q.B.D 33.

[162.] In *Power v. DUTC* [1926] I.R. 302, a claim under the Fatal Accidents Act 1846, a statement by the deceased person made before his death was admissible.

[163.] *Evans v. Merthyr Tydfil Urban District Council* [1899] 1 Ch. 24; *White v. Dowling* (1845) 8 Ir. L.R. 128.

[164.] *G.(A.) v. G.(T.)* [1970] 2 Q.B. 643.

APPENDIX - RELATED LEGISLATION

CONTENTS

Children Act 1997

(1992 No.12)

PART III

EVIDENCE OF CHILDREN

Interpretation

19.—(1) In this Part, unless the context otherwise requires—

"child" means a person who is not of full age;

"statement" means any representation of fact or opinion however made;

"video-recorded" means recorded on any medium (including a film) from which a moving image may by any means be produced, and includes the accompanying soundtrack, if any, and "video-recording" has a corresponding meaning.

(2) Where the age of a person at any time is material for the purpose of any proceedings to which this Part applies, his or her age at that time shall, for the purposes of such proceedings, be deemed, unless the contrary is proved, to be or to have been that which appears to the court to be his or her age at that time.

Application of Part III

20.—This Part applies to—

(a)   civil proceedings before any court, commenced after the commencement of this Part, concerning the welfare of a child; or

(b)   with the necessary modifications, in the same manner as it applies to a child, to civil proceedings before any court, commenced after the commencement of this Part, concerning the welfare of a person who is of full age but who has a mental disability to such an extent that it is not reasonably possible for the person to live independently.

Evidence through television link

21.—(1) In any proceedings to which this Part applies a child may, with the leave of the court, give evidence (whether from within or outside the State) through a live television link.

(2) Evidence given under subsection (1) shall be video-recorded.

(3) Any child who, in giving evidence under subsection (1) from outside the State, makes a statement material in the proceedings which the child knows to be false or does not believe to be true shall be guilty of perjury, or, if section 28 applies, shall be guilty of an offence specified in subsection (2) of that section.

(4) Proceedings for an offence under subsection (3) may be taken, and the offence may, for the purposes of the jurisdiction of the court, be treated as having been committed, in any place in the State.

(5) Where evidence is given by a child under subsection (1) that any person was known to him or her before the date of commencement of the proceedings, the child shall not be required to identify the person during the course of those proceedings, unless the court directs otherwise.

Evidence through intermediary

22.—(1) Where in proceedings to which this Part applies the evidence of a child is being given or to be given through a live television link, the court may, of its own motion or on the application of a party to the proceedings, if satisfied that, having regard to the age or mental condition of the child, any questions to be put to the child should be put through an intermediary, direct that any such question be so put.

(2) Questions put to a child through an intermediary under this section shall be either in the words used by the questioner or in words that convey to the child, in a way that is appropriate to his or her age or mental condition, the meaning of the questions being asked.

(3) An intermediary referred to in subsection (1) shall be appointed by the court and shall be a person who, in its opinion, is competent to act as such.

Admissibility of hearsay evidence

23.—(1) Subject to subsection (2), a statement made by a child shall be admissible as evidence of any fact therein of which direct oral evidence would be admissible in any proceeding to which this Part applies, notwithstanding any rule of law relating to hearsay, where the court considers that—

    (a)   the child is unable to give evidence by reason of age, or

    (b)   the giving of oral evidence by the child, either in person or under section 21, would not be in the interest of the welfare of the child.

    (2)(a)   Any statement referred to in subsection (1) or any part thereof shall not be admitted in evidence if the court is of the opinion that, in the interests of justice, the statement or that part of the statement ought not to be so admitted.

    (b)   In considering whether the statement or any part of the statement ought to be admitted, the court shall have regard to all the circumstances, including any risk that the admission will result in unfairness to any of the parties to the proceedings.

(3) A party proposing to adduce evidence admissible in proceedings to which this Part applies by virtue of subsection (1), shall give to the other party or parties to the proceedings—

    (a)   such notice, if any, of that fact, and

    (b)   such particulars of or relating to the evidence,

as is reasonable and practicable in the circumstances for the purpose of enabling such party or parties to deal with any matter arising from its being hearsay.

(4) Subsection (3) shall not apply where the parties concerned agree that it should not apply.

Weight of hearsay evidence

24.—(1) In estimating the weight, if any, to be attached to any statement admitted in evidence pursuant to section 23, regard shall be had to all the circumstances from which any inference can reasonably be drawn as to its accuracy or otherwise.

(2) Regard may be had, in particular, as to whether—

(a) the original statement was made contemporaneously with the occurrence or existence of the matters stated,

(b) the evidence involves multiple hearsay,

(c) any person involved has any motive to conceal or misrepresent matters,

(d) the original statement was an edited account or was made in collaboration with another for a particular purpose, and

(e) the circumstances in which the evidence is adduced as hearsay are such as to suggest an attempt to prevent proper evaluation of its weight.

Evidence as to credibility

25.—Where information is given in a statement admitted in evidence pursuant to section 23—

(a) any evidence which, if the child who originally supplied the information had been called as a witness, would have been admissible as relevant to his or her credibility as a witness shall be admissible for that purpose,

(b) evidence may, with the leave of the court, be given of any matter which, if that child had been called as a witness, could have been put to him or her in cross-examination as relevant to his or her credibility as a witness but of which evidence could not have been adduced by the cross-examining party, and

(c) evidence tending to prove that the child, whether before or after supplying the information, made (whether orally or not) a statement which is inconsistent with it shall, if not already admissible, be admissible for the purpose of showing that the witness has contradicted himself or herself.

Copies of documents in evidence

26.—(1) Where information contained in a document is admissible in evidence in proceedings to which this Part applies, the information may be given in evidence, whether or not the document is still in existence, by producing a copy of the document, or of the material part of it, authenticated in such manner as the court may approve.

(2) It is immaterial for the purposes of subsection (1) how many removes there are between the copy and the original, or by what means (which may include facsimile transmission) the copy was produced or any intermediate copy was made.

(3) In this section "document" includes a sound recording and a video-recording.

Transfer of proceedings

27.—Where in proceedings to which this Part applies the court is of the opinion that it is desirable that evidence be taken by live television link or by means of a video-recording and facilities for doing so are not available, it may, by order, transfer the proceedings to a court where those facilities are available and, where such an order is made, the jurisdiction of the court to which the proceedings have been transferred may be exercised—

  (a) in the case of the Circuit Court, by the judge of the circuit concerned, and

  (b) in the case of the District Court, by the judge of that court for the time being assigned to the district court district concerned.

Oath or affirmation not necessary for child witnesses

28.—(1) Notwithstanding any rule of law, in any civil proceedings (whether or not they are proceedings to which this Part applies) the evidence of a child who has not attained the age of 14 years may be received otherwise than on oath or affirmation if the court is satisfied that the child is capable of giving an intelligible account of events which are relevant to the proceedings.

(2) Any child whose evidence is received in accordance with subsection (1) and who makes a statement material in the proceedings concerned which the child knows to be false or does not believe to be true, shall be guilty of an offence and on conviction shall be liable to be dealt with as if guilty of perjury.

(3) Subsection (1) shall apply to a person with mental disability who has attained the age of 14 years as it applies to a child who has not attained that age.

(4) Unsworn evidence received by virtue of this section may corroborate evidence (sworn or unsworn) given by any other person.

Criminal Evidence Act 1992

(1992 No. 12)

An Act to amend the law of evidence in relation to criminal proceedings and to provide for connected matters.

[7TH JULY, 1992]

BE IT ENACTED BY THE OIREACHTAS AS FOLLOWS:

PART I

PRELIMINARY

Short title and Commencement

1.—(1) This Act may be cited as the Criminal Evidence Act, 1992.

(2) This Act (except Part III and section 29) shall come into operation three months after the date of its passing.

(3) Part III and section 29 shall come into operation on such day or days as may be fixed therefor by order or orders of the Minister for Justice and different days may be so fixed for different purposes and different provisions; and, in particular, any of the provisions of sections 13 to 16 and section 29 may be brought into operation on different days for different courts and for different circuits and district court districts.

(4) (a) The provisions of this Act (other than Part III (except sections 15, 16 (1) (b) and 18) and section 29) shall not apply to criminal proceedings instituted before the commencement of the provisions concerned.

   (b) For the purposes of paragraph (a) criminal proceedings are instituted—

      (i) when a summons or warrant of arrest is issued in respect of an offence,

      (ii) when a person is arrested without a warrant, or

when a person is remanded for trial pursuant to section 177 or 178 (as amended by section 3 of the Defence (Amendment) Act, 1987) of the Defence Act, 1954.

Interpretation (general)

2.—(1) In this Act—

"the Act of 1935" means the Criminal Law Amendment Act, 1935;

"court" includes court-martial;

"criminal proceedings" includes proceedings before a court-martial and proceedings on appeal;

"document" includes—

> (i) a map, plan, graph, drawing or photograph, or
>
> (ii) a reproduction in permanent legible form, by a computer or other means (including enlarging), of information in non-legible form;

"information" includes any representation of fact, whether in words or otherwise;

"information in non-legible form" includes information on microfilm, microfiche, magnetic tape or disk;

["sexual offence" means rape, an offence under section 3 of the Criminal Law (Sexual Offences) Act, 1993, sexual assault (within the meaning of section 2 of the Criminal Law (Rape) (Amendment)Act, 1990), aggravated assault (within the meaning of section 3 of that Act), rape under section 4 of the Criminal Law(Rape) (Amendment) Act, 1990, or an offence under —

(a)   section 3 (as amended by section 8 of the Act of 1935) or 6 (as amended by section 9 of the Act of 1935) of the Criminal Law Act, 1885,

(b)   section 4 of the Criminal Law (Sexual Offences) Act, 1993,

(c)   section 1 (as amended by section 12 of the Criminal Justice Act, 1993 and section 5 of the Criminal Law (Incest Proceedings) Act, 1995) or 2 (as amended by section 12 of the Act of 1935) of the Punishment of Incest Act, 1908,

(d)   section 17 (as amended by section 11 of the Act of 1935) of the Children Act, 1908,

(e)   section 1 or 2 of the Act of 1935, or

(f)   section 5 of the Criminal Law (Sexual Offences) Act, 1993,

excluding an attempt to commit any such offence;]

"video recording" means any recording, on any medium, from which a moving image may by any means be produced and includes the accompanying soundtrack (if any), and cognate words shall be construed accordingly.

Amendment history

The definition of "sexual offence" was substituted by s. 16 of the Criminal Justice (Miscellaneous Provisions) Act 1997 (No.4 of 1997), with effect from March 4, 1997.

(2) Nothing in Part II or in section 30 shall prejudice the admissibility in evidence in any criminal proceedings of information contained in a document that is otherwise so admissible.

(3) Where in any criminal proceedings the age of a person at any time is material for the purposes of any provision of this Act, his age at that time shall for the purposes of that provision be deemed, unless the contrary is proved, to be or to have been that which appears to the court to be or to have been his age at that time.

(4) In this Act—

    (a)   a reference to a Part or section is to a Part or section of this Act, unless it is indicated that reference to some other enactment is intended,

    (b)   a reference to a subsection or paragraph is to the subsection or paragraph of the provision in which the reference occurs, unless it is indicated that reference to some other provision is intended.

(5) A reference in this Act to any enactment shall be construed as a reference to that enactment as amended, adapted or extended by or under any subsequent enactment (including this Act).

Repeals

3.—The enactments specified in the Schedule to this Act are hereby repealed to the extent specified in column (3) thereof.

PART II

ADMISSIBILITY OF DOCUMENTARY EVIDENCE

Definition (Part II)

4.—In this Part "business" includes any trade, profession or other occupation carried on, for reward or otherwise, either within or outside the State and includes also the performance of functions by or on behalf of—

    (a)   any person or body remunerated or financed wholly or partly out of moneys provided by the Oireachtas,

    (b)   any institution of the European Communities,

    (c)   any national or local authority in a jurisdiction outside the State, or

    (d)   any international organisation.

Admissibility of documentary evidence

5.—(1) Subject to this Part, information contained in a document shall be admissible in any criminal proceedings as evidence of any fact therein of which direct oral evidence would be admissible if the information—

    (a)   was compiled in the ordinary course of a business,

    (b)   was supplied by a person (whether or not he so compiled it and is identifiable) who had, or may reasonably be supposed to have had, personal knowledge of the matters dealt with, and

    (c)   in the case of information in non-legible form that has been reproduced in permanent legible form, was reproduced in the course of the normal operation of the reproduction system concerned.

(2) Subsection (1) shall apply whether the information was supplied directly or indirectly but, if it was supplied indirectly, only if each person (whether or not he is identifiable) through whom it was supplied received it in the ordinary course of a business.

(3) Subsection (1) shall not apply to—

    (a)   information that is privileged from disclosure in criminal proceedings,

    (b)   information supplied by a person who would not be compellable to give evidence at the instance of the party wishing to give the information in evidence by virtue of this section, or

    (c)   subject to subsection (4), information compiled for the purposes or in contemplation of any—
    (i) criminal investigation,
    (ii) investigation or inquiry carried out pursuant to or under any enactment,
    (iii) civil or criminal proceedings, or
    (iv) proceedings of a disciplinary nature.

(4) Subsection (3) (c) shall not apply where—

    (a)   (i) the information contained in the document was compiled in the presence of a judge of the District Court and supplied on oath by a person in respect of whom an offence was alleged to have been committed and who is ordinarily resident outside the State,
    (ii) either [section 4F] (which deals with the taking of a deposition in the presence of such a judge and the accused) of the Criminal Procedure Act, 1967, could not be invoked or it was not practicable to do so, and
    (iii) the person in respect of whom the offence was alleged to have been committed either has died or is outside the State and it is not reasonably practicable to secure his attendance at the criminal proceedings concerned,

  or

    (b)   the document containing the information is—
    (i) a map, plan, drawing or photograph (including any explanatory material in or accompanying the document concerned),
    (ii) a record of a direction given by a member of the Garda Síochána pursuant to any enactment,
    (iii) a record of the receipt, handling, transmission, examination or analysis of any thing by any person acting on behalf of any party to the proceedings, or
    (iv) a record by a registered medical practitioner of an examination of a living or dead person.

Amendment history
Subsection (4)(a)(ii) was amended by s. 18 of the Criminal Justice Act 1999 (No.10 of 1999), which came into effect on October 1, 2001 (Criminal Justice Act, 1999, (Part III) (Commencement) Order 2001)

(5) Without prejudice to subsection (1)—

(a) where a document purports to be a birth certificate issued in pursuance of the Births and Deaths Registration Acts, 1863 to 1987, and

(b) a person is named therein as father or mother of the person to whose birth the certificate relates,

the document shall be admissible in any criminal proceedings as evidence of the relationship indicated therein.

(6) Where information is admissible in evidence by virtue of this section but is expressed in terms that are not intelligible to the average person without explanation, an explanation of the information shall also be admissible in evidence if either—

(a) it is given orally by a person who is competent to do so, or

(b) it is contained in a document and the document purports to be signed by such a person.

Evidence of admissibility

6.—(1) In relation to information contained in a document which a party to criminal proceedings wishes to give in evidence by virtue of section 5, a certificate—

(a) stating that the information was compiled in the ordinary course of a specified business,

(b) stating that the information is not of a kind mentioned in paragraph (a) or (b) of section 5 (3),

(c) either stating that the information was not compiled for the purposes or in contemplation of any investigation, inquiry or proceedings referred to in section 5 (3) (c) or, as the case may be, specifying which of the provisions of section 5 (4) applies in relation to the document containing the information,

(d) stating that the information was supplied, either directly or, as the case may be, indirectly through an intermediary or intermediaries (who, or each of whom, received it in the ordinary course of a specified business), by a person who had, or may reasonably be supposed to have had, personal knowledge of the matters dealt with in the information and, where the intermediary, intermediaries or person can be identified, specifying them,

(e) in case the information is information in non-legible form that has been reproduced in permanent legible form, stating that the reproduction was effected in the course of the normal operation of a specified system,

(f) where appropriate, stating that the person who supplied the information cannot reasonably be expected to have any, or any adequate, recollection of the matters dealt with in the information, having regard to the time that has elapsed since he supplied it or to any other specified circumstances,

(g) unless the date on which the information was compiled is already shown on the document, specifying the date (or, if that date is not known, the approximate date) on which it was compiled,

(h) stating any other matter that is relevant to the admissibility in evidence of the information and is required by rules of court to be certified for the purposes of this subsection,

and purporting to be signed by a person who occupies a position in relation to the management of the business in the course of which the information was compiled or who is otherwise in a position to give the certificate shall be evidence of any matter stated or specified therein.

(2) For the purposes of subsection (1) it shall be sufficient for a matter to be stated or specified to the best of the knowledge and belief of the person stating or specifying it.

(3) Notwithstanding that a certificate may have been given pursuant to subsection (1), the court—

(a) shall, where a notice has been served pursuant to section 7 (2) objecting to the admissibility in evidence of the whole or any specified part of the information concerned, and

(b) may, in any other case,

require oral evidence to be given of any matter stated or specified in the certificate.

(4) If any person in a certificate given in evidence in any proceedings by virtue of subsection (1) makes a statement material in those proceedings which he knows to be false or does not believe to be true, he shall be guilty of an offence and shall be liable—

(a) on summary conviction, to a fine not exceeding €634.87 [£500] or imprisonment for a term not exceeding 6 months or both, or

(b) on conviction on indictment, to a fine or imprisonment for a term not exceeding 2 years or both.

Notice of documentary evidence

7.—(1) Information in a document shall not, without the leave of the court, be admissible in evidence by virtue of section 5 at a trial unless—

(a) a copy of the document and, where appropriate, of a certificate [pursuant to section 4B(1) or 4C(1) of the Criminal Procedure Act, 1967], or

(b) not later than 21 days before the commencement of the trial, a notice of intention so to give the information in evidence, together with a copy of the document and, where appropriate, of the certificate, is served by or on behalf of the party proposing to give it in evidence on each of the other parties to the proceedings.

Amendment history

Subsection (1)(a) was amended by s.18 of the Criminal Justice Act 1999 (No. 10 of 1999), with effect from October 1, 2001 (Criminal Justice Act, 1999 (Part III) (Commencement) Order, 2001).

(2) A party to the proceedings on whom a notice has been served pursuant to subsection (1) shall not, without the leave of the court, object to the admissibility in evidence of the whole or any specified part of the information concerned unless, not later than 7 days before the commencement of the trial, a notice objecting to its admissibility is served by or on behalf of that party on each of the other parties to the proceedings.

(3) A document required by this section to be served on any person may, subject to subsection (4), be served—

(a) by delivering it to him or to his solicitor,

(b) by addressing it to him and leaving it at his usual or last known residence or place of business or by addressing it to his solicitor and leaving it at the solicitor's office,

(c) by sending it by registered post to him at his usual or last known residence or place of business or to his solicitor at the solicitor's office, or

(d) in the case of a body corporate, by delivering it to the secretary or clerk of the body at its registered or principal office or sending it by registered post to the secretary or clerk of that body at that office.

(4) A document required by this section to be served on an accused shall be served personally on him if he is not represented by a solicitor.

Admission and weight of documentary evidence

8.—(1) In any criminal proceedings information or any part thereof that is admissible in evidence by virtue of section 5 shall not be admitted if the court is of opinion that in the interests of justice the information or that part ought not to be admitted.

(2) In considering whether in the interests of justice all or any part of such information ought not to be admitted in evidence the court shall have regard to all the circumstances, including—

(a) whether or not, having regard to the contents and source of the information and the circumstances in which it was compiled, it is a reasonable inference that the information is reliable,

(b) whether or not, having regard to the nature and source of the document containing the information and to any other circumstances that appear to the court to be relevant, it is a reasonable inference that the document is authentic, and

(c) any risk, having regard in particular to whether it is likely to be possible to controvert the information where the person who supplied it does not attend to give oral evidence in the proceedings, that its admission or exclusion will result in unfairness to the accused or, if there is more than one, to any of them.

(3) In estimating the weight, if any, to be attached to information given in evidence by virtue of this Part, regard shall be had to all the circumstances from which any inference can reasonably be drawn as to its accuracy or otherwise.

Evidence as to credibility of supplier of information

9.—Where information is given in evidence by virtue of this Part—

(a) any evidence which, if the person who originally supplied the information had been called as a witness, would have been admissible as relevant to his credibility as a witness shall be admissible for that purpose,

(b) evidence may, with the leave of the court, be given of any matter which, if that person had been called as a witness, could have been put to him in cross-examination as relevant to his credibility as a witness but of which evidence could not have been adduced by the cross-examining party, and

(c) evidence tending to prove that that person, whether before or after supplying the information, made (whether orally or not) a statement which is inconsistent with it shall, if not already admissible by virtue of section 5, be admissible for the purpose of showing that he has contradicted himself.

Amendment of Criminal Procedure Act, 1967

10.—Omitted. Amends s.6 of the Act.

Evidence of resolution of Dáil or Seanad

11.—In any criminal proceedings evidence of the passing of a resolution by either House of the Oireachtas, whether before or after the commencement of this section, may be given by the production of a copy of the Journal of the proceedings of that House relating to the resolution and purporting to have been published by the Stationery Office.

PART III

EVIDENCE IN CERTAIN PROCEEDINGS

Offences to which Part III applies

12.—This Part applies to—

(a) a sexual offence,

(b) an offence involving violence or the threat of violence to a person, [...]

(c) an offence consisting of attempting or conspiring to commit, or of aiding, abetting, counselling, procuring or inciting the commission of, an offence mentioned in [paragraph (a) or (b), or]

[(d) an offence under section 3, 4, 5 or 6 of the Child Trafficking and Pornography Act, 1998.]

Amendment history
Paragraphs (b) and (c) were amended, and para. (d) substituted, by s. 10 of the Child Trafficking and Pornography Act 1998 (No.22 of 1998), with effect from July 29, 1998.

Evidence through television link

13.—(1) In any proceedings [(including proceedings under section 4E or 4F of the Criminal Procedure Act, 1967)] for an offence to which this Part applies a person other than the accused may give evidence, whether from within or outside the State, through a live television link—

(a) if the person is under 17 years of age, unless the court sees good reason to the contrary,

(b) in any other case, with the leave of the court.

Amendment history
Subsection (1) was amended by s.18 of the Criminal Justice Act 1999 (No.10 of 1999), with effect from October 1, 2001 (Criminal Justice Act, 1999, (Part III) (Commencement) Order 2001).

(2) Evidence given under subsection (1) shall be video recorded.

(3) While evidence is being given through a live television link pursuant to subsection (1) (except through an intermediary pursuant to section 14 (1)), neither the judge, nor the barrister or solicitor concerned in the examination of the witness, shall wear a wig or gown.

Evidence through intermediary

14.—(1) Where—

(a) a person is accused of an offence to which this Part applies, and

(b) a person under 17 years of age is giving, or is to give, evidence through a live television link,

the court may, on the application of the prosecution or the accused, if satisfied that, having regard to the age or mental condition of the witness, the interests of justice require that any questions to be put to the witness be put through an intermediary, direct that any such questions be so put.

(2) Questions put to a witness through an intermediary under this section shall be either in the words used by the questioner or so as to convey to the witness in a way which is appropriate to his age and mental condition the meaning of the questions being asked.

(3) An intermediary referred to in subsection (1) shall be appointed by the court and shall be a person who, in its opinion, is competent to act as such.

Procedure in District Court in relation to certain offences

[**15.**— (1) Where—

(a) under Part IA of the Criminal Procedure Act, 1967, the prosecutor consents to the sending forward for trial of an accused person who is charged with an offence to which this Part applies,

(b) the person in respect of whom the offence is alleged to have been committed is under 17 years of age on the date consent is given to the accused being sent forward for trial, and

(c) it is proposed that a video-recording of a statement made by the person referred to in paragraph (b) of this subsection during an interview as mentioned in section 16(1)(b) shall be given in evidence pursuant to that section,

the prosecutor shall, in addition to causing the documents mentioned in section 4B(1) of that Act to be served on the accused—

(i) notify the accused that it is proposed so to give evidence, and

(ii) give the accused an opportunity of seeing the video-recording of the interview.

(2) If the person in respect of whom the offence is alleged to have been committed is available for

cross-examination at the hearing of an application under section 4E of the Criminal Procedure Act, 1967, the judge hearing the application may consider any statement made in relation to that offence by that person on a video-recording mentioned in section 16(1)(b) of this Act.

(3) If the accused consents, an edited version of the video-recording of an interview mentioned in section 16(1)(b), may, with leave of the judge hearing an application referred to in subsection (2) of this section, be shown at the hearing of the application, and, in that event, subsection (2) and section 16(1)(b) shall apply in relation to that version as it applies in relation to the original video-recording.]

Amendment history
Section 15 was substituted by s. 19 of the Criminal Justice Act 1999 (No.10 of 1999), with effect from October 1, 2001 (Criminal Justice Act, 1999 (Part III) (Commencement) Order 2001).

Videorecording as evidence at trial

16.—(1) Subject to subsection (2) –

[(a) a videorecording of any evidence given, in relation to an offence to which this Part applies, by a person under 17 years of age through a live television link in proceedings under Part IA of the Criminal Procedure Act, 1967, and]

Amendment history
Subsection (1)(a) was substituted by s. 20 of the Criminal Justice Act 1999 (No. 10 of 1999), with effect from October 1, 2001 (Criminal Justice Act, 1999 (Part III) (Commencement) Order 2001.

(b) a video recording of any statement made by a person under 14 years of age (being a person in respect of whom such an offence is alleged to have been committed) during an interview with a member of the Garda Síochána or any other person who is competent for the purpose,

shall be admissible at the trial of the offence as evidence of any fact stated therein of which direct oral evidence by him would be admissible:

[Provided that, in the case of a video recording mentioned in paragraph (b), the person whose statement was video recorded is available at the trial for cross-examination.]

Amendment history
The proviso to subs. (1)(b) was inserted by s.20 of the Criminal Justice Act 1999 (No. 10 of 1999), with effect from October 1, 2001 (Criminal Justice Act, 1999 (Part III) (Commencement) Order 2001.

(2) (a) Any such videorecording or any part thereof shall not be admitted in evidence as aforesaid if the court is of opinion that in the interests of justice the videorecording concerned or that part ought not to be so admitted.

(b) In considering whether in the interests of justice such videorecording or any part thereof ought not to be admitted in evidence, the court shall have regard to all the circumstances, including any risk that its admission will result in unfairness to the accused or, if there is more than one, to any of them.

(3) In estimating the weight, if any, to be attached to any statement contained in such a video recording regard shall be had to all the circumstances from which any inference can reasonably be drawn as to its accuracy or otherwise.

(4) In this section "statement" includes any representation of fact, whether in words or otherwise.

Transfer of proceedings

17.—In any proceedings for an offence to which this Part applies in any circuit or district court district in relation to which any of the provisions of sections 13 to 16 or section 29 is not in operation the court concerned may, if in its opinion it is desirable that evidence be given in the proceedings through a live television link or by means of a videorecording, by order transfer the proceedings to a circuit or district court district in relation to which those provisions are in operation and, where such an order is made, the jurisdiction of the court to which the proceedings have been transferred may be exercised—

(a) in the case of the Circuit Court, by the judge of the circuit concerned, and

(b) in the case of the District Court, by the judge of that court for the time being assigned to the district court district concerned.

Identification evidence

18.—Where—

(a) a person is accused of an offence to which this Part applies, and

(b)   evidence is given by a person (in this section referred to as "the witness") through a live television link pursuant to section 13 (1),

then—

(i) in case evidence is given that the accused was known to the witness before the date on which the offence is alleged to have been committed, the witness shall not be required to identify the accused at the trial of the offence, unless the court in the interests of justice directs otherwise, and

(ii) in any other case, evidence by a person other than the witness that the witness identified the accused at an identification parade as being the offender shall be admissible as evidence that the accused was so identified.

Application of Part III to persons with mental handicap.

19.—The references in sections 13 (1) (a), 14 (1) (b), 15 (1) (b) and 16 (1) (a) to a person under 17 years of age and the reference in section 16 (1) (b) to a person under 14 years of age shall include references to a person with mental handicap who has reached the age concerned.

PART IV

COMPETENCE AND COMPELLABILITY OF SPOUSES AND FORMER SPOUSES
TO GIVE EVIDENCE

Definitions (Part IV)

20.—In this Part—

["decree of divorce" means a decree under section 5 of the Family Law (Divorce) Act, 1996, or any decree that was granted under the law of a country or jurisdiction other than the State and is recognised in the State.]

"decree of judicial separation" includes a decree of divorce a mensa et thoro or any decree made by a court outside the State and recognised in the State as having the like effect;

["former spouse" includes a person who, in respect of his or her marriage to an accused –

(a) has been granted a decree of judicial separation, or

(b) has entered in to a separation agreement, or

(c) has been granted a decree of divorce.]

"separation agreement" means an agreement in writing which provides for the spouses concerned living separately and apart from each other.

Amendment history

The definition of "decree of divorce" was inserted, and the definition of "former spouse" was substituted, by s. 49 of the Family Law (Divorce) Act 1996 (No. 33 of 1996), with effect from February 27, 1997.

Competence of spouses and former spouses to give evidence

21.—In any criminal proceedings the spouse or a former spouse of an accused shall be competent to give evidence at the instance—

(a) subject to section 25, of the prosecution, and

(b) of the accused or any person charged with him in the same proceedings.

Compellability to give evidence at instance of prosecution

22.—(1) In any criminal proceedings the spouse of an accused shall, subject to section 25, be compellable to give evidence at the instance of the prosecution only in the case of an offence which—

(a) involves violence, or the threat of violence, to—
  (i) the spouse,
  (ii) a child of the spouse or of the accused, or
  (iii) any person who was at the material time under the age of 17 years,

(b) is a sexual offence alleged to have been committed in relation to a person referred to in subparagraph (ii) or (iii) of paragraph (a), or

(c) consists of attempting or conspiring to commit, or of aiding, abetting, counselling, procuring or inciting the commission of, an offence falling within paragraph (a) or (b).

(2) In any criminal proceedings a former spouse of an accused shall, subject to section 25, be compellable to give evidence at the instance of the prosecution unless—

(a) the offence charged is alleged to have been committed at a time when the marriage was subsisting and no decree of judicial separation or separation agreement was in force, and

(b) it is not an offence mentioned in subsection (1).

(3) The reference in subsection (1) to a child of the spouse or the accused shall include a reference to—

(a) a child who has been adopted by the spouse or the accused under the Adoption Acts, 1952 to 1991, or, in the case of a child whose adoption by the spouse or the accused has been effected outside the State, whose adoption is recognised in the State by virtue of those Acts, and

(b) a person in relation to whom the spouse or the accused is in loco parentis.

Compellability to give evidence at instance of accused

23.—Subject to section 25, in any criminal proceedings the spouse or a former spouse of an accused shall be compellable to give evidence at the instance of the accused.

Compellability to give evidence at instance of co-accused

24.—(1) Subject to section 25, in any criminal proceedings—

(a) the spouse of an accused shall be compellable to give evidence at the instance of any person charged with the accused in the same proceedings only in the case of an offence mentioned in section 22 (1),

(b) a former spouse of an accused shall be compellable to give evidence at the instance of any person charged with the accused in the same proceedings unless—

(i) the offence charged is alleged to have been committed at a time when the marriage was subsisting and no decree of judicial separation or separation agreement was in force, and

(ii) it is not an offence mentioned in section 22 (1).

(2) Subsection (1) is without prejudice to the power of a court to order separate trials of persons charged in the same proceedings if it appears to it to be desirable in the interests of justice to do so.

Saving

25.—Where persons (being either a husband and wife or persons who were formerly husband and wife) are charged in the same proceedings, neither shall at the trial be competent by virtue of section 21 (a) to give evidence at the instance of the prosecution, or be compellable by virtue of section 22, 23 or 24 to give evidence, unless the person concerned is not, or is no longer, liable to be convicted at the trial as a result of pleading guilty or for any other reason.

Right to marital privacy

26.—Nothing in this Part shall affect any right of a spouse or former spouse in respect of marital privacy.

PART V

MISCELLANEOUS

Oath or affirmation not necessary for child etc., witness

27.—(1) Notwithstanding any enactment, in any criminal proceedings the evidence of a person under 14 years of age may be received otherwise than on oath or affirmation if the court is satisfied that he is capable of giving an intelligible account of events which are relevant to those proceedings.

(2) If any person whose evidence is received as aforesaid makes a statement material in the proceedings concerned which he knows to be false or does not believe to be true, he shall be guilty of an offence and on conviction shall be liable to be dealt with as if he had been guilty of perjury.

(3) Subsection (1) shall apply to a person with mental handicap who has reached the age of 14 years as it applies to a person under that age.

Abolition of requirement of corroboration for unsworn evidence of child, etc.

28.—(1) The requirement in section 30 of the Children Act, 1908, of corroboration of unsworn evidence of a child given under that section is hereby abolished.

(2) (a) Any requirement that at a trial on indictment the jury be given a warning by the judge about convicting the accused on the uncorroborated evidence of a child is also hereby abolished in relation to cases where such a warning is required by reason only that the evidence is the evidence of a child and it shall be for the judge to decide, in his discretion, having regard to all the evidence given, whether the jury should be given the warning.

(b) If a judge decides, in his discretion, to give such a warning as aforesaid, it shall not be necessary to use any particular form of words to do so.

(3) Unsworn evidence received by virtue of section 27 may corroborate evidence (sworn or unsworn) given by any other person.

Evidence through television link by persons outside State

29.—(1) Without prejudice to section 13 (1), in any criminal proceedings a person other than the accused who is outside the State may, with the leave of the court, give evidence through a live television link.

(2) Evidence given under subsection (1) shall be videorecorded.

(3) Any person who while giving evidence pursuant to subsection (1) makes a statement material in the proceedings which he knows to be false or does not believe to be true shall, whatever his nationality, be guilty of perjury.

(4) Proceedings for an offence under subsection (3) may be taken, and the offence may for all incidental purposes be treated as having been committed, in any place in the State.

Copies of documents in evidence

30.—(1) Where information contained in a document is admissible in evidence in criminal proceedings, the information may be given in evidence, whether or not the document is still in existence, by producing a copy of the document, or of the material part of it, authenticated in such manner as the court may approve.

(2) It is immaterial for the purposes of subsection (1) how many removes there are between the copy and the original, or by what means (which may include facsimile transmission) the copy produced or any intermediate copy was made.

(3) In subsection (1) "document" includes a film, sound recording or videorecording.

Section 3

SCHEDULE

ENACTMENTS REPEALED

Omitted.

Acts referred to

Children Act, 1908	1908, c. 67
Criminal Justice (Legal Aid) Act, 1962	1962, No. 12
Criminal Law Amendment Act, 1885	1885, c. 69
Criminal Law Amendment Act, 1935	1935, No. 6
Criminal Law (Rape) (Amendment) Act, 1990	1990, No. 32
Criminal Procedure Act, 1967	1967, No. 12
Defence Act, 1954	1954, No. 18
Defence (Amendment) Act, 1987	1987, No. 8
Punishment of Incest Act, 1908	1908, c. 45

Criminal Justice Act 1984

(1984 No. 22)

Regulations regarding treatment of persons in custody

7.—(1) The Minister shall make regulations providing for the treatment of persons in custody in Garda Síochána stations.

(2) The regulations shall include provision for the assignment to custody the member of the Garda Síochána in charge of a Garda Síochána station, or to some other member, of responsibility for overseeing the application of the regulations at that station, without prejudice to the responsibilities and duties of any other member of the Garda Síochána.

(3) A failure on the part of any member of the Garda Síochána to observe any provision of the regulations shall not of itself render that person liable to any criminal or civil proceedings or of itself affect the lawfulness of the custody of the detained person or the admissibility in evidence of any statement made by him.

(4) A failure on the part of any member of the Garda Síochána to observe any provision of the regulations shall render him liable to disciplinary proceedings.

(5) A draft of every regulation proposed to be made under this section shall be laid before each House of the Oireachtas and the regulation shall not be made until a resolution approving the draft has been passed by each such House.

Criminal Justice Act, 1984 (Treatment of Persons in Custody in Garda Síochána Stations) Regulations, 1987

(S.I. No. 119/1987)

CONTENTS.

Preliminary and General

Arrested persons

Persons other than arrested persons

Provisions applicable generally

S.I. No. 119 of 1987.

Preliminary and General

I, GERARD COLLINS, Minister for Justice, in exercise of the powers conferred on me by section 7 of the Criminal Justice Act, 1984 (No. 22 of 1984), hereby make the following Regulations with respect to which, pursuant to that section, a draft has been laid before each House of the Oireachtas and a resolution approving of the draft has been passed by each such House:

Title and commencement.

1. (1) These Regulations may be cited as the Criminal Justice Act, 1984 (Treatment of Persons in Custody in Garda Síochána Stations) Regulations, 1987.

(2) These Regulations shall come into operation one month after the date on which they are made.

Interpretation.

2. (1) In these Regulations:-

"the Act" means the Criminal Justice Act, 1984 (No. 22 of 1984);

"adult" means a person not below the age of eighteen years and

"adult relative" shall be construed accordingly;

"arrested person" means a person who is taken on arrest to, or arrested in, a station;

"custody" means custody in a Garda Síochána station;

"custody record" means a record kept under Regulation 6;

"district" means a Garda Síochána district;

"doctor" means a registered medical practitioner;

"member" means a member of the Garda Sochána;

"member in charge" has the meaning assigned to it by Regulation 4(1);

"station" means a Garda Síochána station;

"superintendent" means a superintendent of the Garda Síochána and, in relation to a district, means a superintendent who is in charge of the district and includes an inspector of the Garda Síochána who is in charge of the district in the superintendent's absence.

(2) In these Regulations a reference to a person signing a document shall include, in the case of a person unable to write, a reference to the person making his mark.

(3) In Regulations 12(8) and 18(1) "appropriate adult", in relation to a person in custody, means-

    (a)   in case the person is married and his spouse is an adult and is readily available, his spouse, and

    (b)   in any other case, his parent or guardian or, where a parent or guardian is not readily available, an adult relative or some other responsible adult, as may be appropriate, in attendance at the station pursuant to subparagraph (b) or (c) of Regulation 13(2).

(4) If and for so long as the member in charge of a station in which a person is in custody has reasonable grounds for believing that the person is not below the age of seventeen years, the provisions of these Regulations shall apply as if he had attained that age.

(5) In these Regulations a reference to a Regulation is a reference to a regulation of these Regulations and a reference to a paragraph or subparagraph is a reference to the paragraph or subparagraph of the provision in which the reference occurs, unless it is indicated that reference to some other Regulation or provision, as may be appropriate, is intended.

General.

3. (1) In carrying out their functions under these Regulations members shall act with due respect for the personal rights of persons in custody and their dignity as human persons, and shall have regard for the special needs of any of them who may be under a physical or mental disability, while complying with the obligation to prevent escapes from custody and continuing to act with diligence and determination in the investigation of crime and the protection and vindication of the personal rights of other persons.

(2) There shall be no unnecessary delay in dealing with persons in custody.

Member in charge.

4.(1) In these Regulations "member in charge" means the member who is in charge of a station at a time when the member in charge of a station is required to do anything or cause anything to be done pursuant to these Regulations.

(2) The superintendent in charge of a district shall issue instructions in writing from time to time, either generally or by reference to particular members or members of particular ranks or to particular circumstances, as to who is to be the member in charge of each station in the district.

(3) As far as practicable, the member in charge shall not be a member who was involved in the arrest of a person for the offence in respect of which he is in custody in the station or in the investigation of that offence.

(4) The superintendent in charge of a district shall ensure that a written record is maintained in each station in his district containing the name and rank of the member in charge at any given time.

Duties of member in charge.

5. (1) The member in charge shall be responsible for overseeing the application of these Regulations in relation to persons in custody in the station and for that purpose shall visit them from time to time and make any necessary enquiries.

(2) Paragraph (1) is without prejudice to the responsibilities and duties of any other member in relation to persons in custody.

(3) Where it appears to the member in charge that a direction given or action taken by a member of higher rank is inconsistent with the proper application of these Regulations, he shall inform that member accordingly and, unless the matter is resolved, report it without delay to another member of or above the rank of superintendent.

(4)(a) Where, by reason of the number of persons in custody or other circumstances, the member in charge is unable to carry out adequately the duty imposed on him by paragraph (1) in relation to visiting persons in custody and making any necessary enquiries, he may authorise in writing another member to carry out that duty.

(b) The authorisation shall specify the reasons for giving it and shall terminate when these reasons no longer apply.

(c) In the case of the Bridewell Station, Dublin, the member with particular responsibility for the cell area shall be deemed to have been authorised under subparagraph (a) by the member in charge and subparagraph (b) shall not apply.

Custody record.

6. (1) A record (in these Regulations referred to as the custody record) shall be kept in respect of each person in custody.

(2) The member in charge shall record or cause to be recorded in the custody record as soon as practicable such information as is required to be recorded by these Regulations. Each entry in the record shall be signed or initialled by the member making it.

(3) Where a person in custody is transferred to another station, the member in charge of the station from which he is transferred shall send with him the custody record relating to him, or a copy of it, to the member in charge of that other station.

(4) Without prejudice to the responsibility of any other member for the accuracy and completeness of any entry which he has made in a custody record, the member in charge shall be responsible for the accuracy and completeness of all entries made in the custody record while he is the member in charge.

(5) Paragraph (2) does not apply to a record referred to in Regulation 10(5) or paragraph (10) or (11) of Regulation 12.

Arrested persons

Record of arrest and detention

7. (1) in relation to an arrested person, a record shall be made of-

(a) the date, time and place of arrest and the identity of the arresting member (or other person effecting the arrest),

(b) the time of arrival at the station,

(c) the nature of the offence or other matter in respect of which he was arrested, and

(d) any relevant particulars relating to his physical or mental condition.

(2) In the case of a person who is being detained in a station pursuant to section 4 of the Act the member in charge at the time of the person's arrival at the station shall, when authorising the detention, enter in the custody record and sign the following statement:

"I have reasonable grounds for believing that the detention of (insert here the name of the person detained) is necessary for the proper investigation of the offence(s) in respect of which he/she has been arrested."

> (3)(a) Where a direction has been given by an officer of the Garda Síochána under section 4(3)(b) of the Act that a person be detained for a further period not exceeding six hours, the fact that the direction was given, the date and time when it was given and the name and rank of the officer who gave it shall be recorded.
>
> (b) The direction or (if it was given orally) the written record of it shall be signed by the officer giving it and-
> (i) shall state the date and time when it was given and the officer's name and rank and that the officer had reasonable grounds for believing that such further detention was necessary for the proper investigation of the offence concerned, and
> (ii) shall be attached to and form part of the custody record.

(4) Where a direction has been given under section 30 of the Offences against the State Act, 1939 (No. 13 of 1939), that a person be detained for a further period not exceeding twenty-four hours, the fact that the direction was given, the date and time when it was given and the name and rank of the officer who gave it shall be recorded.

Information to be given to an arrested person.

8. (1) The member in charge shall without delay inform an arrested person or cause him to be informed-

> (a) in ordinary language of the offence or other matter in respect of which he has been arrested,
>
> (b) that he is entitled to consult a solicitor, and
>
> (c) (i) in the case of a person not below the age of seventeen years, that he is entitled to have notification of his being in custody in the station concerned sent to another person reasonably named by him, or
> (ii) in the case of a person under the age of seventeen years, that a parent or guardian (or, if he is married, his spouse) is being given the information required by Regulation 9(1)(a)(i) and is being requested to attend at the station without delay.

The information shall be given orally. The member in charge shall also explain or cause to be explained to the arrested person that, if he does not wish to exercise a right specified in subparagraph (b) or (c)(i) immediately, he will not be precluded thereby from doing so later.

(2) The member in charge shall without delay give the arrested person or cause him to be given a notice containing the information specified in subparagraphs (b)

and (c) of paragraph (1) and such other information as the Commissioner of the Garda Síochána, with the approval of the Minister for Justice, may from time to time direct.

(3) Paragraphs (1) and (2) apply only in relation to the member in charge of the station to which an arrested person is taken on arrest or in which he is arrested.

(4) The time of the giving of the information specified in paragraph (1) and the notice specified in paragraph (2) shall be recorded. The member in charge shall ask the arrested person or cause him to be asked to sign the custody record in acknowledgement of receipt of the notice. If he refuses to sign, the refusal shall be recorded.

Notification to solicitor or other persons.

9. (1)(a) Where an arrested person is under the age of seventeen years, the member in charge of the station concerned shall as soon as practicable-

    (i)   inform or cause to be informed a parent or guardian of the person-

        (I)   of his being in custody in the station,

        (II) in ordinary language of the offence or other matter in respect of which he has been arrested, and

        (III) of his entitlement to consult a solicitor, and

    (ii)   request the parent or guardian to attend at the station without delay.

  (b) If the member in charge is unable to communicate with a parent or guardian, he shall inform the arrested person or cause him to be informed without delay of that fact and of his entitlement to have notification of his being in custody in the station concerned sent to another person reasonably named by him.

  (c) If the arrested person is married, this paragraph shall have effect with the substitution of references to his spouse for the references to a parent or guardian.

(2) (a) Where an arrested person has asked for a solicitor or has asked that a person reasonably named by him should be notified of his being in custody in the station concerned-

    (i)   the member in charge shall notify or cause to be notified the solicitor or that person accordingly as soon as practicable, and

    (ii)   if the solicitor or the named person cannot be contacted within a reasonable time or if the solicitor is unable or unwilling to attend at the station, the person shall be given an opportunity to ask for another solicitor or that another person reasonably named by him should be notified as aforesaid and, if the person asks for another solicitor or asks that another person reasonably named by him should be notified as aforesaid, the member in charge shall notify or cause to be notified that other solicitor or person accordingly as soon as practicable.

  (b) If the arrested person is under the age of seventeen years, subparagraph (a) shall also apply in relation to a request for a solicitor by a parent of his or his guardian or spouse or by an adult who is present during the questioning of the arrested person in accordance with subparagraph (b) or (c) of Regulation 13(2) with the substitution of references to a parent of his, his guardian or spouse or such an adult for the references to an arrested person.

(3) Where an arrested person is being transferred to another station, the member in charge of the station from which he is being transferred shall inform any person who has been notified or informed under this Regulation, or cause him to be informed, of the transfer as soon as practicable.

(4) Any request made by a person under this Regulation and the time at which it was made and complied with and any action taken by a member under this Regulation and the time at which it was taken shall be recorded.

Enquiries.

10. (1) Information as to the station where an arrested person is in custody shall be given-

   (a)   if the arrested person consents, in response to an enquiry by a solicitor whose presence has not been requested by him;

   (b)   if the arrested person consents and the member in charge is satisfied that giving the information will not hinder or delay the investigation of crime, in response to an enquiry by any other person.

(2) As soon as practicable after a person is taken on arrest to, or arrested in, a station other than a district headquarters, the member in charge of the station shall notify the district headquarters for the district or cause it to be notified accordingly and shall also, as soon as practicable, notify the district headquarters for the district or cause it to be notified if the person is transferred to another station or ceases to be in the custody of the Garda Síochána.

(3) Where a person is in custody in a district other than that in which he resides, the member in charge shall also, as soon as practicable, notify or cause to be notified the district headquarters for the district in which the person resides.

(4) A notification to a district headquarters under this Regulation and the time of the notification shall be recorded.

(5) A record shall be kept in each district headquarters of persons whose whereabouts have been notified to it under this Regulation and of the times of the notifications.

(6) The Commissioner of the Garda Síochána may from time to time designate a station or stations in the Dublin Metropolitan Area for the purpose of receiving notifications under this Regulation and, if and for so long as a station or stations is or are so designated, then notwithstanding anything in this Regulation, as respects a district in that Area-

   (a)   the said notifications shall be made to the station, or one of the stations, so designated and, in case the person in custody resides in a district outside that Area, to the district headquarters for that district, and

(b) paragraphs (4) and (5) shall have effect as if the reference in paragraph (4) to a district headquarters were a reference to a station so designated and as if the reference in paragraph (5) to each district headquarters were a reference to the station or, as the case may be, each of the stations so designated.

(7) In this Regulation "district headquarters" means the Garda Síochána headquarters for a district.

Visits and communications.

11. (1) An arrested person shall have reasonable access to a solicitor of his choice and be enabled to communicate with him privately.

(2) Where an arrested person has not had access to a solicitor in accordance with paragraph (1) and a solicitor whose presence has not been requested by the arrested person presents himself at the station and informs the member in charge that he wishes to visit that person, the person shall be asked if he wishes to consult the solicitor and, if he does so wish, the said paragraph (1) shall apply accordingly.

(3) A consultation with a solicitor may take place in the sight but out of hearing of a member.

(4) An arrested person may receive a visit from a relative, friend or other person with an interest in his welfare provided that he so wishes and the member in charge is satisfied that the visit can be adequately supervised and that it will not hinder or delay the investigation of crime.

(5) (a) An arrested person may make a telephone call of reasonable duration free of charge to a person reasonably named by him or send a letter (for which purpose writing materials and, where necessary, postage stamps shall be supplied on request) provided that the member in charge is satisfied that it will not hinder or delay the investigation of crime. A member may listen to any such telephone call and may terminate it if he is not so satisfied and may read any such letter and decline to send it if he is not so satisfied.

(b) Subparagraph (a) is without prejudice to the provision of paragraph (1).

(6) Before an arrested person has a supervised visit or communicates with a person other than his solicitor, he shall be informed that anything he says during the visit or in the communication may be given in evidence.

Interviews (general).

12. (1) Before an arrested person is interviewed, the member conducting the interview shall identify himself and any other member present by name and rank to the arrested person.

(2) The interview shall be conducted in a fair and humane manner.

(3) Not more than two members shall question the arrested person at any one time and not more than four members shall be present at any one time during the interview.

(4) If an interview has lasted for four hours, it shall be either terminated or adjourned for a reasonable time.

(5) As far as practicable interviews shall take place in rooms set aside for that purpose.

(6) Where an arrested person asks for a solicitor, he shall not be asked to make a written statement in relation to an offence until a reasonable time for the attendance of the solicitor has elapsed.

(7) (a) Except with the authority of the member in charge, an arrested person shall not be questioned between midnight and 8 a.m. in relation to an offence, which authority shall not be given unless-

    (i)   he has been taken to the station during that period,

    (ii)   in the case of a person detained under section 4 of the Act, he has not consented in writing to the suspension of questioning in accordance with subsection (6) of that section, or

    (iii)   the member in charge has reasonable grounds for believing that to delay questioning the person would involve a risk of injury to persons, serious loss of or damage to property, destruction of or interference with evidence or escape of accomplices.

    (b)   Subparagraph (a) (i) is subject to the provisions of Regulation 19 (2).

(8)(a) Where an arrested person is deaf or there is doubt about his hearing ability, he shall not be questioned in relation to an offence in the absence of an interpreter, if one is reasonably available, without his written consent (and, where he is under the age of seventeen years, the written consent of an appropriate adult) or in the circumstances specified in paragraph (7) (a) (iii).

    (b)   A consent shall be signed by the arrested person and be recorded in the custody record or a separate document.

    (c)   Where an arrested person has requested the presence of an interpreter under subparagraph (a) and one is not reasonably available, any questions shall be put to him in writing.

(9) An arrested person who is under the influence of intoxicating liquor or drugs to the extent that he is unable to appreciate the significance of questions put to him or his answers shall not be questioned in relation to an offence while he is in that condition except with the authority of the member in charge, which authority shall not be given except in the circumstances specified in paragraph (7) (a) (iii).

(10) If, while being interviewed, an arrested person makes a complaint to a member in relation to his treatment while in custody, the member shall bring it to the attention of the member in charge, if he is not present at the interview, and record it or cause it to be recorded in the record of the interview.

(11)(a) A record shall be made of each interview either by the member conducting it or by another member who is present. It shall include particulars of the time the interview began and ended, any breaks in it, the place of the interview and the names and ranks of the members present.

(b) Where an interview is not recorded by electronic or other similar means, the record shall-

(i) be made in the notebook of the member concerned or in a separate document and shall be as complete as practicable,

(ii) if it is practicable to do so and the member concerned is of opinion that it will not interfere with the conduct of the interview, be made while the interview is in progress or otherwise as soon as practicable afterwards, and

(iii) be signed by the member making it and include the date and time of signature.

(12)(a) A record shall be made of the times during which an arrested person is interviewed and the members present at each interview.

(b) Where an authority is given pursuant to this Regulation, the fact that it was given, the name and rank of the member giving the authority and the reasons for doing so shall be recorded.

(c) The fact that an arrested person has consented in writing under section 4 (6) of the Act to the suspension of questioning between midnight and 8 a.m. shall be recorded and the consent shall be attached to and form part of the custody record.

(d) The particulars specified in section 4 (6) (d) of the Act shall be recorded.

Interviews (persons under seventeen years).

13. (1) Except with the authority of the member in charge, an arrested person who is under the age of seventeen years shall not be questioned in relation to an offence or asked to make a written statement unless a parent or guardian is present, which authority shall not be given unless-

(a) it has not been possible to communicate with a parent or guardian in accordance with Regulation 9 (1) (a),

(b) no parent or guardian has attended at the station concerned within a reasonable time of being informed that the person was in custody and of being requested so to attend,

(c) it is not practicable for a parent or guardian to attend within a reasonable time, or

(d) the member in charge has reasonable grounds for believing that to delay questioning the person would involve a risk of injury to persons or serious loss of or damage to property, destruction of or interference with evidence or escape of accomplices:

Provided that a parent or guardian may be excluded from the questioning with the authority of the member in charge which authority shall not be given unless-

(i) the parent or guardian concerned is the victim of, or has been arrested in respect of, the offence being investigated,

(ii) the member in charge has reasonable grounds-

(I)   for suspecting him of complicity in the offence, or

(II) for believing that he would, if present during the questioning, be likely to obstruct the course of justice, or

(III) while so present, his conduct has been such as to amount to an obstruction of the course of justice.

(2) Where an arrested person who is under the age of seventeen years is to be questioned in relation to an offence in the absence of a parent or guardian, the member in charge shall, unless it is not practicable to do so, arrange for the presence during the questioning of-

(a)   the other parent or another guardian,

(b)   if the other parent or another guardian is not readily available or his presence, having regard to the proviso to paragraph (1), is not appropriate, an adult relative, or

(c)   if the other parent or another guardian or an adult relative is not readily available or the presence of the other parent or another guardian is, having regard to the said proviso, not appropriate, some other responsible adult other than a member.

(3) Where a request for the attendance of a solicitor is made during the questioning by the parent or guardian, spouse, adult relative or other adult present, Regulation 12(6) shall apply as if the request had been made by the arrested person.

(4) Where an authority is given to a member to question an arrested person in the absence of a parent or guardian, or to exclude a parent, guardian or other person from the questioning pursuant to paragraph (1) or (2), the fact that the authority was given, the name and rank of the member giving it, the reasons for doing so and the act ion taken in compliance with the said paragraph (2) shall be recorded.

(5) (a)   This Regulation is without prejudice to the provisions of Regulation 12.

(b)   This Regulation (other than paragraph (3)), in its application to a person under the age of seventeen years who is married to an adult, shall have effect with the substitution of references to the person's spouse for the references (other than those in subparagraphs (a), (b) and (c) of paragraph (2)) to a parent or guardian and as if "a parent or guardian" were substituted for "the other parent or another guardian" in each place where it occurs in those subparagraphs.

Foreign nationals.

14. (1) The member in charge shall without delay inform or cause to be informed any arrested person who is a foreign national that he may communicate with his consul and that, if he so wishes, the consul will be notified of his arrest. The member in charge shall, on request, cause the consul to be notified as soon as practicable. Any communication addressed to him shall be forwarded as soon as practicable.

(2) Consular officers shall be entitled to visit one of their nationals, or a national of another State for whom, by formal or informal arrangement, they offer consular

assistance, who is an arrested person and to converse and correspond with him and to arrange for his legal representation.

(3) This Regulation is without prejudice to the application to a national of a foreign country of the provisions of a consular convention or arrangement between the State and that country.

(4) If the member in charge has reasonable grounds for believing that an arrested person who is a foreign national is a political refugee or is seeking political asylum, a consular officer shall not be notified of his arrest or given access to or information about him except at the express request of the foreign national.

(5) A record shall be made of the time when a foreign national was informed or notified in accordance with this Regulation, when any request was made, when the request was complied with and when any communication was forwarded to a consul.

(6) In this Regulation "consul" means, in relation to a foreign national, the diplomatic or consular representative of that person's own country either in the State or accredited to the State on a non- residential basis, or a diplomatic or consular representative of a third country which may formally or informally offer consular assistance to a national of a country which has no resident representative in the State.

Charge sheets.

15. (1) Where a person in custody is charged with an offence, a copy of the charge sheet containing particulars of the offence shall be given to him as soon as practicable. Where the person charged is under the age of seventeen years, a copy of the charge sheet shall also be given to the person's parent or guardian or (where the person is married to an adult) to the spouse if present when the person is charged or, if not present, shall be forwarded as soon as practicable.

(2) A record shall be made of the time when the person was charged with an offence. The charge sheet number (or numbers) shall also be recorded. Where a copy of a charge sheet is given to a person in the station, he shall be asked to sign the custody record in acknowledgement of its receipt. If he refuses to sign it, the refusal shall be recorded.

Persons other than arrested persons

Provisions relating to persons other than arrested persons.

16. (1) This Regulation applies to a person in custody other than an arrested person.

(2) Information as to the station where a person to whom this Regulation applies is in custody shall be given in response to an enquiry by-

    (a)   his solicitor,

    (b)   if the person consents, another solicitor,

(c) if the person consents and the member in charge is satisfied that giving the information will not prejudice the person's safe custody, any other person.

(3) Regulation 10, except paragraph (1), shall have effect in relation to a person to whom this Regulation applies and who is expected to remain in custody overnight.

(4) (a) Where a person to whom this Regulation applies has asked for a solicitor, the member in charge shall notify the solicitor or cause him to be notified accordingly.

(b) If the solicitor cannot be contacted within a reasonable time or if he is unable or unwilling to attend at the station, the person shall be given an opportunity to ask for another solicitor.

(5) (a) Paragraphs (1) and (2) of Regulation 11 shall have effect in relation to a person to whom this Regulation applies.

(b) Such a person may receive a visit from a relative, friend or other person with an interest in his welfare provided that he so wishes and the member in charge is satisfied that the visit can be adequately supervised and that it will not be prejudicial to the interests of justice.

(6) Regulation 14, except paragraph (1), shall have effect in relation to a foreign national to whom this Regulation applies.

Provisions Applicable Generally

Searches.

17. (1) A member conducting a search of a person in custody shall ensure, so far as practicable, that the person understands the reason for the search and that it is conducted with due respect for the person being searched.

(2) A person in custody shall not be searched by a person (other than a doctor) of the opposite sex.

(3) Where a search of a person in custody involves removal of clothing, other than headgear or a coat, jacket, glove or similar article of clothing, no person of the opposite sex shall be present unless either that person is a doctor or the member in charge considers that the presence of that person is necessary by reason of the violent conduct of the person to be searched.

(4) A search of a person in custody involving removal of underclothing shall, where practicable, be carried out by a doctor.

(5) Where clothing or footwear of a person is retained, replacements of a reasonable standard shall be provided.

(6) A record shall be made of a search of a person in custody including the name of the person conducting the search and the names of those present.

(7) Particulars of any property taken from or handed over by a person in custody shall be recorded. The person shall be asked to sign the record of such property as being correct. If he refuses to do so, the refusal shall be recorded at the time of refusal.

Fingerprints, etc.

18. (1) (a) Fingerprints, palm prints or photographs shall not be taken of, or swabs or samples taken from, a person in custody (otherwise than pursuant to a power conferred on a member by law) except with his written consent and, where he is under the age of seventeen years, the written consent of an appropriate adult.

    (b) A consent shall be signed and be recorded in the custody record or a separate document.

(2) The fact that fingerprints, palm prints, photographs, swabs or samples have been taken of or from a person in custody shall be recorded.

(3) Where the authority of a member of the Garda Síochána of a specified rank is required for the taking of fingerprints, palm prints or photographs of a person in custody, the name and rank of the member giving the authority shall be recorded.

Conditions of custody.

19. (1) A person shall be kept in custody only in a station which has facilities to enable him to be treated in accordance with these Regulations for the period during which he is expected to be in custody in that station.

(2) A person in custody shall be allowed such reasonable time for rest as is nencessary.

(3) A person in custody shall be provided with such meals as are nencessary and, in any case, at least two light meals and one main meal in any twenty-four hour period. He may have meals supplied at his own expense where it is practicable for the member in charge to arrange this.

(4) Access to toilet facilities shall be provided for a person in custody.

(5) Where it is necessary to place persons in custody in cells, as far as practicable not more than one person shall be kept in each cell. Persons of the opposite sex shall not be placed in a cell together. A violent person shall not be placed in a cell with other persons if this can be avoided.

(6) Where a person is kept in a cell, a member shall visit him at intervals of approximately half an hour. A drunken person or a person under the influence of drugs shall be visited and spoken to and if necessary roused for this purpose at intervals of approximately a quarter of an hour for a period of two hours or longer if his condition warrants it.

(7) A member shall be accompanied when visiting a person in custody of the opposite sex who is alone in a cell.

(8) A person in custody under the age of seventeen years shall not be kept in a cell unless there is no other secure accommodation available and where practicable shall not be placed in a cell with an adult other than an adult relative.

Persons in custody not to be ill-treated.

20. (1) No member shall subject a person in custody to ill-treatment of any kind or the threat of ill-treatment(whether against the person himself, his family or any other person connected with him) or permit any other person to do so.

(2) No member shall use force against a person in custody except such reasonable force as is necessary-

   (a)   in self-defence,

   (b)   to secure compliance with lawful directions,

   (c)   to prevent his escape, or

   (d)   to restrain him from injuring himself or others, damaging property or destroying or interfering with evidence.

(3) If a member uses force which causes injury to a person in custody, he shall, if he is not the member in charge, report the circumstances to that member, who shall report the matter to the superintendent in charge of the district. If the force is used by the member in charge, he shall report the circumstances to that superintendent.

(4) If it comes to the notice of a member that there has been a contravention of paragraph (1), (2) or (3) by another member-

   (a)   he shall report the matter to the member in charge or (in case the contravention is by the member in charge) to the superintendent in charge of the district, and

   (b)   unless the matter has already been reported to that superintendent, the member in charge shall report it to him.

(5) The action taken in accordance with paragraph (3) or (4) shall be recorded.

(6) On receiptof a report under paragraph (3) or (4) by a superintendent, he shall investigate the matter without delay or cause it to be so investigated.

(7) If a person in custody makes a complaint concerning the conduct of a member (whether before or after his arrest) or, if such a complaint is made on his behalf, the fact that a complaint was made shall be recorded. Particulars of the complaint shall be recorded in a separate document, a copy of which shall be attached to and form part of the custody record. If the complaint alleges physical ill-treatment, the member in charge shall arrange for the person to be medically examined as soon as practicable unless, in a case where the allegation relates to another member, he considers the complaint to be frivolous or vexatious.

Medical treatment.

21. (1) If a person in custody-

   (a)   is injured,

   (b)   is under the influence of intoxicating liquor or drugs and cannot be roused,

   (c)   fails to respond normally to questions or conversation (otherwise than owing to the influence of intoxicating liquor alone),

   (d)   appears to the member in charge to be suffering from a mental illness, or

   (e)   otherwise appears to the member in charge to need medical attention,

The member in charge shall summon a doctor or cause him to be summoned, unless the person's condition appears to the member in charge to be such as to necessitate immediate removal to a hospital or other suitable place. The member in charge shall ensure that any instructions given by a doctor in relation to the medical care of a person in custody are complied with.

(2) Notwithstanding that paragraph (1) may not apply, medical advice shall be sought if the person in custody claims to need medication relating to a heart condition, diabetes, epilepsy or other potentially serious condition or the member in charge considers it necessary because the person has in his possession any such medication.

(3) The removal of a person in custody to a hospital or other suitable place and the time of removal shall be recorded. Any instructions given by a doctor regarding the medical care of a person in custody and the steps taken to comply with them shall also be recorded.

(4) If a person in custody asks to be examined by a doctor of his choice at his own expense, the member in charge shall, if and as soon as practicable, make arrangements accordingly. This shall not preclude his examination by another doctor summoned by the member in charge provided that the person in custody consents to the examination.

(5) A record shall be made of any medical examination sought by the member in charge or person in custody, the time the examination was sought and the time it was carried out. If it is not practicable to accede to a request by a person in custody for medical examination by the doctor of his choice at his own expense, the relevant circumstances shall also be recorded.

(6) Where a person in custody has been removed to a hospital or other suitable place, an immediate relative and any other person required to be notified under Regulation 9 of the person's detention shall be so informed as soon as practicable. The time at which the relative and other person were informed shall be recorded.

Mentally handicapped persons.

22. (1) The provisions of these Regulations relating to persons under the age of seventeen years shall apply, in addition to any other applicable provisions, in relation to a person in custody not below that age whom the member in charge suspects or knows to be mentally handicapped.

(2) In the application of Regulation 13(2)(c) to such a person, the responsible adult referred to in that provision shall, where practicable, be a person who has experience in dealing with the mentally handicapped.

Other matters to be recorded.

23. Particulars relating to any of the following matters (including the relevant time and the act ion, if any, taken by a member in relation thereto) shall also be recorded:

    (a)   visits to persons in custody by the member in charge or other members,

    (b)   any other visits to them,

    (c)   telephone and other enquiries concerning them,

    (d)   telephone calls made or letters sent by them,

(e) any requests made by them or by persons attending at the station and seeking to visit them,

(f) meals supplied to them,

(g) the ending of their custody (release, station bail, etc.).

Preservation of custody records.

24. (1) Custody records shall be preserved for at least twelve months or, if any proceedings to which a custody record would be relevant are instituted or any complaint is made in respect of the conduct of a member while a person was in custody, until the final determination of the proceedings or complaint, whichever is the later.

(2) When a person ceases to be in custody, he or his legal representative shall, on request made within twelve months thereafter, be supplied as soon as practicable with a copy of the custody record relating to him or of such entries in it as he may specify.

GIVEN under my Official Seal, this 16th day of April, 1987.
GERARD COLLINS,
Minister for Justice.

EXPLANATORY NOTE.

The regulations contain detailed provisions regarding the treatment of persons in custody in Garda stations.

Criminal Justice (Evidence) Act 1924

(No. 37/1924)

Competency of witnesses in criminal cases

1.—Every person charged with an offence, and the wife or husband, as the case may be, of the person so charged, shall be a competent witness for the defence at every stage of the proceedings, whether the person so charged is charged solely or jointly with any other person: Provided as follows:—

(a) a person so charged shall not be called as a witness in pursuance of this Act except upon his own application:

(b) the failure of any person charged with an offence, or of the wife or husband, as the case may be, of the person so charged, to give evidence shall not be made the subject of any comment by the prosecution:

(c) the wife or husband of the person charged shall not, save as in this Act mentioned, be called as a witness in pursuance of this Act except upon the application of the person so charged:

(d) nothing in this Act shall make a husband compellable to disclose any communication made to him by his wife during the marriage, or a wife compellable to disclose any communication made to her by her husband during the marriage:

(e) a person charged and being a witness in pursuance of this Act may be asked any question in cross-examination notwithstanding that it would tend to criminate him as to the offence charged:

(f) a person charged and called as a witness in pursuance of this Act shall not be asked, and if asked shall not be required to answer, any question tending to show that he has committed or been convicted of or been charged with any offence other than that wherewith he is then charged, or is of bad character, unless—

(i) the proof that he has committed or been convicted of such other offence is admissible evidence to show that he is guilty of the offence wherewith he is then charged; or

(ii) he has personally or by his advocate asked questions of the witnesses for the prosecution with a view to establish his own good character, or has given evidence of his good character, or the nature or conduct of the defence is such as to involve imputations on the character of the prosecutor or the witnesses for the prosecution; or

(iii) he has given evidence against any other person charged with the same offence:

(g) every person called as a witness in pursuance of this Act shall, unless otherwise ordered by the court, give his evidence from the witness box or other place from which the other witnesses give their evidence:

(h) nothing in this Act shall affect the right of the person charged to make a statement without being sworn.

Criminal Law (Rape) (Amendment) Act 1990

(1990 No. 32)

Corroboration of evidence in proceedings in relation to offences of a sexual nature

7.—(1) Subject to any enactment relating to the corroboration of evidence in criminal proceedings, where at the trial on indictment of a person charged with an offence of a sexual nature evidence is given by the person in relation to whom the offence is alleged to have been committed and, by reason only of the nature of the charge, there would, but for this section, be a requirement that the jury be given a warning about the danger of convicting the person on the uncorroborated evidence of that other person, it shall be for the judge to decide in his discretion, having regard to all the evidence given, whether the jury should be given the warning; and accordingly any rule of law or practice by virtue of which there is such a requirement as aforesaid is hereby abolished.

(2) If a judge decides, in his discretion, to give such a warning as aforesaid, it shall not be necessary to use any particular form of words to do so.

Criminal Procedure Act 1865

28° VICTORIÆ, c. 18.

(Denman's Act)

Arrangement of Sections

AN ACT FOR AMENDING THE LAW OF EVIDENCE AND PRACTICE ON CRIMINAL TRIALS.

[9TH MAY 1865.]

'WHEREAS it is expedient that the Law of Evidence and Practice on Trials for Felony and Misdemeanor and other Proceedings in Courts of Criminal Judicature should be more nearly assimilated to that on Trials at Nisi Prius:' Be it enacted by the Queen's most Excellent Majesty, by and with the Advice and Consent of the Lords Spiritual and Temporal, and Commons, in this present Parliament assembled, and by the Authority of the same, as follows ; that is to say,

Provisions of Sect. 2. of this Act to apply to Trials commenced on or after July 1, 1865

1. That the Provisions of Section Two of this Act shall apply to every Trial [...] which shall be commenced on or after the First Day of July One thousand eight hundred and sixty-five, and that the Provisions of Sections from Three to Eight, inclusive, of this Act shall apply to all Courts of Judicature, as well Criminal as all others, and to all Persons having, by Law or by Consent of Parties, Authority to hear, receive, and examine Evidence.

Amendment history

The words "for felony or misdemeanour" were deleted by s.16 of the Criminal Law Act 1997 (No. 14 of 1997), with effect from July 22, 1997.

Summing up of Evidence in Cases of Felony and Misdemeanor

2. If any Prisoner or Prisoners, Defendant or Defendants, shall be defended by Counsel, but not otherwise, it shall be the Duty of the presiding Judge, at the Close of the Case for the Prosecution, to ask the Counsel for each Prisoner or Defendant so defended by Counsel whether he or they intend to adduce Evidence, and in the event of none of them thereupon announcing his Intention to adduce Evidence, the Counsel for the Prosecution shall be allowed to address the Jury a Second Time in support of his Case, for the Purpose of summing up the Evidence against such Prisoner or Prisoners, or Defendant or Defendants; and upon every Trial [...], whether the Prisoners or Defendants, or any of them, shall be defended by Counsel or not, each and every such Prisoner or Defendant, or his or their Counsel respectively, shall be allowed, if he or they shall think fit, to open his or their Case or Cases respectively; and after the Conclusion of such Opening or of all such Openings, if more than One, such Prisoner or Prisoners, or Defendant or Defendants, or their Counsel, shall be entitled to examine such Witnesses as he or they may think fit, and when all the Evidence is concluded to sum up the Evidence respectively; and the Right of Reply, and Practice and Course of Proceedings, save as hereby altered, shall be as at present.

Amendment history

The words "for felony or misdemeanour" were deleted by s.16 of the Criminal Law Act 1997 (No. 14 of 1997), with effect from July 22, 1997. Note the procedure of speeches is affected by s.24(1) of the Criminal Justice Act 1984 (No. 22 of 1984).

How far Witness may be discredited by the Party producing

3. A Party producing a Witness shall not be allowed to impeach his Credit by general Evidence of bad Character, but he may, in case the Witness shall, in the Opinion of the Judge, prove adverse, contradict him by other Evidence, or, by Leave of the Judge, prove that he has made at other Times a Statement inconsistent with his present Testimony; but before such last-mentioned Proof can be given the Circumstances of the supposed Statement, sufficient to designate the particular Occasion, must be mentioned to the Witness, and he must be asked whether or not he has made such Statement.

As to Proof of contradictory Statements of adverse Witness

4. If a Witness, upon Cross-examination as to a former Statement made by him relative to the Subject Matter of the Indictment or Proceeding, and inconsistent with his present Testimony, does not distinctly admit that he has made such Statement, Proof may be given that he did in fact make it; but before such Proof can be given the Circumstances of the supposed Statement, sufficient to designate the particular

Occasion, must be mentioned to the Witness, and he must be asked whether or not he has made such Statement.

Cross-examinations as to previous Statements in Writing

5. A Witness may be cross-examined as to previous Statements made by him in Writing or reduced into Writing relative to the Subject Matter of the Indictment or Proceeding, without such Writing being shown to him; but if it is intended to contradict such Witness by the Writing, his Attention must, before such contradictory Proof can be given, be called to those Parts of the Writing which are to be used for the Purpose of so contradicting him: Provided always, that it shall be competent for the Judge, at any Time during the Trial, to require the Production of the Writing for his Inspection, and he may thereupon make such Use of it for the Purposes of the Trial as he may think fit.

Proof of previous Conviction of Witness may be given

6. A Witness may be questioned as to whether he has been convicted of any Felony or Misdemeanor, and upon being so questioned, if he either denies or does not admit the Fact, or refuses to answer, it shall be lawful for the cross-examining Party to prove such Conviction; and a Certificate containing the Substance and Effect only (omitting the formal Part) of the Indictment and Conviction for such Offence, purporting to be signed by the Clerk of the Court or other Officer having the Custody of the Records of the Court where the Offender was convicted, or by the Deputy of such Clerk or Officer, (for which Certificate a Fee of Five Shillings and no more shall be demanded or taken,) shall, upon Proof of the Identity of the Person, be sufficient Evidence of the said Conviction, without Proof of the Signature or official Character of the Person appearing to have signed the same.

Documentary Evidence Act 1925

(No. 24/1925)

An Act to regulate the mode of proof of official documents, to make provision for the punishment of offences in relation to official documents, and for other purposes connected therewith.

[3RD JULY, 1925.]

BE IT ENACTED BY THE OIREACHTAS OF SAORSTÁT EIREANN AS FOLLOWS:—

Meaning of "Stationery Office".

1.—In this Act and in every other Act of the Oireachtas the expression "the Stationery Office" means and, in the case of an Act passed before this Act, shall be deemed always to have meant the Stationery Office established and maintained by the Government of Saorstát Eireann.

Proof of Acts of the Oireachtas.

2.—Prima facie evidence of this or any other Act of the Oireachtas whether public, or private, and whether passed before or after the passing of this Act, or of the Journal of the Proceedings of either House of the Oireachtas, may be given in all Courts of Justice and in all legal proceedings by the production of a copy of such Act or Journal printed under the superintendence or authority of and published by the Stationery Office.

Proof of proclamations and certain orders.

3.—Prima facie evidence of any proclamation, order or other official document issued or made by the Governor-General on the advice of the Executive Council and of any proclamation issued by the Executive Council may be given in all Courts of Justice and in all legal proceedings in all or any of the ways hereinafter mentioned, that is to say:—

(a) by the production of a copy of the Iris Oifigiúl, purporting to contain such proclamation, order, or other official document; or

(b) by the production of a copy of such proclamation, order or other official document printed under the superintendence or authority of and published by the Stationery Office; or

(c) by the production of a copy of or extract from such proclamation, order or other official document purporting to be certified to be true by the Secretary to the Executive Council or by some other officer of the Executive Council authorised in that behalf by the President.

Proof of rules, regulations and byelaws.

4.—(1) Prima facie evidence of any rules, orders, regulations, or byelaws to which this section applies, may be given in all Courts of Justice and in all legal proceedings by the production of a copy of the Iris Oifigiúil purporting to contain such rules, orders, regulations, or byelaws or by the production of a copy of such rules, orders, regulations, or byelaws printed under the superintendence or authority of and published by the Stationery Office.

(2) This section applies to all rules, orders, regulations and byelaws made under the authority of any British Statute or any Act of the Oireachtas by—

    (a) the Governor-General on the advice of the Executive Council, or

    (b) the Executive Council, or

    (c) a Minister, or

    (d) any statutory body, corporate or unincorporate, exercising throughout the whole of Saorstát Eireann any function of government or discharging throughout the whole of Saorstát Eireann any public duties in relation to public administration.

Presumption of printing and publication b the Stationery Office.

5.—(1) Every copy of an Act of the Oireachtas, proclamation, order, rule, regulation, bye-law, or other official document which purports to be published by the Stationery Office or to be published by the authority of the Stationery Office shall, until the contrary is proved, be presumed to have been printed under the superintendence and authority of and to have been published by the Stationery Office.

(2) Where an Act of the Oireachtas, whether passed before or after the passing of this Act, provides that a copy of any proclamation, order, rule, regulation, byelaw, or other official document shall be conclusive evidence or be prima facie evidence, or be evidence, or have any other effect when purporting to be printed under the superintendence and authority, or the superintendence, or the authority, of the Stationery Office, such copy shall also be conclusive evidence or prima facie evidence or evidence or have the said effect (as the case may require) if it purports to be published by the Stationery Office or to be published by the authority of the Stationery Office.

Offences and penalties.

6.—(1) Every person who shall print or publish any copy of an Act of the Oireachtas or any copy of a proclamation, order, rule, regulation, byelaw, or other official document made or issued—

    (a) by the Executive Council, or

    (b) by the Governor-General on the advice of the Executive Council, or

    (c) by any Minister who is the head of a Department of State established by the Ministers and Secretaries Act, 1924 (No. 16 of 1924), or

    (d) by any body, corporate or unincorporate, exercising throughout the whole of Saorstát Eireann any function of government or discharging throughout the whole of Saorstát Eireann any public duties in relation to public administration,

which copy shall falsely purport to have been printed under the superintendence or the authority of the Stationery Office or to have been published by or by the authority of the Stationery Office shall be guilty of felony and shall be liable on conviction thereof to suffer penal servitude for any term not exceeding seven years or imprisonment with or without hard labour for any term not exceeding two years.

(2) Every person who shall print or publish any document which purports to be a copy of an Act of the Oireachtas or of any such proclamation, order, rule, regulation, byelaw or other official document as is mentioned in the foregoing sub-section and which is in any material respect (whether by addition, omission, or otherwise) not a true copy of such Act or document shall be guilty of felony and shall be liable on conviction thereof to suffer penal servitude for any term not exceeding seven years or imprisonment with or without hard labour for any term not exceeding two years.

(3) If any person shall tender in evidence in any Court of Justice or any legal proceedings a copy of any Act of the Oireachtas or of any such order, rule, regulation, byelaw, or other, official document as is mentioned in sub-section (1) of this section which copy purports and is represented by such person to have been printed under the superintendence or the authority of the Stationery Office or to have been published by or by the authority of the Stationery Office and was to the knowledge of such person not so printed or not so published, such person shall be guilty of a misdemeanour and shall be liable, oil conviction thereof to stiffer penal servitude for any term not exceeding five years or imprisonment with or without hard labour for any term not exceeding two years.

(4) If any person shall tender in evidence in any Court of Justice or in any legal proceedings a document which purports and is represented by such person to be a copy of an Act of the Oireachtas or of any such proclamation, order, rule, regulation, byelaw, or other official document as is mentioned in sub-section (1) of this section and is to the knowledge of such person in any material respect (whether by addition, omission, or otherwise) not a true copy of such Act or document, such person shall be guilty of a misdemeanour and shall be liable on conviction thereof to suffer penal servitude for any term not exceeding five years or imprisonment with or without hard labour for any term not exceeding two years.

Authentication of official documents under Ministers and Secretaries Act, 1924.

7.—(1) A Minister who is head of a Department of State established under the Ministers and Secretaries Act, 1924 (No. 16 of 1924) may at any time or times authorise more than one person to authenticate by his signature the seal of such Minister, and where more than one person is so authorised by any such Minister the seal of such Minister shall be sufficiently authenticated for the purposes of sub-section (1) of section 15 of the said Act if it is authenticated by the signature of one of the persons who are for the time being so authorised.

(2) Any such Minister as aforesaid may at any time or times authorise more than one officer of his Department of State to authenticate orders and instruments under sub-section (4) of section 15 of the Act aforesaid, and where more than one such officer is so authorised any order or instrument which can under that sub-section be authenticated by the signature of such Minister shall be sufficiently authenticated by the signature of any one of the officers who are for the time being so authorised.

(3) This section shall be deemed to have had effect as from the commencement of the said Ministers and Secretaries Act, 1924.

Application of certain British Statutes.

8.—The Evidence Act, 1845, the Documentary Evidence Act, 1868, and the Documentary Evidence Act, 1882, shall not apply to any document to which this Act applies but in all other respects the said Acts shall continue to have the same force and effect as they respectively had immediately before the passing of this Act.

Short title.

9.—This Act may be cited as the Documentary Evidence Act, 1925.

Index

GRIFFITH COLLEGE DUBLIN
South Circular Road, Dublin 8.
Tel.4545640 Fax: 4549265